THE TOM CLANCY
COMPANION

Novels by Tom Clancy

THE TOM CLANCY COMPANION

Edited by Martin H. Greenberg

Introduction by Larry Bond

Fontana
An Imprint of HarperCollins*Publishers*

Acknowledgments

I'd like to thank Mary Prisco and Audrey Hanson for their help in preparing this book, and Tom Clancy for his cooperation, patience and good humor.

Martin H. Greenberg

Contents

Introduction

I'VE KNOWN TOM for almost ten years now. We first met when he bought a copy of a war game that I had written. He used it as a data source, one of many he found for *The Hunt for Red October*. In the course of his work, he wrote a letter to me with a few questions. I answered it, and we started corresponding. We shared many interests, discussing defense issues, politics, and history in a series of letters and phone calls that stretched effortlessly over the years. We still talk, although not as often as I'd like. We're both pretty busy.

We'd talked on the phone quite a bit before I ever got out to his house. At that time, he lived in rural Maryland, a little over an hour's drive outside Washington, D.C. The house wasn't as large as the one he lives in now, but was filled with a happy family and very many books.

Tom is a big guy, with a square face, slightly curly brown hair, and Coke-bottle glasses. He has an easy, relaxed manner, and an Irishman's temper.

He showed me a manuscript of *Hunt* and asked me about some of the dialogue, terms used by the Navy characters. I wish I could say that I realized at once what I was looking at, but I just thought it was a good story, certainly not a blockbuster novel or the start of a whole new genre in fiction.

I watched Tom as *Hunt* took off, and watched him handle the success with increasing levels of incredulity. He survived *The New York Times* Bestseller list, TV interviews, and finally a visit to the White House to meet the President himself. We've all imagined ourselves getting a taste of this, and Tom was very much an average guy, coping with ever-increasing fame.

Following *Hunt,* Tom of course wanted to work on another book. He'd always wanted to be a writer, and his first book's success was the vote of confidence he needed to leave the insurance business behind.

It seems strange to talk about it as history, but the Soviet Union in the early 1980s was a powerful and threatening enemy. The Afghan invasion was still a recent event. Tanks, planes, and ships were being turned out like rolls at a bakery, and Soviet arms were flowing to terrorist organizations around the world.

While the threat to Europe itself from the Soviets was never that probable, the sheer mass of weapons and men stationed in Eastern Europe made the threat of a Soviet invasion real. As a defense analyst, I studied the "Central Front" scenario, writing war games that tested the strengths of the two sides. One of those war games was a study of the effort to reinforce Europe in time of war. When Tom heard about it, he thought the topic would be a great one for a book: A hypothetical "Central Front" war, with the action centering on the struggle for the North Atlantic.

Tom and I started work on what would become *Red Storm Rising.* We plotted out the book together, then, while I researched the military issues, Tom wrote the book. This included visits to military bases with Tom, writing operations plans, and wargaming out some of the battles in the book. I also edited the text for the correctness of military terms and added in some of the dialogue for the naval engagements.

I watched the book grow from an outline, chapter by chapter, and worked with Tom to find information, solve problems, and keep the plot threads from becoming tangles. In effect, I apprenticed under Tom, watching how it was done. I learned enough to strike out on my own.

I can say I've known Tom "since the beginning," and have watched him develop as each book has appeared. He has handled the fame well. I've also watched the media build up a myth about him: techno-freak and super-patriot. While parts of that description are true, they've ignored the real reason for his fame.

When you talk to Tom, either face-to-face or over the phone, you are struck by a couple of things. First is his storytelling ability. Anecdotes, funny stories, and historical incidents fill his conversation, and he tells them well.

The second thing you notice is his encyclopedic memory. This is a very useful skill for a writer, not only in remembering the basic facts, but adding all those small details that give a story verisimilitude.

When we were researching *Red Storm,* Tom and I spent a fascinating evening with Arkady Shevchenko, whose book, *Breaking with Moscow,* described his defection from the Soviet Union. In 1985, the inner workings of the Politburo were still a mystery. Some of the scenes in *Red Storm* were to be Politburo meetings. The chance to interview Shevchenko, who had actually attended many of those meetings, was an exciting opportunity to bring the book within a hairsbreadth of reality.

Tom asked questions about the Politburo itself, of course, but he also asked about the room where they met. What did it look like, ornate or Spartan? Did they serve tea or vodka during the meetings? How often did they meet? Who could call a meeting? Did they ever argue or was it all calm and precise?

By probing across a wide range of questions, Tom sought to get more than just the bare facts of the Politburo's structure or function. He wanted to know how the men on it worked, how they made their decisions, and what kind of men they were.

This is another of Tom's skills—building great characters. The technology in a techno-thriller serves the same purpose as horses serve in a Western. It moves the characters along, but it's the characters that people remember. If Ramius and Ryan hadn't been real and interesting, *The Hunt for Red October* would have lain on the shelves in obscurity.

Tom likes to "get inside the character's heads," a process every author strives for, but he obviously succeeds at. He makes characters real by understanding their motivations, their beliefs, and their mind-set. This means making all the major characters, not just the heroes, real.

Sometimes the technology can hide the importance of characterization. Everyone talks about the hardware in Tom's books, as if he had a special pipeline to the Pentagon. Although he'd never been on a submarine a day in his life, he learned about *submariners* by talking to engineers from a nearby nuclear power plant. Many of them had served on nuclear subs, and Tom studied their character, their speech, and their attitudes. The facts of a submarine's function and performance came from reading several widely available books.

Any author has to do research if a book is to feel right. A romance author will visit the places where the lovers will meet. A historical writer will research uniforms and language, and so on.

One lesson I learned from Tom is how to do research. The best way is to talk to a person who should know. Don't be afraid to ask questions. If you are writing about airplanes, talk to a pilot. If one of your characters is a gourmet cook, find one and talk to him or her. This sounds obvious, but there are writers who don't do this, and their work suffers.

Tom is interested in the hardware, of course. He likes the technology. It's one reason he writes about it. If he is a techno-freak, it is in the sense that he understands it, and sees it as an ally in a world of challenges.

The results of Tom's books have been gratifying. *The Hunt for Red October* gave readers a window into the world of nuclear submarines. *Red Storm Rising* showed Americans how their military might fight a war with Russia, if it came to that. The book was close enough to reality to become a text at several military colleges.

Each time Tom writes a book, whether it is about terrorism or antisatellite warfare or drug running, the reader can expect a painless education in addition to an E-ticket ride.

Tom's unique position in the publishing industry is matched by his unique skill as a storyteller and writer. In addition to starting a new genre, he has turned out a series of books that have affected public opinion, expanded our horizons, and deprived us of many nights' sleep. May he continue to do so.

—Larry Bond

1. Tom Clancy's Fiction
The Birth of the Techno-Thriller

by Marc A. Cerasini

TOM CLANCY'S REMARKABLE first novel, *The Hunt for Red October,* marks the birth of a genre. In it he fused traditional military fiction with near-future apocalyptic science fiction, touches of espionage fiction, and a large dose of social realism to create a brand-new type of novel that we shall hereafter call the techno-thriller.

Although in creating the techno-thriller Clancy borrowed quite freely from other genres of fiction, he also infused his novel with unique philosophical elements that clearly signaled readers—and other writers, as well—that a definite thematic shift in the politics of popular fiction was at hand. *The Hunt for Red October* tackled the thorny issue of Cold War politics at what proved to be a crucial juncture in Soviet-American relations. At the time the book appeared, vital decisions had to be made by the American electorate.

In the decade of the eighties, Americans of all walks of life were asking themselves whether we should commit ourselves to another expensive round of military spending to counter the Soviet buildup of the 1970s. The conservatives, led by Ronald Reagan, said yes, and history proved them

5

right. Clancy agreed with conservative policies, and in his fiction he tried to outline the arguments for increased international vigilance while at the same time entertaining his readers.

Clancy could not possibly have known how influential and far-reaching his work would become, but it is doubtful he would have allowed such considerations to affect his judgment, in any case. His work springs from deeply held personal convictions, not fashionable dogmas. Here is an author who writes what he believes.

In *The Hunt for Red October,* we can find the seeds of virtually all Tom Clancy's subsequent fiction, a comprehensive overview of the author's philosophy. It is a grand sea story with the distinctly American archetype of the wandering Yankee embodied in Jack Ryan, Clancy's durable protagonist. The traditional flight from civilization that has been a vital theme of American literature and the exuberance, optimism, and pioneering spirit that infuse our fiction, are all components of Clancy's work as well.

Clancy's accomplishments—the fusion of aspects of other genres of popular fiction into a new one, the addition of social relevance and social realism, and the echoes of themes and archetypes from "mainstream" American literature—combine to give his work its phenomenal commercial appeal and a continuing grip on the popular imagination. The power of his fiction and the breadth of its influence have made Tom Clancy so well-known that, during the 1980s, the author was regarded by members of the media as a sort of de facto spokesman for the Reagan administration. But Clancy clearly owes less allegiance to a particular administration or political party than he does to the libertarian value of individual freedom—an inalienable right he consistently and staunchly defends in his fiction.

A DIFFERENT KIND OF FICTION

It was in 1984 that Ronald Wilson Reagan won re-election after his stormy first term that featured everything from a breakdown of superpower relations to an assassination attempt. It was a time of East/West tension that preceded glasnost, a time of increasing international terrorism and Third World intransigence, a time that reawakened the dreams of a new, more powerful America—and gave birth to a new kind of fiction. It was the year that Tom Clancy's *The Hunt for Red October* was published in hardcover, without fanfare, by the Naval Institute Press.

Before Tom Clancy and *The Hunt for Red October,* the social malaise that paralyzed the political life of our nation in the seventies gripped the popular culture—more specifically, the motion pictures and popular fiction of the day. Military films and fiction, long a staple of popular entertainment, became an anathema overnight. Military-oriented war fiction, which had survived every single conflict America had fought—from the Revolutionary War through Korea, whether the war was politically popular or not—could not survive the defeat of Vietnam. Traditional war novels, tales of personal heroism and self-sacrifice that reinforced higher values of social responsibility, the type of fiction characteristic of the years following the Second World War, were replaced with the fiction of cynicism and defeat.

A spate of antiwar novels, from Michael Herr's *Dispatches* to Gustav Hasford's *The Short Timers* and its sequel, *The Phantom Blooper,* not to mention their Hollywood equivalents—films like *Platoon* and *The Deer Hunter*—gained popularity. The image of Colonel Kurtz from Francis Ford Coppola's *Apocalypse Now* replaced the image of Sergeant York in our popular culture. The villains became, not invaders from another land, but members of our own government whom we elected to serve us, not to mention dozens of evil cadres of officers in our own military. Right-wing villains would soon become a cliché. By the mid-1970s, positive portrayals of the military were expunged from mainstream literature and motion pictures.

By silent consensus, and long before the term "politically correct" was coined, positive representations of soldiers and the military were effectively exiled from "real" fiction and relegated to macho men's adventure fiction and, oddly enough, to the realm of science fiction.

Still branded as second-class literature in 1970, science fiction proved to be the last haven for thoughtful, well-written pro-military and military-oriented fiction. Even during the Vietnam protest years, Robert Heinlein found favor with younger readers—admittedly, more for the countercultural appeal of *Stranger in a Strange Land* (1962) than for the gleeful militarism and the peaeans to the virtues of strength and self-reliance found in *Starship Trooper* (1960).

Military science fiction had other well-established popular practitioners, like that champion of libertarianism, H. Beam Piper, and the visionary proponent of space technology, Martin Caidin. Even Frank Herbert, another speculative-fiction author adopted by the counterculture of the sixties and the venerable author of *Dune,* wrote a near-future thriller of twenty-first-century submarine warfare called *Under Pressure* (1956).

In the late 1960s and early seventies, newer, younger science fiction authors were willing to assume the mantle of Heinlein, Piper, and others and produce tales of futuristic, technological warfare. While a number of these works were thinly veiled allegories of East/West superpower relations or the Vietnam War, the outright portrayal of communists as inherently evil was *passé* even in speculative fiction. Some of the authors of new military SF, like Jerry Pournelle and David Drake, were quite influential—Pournelle was to write several important bestselling works in collaboration with Larry Niven, including *The Mote in God's Eye* (1974), *Lucifer's Hammer* (1977), and a techno-thriller about conventional warfare fought against interstellar invaders, *Footfall* (1985). These works, and Pournelle's own tales of the futuristic mercenary soldier, John Christian Falkenberg, which feature a united Earth government ruled by a Soviet-American Co-dominium, have strong pro-military elements.

Yet even in science fiction the social changes rocking America were making their presence felt. In 1974, Vietnam veteran turned science fiction author Joe Haldeman felt compelled to write the award-winning science-fiction classic, *The Forever War* (1974), a distinctly antiwar novel written as a retort to *Starship Trooper*'s gleeful militarism. Haldeman was also one of the first authors to write a conventional Vietnam War novel, *War Year* (1972). The politics of protest began in earnest in the late 1960s, and SF was not immune. Authors like Harlan Ellison, Philip K. Dick, and Roger Zelazny were writing their own "military" action novels, with a decidedly antimilitary, antiwar twist.

But even during this era there were works, both novels and motion pictures, that could be considered precursors to Clancy's unique fusion of genres. In Hollywood in the 1970s, producers discovered that no matter what people thought about war and the military, a war film could still be produced and accepted by a mass audience if it was disguised well enough. In 1976 George Lucas made *Star Wars,* a rather clever reincarnation of the traditional war film, *à la* the unabashedly patriotic films of the 1940s.

Lucas used the films of John Wayne, Van Johnson, and Ronald Reagan as models for a singularly successful science-fiction/war epic. By carefully dodging moral and political gray areas and making the villains clear-cut fascists, the good guys honest and noble, Lucas managed to avoid the criticism a war film might otherwise have been subjected to during that decade. The setting, "a long time ago in a galaxy far, far away," safely placed the film within the boundaries of fantasy, and Lucas, by cleverly covering the villains' faces and bodies with inhuman, robotlike masks and battle armor, avoided criticism for overt violence—faceless, the men Luke Skywalker joyfully gunned down looked somehow less than human.

The *Star Wars* films were a resounding success and proved to Hollywood producers that, whatever their politics, Americans loved action. But the cosmetic lengths Lucas had to go to to hide the true nature of his films speak volumes about the antimilitary feelings still prevalent in the mid-1970s.

In prose, the best-known forerunners of Clancy are Clive Cussler's Dirk Pitt adventures, which also fuse technology with superpower politics and a dose of science fiction, and Craig Thomas's seminal novel, *Firefox* (1977), and its sequels. But although there are similarities to Clancy's work, we can also find strong differences in theme and approach among these authors.

Cussler's Dirk Pitt, for instance, is an international adventurer more along the lines of a James Bond than a Jack Ryan. Cussler's plots are not anchored in reality so much as in the wild flights of fancy more reminiscent of Kenneth Robson's Doc Savage adventures than Clancy's Jack Ryan novels. Though Cussler's novels are enjoyable, they lack the philosophical and political dimensions found in Clancy's work, and much of the depth.

Craig Thomas's *Firefox,* about a super Stealth aircraft invented by the Soviets and stolen by an American pilot, while strong on technology and superpower politics, still features as its protagonist the kind of wounded Vietnam-veteran antihero favored in the 1970s. Thomas's Gaunt is not a military officer, but a hostile outsider conscripted by the military against his wishes and forced to perform a dangerous espionage mission by the governments of the United States and Great Britain.

Though similarities exist, Clancy's fusion of genres was unique. He blended the technological flavor of science fiction with the traditional values of honor, heroism, and self-sacrifice featured in the best military fiction, and he added a large dose of the kind of strong anticommunist thinking found in the espionage fiction of Len Deighton, John le Carré, and others. In the process, Clancy produced a highly profitable and very popular hybrid that is still going strong.

THE HUNT FOR RED OCTOBER

The perfect yarn.
—President Ronald Wilson Reagan

In the first few pages of *The Hunt for Red October,* the battle lines are drawn and the differing natures of the combatants are clearly delineated. All good popular fiction should engage the reader and get him or her "off the fence." From the first few pages of *Hunt,* Clancy's readers are asked to choose sides, though the author is careful to stack the deck by giving us a bleak picture of one side of the coming conflict. A mere four paragraphs into the narrative, Marko Ramius, the half-Russian, half-Lithuanian naval officer who is at the center of the events about to unfold, bitterly muses about the filthy condition of a polluted, oil-coated fjord—the last sight he will see of the *Rodina,* his homeland. He compares the Soviet Union to "a slovenly giant," adding that it is "an altogether apt simile. . . . The Soviet giant cared little for the dirt it left on the face of the earth."

This comparison, and the hundreds that follow during the course of this adventure classic, are at the thematic heart of Tom Clancy's fiction. Marko's thoughts are remarkably un-Soviet, and they spring from a most remarkable man.

Ramius, Captain First Rank of the Soviet Navy, a veteran of countless tours of duty, the son of an honored Soviet hero, a trusted member of the Kremlin inner circle, an architect of the Soviet undersea forces, and one of the designers of the most impressive feat of Soviet maritime engineering, the *Typhoon*-class nuclear submarine *Red October,* is about to defect. And he is taking the *Red October,* the first submarine to incorporate a new, silent underwater drive system dubbed "the caterpillar," with him.

A brazen act of treason, but Ramius has his reasons. In subsequent passages we learn that "Marko's father had been a true Soviet hero," an exalted position, to be sure, but we find that "Marko was deeply ashamed to be his son." We discover that his mother "died giving birth to him, and he was raised by his paternal grandmother in Lithuania." During this period, "his father strutted through the Party Central Committee in Vilnius, awaiting his promotion to Moscow." Mourning the mother he never knew and estranged from his Russian father, Ramius was exposed to religion (he was baptized a Roman Catholic) and reared near the sea, which instilled a deep love for nature in young Marko. When we first meet him, he is outraged by the treatment accorded the environment by the callous Soviet machine. But Mother Nature is not his only concern, nor the sole reason for his treason.

Rage is an element in Ramius's plot: "Marko planned to wreak his own vengeance on the Soviet Union, enough, perhaps, to satisfy the thousands of his countrymen who had died before he was even born." A reference to the Soviet-engineered famines in the Ukraine during Stalin's reign and a subtle hint by the author that nationalism is not dead in the USSR, despite fifty years of Soviet occupation and forced social engineering.

Ramius's bitter musings are cut short by a comment from the *zampolit,* or Political Officer, Ivan Putin. Putin, whose "voice was always too loud, his humor too affected," is described as "the perfect political officer." Putin is an operative of the KGB, and an officer like him is placed aboard every

Soviet naval vessel to monitor the reliability and performance of the Soviet officers and men. Big Brother, Clancy tells us, is always watching the Soviet citizens. In the capacity of Political Officer, Putin is a flesh-and-blood embodiment of the Communist Party and the State itself.

In a particularly grisly sequence, Ramius will murder Putin with his bare hands. But for now, Putin and Ramius spar only with words, and Ramius enjoys this rhetorical exercise—in no small part because it will be for the last time. We learn many things about Ramius in the pages that follow, including a highly personal motive for revenge that has nothing to do with Lithuanian nationalism or Soviet transgressions against his country.

The tragedy that set Marko Ramius on a course of treason is one the officers serving aboard the *Red October* also experienced to a lesser degree, and one in which even the Party toad Putin played his own small role. Clancy wisely chose two opposing viewpoints, Ramius's and Putin's, to inform readers about the real reason for Marko's treason—the death of his beloved wife.

"For Putin the death of Natalia Bogdanova Ramius had been a cause of grief, but beyond that the act of an uncaring God whose existence he regularly denied. For Ramius it had been a crime committed not by God but the State. An unnecessary, monstrous crime, one that demanded punishment."

Clancy will compare and contrast the differences of the opposing characters and ideologies continually throughout this work, just as he compares and contrasts the two protagonists, Marko Ramius and Jack Ryan. The comparisons of Soviet and American society, sometimes subtle, but more often straightforward, demonstrate the inherent evils of the Soviet system through example rather than rhetoric. And the manner in which the author contrasts his protagonists—the products of two different political systems—serves to explode the stereotypes of the New Soviet Man and the agressive, avaricious capitalist.

For example, Ramius, we learn, lost his wife to a hack doctor with Party connections—and therefore unpunishable—who botched a simple appendectomy and then let his patient die of infection. The drugs Ramius's wife was treated with might even have contributed to her death—again, the blame for the ineffectiveness of the drugs is laid at the door of the callous Soviet bureaucracy.

This is the prime example, but certainly not the *only* example, of one interesting facet of *The Hunt for Red October*. Throughout this novel, characters trapped inside the Soviet system tend to blame that system for their woes. The American characters, on the other hand, are much more generous in their appraisal of their personal misfortune.

For instance, later in the narrative we meet an ex–U.S. naval officer, Skip Tyler, who lost a leg in a traffic accident, an injury that ended his military career. A tragedy, to be sure, but Tyler seems neither embittered by the loss nor judgmental about the drunk driver responsible—he even expresses pity for the drunk, a shipfitter with a wife and family, who was killed in the same accident.

In *Hunt* it seems that the New Soviet Man is really a bad model of the old capitalist stereotype—aggressive, greedy, and self-serving. The American and British characters, supposedly the product of selfish capitalism, are shown as generous, self-sacrificing, and infused with a sense of society's wholeness. Though their actions may spring from self-interest, we are clearly shown through Clancy's characters that enlightened self-interest is infinitely better than forced compliance with the goals of the State.

Ramius, born and bred in the Party system and wise to its ways, is certain it was the Soviet system that caused him so much pain, and he will have his revenge. For the loss of his beloved wife, and for a thousand other petty indignities—such as Putin's off-the-cuff comment to Ramius on the bridge of the *Red October,* about which the Captain fumes, "You son of a bitch . . . saying in front of my men that you must pass on my fitness to command!"—Ramius will have his revenge. We see by this telling scene involving Putin that Ramius is also proud, a failing his critics use against him when they contemptuously refer to Ramius's command as "the Vilnius Academy"—a slur on his Lithuanian ancestry—and accuse the Captain of nurturing his own "personality cult."

Ramius's pride is evident in the fact that he cannot merely slink off and vanish—he feels compelled to rub salt into the wounds he is about to inflict, and sends a letter to a relative by marriage, an admiral in the Kremlin, informing him of his intention to defect and take the submarine. It is a rash move, made only because of pride. It would have been far safer for Ramius to just disappear. But this illustrates that vengeance is Marko's deepest motivation, not a longing for the freedom or material comforts of the West.

Ramius is joined in his flight by the officers aboard the submarine, including Gregoriy Kamarov, the ship's navigator and "the first officer Ramius recruited." Kamarov is a man Marko regards as more than a fellow officer or shipmate—he is a kind of favored son to the older, childless Ramius. Only the Political Officer, Putin, the ship's medical officer, Dr. Petrov (whom Marko refers to as "useless"), and the common seamen aboard the sub are not involved in the bid for freedom.

Putin and Ramius share knowledge of their secret orders for this mission, which are locked in a safe to which both officers have a key. For the plot to succeed, Ramius must replace the real orders with the false ones he had previously prepared—just one of the many reasons Putin must die.

Ramius coolly kills the Political Officer and makes it appear an accident. He then replaces the real orders with his own and posts them for the crew to read. But unknown to Ramius, and even to the dead *zampolit,* a KGB plant is among the cooking staff and has seen the real orders. He immediately recognizes something is wrong, but for now the spy will bide his time and not make a move.

The *Red October* moves out of the fjord and dives below the surface of the ocean.

The first chapter of this work is amazingly rich. In a seemingly effortless fashion, Clancy introduces us to the core cast of Soviet characters, offers his readers a taste of the communist system, gives us details about submarine technology, and even hints at the existence of the cook/KGB mole. It is a masterful piece of fiction that grabs and holds our interest.

Now the hunt is on.

As the Russian submarine begins its dangerous journey, it is detected by the sonar officer aboard a *Los Angeles*-class American nuclear submarine— and we finally meet some of the players on the other side. We will find that the American and British cast of *Hunt* are cut from a very different cloth than their Soviet counterparts.

When we are first introduced to Jack Ryan—a character who will become central to the Clancy universe and may well be an idealized portrait of the author himself—Ryan is seen writing the introduction to his new book, a biography of Admiral Halsey called *Fighting Sailor.* Ryan, we discover, is an author, a husband, and a doting father. But before he was all of these things, Jack Ryan was a United States Marine. His career was tragically cut short by a helicopter accident in the line of duty, an accident that almost cost the young soldier his life and meant long months of recuperation. Ryan has found a place as an academic, and in the role of a minor adviser to the Central Intelligence Agency. It is also hinted that he is being groomed for a position on the staff of Vice Admiral James Greer, and, as we shall see, will in time become the Admiral's protégé.

Ryan, we learn, came to the attention of the CIA with the events later described in Clancy's third novel, *Patriot Games.* Because of Ryan's heroism in that international terrorist incident, and because of the honorary knighthood subsequently bestowed on him by the Queen, the young man was placed in the Central Intelligence Agency and was named a liaison in joint American/British projects—of which the coming hunt for a defecting Russian submarine will be the most ambitious and dangerous one yet.

From information gathered from a variety of seemingly unconnected sources, and with the help of Skip Tyler, the one-legged former submariner and now defense adviser to the Navy referred to earlier, as well as a hundred other men he will never meet, Ryan deduces that Ramius is defecting with the new technology.

Help in bringing Ramius out of the "cold" will come from these and still *other* sources, including British and American military officers and specialists, the intelligence communities of several countries, and a U.S. mole deep in the Kremlin known only as the Cardinal, who subsequently appears in *The Cardinal of the Kremlin* as the central character.

There are a host of secondary characters who step in and out of the action as needed, and they grow or fade in importance as the author manipulates our expectations. A helicopter full of intelligence officers, added as a key component of the scheme to grab the *Red October,* crashes into the sea with the loss of all hands. A minor sonar operator aboard the U.S.S. *Dallas* becomes the first man to decipher the distinctive cavitation of the Soviet sub, and the youngest submarine commander in the U.S. Navy becomes the first to track the *Red October* and the first to communicate with her treasonous captain. These characters, whether major and minor, are all nevertheless important to the tone of the novel. The American military officers are seen as products of their institutions and are portrayed as competent, dedicated professionals.

In a techno-thriller of the Clancy mold, the characters are sometimes less important than the military organizations they represent. The protagonists are often portrayed as highly trained, highly motivated components of a larger military "organism" as well as individuals with their own personal concerns.

Characters like Bart Mancuso, commander of the *Los Angeles*–class nuclear submarine, the *Dallas,* serve to illustrate the sharp differences between the democratic and the communist systems and the way these systems treat their citizens. The Soviet officers are not permitted to think for themselves and must contact their superiors before they take even the simplest action. They are watched constantly, and are always under suspicion. The American and British officers, on the other hand, are expected to think on their feet, make their own command decisions, and take the initiative. They are given much freedom, and, in the case of American submarine commanders, a great deal of responsibility—more so than their Soviet counterparts.

The Western characters in Clancy's novels seem to understand the importance of acting as a team and for the good of the community. Ironically, the so-called communists—especially the politicians and high military officers—are portrayed as backstabbing opportunists more concerned with their own personal aggrandizement than the welfare of their empire. This observation by Clancy, which flips the traditional notion of the New Soviet Man and the capitalist "running dog" on its ears, is not offhand. Tom Clancy is careful to make a distinction between what people say and what they actually do. Appearances are more important than actions in a totalitarian system. The Soviet characters mouth the appropriate Communist Party rhetoric about the good of the worker and the glory of self-sacrifice even as they take their perks for granted and enjoy the luxuries of a parasitic political aristocracy.

Yet Clancy creates sympathetic characters on both sides of the fence; most readers can find sympathetic, even likable Soviet characters in his novels, especially in *Red Storm Rising,* and some of the American characters are shown to be ambitious, petty, mean-spirited, and a threat to national security and freedom in general. In the best passages of Clancy's fiction, the Russians are seen as a much more complex people than the popular stereotypes. The author has nothing against the Russian people, he only objects to the Soviet system of government; often his Russian characters are seen as victims of that system.

Victimization is the key to understanding some of the characters in *Hunt.* Ramius is defecting because of the tragedy surrounding his wife's death, a death he blames on the Soviet system. The Cardinal, we learn, turned traitor in part because of the loss of several members of his family—including his two sons—to Soviet adventurism and bureaucratic mismanagement. These losses, and how they affect the characters, are crucial to understanding the central importance of the family in Clancy's world view.

The primacy of the family in society is alluded to in dozens of passages in *Hunt,* and characters on both sides of the conflict feel they are doing their best to protect their families and their homes. The singular rootlessness of the cadre of officers recruited by Ramius—all are men without wives, children, or even immediate family members—is vital in understanding the reasons for their treason. These men would not have defected, no matter how they hated the Soviet system, if they had possessed strong familial bonds or their family members had not been victims of State mischief. But the State was deemed more important than their "petty" individual concerns, and for this reason they rebel.

The more "evil" Soviet characters, men like Captain Tupelov, a former student of Ramius's who will face his mentor in mortal combat at the climax of the novel, are shown to lack any kind of bond with their fellow man. Throughout the novel, Captain Tupelov is contrasted with Captain Kamarov—the "adopted" son of Ramius—and the men are indeed opposites. Tupelov dies trying to best his master and take his place as the head of the "Vilnius academy." Kamarov dies trying to bring the *Red October* to the Americans and save his surrogate father's life.

Hope is in the heart of the heroes of Clancy's fiction. Ambition and greed drive his villains.

As the *Red October* rushes toward her final fate and freedom, the Soviets send their fleet to stop her. The aggressive stance of the Russians worries the government of the United States, which moves its fleet to counter the threat. Plotters aboard the *Red October,* meanwhile, are contaminating the radiation-exposure badges that each crewman wears with the on-board X-ray machine, convincing Dr. Putin there is a radiation leak in the submarine's reactor. Further evidence—faked, of course—is presented by Ramius, evidence that suggests the *Red October* has been sabotaged. The defectors are paving their way to freedom and setting the stage for the final showdown.

Skip Tyler, poised thousands of miles away in the bowels of CIA headquarters, has come up with a possible plot to grab the Russian sub and make the Soviets think it is lost at the bottom of the sea. Tyler is an important character in *Hunt,* though this is belied by his short time onstage. But it is Tyler's life and viewpoint—even more than Jack Ryan's—that is used to illustrate the best features of the American character. Tyler takes the loss of his leg and his naval career with much more grace than the Soviet characters accept their personal losses, and it is Tyler, not Ryan, who develops the plan to grab the Russian sub.

In his seminal work on American literature, *Love and Death in the American Novel* (1960), Leslie A. Fiedler uncovered and outlined a recurring theme in American literature: the theme of the flight from the responsibilities of civilization and the bonds of the family. We can find a similar "flight" in *The Hunt for Red October,* but the flight is not *away* from civilization and responsibility but *to* civilization and *to* responsibility. Jack Ryan is not fleeing responsibility, he is embracing it. In many ways, Ryan already has. He is a husband, a father, an author, and a teacher. But *Hunt* is a coming-of-age story with Ryan at its core—the tale of Jack Ryan's acceptance into the adult world of power and the wielding of power. For Jack, and, to a lesser extent, Skip Tyler, the events that lead to increased self-awareness and empowerment are initiated by the foreign-born Ramius, and lead not from responsibility and adulthood but to them. Though the characters meet only at the novel's climax, Ryan and Ramius are brothers under the skin. Each man's fate is intertwined with the other's. Each man begins a quest and finds a new way of living.

Clancy, in reversing the traditional theme of the flight from civilization, is acknowledging an important change in the American psyche. America is no longer a young, pioneer nation moving freely and unnoticed among other nations. It has become a superpower—a catalyst for change in the modern world. This is not the role of a youthful nation strutting upon the scene, nor does it allow for the luxury of a flight from responsibility.

In the revolutionary changes experienced in the twentieth century, governments all over the world have fallen and been replaced. The United States, once a bold experiment in democracy, is now the possessor of one of the oldest established governments in the world. We are a country entering middle age, and, as such, need a new kind of role model, a new archetypal hero.

With *The Hunt for Red October,* we may have met the new popular culture "hero"—not a powerful youth exulting in his physical prowess and exercising his might in a just cause, but an individual entering middle age who does not confront his enemy in physical combat but who can send other men to do it. Clancy's new hero is not physically powerful—he *wields* power. In this respect Tom Clancy's fiction has more in common with James Clavell's novels than the tales of Robert Ludlum, Craig Thomas, John le Carré, and the other espionage authors. Clavell's protagonists are not so much men of action as men of vision. His novels, from *Shogun* (1976) to *Noble House* (1981), are more concerned with the accumulation and uses of power than in physically confronting or confounding an enemy.

James Clavell's characters are builders, not destroyers, and they have much in common with the balanced, responsible characters who help maintain civilization in Clancy's fiction. Despite the apocalyptic destruction featured in his second novel, *Red Storm Rising,* Clancy's protagonists would much rather outsmart than outfight their rivals. In Clancy's world it is the role of men and women of power and influence to be vigilant. They are the guardians, the examples, the leaders, and Clancy's novels can be considered cautionary tales warning of the consequences of neglect, carelessness, or political inaction.

RED STORM RISING

> Cry "Havoc!" and let slip the dogs of war.
> —William Shakespeare, *Julius Caesar,* III, i, 273

Tom Clancy's second novel, *Red Storm Rising* (1986) was as revolutionary a development in its own way as his first work of fiction. Before *Red Storm Rising,* the few novels written after the Second World War that explored the possibility of a World War III were almost exclusively apocalyptic in theme.

A superpower confrontation in our post-Hiroshima age was consistently envisioned as a short nuclear exchange that would destroy most, if not all, life on Earth.

Novels like Britisher Nevil Shute's *On the Beach* (1957, filmed in 1959), Americans Eugene Burdick's and Harvey Wheeler's *Fail-Safe* (1962, filmed in 1964), and Walter M. Miller's *A Canticle for Leibowitz* (1957) are representative of the post–World War II, pre-Clancy model. The future-war novels in this period came in three basic molds. They chronicled the misery suffered by the few survivors of a nuclear exchange *immediately after* the holocaust *(On the Beach)*. They outlined life in the decades or even centuries that followed Armageddon *(A Canticle for Leibowitz)*. Or they were alarmist tales that warned of the dangers of the Cold War *(Fail-Safe)*. Often a single work combined these themes. Virtually all of the novels and stories of this kind were considered science fiction rather than mainstream fiction or adventure fare. But this was not always the case.

In the early part of the twentieth century, the fiction of future war enjoyed widespread popularity, especially in France and England. Though some of this fiction was similar in theme to later works by Shute and Miller in that it postulated a war that would end all wars, usually by means of human extinction, much turn-of-the-century future-war fiction was closer thematically to Clancy's in that these works illustrated technology's impact on modern warfare. H. G. Wells's "The Land Leviathans" (1903) envisioned the use of tanks on the modern battlefield; *The War in the Air* (1908), the use of aircraft. Wells even wrote the first "atomic bomb" story, *The World Set Free,* in 1914. In essence, these novels were "proto" techno-thrillers.

Another type of fiction popular at that time was "invasion fiction," in which the warning was sounded not against the ravages of war, but against the threat certain nations or peoples posed to their more peaceful neighbors. Anti-German fiction abounded before the First and Second wars: the first techno-thriller boom occurred between 1890 and 1910. Erskine Childers's *The Riddle of the Sands* (1903, filmed in 1979) and William Le Queux's *The Invasion of 1910* (1906) had a considerable impact on the British public when they first appeared. Le Queux, now acknowledged as one of the early writers of espionage fiction, made a healthy living fostering anti-German hysteria. While he focused on the threat presented by the Germans, other authors, most notably Jack London, warned of the menace from the East in various "Yellow Peril" novels. London was especially vociferous about the military threat posed by Japan.

Though this first torrent of invasion fiction was pretty mundane, it did have a strong impact on readers before the Great War. The tone of Le

Queux's fiction no doubt influenced popular opinion in Britain and helped to lead public acceptance of the First World War.

Future-war fiction before the Second World War was pretty straightforward—even technology's impact on the battlefield was held to a minimum. The atomic bomb changed things—future-war fiction after the Second World War and prior to Clancy is notable for its alarmist tone.

Now, only a few years after the debut of *Red Storm Rising,* a novel depicting a *conventional,* non-nuclear confrontation between NATO and the Warsaw Pact doesn't seem so revolutionary, as dozens of novels have been published on that theme. But this seemingly simple concept certainly was revolutionary in August 1986, when *Red Storm Rising* first appeared. Before *Red Storm Rising,* about the only work to depict a conventional confrontation between the Soviets and the United States was John Milius's film *Red Dawn* (1984), which told the story of a Soviet invasion through Mexico into America's heartland and a small guerrilla force of American teenagers that helped defeat them. This film was almost universally vilified as right-wing propaganda when it first appeared, though it did well enough at the box office. In prose, such a story was still a few years away.

Clancy went against type to produce his epic novel of World War III, and *Red Storm Rising* was one of the very few novels to recognize the simple truth that if wars are fought for national interest and security, a full nuclear exchange would guarantee neither. Both NATO and the Warsaw Pact have long recognized this truth and have planned accordingly.

Though Clancy *may* have written this novel partially as a response to the many critics of Ronald Reagan's military buildup of the 1980s, *Red Storm Rising* is *not* a jingoistic, anticommunist propaganda piece. Above and beyond any political message Clancy meant to convey, the author seems to have felt the need to exorcise future-war fiction of the nuclear specter while at the same time exploring more conventional, but no less deadly, technological advances on the modern battlefield. That thematic difference alone makes *Red Storm Rising* no less unique than *The Hunt for Red October.* Tom Clancy actually brought the techno-thriller back to its roots in turn-of-the-century invasion fiction by writing the modern equivalents of Le Queux's prophetic tales.

Red Storm Rising was Clancy's second work, and his only novel thus far that does not feature as the central character his protagonist, Jack Ryan. Perhaps Clancy had not yet decided to use Ryan again. But it is more probable the author did not want Ryan to inhabit this particular reality— the events depicted in *Red Storm Rising* would change the world forever. Jack Ryan lives in a world closer to *our own;* the world of *Red Storm Rising* is *another* reality. His absence does not hurt this novel—rather it frees it.

Not bound by our political reality, Clancy's imagination was allowed to soar, with spectacular results.

But Tom Clancy did not write *Red Storm Rising* alone. He had the help of a former Naval Intelligence operative named Larry Bond and a $15 war game Mr. Bond created, a game published by Game Designers' Workshop and called "Harpoon." Clancy, an early fan of Harpoon, met Larry Bond in 1982 when his first novel was in pre-production. The author acknowledges that *The Hunt for Red October* was inspired by Harpoon, and this game has been adopted by the United States Navy as a training tool.

Clancy and Bond struck up a friendship and worked together on a scenario called "Convoy-84," a macro–war game or "campaign" using the Harpoon rules system and featuring a second battle for the North Atlantic, fought with high-tech modern weaponry. It is from this wargamers' scenario that *Red Storm Rising* was born. The roots of the novel are apparent in the inordinate amount of time spent depicting the resupply of Europe by seagoing convoys after hostilities between the superpowers commence.

Clancy's fiction, along with the novels of Larry Bond and others, may be wargaming's first step toward reaching a mass audience. Wargaming began with a small cadre of hard-core enthusiasts, but the phenomenon is growing. And, like science fiction, wargaming also has technology on its side. With the growth of war-game-related participation "sports" like "Paintball"—in which two "armies" battle each other with weapons that fire balloons filled with multicolored dyes—and computer games based on attack-fighter HUD displays and bestselling techno-thrillers, not to mention the recent breakthroughs in "virtual reality" computer hardware and software and its potential for unimaginably complex, interactive gaming, wargaming may take on a life of its own in the decades ahead.

Of course, a knowledge of wargaming is not a prerequisite for enjoying *Red Storm Rising,* but those readers who have participated in one or more of these games will have little trouble recognizing elements of gaming in this novel. Despite this little-known inspiration for *Red Storm Rising,* Tom Clancy did not write a story about soulless machines clashing on the battlefield of the future, he wrote a very human story that is surprisingly apolitical without being politically naive.

The action begins when Muslim terrorists attack the Soviet Union's centralized oil-production facility in western Siberia. The terrorists, one of them an insider who works at the project, die in the attack, but not before they destroy the USSR's ability to supply itself with petroleum. Faced with massive shortages and the threat of economic collapse, the Politburo formulates a daring plan to attack and claim the oil-rich regions of the Mideast. As part of this plan, the Soviets launch a *maskirovka* that will lull the

West into complacency. The Soviets will "make nice" with the NATO alliance even as they plan for a war in Europe, for the Politburo has deduced that before they can claim the Mideast as their own, they must first neutralize NATO. But they get some bad advice. We learn near the close of the novel that a factional fight within the KGB has allowed overly optimistic assessments of NATO's inability to counter the Soviet offensive to be used in Soviet pre-war planning instead of more realistic assessments of NATO's strength—with disastrous consequences.

As the Soviets prepare for an invasion of the West, they also mount an elaborate scheme to justify that war. With a brilliant plot device, Clancy illustrates the cool viciousness of the Soviet system. A group of Soviet schoolchildren is blown up in the first "terrorist" incident in Russian history. The bombing was, of course, engineered by the KGB, who then pin the blame for the atrocity on a West German "spy." As East-West tensions mount, we are introduced to some of the main characters.

In NATO's corner we meet Robert Toland, who quit active duty in the United States Navy after he ran his ship onto a sandbar and effectively ended his career. Toland is recalled to active duty when he recognizes several telling events within the Soviet Union, actions that lead him to believe the Russians are arming for war. And there's Danny McCafferty, commander of the U.S.S. *Chicago,* who will battle the Soviet threat beneath the high seas.

We also meet "Buns" Nakamura, who fires rockets at orbiting Soviet spy satellites from an F-15 and becomes the first female ace in the United States Air Force. And then there is Clancy's Everyman—First Lieutenant Mike Edwards, a United States Air Force meteorologist stationed in Iceland. Edwards and a squad of Marines are the only Americans left in Iceland after the Soviets launch a successful surprise attack on the U.S. air base at Keflavik, capturing it intact and killing or capturing the American personnel.

On the Russian side we find a bevy of "old men" who rule the Politburo, including Mikhail Eduardovich Sergetov, who is an early opponent of the war, and Boris Kosov, Chairman of the KGB and leader of the faction opposed to the war. But Clancy's sympathies in *Red Storm Rising* lie with the soldiers, and once hostilities commence, the attention shifts to men like Marshal Rozhkov, Commander in Chief of Ground Forces, and Pavel Alekseyev, deputy commander of the Southwestern Theater of the war. It is interesting to note that only near the close of the novel do readers meet the General who led the NATO forces to victory. Though Clancy concentrates on the Soviet hierarchy, from the old men in the Kremlin to the generals on the field, the Allied characters are almost all citizen soldiers—

helicopter pilots, naval officers, tank crewmen, pilots. We meet few Americans beyond the rank of captain.

When the war finally begins, NATO, while not totally prepared, is at least ready. The Soviets learn, to their chagrin, that their *maskirovka* was not nearly as successful as they hoped. Furthermore, the Red Army is caught with its pants down when, out of the night sky, the Stealth aircraft makes a nonappearance (at least on Soviet radar), bombing vital bridgeheads in Germany and halting the Soviet advance long enough for the West to mount a counterattack. In a sequence that will demonstrate just how much public knowledge of military technology has changed in recent years, Clancy utilized the now-antiquated "Frisbee" design dubbed the F-19A Ghostrider. We now know that the real thing, the F-117 Black Jet revealed to the public just a few years after *Red Storm Rising* was published, looks nothing at all like this early design disseminated, no doubt, as disinformation by a security-conscious Pentagon. Of course, Tom Clancy *was* right that the United States Air Force already had Stealth aircraft secretly deployed by 1986.

The middle portion of *Red Storm Rising* is given over to the NATO resupply efforts, the result of Clancy's fascination with the Navy and his enthusiasm for the war game that was the inspiration for this novel. The war soon degenerates into a meat grinder on land as the Soviet advances in West Germany are met with antitank and antipersonnel weapons, and a graveyard at sea, as the Americans' attempt to resupply and reinforce NATO is thwarted by Russian bombers and submarines. Soon the original objective—seizing the Arab oil fields—is forgotten. The fog of war leads whole nations astray.

As one of Clancy's characters observes, all plans go out the window after the first shot has been fired. The Soviets learn this lesson repeatedly as their "quick victory" becomes bogged down in German mud and blood. Indeed, control of the war becomes the focus of the second half of the novel, when the threat of nuclear exchange looms larger. The Kremlin's loss of control and its willingness to use nuclear arms are the catalyst for change at the close of the novel, when once-loyal officers in the Red Army rise up and eliminate both the Politburo and the head of the KGB.

How war changes things, on a personal as well as a societal scale, is another theme explored in Clancy's novel. Technology, it seems, is not the only thing that evolves during wartime—individuals, too, grow, mature, and change, and of course die. This is a reflection of reality. Before the American Civil War, Ulysses S. Grant was a drunkard who failed at everything he ever tried. By war's end he was a national hero, and a decade later, he was President. There are similar, if less spectacular, transformations to be found in *Red Storm Rising*.

In a revealing scene near the end of the novel, Mikhail Sergetov marvels at how much his son has matured during the conflict, though he laments that it took a war to make him a man. On the NATO side, the disgraced Bob Toland is given a second chance at a military career when he devises a clever scheme to hit Soviet airfields after their bombing raids on Allied shipping. Buns Nakamura goes from a ferry pilot to a "real" combat pilot at the front (women are barred from combat in the American military) to an ace after she surprises a flight of Russian bombers—she then becomes the first satellite-killer in history.

Most striking is the case of Clancy's Everyman hero, Mike Edwards. Trapped in Iceland, Lieutenant Edwards goes from the modern equivalent of a ninety-day wonder to a hardened combat veteran when he leads a squad of Marines through Iceland, all the while reporting on Soviet activity in the region. More important, the war allows him to exorcise a very personal demon. Back in the States, his childhood sweetheart was raped and murdered by a man who was later permitted by the courts to plead insanity. In Iceland, Edwards and his Marines stumble upon the rape of a young Icelandic woman by drunken Red Army soldiers. Going against the direct orders from his superiors in Scotland, Edwards intervenes and rescues the woman, executing the captured Russian soldiers with his own hands after pronouncing them guilty of war crimes. His actions as judge, jury, and executioner seem to purge the demons of his past and permit him to become emotionally attached to Vigdis, the woman he rescued. In essence, his experiences in war allow him to go on with his life after the conflict is over.

Of course, not all the changes brought about by war are positive. Commander Ed Morris is so enamored of his command that at the beginning of the novel he proudly sports a personalized automobile license plate bearing the serial number of his ship. After the ship is struck by a Soviet torpedo and many members of his crew die, Morris muses bitterly that not many men are forced to drive around with the number of their failure branded on their car. And, though he pulls himself together enough to return to combat duty, he will suffer from nightmares for as long as he lives.

But the most striking change comes at the close of the novel, when the government that has dragged the people of the Soviet Union into this disastrous conflict is violently deposed. The revolution is prompted by a successful Tomahawk missile attack on the Russian mainland, an attack that for about ten minutes has the Soviet high command convinced that nuclear Armageddon is at hand. The realization that the war is spiraling out of control forces one of the rival factions in the KGB to attempt to take over the government and sue for peace. This is just about the only reference to the nuclear arsenal in the entire novel.

Some critics accuse Clancy of sanitizing war, but it is hard to justify this assertion after reading the novel. Heads being blown off, men being eaten up by mortar fire and burned to death in fuel-air explosions and smashed tanks are not images that are consistent with a sanitized struggle, though Clancy does eschew the use of chemical and biological weapons. Again, this was done purely for dramatic purposes. The war in *Red Storm Rising* is fought much like the Second World War—with unwritten codes of conduct and gentlemanly, if unspoken, agreements among the combatants. This is consistent with Clancy's vision of a conventional war, and the historical precedents are already in place. Though both the Nazis and the Allies had large chemical-weapons arsenals at the beginning of the Second World War, neither side used them in combat for fear that the other side would respond in kind—spiraling the war out of "control."

Another area in which Clancy's work comes under fire is in the performance of the weapons systems in his novels. Many experts claim that in Clancy's universe the tools of war work too well. Retired Colonel Carl Bernard, who fought in the Second World War, Korea, and Vietnam, stated in an article about Tom Clancy published in the August 8, 1988, *Newsweek,* "anything more complex than a can opener doesn't work and it doesn't work a lot." Clancy himself dismisses these critics and claims to downgrade all weapons performance 50 percent from the manufacturers' specs.

Strong criticism was leveled against the performance of the Tomahawk Cruise Missile in particular. Detractors claimed that the Tomahawk would never live up to the promises of its manufacturer. But this weapon's impressive performance in the 1991 Gulf War has proved these critics wrong.

Another aspect of "real life" Clancy avoided was how the war affected life on the home front. Scant attention is paid to middle America's reaction to the war, except in the military. In the beginning of the novel, Clancy demonstrates how the Soviet propaganda machine cleverly manipulates Western media organs in their bold *maskiarovka,* and some of the characters introduced early in the novel were print and television journalists. But after the hostilities begin, these characters are all but forgotten, and almost no mention is made of media impact on American civilians or how the war is covered, though at one point the author mentions that some of the footage from the European theater is being broadcast live via satellite from the battlefield.

In the final analysis, *Red Storm Rising* must be judged a huge success. The story is powerful and inspiring, suspenseful and fast-paced. Even better, there is a marked improvement in Clancy's writing style. At times his prose soars into a kind of poetry, especially in the battle sequences. The novel stirs readers' blood and whips our emotions into a martial frenzy. Readers react emotionally to the action in the novel, and characters on both sides elicit our sympathy and respect. The victories, for both sides, make our spirits soar; the defeats fill us with grief. In this way, *Red Storm Rising* is decidedly apolitical—we can find something to admire in characters from the Kremlin to Washington, from the Warsaw Pact or NATO, whether soldier or civilian. In the final analysis, *Red Storm Rising* is a novel of war, not of politics.

If *The Hunt for Red October* brought the techno-thriller to the forefront of popular culture, *Red Storm Rising* gave this sub-genre another direction. Like the invasion fiction of the early part of this century, Tom Clancy's *Red Storm Rising* has touched a chord in the American psyche and inspired many imitators. Since the publication of his second novel, dozens of Third World War scenarios have appeared, varying in quality, approach, and setting. Some authors have taken Clancy's cue and have written tales about a confrontation between the Soviets and the West, while other authors have explored very different scenarios.

With *The Hunt for Red October,* Tom Clancy created and defined the techno-thriller. In *Red Storm Rising* he brought old-fashioned invasion fiction back into fashion. For his third work, the author chose to return to more personal matters, to a "smaller" story, and to his durable protagonist, Jack Ryan.

PATRIOT GAMES

Patriot Games was a breath of fresh air to fans of action fiction who found the usual adventure fare lacking in intelligence and wit, and who also resented the moral ambiguity of John le Carré's, Len Deighton's, or Robert Ludlum's espionage fiction. With *Patriot Games,* Clancy set out to win female readers as well, with equally spectacular results.

This is not to suggest that Clancy wrote *Patriot Games* as a calculated piece of commercial fluff—the novel touches upon too many serious issues for such a conclusion—but there is no denying Clancy's shrewdness in his choice of subject, and he won over a whole new segment of the reading public with this elegant story of a savage terrorist attack on members of the British royal family.

Since their storybook marriage in 1981, Charles and Diana, the Prince and Princess of Wales, have captured the hearts of people on both sides of the Atlantic. The birth of their two children became news worldwide, and hardly a day goes by without Charles or Diana stepping once more into the limelight.

Tom Clancy capitalized on Britain's and America's fascination with British royalty in *Patriot Games,* and he also chose this project as the vehicle for the return of his protagonist, Jack Ryan. We learn more about Ryan in this outing, and his personal history is also most revealing.

The plot of *Patriot Games* is a simple one. Jack Ryan, on a working vacation in London with his wife and child, happens to be near when Irish terrorists attack the Prince and Princess and their infant son in a cleverly executed ambush on the streets of the British capital. Though Ryan later deduces that the Ulster Liberation Army—the ULA—was intent on kidnapping, not murder, it surely would have been successful in either case were it not for the training and instincts instilled in Jack Ryan by the Marine Corps.

Ryan disarms one terrorist and kills another—a third manages to escape. Though gravely wounded in the confrontation, Ryan survives to become a hero on both sides of the Atlantic. He is knighted by the Queen and, in a grandly entertaining scene, Ryan talks some sense into the Prince, who is ashamed of his own inaction during the terrorist incident. Ryan also attracts the interest of the terrorists themselves, members of an outlawed splinter group of the Irish Republican Army.

We learn much about Irish politics and the history of the "troubles" in Northern Ireland. Though Clancy—and Jack Ryan—are of Irish stock, neither the author nor his fictional counterpart show much sympathy for the IRA, the Sinn Fein, the Irish National Liberation Army, or similar groups.

The ULA seeks revenge by harming Ryan's pregnant wife and young child in a cowardly attack staged in the United States. This attack coincides with the Provisional Wing of the Irish Republican Army's fund-raising activities in America and is intended to discredit them as well. This shocking incident ultimately precipitates Ryan's involvement with Admiral Greer and the Central Intelligence Agency.

Ryan's family recovers, but when the royal family later comes to America to visit the Ryans in their home, both families are again attacked by the ULA, who all but slaughter the security forces assigned to guard the two families. In an exciting sequence, a counterattack is mounted and the ULA is destroyed. In the poignant final scene, Jack Ryan's second child is born.

Though published in 1987, *Patriot Games* was, chronologically, the first Jack Ryan adventure, as the events happen before the *Red October* incident. Allusions are made throughout *The Hunt for Red October* to the incidents in *Patriot Games,* though few details are then given. It is interesting to note that Clancy had something like a plan in place for his protagonist, despite the author's own admission that he seldom works with an outline when writing a novel.

Only marginally a techno-thriller (satellite technology is employed to monitor terrorist activities and training in the Middle East, and via satellite, we watch the capture of a French terrorist group in *real time*—the picture shot from earth orbit and beamed to CIA headquarters at Langley), *Patriot Games* more resembles a roman à clef. Mirror images of the real royal family are used as characters in this novel, and other figures, men like Admiral Greer, come to resemble identifiable members of America's real-life intelligence community. This pattern will continue in subsequent Jack Ryan adventures.

But the presence of the royal family doesn't make *Patriot Games* a glitz-and-glamour novel—these characters aren't used as expensive scenery. Clancy utilizes the royal family, and the family of Jack Ryan, for a *thematic* purpose. The importance—or, rather, the necessity—of the family unit to the continued health of human society is the central theme of this novel.

Throughout *Patriot Games,* the reader is struck by the author's repeated, calculated juxtapositioning and continual contrast and comparisons of Ryan's family and the royal family to the violent, rootless men who choose a life of political terrorism. Clancy's vision of the British royal family is nothing more than Ryan's family—or our own—in *macrocosm.* The Windsors might be a little more reserved, a little less accessible than your neighbors, but they are still a recognizable family with human responses and emotions. In this novel they come to symbolize civilization and society on the grand scale, just as the Ryans represent society in *microcosm.* Both are seen as representative of the *family*—the smallest yet most vital unit in civilization. Destroy the royal family and you destroy British society. By extension, if you destroy the family as an institution, you destroy civilization as a whole.

There are numerous references in *Patriot Games* to the importance of the family. After the attack, Ryan upbraids the Prince for feeling guilty that he did not act in a more decisive manner, that he did not kill the terrorists himself. Ryan convinces him that he did *"exactly* the right thing," for the Prince shielded his wife and child and waited for the help he knew was on the way. Later on in that same conversation, Ryan calls rearing a family "what it's all about."

Though Ryan would give his life to defend his country and the rule of law, he also concedes, in a telling scene, that the rule of law isn't as important to him as his own immediate family, and that he would violate those laws to protect his loved ones, though not without misgivings. Ryan muses that, *"If we can do it* [stop terrorism] *by civilized rules, well and good—but if not, then we have to do the best we can, and rely on our consciences to keep us from going over the edge."* He follows that statement with an even more revealing passage. "He [Ryan] thought that he could trust his conscience. He was holding it [his wife] in his arms." To Ryan—and Clancy—the family is the first and most important step toward socialization. It is revealing that Clancy chose to end the novel with the birth of the Ryans' second child. The future and all our hopes rest, it seems, on the survival of the family unit.

The "bad guys" in *Patriot Games,* on the other hand, are universally misfits, men without hope—they have no lovers, no families, and, by extension, no future. They possess neither comprehensible human emotions nor the normal societal bonds that make men truly civilized. The ULA has replaced hearth and home with Marxist rhetoric and political violence. Despite their claim to fight for a better world, its members are driven by their insatiable appetites for blood, for power, and for vengeance. The terrorists are stripped of emotion, or rather, their political convictions have subsumed their human emotions. "It was the terrorists who had cast themselves out of the civilized community," Ryan muses at one point. A guard who rescues one of the Irish terrorists from a vicious prison rape is later shot by that same terrorist, who remarks, in traditional "Marxist/Leninist-speak" as he pulls the trigger, "Gratitude, Mr. Highland, is a disease of dogs."

We glean some facts about Jack Ryan's personal history in *Patriot Games*—we learn about the helicopter accident that cut his military career short, and about his parents, who were killed in a plane crash in Chicago just eighteen months after his Marine Corps career ended. Perhaps that tragic loss explains the important place his own family occupies in Ryan's life.

Although, as we have seen, *Patriot Games* was not written as a glitzy, romantic swashbuckler, there are certainly scenes and incidents in it that echo the kinds of things one would expect to find in such a melodrama. The wish-fulfillment aspect of *Patriot Games,* especially, appeals to everyone's Walter Mitty streak—who would not like to save the royal family, become a knight, and then save one's own loved ones in yet another public display of heroism? What man would not want to win for his wife the title "Lady"; what woman would not want to be married to a man so brave, a man who could win such an honor? In one brief, shining moment, a common, unassuming Everyman like Jack Ryan is transformed into an international hero. Such a dramatic metamorphosis appeals to everyone.

There are romantic sequences as well, like the wonderful scene in which Ryan and his wife witness the Ceremony of the Keys at the Tower of

London. Glitzy scenes include a first-class ride on the SST and a tour of Buckingham Palace conducted by the royals themselves. There are charming, heartwarming scenes to be found, as when Ryan is informed by his wife that he will again be a father.

Clancy also began to introduce seemingly minor characters who take up great importance by the close of the novel and in subsequent works. In *Patriot Games* we meet Robbie Jackson, a hotshot Tomcat pilot for the Navy. Jackson and his wife appear to be secondary characters, but at the climax, it is Jackson who first gets the drop on the terrorists and saves Ryan and the royal family. Jackson becomes even more important in *Clear and Present Danger* and *The Sum of All Fears.* Clancy has also introduced minor characters who stay minor in the novel in which they first appear but become much more central to the next work or even the work after that.

Finally, allusions to other concerns—concerns that are explored in Clancy's subsequent novels—are made throughout *Patriot Games.* Ryan habitually ponders such heady notions as the rule of law, the nature of society, and the often desperate situations that cause governments to utilize the military to eliminate what is essentially a criminal threat. This last theme, especially, is explored in Clancy's fifth novel, *Clear and Present Danger.*

For his next work, Clancy once again turns his attention to "the Evil Empire."

THE CARDINAL OF THE KREMLIN

> The stories I tell are true and because they are I had no choice but to disguise the people who lived them.
>
> —Bette B. Lord, *Legacies*

The Cardinal of the Kremlin is the closest Tom Clancy ever came to writing a traditional espionage novel. Clancy blended elements of a roman à clef and his own unique brand of thriller with more traditional aspects of espionage fiction—such as the attention to the everyday details of the tradecraft of spying and an exploration of the motives of those who take up this dangerous vocation. As with virtually all espionage fiction written about the Cold War, the protagonists' main tasks are to avoid a superpower confrontation (which may or may not involve a nuclear threat), and at the same time to capture or learn some vital piece of information that has a destabilizing effect on the existing balance of power. In the case of *Cardinal,* what Hitchcock liked to call the "McGuffin" is a technological break-through at a super-secret Soviet SDI installation at Dushanbe, on the border of Afghanistan.

Many themes from Clancy's two previous Jack Ryan novels are echoed in *Cardinal,* but the author also adds a few new ingredients to the mixture, ingredients that reflect the changing political situation in the USSR during the period the novel was written. When Clancy began work on *The Cardinal of the Kremlin,* three major issues were dominating superpower relations: the reforms Gorbachev introduced to the Soviet people, the disastrous war in Afghanistan that threatened relations with the West and had the ruinous potential of a Vietnam, and the ongoing controversy over the Strategic Defense Initiative, or SDI, and that technology's impact on the balance of power and, by extension, arms negotiations.

It was around this time that Western democracies began to suspect that Gorbachev might indeed be serious about reform. At the time *Cardinal* was published, both the American government and the governments of Europe and Japan were becoming more convinced than ever that Gorbachev was serious about reforming his own system and improving relations with the Western democracies.

The war in Afghanistan became a major stumbling block to real reform, however. The West saw Soviet intervention there to be a form of imperial-ism that precluded serious considerations about allowing the Soviet Union any new economic or political concessions. These two factors tended to cancel each other out in the international community, which led to confu-sion about Gorbachev's true motives.

In mediaspeak, the SDI program was stuck with the pejorative "Star Wars," and this crucial research was never really a political issue until President Ronald Reagan made his now-famous speech about the impor-tance of space-based defenses. This focused media attention on the Ameri-can program, which had quietly been making steady progress for almost a decade, and, to a much lesser extent, on the Soviet program, which had been active for a quarter of a century.

With the help of politicians hostile to defense programs, and of the American media, which were generally hostile to Reagan's administration anyway, the Soviets were able to make a political issue out of SDI, convinc-ing arms negotiators that this technology was "destabilizing"—but only in *American* hands, of course. The reality was that America was only then beginning to make real progress.

Tom Clancy was able to meld these very real, very different political situations into a single thriller novel that crackles with suspense and moves at breakneck speed, a thriller that also casts some light on the events that shaped U.S./USSR relations at that critical juncture. *The Cardinal of the Kremlin* also touches on a number of issues close to the author's heart, issues consistent with Clancy's personal philosophy as it was expressed in his earlier work.

In contrast to the comparatively simple plot of *Patriot Games, The Cardinal of the Kremlin* is a complex story, though told with both clarity and brevity. The plot centers on the Cardinal, a highly placed CIA mole in the Kremlin, who has been supplying the West with Soviet intelligence information for decades. This character is first alluded to in *The Hunt for Red October*, but it is here that we learn the whole story.

The novel opens in Afghanistan, but the action really begins when a U.S. Army team of researchers accidentally learns about a secret Soviet SDI installation. Admiral Greer, who has been "running" the Cardinal for decades, asks the mole to supply information about Soviet SDI capabilities.

The man code-named the Cardinal—a traitor to the Communist Party who has been trading secrets for a generation—is really Colonel Mikhail Semyonovich Filitov, three times decorated a Hero of the Soviet Union. Presently the Cardinal is being "handled" by a husband-and-wife CIA spy-team station in the U.S. Embassy in Moscow. When instructed to find out about the Dushanbe SDI site, Filitov sends a promising young colonel on his staff, Bondarenko, to tour the complex and write a confidential report. Bondarenko complies, and Filitov attempts to forward that information to the CIA. The information exchange is compromised and two operatives are lost—one is captured by the KGB, the other is murdered by common criminals as he is trying to flee the KGB's grasp in Moscow. Although the microfilm on which the information was encrypted was exposed, enough of it was salvaged for the KGB to recognize the source of the document—the office of Dimitri Timofeyevich Yazov, Defense Minister of the Soviet Union. A dogged KGB investigator, Vatutin, eventually links Mrs. Foley, one of the U.S. spies, with Yazov's immediate subordinate, Filitov, and they film their information exchange at a Moscow hockey game. A trap is set and Mrs. Foley and Filitov are both captured. The ambitious head of the KGB, Gerasimov, plans to use the Cardinal's treason to discredit the reforms of Narmonov, the novel's liberal president of the Soviet Union and Clancy's Mikhail Gorbachev clone.

This action precipitates a crisis in the White House—should the United States jeopardize the current arms negotiations (in which Jack Ryan is involved) by attempting to rescue the Cardinal? And after the Cardinal is taken by the KGB, will the revelations of his activities help the hard-liners gain the upper hand once more?

The CIA suspects that Gerasimov is staging a power play and intends to outmaneuver Narmonov. The activities of the Cardinal have indeed played right into Gerasimov's ruthless hands. But the KGB head is mistaken when he deduces that one of the two suspects in the Filitov case was killed on Russian soil by the CIA. The KGB feel that since American intelligence violated the unwritten laws of counterespionage, they are free to do the same. Gerasimov masterminds a desperate mission to capture America's foremost SDI scientist. The mission fails, and Ryan, in a face-to-face meeting with the head of the KGB, forces Gerasimov to defect to save his own life, and to bring Filitov with him.

During all this action, events have been brewing half a world away. The Archer, a leader of the Afghan freedom fighters recruited by the CIA, coincidentally observed a laser test at the Dushanbe SDI site. He reports what he witnessed to Ortiz, his CIA weapons supplier. When the Archer observes Ortiz's excitement and fear, he concludes that this new Soviet weapon must be mighty indeed. The Archer sees a means to gain real revenge against the Soviet oppressors and plans a *mujaheddin* attack on the complex.

In Moscow, Filitov and Gerasimov are spirited away on the very aircraft that is flying the American arms negotiators out of that city. At the same time, the Afghan freedom fighters attack Dushanbe with mixed results. Much of the complex is wrecked, but most of the technical personnel are saved by the timely intervention of Colonel Bondarenko. Ryan, forced to stay behind when Gerasimov and Filitov are loaded onto the aircraft, is captured by Vatutin and driven to a dacha outside Moscow. There, in a riveting one-on-one meeting with Narmonov/Gorbachev, Ryan is given a unique opportunity to express America's misgivings about Soviet intentions and a very middle-American vision of our own intentions in dealing with the Soviets in the future. Ryan is then released and sent home on a commercial airliner.

Filitov—"Misha"—three times Hero of the Soviet Union and the Cardinal of the Kremlin, dies in his sleep a few months after he is rescued and debriefed by the CIA. In one of the most poignant and emotional sequences in espionage fiction, he is buried in an unmarked grave near the Civil War battlefield of Antietam in a quiet, secret ceremony.

Readers are treated to a glimpse of virtually all aspects of life in the city of Moscow in *Cardinal.* The life-styles the high Communist Party officials and their sons and daughters enjoy is often compared to the privileges enjoyed by the Czars in Russia's past. Conversely, what little we see of the everyday life of the common people is grim and hopeless.

Resentment of the Soviet system and the special privileges granted to Communist Party members is once again depicted as the prime motive for treason against the *Rodina* in *Cardinal*. Filitov is no casual traitor—he is a man haunted by his actions, a man who must get drunk and have long, rambling "conversations" with the ghosts of the men who fought and died with him in Stalingrad before he commits each act of treason. Filitov is a Hero of the Soviet Union, a man children read about in State schools much as Catholic schoolchildren read about the lives of saints. He is an individual elevated as near to sainthood as the communist system permits—indeed, Clancy's choice of his code name, the Cardinal, is intentionally ironic. Can one imagine a more unlikely traitor?

But Filitov is driven to treason because he cannot trust his masters to do what is right for the people of Russia; he has seen the purges of Stalin, the horrors of war, and the price of Soviet adventurism. Filitov has paid a high price for Soviet incompetence and corruption—he is alone because a Party doctor and State-run factory medicine killed his wife, and the slovenly inefficiency of the State-run defense factories robbed him of his sons.

Resentment of the Soviet system fuels other treasons as well. The courier who works in the public baths and is murdered by Russian thieves while running from the KGB is a veteran of the war in Afghanistan. He objected to the Soviet practice of making bombs to kill and maim children, bombs made to look like innocent toys. This act of conscience left a black mark on his record and cost him his standing with the Party—dooming him to a life as a menial worker.

Hatred of the communists is not limited to Soviet characters—Mrs. Foley's loathing of the communist system was learned at her grandfather's knee, where she heard stories of Soviet atrocities against the Romanovs and other members of the ruling families. The Afghan resistance leader known as the Archer hates the Russians because their bombs killed his whole family.

By contrast, the single American traitor, Bea Taussig, has a personal motive for her betrayal—she is a lesbian in love with the girlfriend of America's most promising scientist, and she helps the KGB grab him on U.S. soil.

In this novel especially, but in virtually every other work of Clancy's that has Soviet protagonists, readers will find that the Russian characters are more complex and much more interesting than their Western counterparts. Clancy seems fascinated with life in the USSR, and doubly fascinated and impressed by individuals and institutions—like the Red Army—that manage to accomplish something good and positive amid the bureaucratic mire and predatory politics of that empire. Men like Colonel Bondarenko, Filitov's protégé, and Vatutin, the determined KGB "policeman" who cracks the Cardinal case, are seen as honest, noble men doing their best in a corrupt, incompetent system—they are not stereotypical villains.

Narmonov, Clancy's Gorbachev clone, comes off exceedingly well in the face-to-face meeting with Jack Ryan, which is at the core of this complex thriller. Until that final confrontation, Ryan, despite his central place in the action of the novel, isn't a particularly important character. This meeting changes that and is most revealing—and it sets the tone for the wonderfully poignant and effective climax.

Men like Gerasimov, the scheming head of the KGB and communist hard-liner, represent the type of individual who has undermined the idealism of the Marxist cause and engendered the treason of men like Filitov. A *chekist,* a toady, and an opportunist, Gerasimov, when forced to defect, mourns not the loss of his homeland—as Marko Ramius does—but the loss of his long-cherished and long-held power and prestige.

Clancy makes it clear to the reader that the Soviet Union's future lies with men like Narmonov, like Filitov, and like Bondarenko. Men like Vatutin, though honorable, are shown to be a threat to the health of the *Rodina*— Vatutin is in reality nothing more than a high-tech torturer, as his interrogation of Filitov and the daughter of a member of the Politburo shows. Though clever (Vatutin deduces that Gerasimov is about to defect and almost stops him, though he manages to capture Jack Ryan only when he jumps out of the negotiators' airplane to help Filitov and Gerasimov board), Vatutin's vision is limited. He is neither a politician nor a soldier, and he can but glimpse the wider implications of Filitov's treason and its ripple effect.

But Clancy doesn't buy the notion of political reform within the Soviet Union, nor does he completely trust the Soviets. The author warns his readers not to be too complacent about Soviet liberalization. In a revealing scene we are privy to Narmonov's inner thoughts, and they are not exactly what one would expect. Narmonov muses about the future of his country and about just how much of a threat an economically rejuvenated Soviet Union will be to America in just thirty years. We see that, realpolitik aside, Narmonov/Gorbachev is still a Marxist/Leninist at heart.

As in *Patriot Games,* many familiar characters join the cast of *The Cardinal of the Kremlin.* There is a visit by Marko Ramius—now Mark Ramsey—who joins Bart Mancuso and "Jonesy" on the U.S.S. *Dallas* for a dangerous mission off the coast of the Estonian city of Talinn. Judge Moore, CIA Chief Ritter, and especially Admiral Greer of American intelligence all take on more importance in Clancy's canon. The author also continues his habit of introducing "minor" characters who take on increased importance in subsequent works. Here we first meet "Clark," the

CIA operative who smuggles Gerasimov's wife and child out of the Soviet Union. "Clark"—whose real name is Kelly—takes on a much larger role in *Clear and Present Danger,* and, especially, in *The Sum of All Fears.*

The reader is treated to dramatic scenes dealing with the Afghanistan War and the *mudjaheddin* who battle the Russians with American-supplied Stinger missiles and near-suicidal courage, and we learn much about the importance of the Strategic Defense Initiative and details of the scientific research surrounding the project. Clancy is particularly concerned that his readers understand how vital this research is, and how it can make the world a safer place.

We find, at the close of *The Cardinal of the Kremlin,* a message of hope and cooperation and a condemnation of the senseless violence and horrors of war. In the climactic scene, appropriately set on the hills near Antietam—the site of the bloodiest battle in American history—Filitov is buried. Attending his secret funeral are CIA chiefs Ritter and Greer, Jack Ryan, General Parks, the young SDI scientist who was kidnapped along with his new wife, and the Russian ambassador, Dalmatov—like Filitov, a former tank commander.

An exchange between Ryan and the Russian ambassador runs as follows.

> "Why here?" Dalmatov asked. . . .
> "I would have preferred Arlington, but then someone might notice. Right over those hills is the Antietam battlefield. . . . It just seemed like the right place," Ryan said. "If a hero must have an unmarked grave, it should at least be close to where his comrades fell."
> "Comrades?"
> "One way or another we all fight for the things we believe in. Doesn't that give us some common ground?"

As in most traditional espionage thrillers, the status quo in superpower relations is restored. But Clancy takes it a single step further and provides a common ground, a common understanding that the two nations can exploit in the future.

The question remains, will they?

CLEAR AND PRESENT DANGER

The wrong way always seems more reasonable.
—George Moore

The next two novels in the Clancy canon, *Clear and Present Danger* and *The Sum of All Fears,* mark still another significant shift in the direction of Tom Clancy's fiction. Both novels deviate sharply from the author's previous efforts, are more complex, and hold several levels of meaning. Neither *Clear and Present Danger* nor *The Sum of All Fears* would appear to be, at least at first glance, particularly commercial, yet Clancy's fifth novel, *Clear and Present Danger,* is his most highly esteemed work—an opinion shared by both critics and fans.

With a good deal of commercial clout and an almost guaranteed audience, Clancy abandoned any and all genre formulas and concentrated on writing his own unique brand of political thriller. Both *Clear and Present Danger* and *The Sum of All Fears* deal with the use and abuse of power—political power, military might, and personal ambition. They also address the hidden and often sinister dangers of a faceless government bureaucracy in which no one can be held accountable for actions judged immoral or illegal by a civilized, democratic society.

Though thematically linked, the plots of these two novels veer off in very different directions. *Clear and Present Danger* illustrates the negative, destructive, and dangerous *abuse* of power, while the early portion of *The Sum of All Fears* explores the constructive, positive, and enlightened *use* of power. *Clear and Present Danger* resembles dystopian fiction, while *The Sum of All Fears* starts out as something akin to utopian fiction but ends on a bittersweet note. Neither novel stands alone, as there are passages in both that illuminate Clancy's major philosophical points—which are consistent in both works—and there is much after-the-fact information presented in *The Sum of All Fears* that illuminates the actions of the previous story.

With his last two novels, Tom Clancy has fought against the tide of American popular literature by writing works that explore the nature of power and, especially in *The Sum of All Fears,* the positive impact that power can have on the citizens of our nation and the world. Although *Clear and Present Danger* is manifestly about political corruption, incompetence, and abuse, it too is a positive work in that "the better angels of our nature," and the values bestowed on us in a free society, ultimately triumph. The clear moral vision of protagonist Jack Ryan and several other characters is instrumental in restoring balance to the affairs of state. The good do *something,* and their actions result in a positive outcome if not a "happy ending."

When the author began work on *Clear and Present Danger,* two issues were dominating the media in the United States. The first was the ongoing problem of drug abuse and the attendant crime, which was reaching epidemic proportions with the introduction of a new form of cocaine to our urban areas; the second was a brewing scandal within the Reagan administration that would come to be known as the Iran/Contra Affair.

In the mid-1980s a new scourge had come to our shores. It was called crack cocaine, or simply crack. Cheap, and requiring little refinement or cutting, crack was seen as a new drug of opportunity by the cartels in Colombia and the street pushers here in America. Crack, by being cheaper than regular cocaine, became more readily available to the less-affluent members of our society. Crack is also highly addictive, a property that guaranteed a steady supply of customers. At a time when education and social strictures against the use of drugs were just beginning to make a dent in the problem, crack arrived, and crack made a terrible problem much, much worse.

Many Americans are aware that the Constitution has nothing at all to say about which drugs we, as citizens, choose to poison ourselves with, and pundits on both sides of the political fence have proposed legalization of drugs to eliminate or curtail the negative effects of street distribution. If one eliminates the profit motive, proponents of legalization insist, much of the problems of attendant crime should disappear. It is a persuasive argument, and there *is* a historical precedent. When Prohibition was imposed on the American people, it did not stop the flow of illegal liquor. It did help make organized crime an immensely profitable enterprise, ensuring the mob's hold on many aspects of American life up to the present. More destructive than that, Prohibition made many otherwise law-abiding Americans into criminals—every single time they sipped a beer or had a tumbler of bathtub gin they were breaking the law. This led to contempt for the institutions of law enforcement and ultimately for the law itself. And a just-say-no campaign would have had no more effect then than it does now.

Conservatives like William F. Buckley have argued that drug laws are no more than the modern equivalent of Prohibition, which didn't work. Indeed, most Americans may feel that drugs are not for them, but many are not morally opposed to drug use. We tend to see drugs as a negative because of the criminal activities that result from illegal distribution—turf wars, gangland assassinations, etc.—and the street crime that results from addicts supporting their expensive and socially sanctioned habits. There have been voices in public office as well who call for the legalization or at the very least the decriminalization of drugs, though this action is politically risky.

The drug war in America began in earnest at about the same time Prohibition did, but when Prohibition was eventually repealed, the government possessed a huge bureaucracy to enforce laws that were no longer on the books, so the strictures against drugs like cocaine, opium, and marijuana remained. The FBI, the Bureau of Alcohol, Tobacco and Firearms, and later, the Drug Enforcement Agency, found a new *raison d'être*. For the next sixty years, these agencies, along with state and local ones, battled a "scourge" that touched only a small percentage of America's citizens. Drugs weren't really a massive social problem until the 1960s, when middle-class American youth was given the green light "to turn on, tune in, and drop out," and drug dealers discovered a vast new market for their products. Since then the problem has grown steadily worse.

But does the drug trade pose a "clear and present danger" to the survival of the United States of America? This is the question Tom Clancy ponders in his fifth novel, *Clear and Present Danger*. The plot is a simple one, though its unfolding is complex.

The CIA is running an antidrug operation inside and outside the borders of Colombia, a nation with friendly relations with this country. The clandestine operation has been ordered by the President, who made a campaign promise to curtail the flow of drugs. The operation is as ingenious as it is illegal. It is run on two fronts: American soldiers are airlifted into Colombia to spy on drug-processing sites and secret airfields. These foot soldiers are covertly recruited because of their light-infantry skills and ethnic backgrounds (Spanish-speakers only) as well as a personal opposition to the drug trade—Clancy's theme of resentment, again, but this time it is a hatred of the criminal element, which has cost key members of the team someone important. Outside of Colombia's borders, an Air Force pilot is drafted to intercept and shoot down drug-running aircraft when they are observed taking off from the Colombian airfields under surveillance by the soldiers. The pilot, too, has a personal vendetta against druggies—his mother was killed by an addict in a mugging incident.

The two clandestine operations are under the direct control of Admiral Cutter, an ambitious peacetime officer of the political kind. Cutter is being used by Bob Ritter and Judge Moore as a pawn—he can take the rap if the mission is compromised and provide the President and the Agency with "plausible deniability." Neither Ritter nor Moore has high regard for Cutter's intellectual faculties, but Cutter has ambition and his own agenda, and will not remain a simple front man for long.

Jack Ryan has just been elevated to Deputy Director, Intelligence (DDI), owing to the illness and imminent death of his mentor and spiritual father, Admiral Greer, the man who recruited Ryan in the first place. Jack has been closed out of this operation, and even his mentor, Greer, knew little about it.

The operation is not in action long before the cartels start to feel the heat. The assassination of an American agent for the Colombians enrages both the President of the United States and Cortez, a former Cuban intelligence agent now working for the Colombian cartel. The President wants revenge and steps up the operations against the drug lords. Cortez fears such retaliation and warns his cartel bosses. It is Cortez who eventually deduces the American scheme to halt the flow of drugs, and he uses the illegal CIA operation for his own benefit.

In the field in Colombia is John Clark, whom we last saw in *Cardinal* when he helped the KGB director's wife and daughter defect from Estonia. Clark is the CIA man in charge of field operations and one of the first to realize that there is something funny about this particular assignment.

Things begin to go awry when a Navy pilot drops a super-secret, undetectable bomb on the mountain fortress of a cartel leader during an important meeting of the crime bosses. The explosion, which is intended to mimic a car bomb, kills most of the major cartel members, as well as some innocent Colombian nationals and even children. When news of the deaths is made public, the President gets cold feet because of the amount of "collateral damage," and orders the operation halted. Cutter is forced to take desperate measures to stop the operation at its source, and meets with Cortez, who has now activated his own scheme to start a war within the cartel in an effort to consolidate his position. Cutter agrees to allow Cortez to implement his plan, but that means abandoning the fifty or so American infantry soldiers on the ground in Colombia—soldiers who are now being mercilessly hunted by cartel mercenaries.

Just in time, Ryan tumbles onto the conspiracy and devises a dangerous last-ditch effort to rescue the soldiers in Colombia. His plan involves Dan Murray at the FBI, Captain Wegener of the U.S. Coast Guard and his cutter, *Panache,* and Colonel Paul Johns and his helicopter crew stationed in Panama. Among the crew of Johns' chopper is a gunner named Buck Zimmer. In the teeth of a tropical storm, Ryan implements his plan when the rest of the CIA is busy with another matter—the funeral service for Admiral Greer, who passes away near the close of the novel. Ryan is almost too late, and American servicemen on the ground and involved in the rescue are killed. Buck Zimmer dies in Ryan's arms. His death begins a chain of events that is not resolved until the middle of Clancy's next novel.

Back in Washington, Ritter and Moore regain their senses and realize the consequences of their actions. Admiral Cutter, now politically isolated, is visited by Clark, who threatens to expose the whole scandal unless the Admiral "does the right thing." Cutter does, by stepping in front of a bus while jogging. Ritter, Moore, and the Congressional oversight committee agree to keep the operation a secret, with no political horseplay. Scandal is averted.

Probably the most ironic aspect of this entire novel is that, despite the fact that the CIA agents were running a secret military operation inside the borders of a friendly nation, which is patently illegal; despite the fact that children and innocent civilians were caught in the crossfire; despite the fact that the whole scheme was run without the approval of Congress or the knowledge of the American people—despite all of these things, the operation actually *worked.* Once the forces of law and order stopped playing by the book and stepped outside the bonds of acceptable civilized behavior, the cartel didn't have a chance. When a government decides to fight fire with fire, it is unstoppable. As one character points out, few people can imagine how much might a nation can bring to bear once the will is there. Once the CIA operatives stepped outside the law, the cartel had plenty to fear. We cannot beat a criminal organization that acts like a nation-state without resorting to the tools nation-states use to settle their differences—and that usually means military might. Yet there are dozens of passages in *Clear and Present Danger* that warn against sending the military to do what is essentially police work.

Clancy also implies that we all have much to fear once the rule of law breaks down, and it is not only high government officials who violate the letter of the law or break the law outright during the course of the novel. When the crew of the Coast Guard vessel *Panache* capture the hired killers who murdered an American real-estate tycoon and his family on the high seas, they know there isn't much of a case against their captives despite a mountain of circumstantial evidence. The captain and crew devise a scheme to "torture" a confession from the perpetrators—and the illegal method *works.*

When a curious defense lawyer uncovers the Coast Guard sailors' actions, he threatens to use that information in the defense—rendering all the fruits of the subsequent investigation "tainted." This might have resulted in the pirates' release and perhaps even a compromise of the evidence that led to the major economic blow dealt to the cartels in Operation Tarpon, but "corruption" again rears its ugly head. The pirates are set up by outraged local cops and murdered in prison, and the men who commit the crime are later cleared by the police as their reward. Again, sticking to the letter of the law would have led to disaster—in this case, the compromise of a major economic sting against the cartel. Bending the law, just a little, or a lot, leads to something like a just punishment.

Drugs and the frustration generated in the war against them corrupt every level of law enforcement in the course of Clancy's novel. This "as above, so below" dynamic continues throughout the course of *Clear and Present Danger.* When the plan begins to unravel, things go wrong on every level. For the higher-ups, like Cutter, exposure of the scandal would probably result in political catastrophe and the end of careers. For middle-management types like Clark and Zimmer, the consequences range from career suicide to literal death. But for the grunts, the men on the lowest rung of the social ladder, the danger is most real. For the cover-up to succeed, these men have to die. It is ironic that the men on the ground, those who will pay the ultimate price for failure, have the least stake in our society. They are only marginally a part of it, to begin with. "Ding" Chavez and the other soldiers like him were a product of America's underclasses and lived on society's fringe. They were "socialized" only by service in the military, and it is their military superior, Cutter, who abandons them when it becomes politically expedient.

When Admiral Cutter's part in the scandal is revealed, Moore, Ritter, and Ryan all agree that it is better to hush up the affair than to unleash on an already disillusioned public yet another government scandal. Ryan, too, is flexible enough to bend the rules for a greater good. Anyway, it is never the violation of the letter of the law that troubles men like Clark, the Coast Guard crew, and even Dan Murray of the FBI—it is the violation of the *intent* of the law, of what is *right,* that bothers them.

But who is to decide the proper course of action? The President—who is neither Reagan nor Bush, but their unnamed successor who seems to embody some of the negative qualities of both—is not zealous enough in pursuit of the truth. When Cutter suggests to the President that he doesn't want to know what is happening, the President readily agrees. Admiral Cutter doesn't seem to feel the pangs of conscience, even when his inaction and dishonesty cost the lives of good men under his command. His chief concern is covering his butt.

Ritter and Moore, who have previously been portrayed as honorable, become converts to the plan because of its initial success and because of their own impatience. Both are blinded to the consequences if their actions are made public. Clark, who has some suspicions about the operation from the start, is less concerned with what is right than with the safety of the men in the field. When Cutter abandons them, Clark feels that the Admiral's action is wrong, but he never questions orders that in this case are patently illegal.

So who is to judge? Who watches the watchmen?

The parallels found in *Clear and Present Danger* to the Iran/Contra scandal cannot be coincidental. Admiral Cutter substitutes for Lieutenant Colonel Oliver North; Bob Ritter takes on the likeness of William Casey, the man who was eventually blamed for Iran/Contra. The operation in Colombia is one that Admiral Greer would never have allowed to occur were he in charge—which is the reason Ryan, his protégé, was shut out of the operation at the beginning. In real life, if not in Clancy's fiction, the dead make convenient scapegoats. Casey was blamed in a very public scandal, Greer wasn't, because the actions of the President and the CIA were never made public. We can see that *Clear and Present Danger,* like Clancy's previous novel, embodies elements of a roman à clef.

But the moral of *Clear and Present Danger* is not so clear. Throughout the novel we see how liberal lawyers compromise the intentions of our founding fathers in order to promote their own agendas within the criminal-justice system. By tying up convictions with technicalities, these judicial activists attack the very concept of justice itself. These lawyers and obstructionists are seen by Clancy as being almost as dangerous as the drug lords themselves. Their actions serve only to undermine the average citizen's faith in government and social institutions—which in the long run serves no one but the agents of chaos.

Clancy makes it clear that times have changed, and due process is perhaps a luxury we can no longer afford, and so, ironically, need more than ever. The government's primary task—some say its *only* task—has always been "to serve and protect." Yet in contemporary America, our government often does neither. Too much of the government's efforts today are directed at artificial issues like abortion rights, redistribution of the "wealth," regulation of private institutions like banking, health care, and insurance, and—what government does best—the levying and collection of taxes. But, by forgetting its primary role, to serve the citizen in the street and protect the nation as a whole, the government of the United States is betraying its people. Social issues like the availability of abortion, the regulation of crucial industries, and the provision of basic services can often be resolved without the intervention of big government. Dubious concepts like the redistribution of wealth usually just mean a heavier tax burden and fewer crucial services for the working poor and the middle classes, and a free ride for welfare bureaucrats, not to mention the generations who remain on the welfare rolls almost thirty years after Lyndon Johnson announced his "war on poverty." Welfare and other programs of "social service" do more harm than good. They tend to undermine the Protestant work ethic that helped build our nation, which in turn lowers productivity. Government "regulation" of industries like the savings and loans has resulted only in disaster. Meanwhile, our streets are not safe—even for children—the murder rate soars, and more and more citizens take to arming themselves for survival.

Can anarchy be far behind?

This is a question Clancy does not address, because at heart he is a law-abiding, fair man who believes in the system envisioned by our founding fathers. Others, myself included, are beginning to have our doubts, and other techno-thriller authors have taken a cue from *Clear and Present Danger* and have written their own novels about the drug war in the future. Some have even taken Clancy's reasoning several steps further.

Several other elements enter the Clancy canon with *Clear and Present Danger,* but are explored more fully in *The Sum of All Fears.* The author introduces minor characters who will take on increasing importance in his sixth novel, including presidential candidate Bob Fowler, former Governor of Ohio (who is mistakenly identified as the governor of Missouri early in *Clear and Present Danger*), and his adviser for foreign affairs, Elizabeth Elliot. "Ding" Chavez, a soldier in the field in Colombia, becomes a CIA spook and works under John Clark in the subsequent novel, as well.

Most important, Clancy introduces a pattern of emotional neglect and abandonment that is stereotypical of the modern postindustrial American male.

When Admiral Greer, Ryan's spiritual father, dies of a protracted bout with cancer, Ryan is unable even to attend the funeral—he is on the life-or-death mission in Colombia, desperately trying to rescue the soldiers abandoned by the Agency and Admiral Cutter. But in doing his duty, Ryan misses the final farewell to one of the most important people in his life. This pattern of neglect will continue in *The Sum of All Fears,* and will come to threaten the emotional well-being of his own family. *The Sum of All Fears* has as one of its themes the personal toll exacted by public service.

Also, in *The Sum of All Fears,* the enlightened, traditional Western values that have served Jack Ryan in good stead in his personal life and during his term in government service become a burden in themselves, and threaten all that he holds dear.

Which is more important, service to a higher cause or one's own family? Clancy's latest novel ponders this important question along with many others.

THE SUM OF ALL FEARS

When Tom Clancy arrived on the literary scene in October 1984, the thriller/espionage genre was dominated by the fear of nuclear war. The theme of virtually every thriller written since the end of the Second World War—from Ian Fleming's to Robert Ludlum's—involved the balance of nuclear terror or the threat of nuclear brinkmanship. Spies and intelligence operatives were called on to help restore the balance of power in the fiction of Ian Fleming, Len Deighton, and later Robert Ludlum and John le Carré. When a nuclear confrontation threatened, the protagonists of these novels were expected to defuse the situation; if a deadly new weapon was invented, it was their duty to learn about it, steal it, or destroy it.

Most of the future-war novels written after 1947 involved the threat, the unfolding, or the aftermath of nuclear annihilation—especially the aftermath, with prophesied horrors such as rampaging mutants, creeping radioactive death, the destruction or crippling of human civilization, and, much later, the threat of nuclear winter.

But by the end of the 1970s the fear of nuclear Armageddon had diminished in the West. When Gorbachev rose to power in 1984, he introduced a series of revolutionary changes in Soviet society that further reduced East/West tensions. By the time Clancy entered the popular culture scene, he was able to write several novels involving East/West confrontations that did not envision a nuclear exchange, though the threat of one was always there and always a factor. But the paranoia that was a profound force in the early days of the Cold War, the days of Khruschev, the Cuban Missile Crisis and its aftermath, had long since dissipated, and with it fear-inspired works like Nevil Shute's *On the Beach* and its imitators.

Tom Clancy must have taken our complacency as something of a challenge. Leave it to the originator of the techno-thriller to conjure up those long-buried but apparently not-forgotten fears from our subconscious in his sixth novel, *The Sum of All Fears*. Though the author preferred the title "The Field of Camlan" for this work, the title the novel ultimately appeared under is the more apt, for *The Sum of All Fears* explores the sum of all the fears human civilization endured during the worst period of the Cold War—back in the bad old days.

This novel and the real events that surrounded its release in August 1991 serve to remind us of just how quickly those uneasy times can return and how fragile our current sense of well-being can be.

The Sum of All Fears is also a novel about the practical application of the current theories about the birth of the "new world order" as envisioned by

George Bush and the other leaders of the democratic West. Clancy's novel follows on the heels of the success of Operation Desert Storm, and formulates a fictional "next step" in the resolution of the ongoing crisis in the Middle East. But such political success can exact a price, and has its casualties. Clancy's novel also ponders the toll exacted by public service, the plight of those whose lives, personal character, and indoctrination did not prepare them for the new world order, and the danger, always present in a democratic society, of electing someone who covets power for the wrong reasons or who is inept at managing it. As Americans, we've seen bad presidents come and go, but so far we have been fairly lucky. Clancy points out that our luck could one day run out.

Through Clancy's story, we see what might happen to the generations of terrorists and malcontents, petty communist bureaucrats, professional KGB thugs, and political fundamentalists when the ideology they've believed in and devoted their lives to—and that has nurtured them in return—crumbles in less than a decade. Clancy demonstrates that our naive optimism that these people will immediately turn around and become happy, peace-loving capitalists is unfounded, and that hazards lie ahead.

The Sum of All Fears is Clancy's most complex and challenging novel to date, and also his most emotionally engaging. The author pulled out all the stops at the climax and offered readers a two-hundred-page roller-coaster ride complete with the threat of nuclear war and the destruction of a cherished American institution. There is an emotional dimension and richness to this work that is compelling and harrowing in its own right.

The Sum of All Fears begins with a potential disaster, then shifts gears and moves into the realm of utopian fiction, only to veer off in an entirely unexpected direction by the novel's close.

After a protracted opening chapter set during the Syrian invasion of Israel in 1973, events move to the present. An Israeli military security officer, shaken by the loss of his wife to another man, acts on his own to quash the new, nonviolent protests by Palestinians in the Occupied Territories. In thrall to a conservative rabbi, the officer shoots and kills the unarmed leader of the nonviolent resistance on live television.

Suddenly, actions on the back burner of the newly elected Fowler administration take the forefront, including a peace initiative dreamed up by Jack Ryan of the CIA and National Security Adviser Dr. Charles Alden. The plan is a simple one: Declare Jerusalem a "Holy City" and run it like the Vatican, patrolled by a special police/security force resembling the Swiss Guards. Holy men from any religion would be welcome there, and Jerusalem would be ruled by a troika of religious men from each of the three major faiths that vie for the rule of that ancient city—Islam, Judaism, and Christianity. The plan works splendidly, but just as it is being implemented, Alden is involved in a sexual scandal that ruins his career and provides enough shocks to his system to kill him with a massive stroke.

Elizabeth Elliot, the abrasive political adviser to Bob Fowler, first introduced in *Clear and Present Danger,* is promoted to Alden's post. Elliot, a liberal and former professor at Bennington, dislikes "Cold Warriors" and "dinosaurs" such as Jack Ryan and contrives to have the credit for the peace plan taken away from Ryan and given to the late Dr. Alden.

Marcus Cabot, Ryan's new superior at the CIA and a Fowler appointee, is not much better than Elliot—he enjoys the perks of his office, and the power, without caring for the work itself.

But the worst of the lot is Bob Fowler, the new President himself, who is an egotistical elitist with leftish pretensions and little practical ability. Fowler is as arrogant as he is inept.

Forces elsewhere in the world, meanwhile, are chafing under the political changes sweeping the Soviet Union and the Middle East. Ismael Qati, an Arab terrorist, is dying of cancer, and his dreams are dying with him, for peace in the Middle East has meant the loss of popular support for the Palestinian terrorist movement of which he was a chief. Before death claims him, Qati wants to commit one more act of political terrorism that will never be forgotten, an event that will hurt his two most hated foes— America and the Soviet Union. He is aided by the discovery of an unexploded Israeli atomic bomb in the garden of an old Druse farmer, a device lost in 1973 during the Syrian invasion and which has remained buried for decades. Qati decides to use the bomb to instigate a world war. With the help of Marvin Russell, an American Indian terrorist who has just seen his brother killed by the FBI in a drug bust; Ghosn, an engineer and lieutenant of Qati's; and Günther Bock, a former East German terrorist *à la* the Baader-Meinhof Group, Qati plans to repair the bomb, plant it, and profit from the chaos that follows.

KGB-trained Günther Bock is especially dangerous. Like his wife, Petra, he was betrayed by their former KGB masters. Petra was captured by the police of the new, united Germany and sentenced to life imprisonment for her terrorist crimes. In prison, subjected to constant mental torture by her jailers, Petra hanged herself.

Fueled by their feelings of betrayal and the knowledge that the world they have envisioned and struggled to create will never be, these unlikely conspirators form a dangerous alliance. Bock connects Qati with a former nuclear-weapons designer for the East Germans, and the old physicist-engineer creates, in a crude workshop in the Middle Eastern desert, a thermonuclear device of considerable magnitude. Russian intelligence, meanwhile, has gotten wind of the East German nuclear project and begins to hunt down the scientists involved. They uncover little, but their investigation is wide enough to make the CIA nervous when they hear about it through a Soviet mole.

Jack Ryan reports to Fowler that there may be nuclear bombs missing from the Soviet arsenal, weapons "lost" during the turmoil following glasnost and German reunification—a report he comes to regret when he later changes his opinion about the validity of the mole's claim.

During all of this, a power play is going on in the inner circle of the Fowler Administration. Elizabeth Elliot sends her own "spy" into the CIA, a young Harvard graduate named Ben Goodley. Ryan makes the best of a bad situation and takes the youth under his wing and does as much for Goodley as Admiral Greer did for him. Elliot also launches an investigation into Jack Ryan's private life and discovers the existence of Buck Zimmer's wife. Ryan has set up Carol Zimmer in her own business as a 7-Eleven owner near his home, fulfilling the promise he made to her dying husband in the previous novel.

Elliot, who has become the widowed Fowler's mistress, assumes that Ryan is having an extramarital affair and gets reporter friends to publish a thinly veiled accusation of this in *The Washington Post*. Cathy Ryan is already suspicious because of her husband's impotence, which is caused by job stress and drinking. Alcohol has already become a bit of a problem, but Cathy assumes she is losing her husband to another woman. The newspaper story seems to confirm her suspicions.

The timely intervention of John Clark, Ryan's driver, and Ding Chavez, now Clark's protégé, saves Ryan's marriage. But the Deputy Director of the CIA decides he's had enough grief from a hostile, incompetent boss and his scheming mistress, and resigns. Before he goes, however, Ryan wants to complete one last operation.

Ryan, through a Russian spy in Tokyo, has learned that the Japanese Prime Minister has cut a secret deal with Mexico and will renege on a trade agreement he made with the United States Government a few months before. Ryan, Clark, and Chavez work out a scheme to eavesdrop on the Japanese trade delegation and deliver a transcript of their discussions to the President before he meets with the Prime Minister.

As a blizzard hits Washington, D.C., the President flies to Camp David, where he will watch the Super Bowl with Elliot instead of attending in person. The Secretaries of State and Defense and other key Cabinet members are on hand in Denver for the big game. Marvin Russell, Qati, and Ghosn smuggle the bomb to Denver and plant it inside the stadium, after which Qati and Ghosn murder Russell, as they murdered the men who reconstructed the bomb.

About an hour into the game, the device detonates, killing sixty thousand people in the blink of an eye. Simultaneously, former members of the East German security police and friends of Bock, disguised as Red Army officers, engineer a clash in Berlin by using a Russian tank to fire on American troops. Within minutes Soviet and NATO tanks and troops are fighting in the streets of Berlin.

Military forces go on alert all over the world. In the skies, American Navy aviators, including Robbie Jackson, Ryan's friend, shoot down a flight of Libyan MiGs. On the high seas, a Russian hunter-killer submarine sinks an American nuclear-missile submarine commanded by the inept, ambitious Captain Ricks.

With contradictory information coming from all sides, his chief advisers dead or missing, and Fowler getting bad advice from Elizabeth Elliot, who is shaken by the swiftness of the crisis, a nuclear confrontation seems imminent. Jack Ryan's advice is being ignored by the President because he no longer trusts his Deputy Director of CIA. When missiles are about to be launched, Ryan prevails by personally taking over the hot line to the Kremlin and exchanging messages with Narmonov, the Chairman of the Soviet Union.

Ryan proves to Fowler that Narmonov is still in charge and that the Red Army coup Elliot suspects has not occurred. Thanks to quick work by Dan Murray and the FBI, the terrorist plot is finally revealed. Qati and Ghosn are captured by Clark and Chavez in Mexico as they are trying to fly to the Middle East. Clark grills Qati and learns of the plot. Qati claims the whole scheme was sponsored by an Iranian ayatollah in the Islamic holy city of Qum, and, in the heat of the moment, Fowler orders a nuclear strike on that city—a direct order that Ryan countermands, insisting that Fowler is no longer in control of his faculties and should be removed from office. Vice President Durling takes charge of the government; Elizabeth Elliot is sedated and taken to the hospital. Fowler is removed from office.

Ryan meets with the terrorists and learns that if Fowler *had* succeeded in destroying Qum with a nuclear strike, he would have played right into Qati's hands, as the terrorist wanted the United States to do just that: make an enemy of Islam for all time. Qati also hoped to cause a Third World War. Destroying the holy city of Qum would have accomplished that as well.

Qati and Ghosn are turned over to an Islamic tribunal, tried, found guilty, and beheaded. Peace is secured, and order once more restored. Jack Ryan is honored by the Saudis and retires from public life.

• • •

Though there is a wealth of major and minor characters featured in *The Sum of All Fears,* the central figure in the novel is a character who appears in only one short scene—the East German–trained terrorist Petra Bock.

Petra, the wife of Günther Bock, is said to have been suckling her twin infant daughters when the German police found and arrested her. Her children were taken from her and no longer even remember she existed. They now live a comfortable bourgeois existence as the adopted children of a police officer from the new, united Germany. Günther was forced to abandon his wife and children or be captured himself.

Petra Bock's estrangement from her children is the perfect metaphor for the sudden loss in the 1980s of the communist ideology that was supposed to nurture the Soviet people from the cradle to the grave, but was abandoned when those selfsame people "matured" and renounced the tenets of socialism in the face of reality. The young people in the Soviet Union today care little for communist ideology—they want blue jeans, movies, rock and roll, and the other amenities of the West. The struggles of their parents and grandparents in the Great Patriotic War and the sacrifice in the decades after the Second World War are no longer cherished memories—chronic shortages of staples, long bread lines, and a poor standard of living have erased such unquestioning support for the *Rodina.*

Like Petra's children, the people of the Soviet Union have forgotten the "mother" that nurtured them, a mother who appeared to be the soul of maternal comfort, but was really a cruel and dangerous murderer.

And Qati, who was Petra's lover, mourns her loss as well. Though Petra was Günther's wife, Qati enjoyed her charms. Here we find another metaphor, this one for communism's traditional support for the "oppressed peoples" of the Third World and the promise of aid and comfort to "revolutionary factions." With the fall of communism, terrorist nations and groups have lost their primary supporter, as well. The loss of the woman Petra and their ideological base push Günther and Qati down a dangerous, near-suicidal path. Qati's terminal cancer, too, can be seen as a metaphor for the withering of the old ways of terrorism during the rise of the new world order.

Marvin Russell, the violent supporter of the American Indian Movement, is a more problematical character. He sees the world through a narrow prism of ideology, blinded to reality by his own Rousseauism, his romantic vision of the primitive life-style of his Native American ancestors. Russell is an Indian, and he wants to despise everything American, yet he demonstrates a pride in all things American—from football to pancakes—while ferrying Qati and Ghosn to Denver. And the two Arabs recognize that Russell's glorification of his ancestors is a silly, romantic conceit, and that the lives of the plains Indians were—to borrow from Hobbes—nasty, brutish, violent, and short.

President Fowler is an example of every inept, naive, and egotistical president we, as Americans, have suffered under; men who believe, despite reality to the contrary, that if they can just bring their own "common sense" and cherished liberal notions to the White House, they will be able to reclaim the hearts of the American people and set an example that will shame the rest of the world's bullies into civilized behavior. Ryan points out to Elizabeth Elliot in *Clear and Present Danger* that thinking the world is a certain way will not make it so, no matter how hard we may wish it. Politicians like Fowler and intellectuals like Elliot, for all their book learning, have not yet grasped that simple lesson.

As Ryan points out in the novel, Fowler reverts to type when the going gets rough. He was a former prosecuting attorney and still thinks like one. Fowler is not cut out for the job of president, and his arrogance prevents him from performing his job well. Because of the changes in the Soviet Union and on the international scene, the President feels supremely confident that the war games he *should* practice with the military are a waste of time, and he does not bother with them. Hence he is ill-prepared when crisis really does loom. Fowler is also seen as lacking the compassion needed to wield so much power. The painful and protracted death of his wife, years before, is said to have burned much human feeling out of the man. In Clancy's universe, power must always be tempered with compassion for one's fellow man. If it is not, the author suggests, then we end up with abominations like Admiral Cutter, Elizabeth Elliot, and Bob Fowler.

Clancy saves most of his contempt for Elizabeth Elliot. She, and those like her in the real world, certainly earn it. A spoiled rich girl playing at left-wing politics, Elliot is as arrogant and narrow-minded as Fowler. She is also much weaker. When the terrorists strike, Elliot cannot forget that she might have died at the football game had the President not changed his mind about attending. She views the attack as a personal one, and it shakes her to her very foundations. She is worthless in the ensuing crisis.

But even before events contrive to undermine her, Elliot is seen as a contemptible human being on almost all fronts. She is sleeping with Fowler to promote her own agenda. She sends the young Harvard man, Ben Goodley, to spy on Ryan, and even tries to destroy Jack's marriage and family life.

Elliot also possesses all the negative traits of the intellectual left. Although she would never think of herself as one, she is a rabid racist. She laments that Ben Goodley, though a promising young asset to the CIA, is a white male instead of being of a more "politically correct" race or gender.

She despises Ryan because he is friends with Clark and Chavez—his driver and bodyguard—and treats them like human beings instead of, in her own words, "furniture." In all respects, Elliot is seen as a thoroughly inadequate human being, and these failings will prove to be her undoing.

Ryan, on the other hand, is portrayed as an honorable man despite the demands of his career in government. He is trying to adhere to his own standards of decency, and in government that is not easy. His traditional values are still an asset, but Ryan is beginning to learn that doing the right thing can be a double-edged sword. If Ryan hadn't rescued the soldiers in Colombia and exposed the illegal covert activities sanctioned by the previous administration in *Clear and Present Danger,* Fowler might not even have been elected in the first place. Ryan blames himself for that near the close of *The Sum of All Fears.*

Jack Ryan's charity toward Buck Zimmer's widow and family are positive actions, but it seems that no good deed goes unpunished when one has powerful enemies, for Elliot uses Jack's relationship with the Zimmers to hurt his wife and threaten his family. If it wasn't for the timely intervention of the "furniture"—Clark and Chavez—Ryan probably would have lost his wife. Ryan's fair treatment of his subordinates encourages loyalty in them. Elizabeth Elliot and Bob Fowler have no such compassion for their underlings; their elitism and arrogance endear them to no one—even the Secret Service agents assigned to protect them don't particularly enjoy their company. Clancy seems to suggest that there is no positive human emotion, no unselfish act, no unsullied thought that people like Elizabeth Elliot cannot twist into something ugly, petty, or evil. She, more so than even Fowler, is a flawed human being who has gone into government work not to be of service to society, but to take advantage of a comfortable position of power and influence for her own personal agenda and aggrandizement.

As in *Hunt* and *Cardinal,* the resentment felt by some of the characters is again a factor in *The Sum of All Fears*—but this time the resentment is not caused by communism, but rather by the *collapse* of communism. Bock, his Stasi cohorts, and Qati and Ghosn have all been betrayed by the fall of Marxist-Leninist governments. Now, rootless men with no future, they make do with the viciousness of their past. They cannot change themselves, but they hope to cause change for the worse. They have no future, and so they would deny everyone a future. Their cruel act of terrorism is unparalleled in human history—never have so few hurt so many and threatened so many more.

The climax of *Clear and Present Danger* features both human and elemental turmoil, as a hurricane threatens the rescue of the soldiers trapped in Colombia. This Shakespearean touch is also found in *The Sum of All*

Fears, when a snowstorm buries Washington, D.C., as the crisis erupts. Like a reminder of the threat of nuclear winter, this elemental menace is hovering in the background of the novel's harrowing climax.

Much has been said here and by others about Tom Clancy's seemingly preternatural ability to prophesize, and to capitalize on situations and events in the real world. Gorbachev's rise was foreshadowed by Clancy's fictional counterpart, Narmonov, in *The Cardinal of the Kremlin,* and both the real and fictional Soviet premiers were former ministers of agriculture. Clancy shrewdly fashioned his fourth novel around SDI and the Soviet intervention in Afghanistan, just as these two issues came to dominate East-West relations.

Other novels, too, benefited from the author's prescience. *Clear and Present Danger* concentrated on the drug war just as crack was changing the face of the drug problem in America, and dealt with the abuse of political power at a time when scandal threatened the second term of Ronald Wilson Reagan.

But even those who had admired Clancy's ability to foretell events in the political arena must have been surprised by the events in the Soviet Union that virtually coincided with the publication of *The Sum of All Fears,* for, within days of the novel's initial appearance in bookstores, the hard-line coup against Gorbachev actually took place. Although this startling and unexpected development was short-lived, it served to remind us all of just how close the Cold War really is, and just how easily the days of superpower mistrust and confrontation can return. As long as nuclear weapons exist— and, like dreams of democracy in the Soviet Union, the bomb is not something that can be locked away and forgotten once unleashed—the threat remains. This message, contained in *The Sum of All Fears,* could not have been better complemented than it was by the events of the failed August coup.

Fortunately, the Russian people had Boris Yeltsin, who went in the eyes of the world from a rather vulgar buffoon to a heroic figure who blocked the tanks, the BMPs, and the oppression of a new hard-line communist government. As in Clancy's novels, one man—a single individual—made all the difference.

Was is it life imitating art or art imitating life? Ask Tom Clancy.

WHY TOM CLANCY?

While it doesn't hurt to get a plug for your first novel from one of the most popular presidents of this century, Ronald Reagan's admiration for Clancy's *The Hunt for Red October* doesn't reach far enough to explain the phenomenal popularity of Clancy's fiction. Since his first novel went into Berkley paperback, each of Clancy's subsequent novels has outsold the previous ones, marking a steady rise in the popularity of this remarkable author. *The Sum of All Fears,* his latest novel, entered the best-seller lists the very first week it went on sale in hardcover.

Tom Clancy's appeal is so widespread, so universal, that he has entered that rarefied realm occupied by only a few other popular writers in this century. His popularity already rivals Stephen King's, though Clancy has been at work only half as long, and has produced but a tiny literary output compared with the prolific King. Danielle Steel, too, has a huge following, though, again, she also has an impressive body of work behind her. Despite his small output, Tom Clancy, like Stephen King and Danielle Steel, has become a literary phenomenon.

What are this author's singular accomplishments? What makes Tom Clancy's work unique?

As we have seen, Clancy fused the traditional thriller/espionage genre with elements of science fiction such as preoccupation with technology and a futurist's vision of political events on the near horizon, to produce the techno-thriller. But, as the author himself has complained when asked about the technological aspects of his fiction, "Why doesn't anyone talk about techno-mysteries?" That is, why stress Clancy's use of technology, since it is neither unique in contemporary fiction nor as pervasive in the author's work as we are led to believe. There is less technical/scientific information in one of Clancy's novels than one would find in a work by Thomas Harris, for instance.

Clancy's vision of future warfare is one of his most enduring achievements. Of all the author's work, *Red Storm Rising* is the most imitated, and this particular novel has given birth to a sub-genre of its own, practiced by authors from Larry Bond to Ralph Peters to Payne Harrison. His vision of futuristic warfare is nothing new. We have seen that near-future, imaginary war novels, as envisioned by authors like William Le Queux and H. G. Wells, were popular during the decades preceding the First World War. Clancy merely updated this classic subgenre of science fiction and portrayed a *conventional* war when everyone else seemed to be thinking *nuclear* war.

Clancy's grasp of current affairs on the international scene is probably also an important factor in his popularity. The tide of international events occurring during the last decade has been unmatched since the Second World War, and we should of course be aware of the revolutionary changes sweeping the world. But since when does a careful analysis of current events guarantee the appeal of a work of fiction?

I think we have to look a little more deeply at Clancy's novels to find the reasons for his audience appeal.

The real secret of Tom Clancy's popularity, I believe, is his deeply held personal and political philosophy, which is reflected in his novels, and the fact that the author prefers to emphasize positives over negatives. Four factors that I believe are vital to his appeal are: (1) his positive portrayal of the United States of America and the political system we enjoy, (2) his positive portrayal of the American military and intelligence agencies, (3) his belief that political and military might can be used for the good of humanity and are not innately evil, and, (4) the fact that the author presents positive male role-models in his fiction, running counter to the fashion in popular literature for the last twenty or so years.

Tom Clancy loves freedom. He is not naive about the problems our society faces, and will continue to face in the future, but he is confident that our enlightened system of Western democratic values provides the tools we need to remedy social or political problems. Rather than blame America, Clancy sees our nation as a beacon and a leader in the decades and perhaps centuries to come, as a force for justice in an unjust world. This is a vision that is vital if America is going to assume its role in the international community and do the job only Americans—because of our unique freedoms and our impressive wealth—can accomplish. The new world order cannot be born without the active intervention of the United States.

The kind of power America may need to wield in the coming decades, and the determination required to make the kind of tough decisions that could lie ahead, also require a willingness by American citizens to allow its government to take a painful stand, and perhaps fight another war like the one fought in Iraq. Individual Americans must be willing to become involved in the political process, and America as a whole should use its economic, political, and even military might in the decades ahead for the good of all.

Clancy's reversal of the trend, so fashionable in the media, in popular fiction, and among the intelligentsia, of bashing the "military-industrial complex" and the intelligence agencies is a big factor in his appeal. Besides the obvious point that many, many Americans work in these areas and may not like being blamed for the ills of the world, we must remember that we need our military. When the military is called to duty, it responds and does what it is ordered to do by the Commander in Chief. And we must not forget that all Americans are potential soldiers, that we are a nation of citizen-soldiers, and, in principle, do not make war without the will and consent of the people of the United States.

The fiction of Tom Clancy and his peers did the world a service by paving the way for Operation Desert Shield, then Desert Storm. The shift in public opinion regarding the use of the military can be traced in part to the popularity of the techno-thriller genre, which educated us about the weapons, the strategies, and the very nature of modern warfare.

Will Tom Clancy's work endure?

Probably. His fiction is certainly not frozen in time, and continues to grow and mature. Although some of his early novels may someday appear dated, Clancy continues to explore new territory and will always remain current—if not well ahead of his time. But even the works that appear to be dated will provide future generations with a clear picture of the crucial period in history that marked the beginning of the end of Marxist-Leninist rule in the Soviet Union and the birth of the new world order. And Tom Clancy will find new areas to explore, new ways to challenge us through his fiction, and new ways to entertain us in the grand manner we have come to expect from this talented and thoughtful author.

2. An Interview With Tom Clancy*

GREENBERG: Can you describe the process, if there is one that you can identify, through which your novels take shape?

CLANCY: You start off with a basic idea: what if? What if an American tourist got in the way of an assassination attempt in London? What if there's a sudden energy crisis in the Soviet Union that forces them to contemplate war as an alternative to total collapse? And you follow that thought to what you hope is a logical conclusion.

GREENBERG: Do you block out scenes in any kind of process that might be of interest to writers?

CLANCY: Every writer has a different system, a different method for structuring a story. Freddie Forsyth, for example, has very highly detailed outlines. So detailed that when he writes he's really filling in the blanks. I

*The following interview was compiled from a series of conversations which took place between Martin H. Greenberg and Tom Clancy during the spring of 1991.

don't use outlines at all. I start working in the morning and write my five or ten or fifteen pages and it's as much a discovery process for me as it is for the reader, with the added advantage on my part that if I don't like it I can change it.

GREENBERG: Is there some part of writing that you could identify as the most enjoyable or more enjoyable than other areas of writing?

CLANCY: There is nothing at all enjoyable about writing. You do it because you love it, but you're not blind to the fact that it is very hard and miserable work.

GREENBERG: Then my next question about the least enjoyable part of it—

CLANCY: The research is the fun part of writing.

GREENBERG: Do you stay away from writing for periods of time—vacations or breaks—or do long periods go by without you doing any writing?

CLANCY: Depends on what you mean by a long period. From the time I finished *Clear and Present Danger* to the time I started *The Sum of All Fears* I essentially tried to take a year off. It turned out to be an illusion on my part. Instead of sitting home and writing I did a lot of running around and giving speeches and making appearances, which actually made my life even more hectic than it generally is.

GREENBERG: Do you have a routine or schedule in terms of writing?

CLANCY: You arise in the morning and go to work just like everybody else.

GREENBERG: And stop when you feel like it.

CLANCY: Well, I usually work from about eight o'clock until lunch, and it's usually all I can stand to do on a continuous basis. The closer I get to deadline the more time I spend at the keyboard. But generally I work from about eight o'clock in the morning until about twelve-thirty.

GREENBERG: Could you tell us a little about your first book and how it came to be written, especially how it came to be published?

CLANCY: Well, the first book, that depends on what you mean by that. But if you mean *The Hunt for Red October,* which is the first one published, in

1982, the right set of circumstances came together, and since I was my own boss and had my own business and could make my own rules I decided that I was going to devote time to do something I've wanted to do really since high school, which was to write a book and have it published and see my name on the cover. So I guess the whole writing, the first draft, was written between November 11, 1982, and February 27, 1983. And the next day I drove it up to the Naval Institute in Annapolis and just left it there and waited for their judgment, which came three weeks later. They said they really liked it, could I rewrite the whole thing.

GREENBERG: And your reaction when they accepted it, I think is predictable, but—

CLANCY: Well, they didn't accept it until the following November. I was, of course, quite pleased, particularly since they offered me a $3,000 advance. I talked them up to $5,000.

GREENBERG: You mentioned that you wanted to write a book and see your name on it. Did you have any vision of what might happen to it before it happened?

CLANCY: Not in my wildest nightmares. When I wrote *Red October* I thought we'd sell maybe 5,000 or 10,000 hardcovers and that would be the end of it. I never really thought about making money. I certainly never thought about best-sellerdom because first the book didn't have any sex. Really, all I was trying to do was write the best book I could and get it published—just to get that monkey off my back—because it was something, it was an ambition that had gone back more than twenty years and that's really all I thought about it. It was just to finish the project, do the best I could, and then get on with my life. No, I never thought about great sales. And when my agent approached me for the first time, one of the first questions I asked him was, "Do you think I'm good enough to do this for a living?" And he said, "Yeah, I think probably you are." It turns out he was right.

GREENBERG: I was going to ask you to talk about each of your novels.

CLANCY: *The Hunt for Red October*—what happened was in August, I guess it was August of 1982, I decided, Clancy, you've always wanted to write a book. You own your own business, you can make your own rules. You can do whatever the hell you want. Why don't you do it? So I did.

Based on a real story—the attempted defection of a Soviet frigate, the *Storozhevoy*. I decided to make the defecting vessel a nuclear-powered missile submarine because it throws a lot more chips into the pot. And really I was just trying to write a reasonably good thriller. And end up trying to treat the—for lack of a better term—the technical issues with reasonable accuracy. Let me make a note here that not too long ago I picked up a murder mystery. I don't read very many of them because I can never figure the damn things out. It makes me feel stupid. I've since learned that cops have the same problems. But anyway, halfway through this mystery the author is going through police lab tests and how the police conduct investigations and all of a sudden I realized here was more technical material in a single 280-page mystery than there was in any two of my books, and they don't call them techno-mysteries. Believe me, I know nothing about how police do laboratory tests, but any mystery writer worth his salt will discuss this in the most excruciating detail because it's a requirement of the genre. And yet those books are not deemed to be technical. All I do in my books is describe with a fair degree of fidelity the tools used by the characters in my books, and why people deem that to be technical, I don't know. I was an English major in college and I don't know how to drive a submarine or an airplane. *Red Storm Rising* began by accident. Larry Bond, who is my co-author, is my son's godfather. And he was over at the house for Tommy's first birthday party. And he told me about a project he was working on. We started discussing it and I said, "Oh hell, I just finished writing a book. This sounds like it would be a fun thing to do. We could write a book out of this and maybe make a few bucks." And he said, "Gee, that sounds interesting," and we shook hands on the idea and that was that. The thing ended up selling a million hardcovers. Let's see, *Patriot Games* was actually the first Ryan book I actually worked on. It predates *Red October* by several years. And of course I—the reason I put Jack Ryan in *Red October* was around chapter 4, when I was writing the thing, I realized there was an element missing. I needed an additional character to really act as the on-screen narrator. The central character that the audience would follow while the plot of the book unfolded. So I had Jack completely fleshed out from—I guess at that point I had maybe a hundred pages of *Patriot Games* written—so I simply dropped him into the plot and included references in *Red October* referring to *Patriot Games,* which book of course was not finished until December of 1986. Jack Ryan grew out of the original concept of *Patriot Games,* which I worked on in 1978 or so. It is kind of slapdash process. Anyway, then, while I was writing *Red October* I came up with this character of the Cardinal and I thought, well, he was kind of an interesting character, we'll have to follow up on him, so that grew into *The*

Cardinal of the Kremlin. Also, the book I just finished, *The Sum of All Fears,* is a project I started working on in 1979. That's when I wrote the first chapter.

GREENBERG: With the opening of the '73 war.

CLANCY: I wrote the opening chapter in either '78 or '79. And I had thought the plot through reasonably before and I knew I could take the world to the brink of a nuclear war but I didn't figure out how to stop it. Well, three-quarters of the way through *Cardinal of the Kremlin* I figured out how I could end *The Sum of All Fears.* So then I put a little—the fact that Ryan meets with Narmonov is the decisive factor and so I had him at the end of *Cardinal* meet Narmonov and they work out a deal and they shake hands on the deal and that's that. And then I had to use *Clear and Present Danger* to put in the new President, who would almost take the world to the brink of war. So really, except for *Red Storm Rising,* which exists in a separate universe from the others, the whole series really is a very logical and connected network of plot lines which would continue to diverge and converge throughout the body of the work.

• • •

GREENBERG: I know that you enjoy reading science fiction and I presume you've read it for many years.

CLANCY: Yes. The first science fiction book I read was *Twenty Thousand Leagues Under the Sea,* by Jules Verne, back when I was in the third grade, and I haven't stopped since. John Varley, for example, I think is the best writer in America, for pure craftsmanship. Varley is one of those people who make me feel quite inferior. And I told him this too, quite recently, to make sure that he knew that I thought that. I really do think he's the best writer in America. There are a lot of really talented people in science fiction—Jerry Pournelle, Larry Niven, Joe Haldeman, the list goes on and on and on. And I wish that Jules Verne was taken a little bit more seriously by critics. For some reason critics regard science-fiction novels as being something other than serious work, and I really don't understand why.

GREENBERG: Do you see any distinctions between SF and many of the things that are published under the techno-thriller label?

CLANCY: Number one, I reject the title of techno-thriller and the claim that I invented it. Actually I argue that if there is such a genre, subgenre, as that it was probably invented by Michael Crichton with the *Andromeda Strain,* but why not just drop the label science fiction entirely and just consider it part of the general category of fiction? Fiction is about speculation, it's about projecting ideas generally into the future rather than into the past. Just make it part of the mainstream, which in many cases I think it is. Maybe one of the problems with science fiction is that it's considered a separate genre when really what you're talking about is the future and you're talking about people and you're talking about ideas and you're talking about ways in which technology or ideas or people can change the world or change the human condition. On that basis, how do you distinguish science fiction from any other kind of fiction?

GREENBERG: Would you care to mention any particular novels that have stayed with you a long time? Those you would recommend to people who are just coming to science fiction?

CLANCY: That's a tough one. I guess you'd argue that *Gulliver's Travels* by Swift is probably the first recognizable science-fiction novel. Then of course Jules Verne. You could argue Edgar Allan Poe. Some people argue Poe, but I don't. H. G. Wells. If you want to consider it a coherent body of literature, you start with Swift and you go to Verne and then H. G. Wells and then modern science fiction sort of blossomed in the twenties and thirties with Jack Williamson and others. Jack London did some stuff that might arguably be called science fiction. And it really came to full flower in the forties and fifties, with Asimov and quite a few others. And the genre keeps getting richer and richer as more talented people get into it. To pick out individual books, I would argue if you want to do a systematic study of science fiction you start with what I would call the classics and just go forward and watch the genre grow as time passes.

• • •

GREENBERG: Have you found that your readers are generally well informed? Can you characterize them?

CLANCY: My mail covers—agewise—a very wide spectrum. And one of the big surprises I had when I started getting mail from *Red October* was roughly a third of it came from women, which is something I never would have believed—my own stupidity or sexism or whatever you want to call it. It never occurred to me that a woman would read my book. That's how stupid I was. I have since learned better. I have since learned that the majority of the books bought in America are bought by women. Causing me to think that yeah, women are at least as smart as men, maybe even smarter. I'd say, generally speaking, I'd say my readers are pretty well informed. But consider that anyone who buys a book is in a minority, and people who buy books are the people actively searching for new ideas. And so it's a selection process that filters out the poorly informed.

GREENBERG: Do you think that people read to have their ideas confirmed as well as to seek new ones?

CLANCY: That's probably true. I make a conscious effort to read things I know I'm going to disagree with, because I like to think I'm intelligent enough to recognize the simple fact that I'm not always right. Hard as it may be for me to admit, I occasionally make mistakes. And in recognition of that, I actively look for ideas I know I'm going to a disagree with.

GREENBERG: Any other thoughts on your readers?

CLANCY: Well, I encourage people not only to read me but to read everybody else in whom they might find some interest. I also urge them to make a conscious effort to read things they think they're going to disagree with because the price of intellectual honesty is the act of examination of contrary ideas. You have to admit to the fact that you're not always right and even somebody you disagree with a lot may have an idea that's better than yours. That's the way you keep your brain from getting fat—to look at other people's ideas and measure them against your own and to decide honestly who's right and who's wrong. Objectivity is a hard thing and you have to exercise it. You have to examine your own ideas continuously to make sure that you are right and not doing something stupid.

GREENBERG: What journals or magazines do you find yourself reading on a regular basis?

CLANCY: I get *Science News.* I used to get *Scientific American.* I think *Science News* is actually better. Also less political. *Aviation Week and Space Technology, Defense News,* no general-interest news magazines because I'm sort of a news junkie. I listen to NPR every day. I see the "MacNeil-Lehrer NewsHour" several times a week; of course I watch CNN. My principal news input comes that way. A few other journals, principally in the area of defense, because I find those rather interesting. But I get *Science News* because I like to keep current on what's happening in science, which is really an even greater passion for me than military or security affairs. Science is progress. That's where the ideas come from. That's where the important developments are happening and so it's something I've always tried to keep track of.

• • •

GREENBERG: A few questions about the movie version of *Hunt*. Your general reaction to it?

CLANCY: It was a successful film. It made money. It was reasonably true to the spirit of the book, although the movie had a lot of technical errors in it and some changes in the story which I do not think were necessary. But you have to remember that the printed word and visual representation on the screen are two different art forms and they have very different roles.

GREENBERG: Would you give us an example or two of some of the mistakes they made.

CLANCY: No, I don't want to get into that. Little stuff that only a fellow in the submarine business would really care about.

GREENBERG: When Jack Ryan takes flight in *Hunt* and in other books, he seems to be in a quest toward responsibility, not away from it. Do you have any sense of how your work fits in with some of these larger themes?

CLANCY: Well, I don't think about "large." A theme to me is a question that a high-school English teacher asks. I live in fear of when I go to talking at high schools and colleges, someone asks me what the theme of my work is, to which I say, that's a twenty-point essay question and you answer it. In the real world, and that's what I try to write about as basically as I can, somebody has to get the job done. I mean, if there's an auto accident, somebody's lying on the street bleeding—somebody has to stop the bleeding and stabilize the patient long enough to get the patient to the hospital so that the doctor can sew him or her back together. Somebody's got to get the job done. Somebody has to take responsibility for what's going on in the world. And Ryan keeps getting stuck with that. Poor dumb bastard. And that's reality. And that's what I write about. If there's a burning building, somebody has to rescue the people and then try to put the fire out. That's why we have firefighters. If a liquor store is being held up or a child is kidnapped, somebody has to respond to that and try to set things right. That's the job of the police and FBI. And those are the people I'm writing about. The real glue of our society are the people who—and in a mental sense they're romantics because they're people who believe in the rules—the people who are willing to take their time and their energy to protect and preserve and restore the things that are broken.

GREENBERG: The question of realistic scenario—do you think to yourself, is this realistic or does it matter in the sense that the idea is a neat one and the people will suspend their disbelief and they're not going to question every detail of the scenario?

CLANCY: Well, fiction is about the suspension of disbelief. I would post the proposition that it is probably impossible for novelists as a group to keep up with reality. The thing I cite in the new book—I had to wait almost twenty years to write this. In 1972, the Black September faction of the Palestine Liberation Organization contracted the Japanese Red Army to shoot up Ben-Gurion International Airport in Israel, which they did, killing mainly Puerto Rican Protestant pilgrims. Now, if I wrote that into a book, if my editor didn't chop it out, I'd probably be institutionalized. But that did in fact happen. The fact of the matter is that novelists are constitutionally unable to be as crazy as the world really is.

GREENBERG: Tom, the family is a central theme in your fiction. Could you talk a little bit about that?

CLANCY: Well, the family is the basic building block of society, period. From my perspective, family is the beginning and end of everything that we're supposed to be working for. I mean if you don't take care of your kids, what the hell good are you? I've certainly had a couple of hard lessons in that. And one of the things I fear is to be lying there waiting to die and thinking, Why didn't I spend more time with my children? That's one of the things. There's not too many things in the world I'm afraid of, but that's one of them.

GREENBERG: I think that's one of the reasons that your work has touched people.

CLANCY: I do talk about a number of different fundamental human values and I don't apologize for that. I've got an absolute rule—if I don't mean it, I don't say it. So if there's something in the book, if it's Jack Ryan's thoughts or the words of the narrator, it's probably me talking and saying something I happen to believe in. The thoughts of ancillary characters do not necessarily reflect my own beliefs.

GREENBERG: But the central character does.

CLANCY: For the most part, yes.

GREENBERG: So in that sense Jack Ryan is to some extent you speaking.

CLANCY: Oh, yes. You put a lot of yourself in all your characters. Jack Ryan has more me than most. Not to be too preachy about it, but when I sketched in the Jack Ryan character, I made a conscious decision that he was going to be something other than James Bond. That he was going to be a normal guy with a wife and kids that he cared about. He did the best he could in a work job. The fact of the matter is that if you look at the Central Intelligence Agency or any security agency, the great majority of the people there are normal, everyday married folks who take their kids to Little League games and fill out their taxes in the first week of April just like everybody else. The idea of a James Bond character with a Bentley who hangs out in casinos and womanizes—I mean, if you were a security officer in the British Secret Service, you'd really worry about having people like that on the payroll.

GREENBERG: Your characters don't wear their values on their sleeve, but they do embrace traditional values and morals. I know you have some views on religion in American life.

CLANCY: If you look at it again, you're looking at social history and Western thought. You'll find that all of our values—about human dignity, about justice, about the value of human life—come from the Judeo-Christians. Unless you admit to the fact—unless you admit to the possibility—that a human being has an immortal soul, then what is the source of human dignity? Then in fact is the elimination of human life no different from the elimination of a steer in the Chicago stockyards? We've tried, we're just now recovering from a seventy-year experiment in a godless state. It is a fact that that experiment was a complete failure. And it was worse than a failure, it was a disaster for the people who undertook it. Unless you admit to the fact that there probably is a God, and man probably has a soul that lives on after the body dies, then why are people different from animals?

GREENBERG: Are you concerned at all about math scores and science education in the United States?

CLANCY: I think the American educational system is a disgrace. What we have is a State-run monopoly—and there's no such thing as a good monopoly. There certainly is no such thing as a well-run State monopoly, and we really need to square that away. As a practical matter, we're probably providing quality education to enough people to keep the country going. However, we're also missing a lot of potentially talented young people who are simply not being educated properly. And that means that although we may be educating enough to keep our country going very well, thank you, there's talent up there that is not being utilized and I don't like to see resources like that wasted.

GREENBERG: Any feelings for what might have gone wrong with public education?

CLANCY: If you take a look at statistical test scores, it worked reasonably well until the early or mid-1960s, and then something went wrong. Exactly what went wrong I'll leave to specialists in the field. The fact of the matter is the system is now broken and it's going to be hard to fix. Possibly, what I think is the easiest way to fix it is to put competition in the system. Competition is the one factor in life that makes people try harder. If you face somebody with a possibility of—give a guy a binary solution, say, either (a) he can do better work and make money or (b) he can stay where he is and lose his job, he will generally chose option (a). That's the reason. The reason monopolies are bad is because there's no competitive drive to improve performance. So what we need to do is put competition in the system, and I would propose doing that by making it easier to put kids in private schools and force the people in the public schools to either lose their jobs or to do better and earn the trust of the American people and get those students back because they can do a better job than say, the Catholic schools like the grammar school I went to in Baltimore. I was just up there a few months ago. When I went there it was hundred percent white. It was a neighborhood school. And hundred percent Catholic. It is now about eighty-five percent black and only fifty percent Catholic. What that means is that a whole lot of black people, half of whom are not even Catholic, are sending their kids to Catholic schools and paying on the order of $3,000 to do so because they want their kids to get a good education. Now $3,000 is a lot of money, particularly for people living in the inner city. They are willing to do that because they are responsible parents and they know that the one thing you've got to give your kids is a good education. The reason they're doing that is because the public schools aren't getting the job done. If we made it easier for people to take that same course of action, in five years you'd end up with a system of education that would be better both in the private sector and in the public sector. And America would profit from that. But simply pumping more money into the system is a waste of time. If you have a bad teacher and you pay him $10,000 more a year, he's not going to transform himself into a good teacher. It didn't work that way with Congress, did it? The only way people improve performance is when they have to. And to put that drive in there you have to have competition. Needless to say, the National Education Association is against that because they know competition is going to hurt them.

GREENBERG: In terms of our political leaders, there's been an ongoing discussion about private lives and public lives. Do you have some feelings about folks who exhibit questionable personal morality; should they be held accountable for that in the political sense or can their performance on the job be separated from their personal lives?

CLANCY: I take an awfully narrow view of personal morality, and I'll express it this way. Let's say your next-door neighbor, a pretty good friend, a guy you've known for five years—all of a sudden you found he was abusing his children. Would you continue to be his friend?

GREENBERG: Not me.

CLANCY: If you find that your senator beats his wife. Even though he's a good senator and he delivers for his constituents, do you think he really deserves to be a senator? Drop it down now. You found that your next-door neighbor—he's got a wife, he's got two kids—you find out he screws around. He's got a couple of gals—he never passes up an opportunity for some extramarital sex. Would your opinion of the man change?

GREENBERG: I think most people's would.

CLANCY: Yeah. Therefore, I ask if we apply that standard to our neighbors, why should we not apply that same standard to the people who represent us in Congress? Again, I take a very provincial view of public life. If a guy can't run his family, if a guy cannot manage his family successfully—be a good husband, be a good father—why the hell do we trust him with anything else?

GREENBERG: Recent polls are troubling in terms of a further decline in respect for important American institutions, like Congress. Is this troubling to you?

CLANCY: Anytime the people express an opinion on something I would regard it as a fundamentally healthy thing. Congress—the American people realize this as much as anyone with a brain would realize—that the Congress is simply not getting the job done. That we expect them to balance the national checkbook and of course they can't do that with their own. They should demand efficiency from government just as we demand efficiency from General Motors, but they don't. Really, you look at Congress and you come up with the conclusion number one, that the majority of people in the United States Congress have the best jobs they will ever have in their life in terms of pay. They could not make that much money in the real world.

CLANCY: Secondly, that because of A, B, their principal objective is not to serve in the national interest, but is in fact to maintain their position, where they make $125,000 or so a year and they get treated like medieval princes.

GREENBERG: And if they last long enough.

CLANCY: They have a better pension than the NFL does.

GREENBERG: Do you think that term limitation is an answer? Do you favor that?

CLANCY: No, I do not. It's just another kind of a cop-out as far as I'm concerned. If the American people want to have better government they better damn well ought to vote for it. That's what democracy means.

GREENBERG: It seems so obvious. Why do you think there's support for it?

CLANCY: One of the most troubling aspects of contemporary American society is that we want a no-fault existence—and there isn't such a thing. Everybody wants to be protected from mistakes. Well, as a general rule if somebody is always protecting you from your mistakes, you have damn little incentive to choose wisely at the beginning. In the case of term limitations as applied here, what you're going to end up with is people who are going to care even less about the bums we have in there because sooner or later the bums are going to be out and a new class of bums is going to go in. It's not just the right of people in a democracy to pay attention to their government. It's their duty to pay attention to their government. Until such time that they do so, they deserve all the crap they get.

GREENBERG: You mentioned General Powell as an American you hold in high esteem. Are there others in the public arena who you feel are outstanding?

CLANCY: Well, let see, Newt Gingrich. He's got a brain. He doesn't mind raising a little hell to get an idea across. On the other side of the aisle, Pat

Moynihan. I disagree with him a lot, but he's one of the few genuine intellects in public life.

GREENBERG: Remember the hell he caught for "benign neglect" so many years ago?

CLANCY: Yeah, but the man has a brain and he has a sense of humor and he's not afraid to say what he thinks and that's pretty damn rare. I've only met the guy once and I like him. I liked him before I met him and I like him now after we've met. Beyond that the two U.S. presidents I've met, Reagan and Bush. I think they've both done reasonably well to this point. There are a lot of good people in public office. Unfortunately there are also a lot of bozos. Bill Sessions, director of the FBI, is the complete gentleman—one of the most honorable people you would ever want to meet. Bill Webster, who is just now leaving CIA—same sort of guy—cut from the same cloth. There are a lot of people like that, but they don't make the news very often because they are not noisy enough.

• • •

GREENBERG: We as citizens, and the military as an institution that serves us, face some very tough choices. What do we spend our defense dollars on now?

CLANCY: At the moment the thing I hear from people in uniform whom I respect would be first of all to throw a lot of money into R and D to try to make a generational leap. In other words, instead of building the next family of weapon systems, simply to hold with what we have now and try to leap beyond the next generation into brilliant systems as opposed to smart systems. Secondly, and more fundamentally, we need to concentrate on what the mission of the U.S. military for the next twenty years is. And I would propose that our mission would be war prevention—which really means intimidating other people out of the idea of fighting wars. Letting them know in very positive, preferably nonviolent terms, that if they incur our wrath they will pay an extremely heavy price for it. Essentially applying the deterrence principle to Third World countries. Now we have the where-withal to do that, but we need to define both the mission in very precise political terms and then also decide how we can carry that mission out most effectively.

GREENBERG: These kinds of scenarios would push us into what kinds of directions in terms of procurement?

CLANCY: The Navy we have now is quite adequate to fulfill that mission. The simplest instrumentality would be simply to say: "There's a submarine sitting off Port Jones, and until we issue different orders, that submarine is going to sink every ship that tries to cross this line, from point A to point B. And if you try to sink the submarine, well, give it your best shot. You'll probably fail." And the people who own merchant ships, who are very sensible people, will probably not want to have their merchant ships lost in a case like this. They will turn around and go in a different direction. And there is nobody in the world, with the possible exception of the Royal Navy, who has the ability to go hunting for an American submarine with any reasonable chance of success. This is like going into the woods looking for bear while armed with a Bowie knife. The bear has longer reach, better senses, and a lot more ferocity. The Royal Navy has some good subs and some very good drivers and they could probably make life difficult for us if they chose to do so. But of course the U.S. Navy and the Royal Navy are very good friends. And our countries are very good friends. Therefore, that eventuality would probably not arise. There is nothing in the world that can defeat a *Los Angeles* class U.S. Navy submarine with any degree of reliability. Nothing in the world exists that can take that ship out with any degree of reliability, and therefore simply by declaring this we could shut down any port in the world. Again, I'm not saying it's a good thing to do or smart thing to do. I'm simply saying the possibility is there. Historically, possibilities like that usually find a way to be implemented sooner or later.

GREENBERG: You've talked in the past about evolutionary technology and revolutionary technology. I gather you think we can get revolutionary technology without a Soviet-level threat. That is, the money will be there for the research and development.

CLANCY: Stealth technology is revolutionary. We proved that in the war with Iraq. The F-15E, which is a fabulous airplane, is an evolutionary development. The F-117A Stealth Fighter, which is of course a bomber, not a fighter, is a revolutionary development because it invalidates all the traditional defenses against aircraft. That's revolutionary. That may be the only piece of truly revolutionary technology in the world right now, but it's ours and we got it and it works. Another example would probably be the AWACS system, which has been around for a while and which changes the way you manage your battle. Nuclear propulsion for ships, and particularly submarines, was revolutionary because it changed the paradigm of how submarines operated. These things do happen periodically, and at the moment we own the ones that really matter.

GREENBERG: And you think that they can continue to be developed in the environment that we're going to face in the next decade or two?

CLANCY: As long as Congress provides funding, I don't see why not.

GREENBERG: You talked about mission before. The mission of all the services will be a form of deterrence, a continuation of what used to be a strategic mission.

CLANCY: Our strategic mission, I think, is war prevention.

GREENBERG: As we see spending falling off in the military sector, this would be a natural area to move into. Which brings me to the procurement process in Washington. I know it's a subject you have strong feelings about.

CLANCY: The procurement process is an utter disaster. The process is corrupt. Corruption starts at the top with the authorization process—funding process and Congress. If you think about it for a minute—the SR-71 was like a three-year project from ink on paper to an airplane lifting off the ground. There is no law of God or nature that says that we can't do that all the time.

GREENBERG: If Johnson can do it. He did it repeatedly at the Skunk Works.

CLANCY: We study things to death. We oversee things to death. And as a result, we end up spending a whole lot of money. The idea of studies was originally intended to save money in the long run. In fact, it costs more money than it saves. You develop an incredible bureaucracy for fear of generating corruption. Well, maybe, presumably, they've been reasonably successful in stopping corruption. But they've also stopped the government from procuring equipment in a timely and cost-effective way. And frankly, I'd put up with ten percent corruption if you could save fifty percent on time and procurement costs. It's a simple economic trade-off.

GREENBERG: Even the requests for proposal themselves seem so dense that it's a miracle we've got the quality we've got—as the Gulf War proved to the extent that there were any surprises about how well everything performed. I think it was because it seemed to do this in spite of the procurement process that was responsible for it.

CLANCY: Well, remember, we were dealing with equipment made by countries with similar procurement procedures which were even more screwed up than ours. I could imagine how good it would be if the Pentagon could develop products as rapidly and as effectively as Apple Computer, for example. As effectively as General Motors or Chrysler or Ford. They go from a new idea for a car to cars in the showroom in a couple of years. Chrysler has a new product out now—it's something like twenty months from developing a car to selling a car. Now, if we can do it with a car, why can't you do it with a jeep? Which is essentially a military version of a car. And maybe a year longer to build a tank or armored vehicle. Maybe two years longer to build an airplane. I really don't see that there's a law of God or nature that says you can't be efficient. I know the SR-71 was developed very, very rapidly. The U-2 was developed very rapidly. The A-7 was developed very very rapidly. And there's no law that says you can't do it today. We've structured a process that really militates against getting results.

GREENBERG: There are some who feel that the level of threat perception has declined so dramatically that it works against improving the system, because the level of threat perception is presumably partly responsible for some efficiencies at certain points in history.

CLANCY: Oh, I don't know that I'd agree with that. I don't think the bureaucrats really care about the threat. A threat to a bureaucrat is losing your desk and telephone, it's not having the Russians drive across the Potomac River bridge. And look at Congress—they all swear an oath to preserve, protect, and defend the Constitution of the United States. You think they're more interested in the Constitution or their districts?

GREENBERG: I'd vote for districts.

CLANCY: Unfortunately, I would tend to agree. Because you find people who, for example, as a general rule detest defense except for those *vital* projects—and they have to be in their own districts.

GREENBERG: Well, I forget who said it, but somebody said years ago that all politics is local.

CLANCY: It was Tip O'Neill. The name Alan Cranston comes to mind. He's always been a supporter of the B-1, which just happens to be made at Rockwell in California.

GREENBERG: I gather the Marines and the Navy and Air Force will be prosperous in that kind of environment. Is that as true of the Army?

CLANCY: Well, the Army just validated its use of heavy forces. Iraq was the first time, really, since Korea, more properly since World War II, that we employed armored divisions in the field. That was like a forty-six-year space from Patton's Third Army to John Yeosock driving his Third Army into Iraq. I think we'll probably want to keep heavy forces around for a while, just on the basis of that historical lesson.

GREENBERG: Related to this—the future of the space program. Does it have a serious future in terms of the kinds of costs involved?

CLANCY: The reason the space program costs as much as it does now is because the only airline that goes into space is NASA, and that is an airline with three airplanes and 20,000 employees. NASA is a government monopoly. And monopolies, particularly government monopolies, by their very nature are hugely inefficient. If we have to depend on NASA to get us into space, invest a lot of money in ground transportation. What we've got to find is a cheaper way to get people and objects into orbit—and private industries will just have to do that because NASA just can't.

GREENBERG: Do you think this is a likely happening?

CLANCY: I see things going on right now. McDonnell Douglas with their clipper project. If they can make that puppy fly, that's going to be another paradigm shift.

GREENBERG: And there will be some incentive in the aerospace industry, I assume, too.

CLANCY: That's why MD is doing it right now.

• • •

GREENBERG: When did you become interested in military science?

CLANCY: Oh, I'm interested in all sorts of technology because, like a lot of Americans, I'm fascinated with gadgets. The military happen to have the best toys.

GREENBERG: Are there certain military historians and military writers whom you'd care to mention?

CLANCY: Probably the best guy in the world is John Keegan. He's a Brit. I've met him, superb guy, great guy, brilliant mind. The mark of a really good historian is a guy who can look at data that people have been poring over for 300 years and find something new in it. That's the mark of a real historian and Keegan is a genius at that. After him I would probably put Alistair Horne, another Brit, then Martin Middlebrook, David Downing; over here, the Belote brothers and Clark Reynolds as naval historians. There's a lot of good ones out there. I read a lot of that because I find military history practically more honest than general social history. It's certainly more honest than academic history because in military history it's rather like a medical mortality and morbidity conference at a hospital. They don't care about personalities; they're looking for what works and what doesn't work, without getting into the theoretical issues. It's a very empirical way of looking at things. It's my judgment that there is such a thing as objective truth out there, and one of the reasons we're here on earth is to find the truth. And military historians look for the truth, I think, more rigorously and more professionally than academic or social historians.

GREENBERG: How about when participants are writing? How do you feel about military memoirs?

CLANCY: You have to be real careful to believe in that stuff. Rule of thumb is that it takes twenty years until the good, objective books on a war come out. You have to wait until all the participants are dead.

GREENBERG: So if General Norman Schwarzkopf writes a book on the Gulf War, we better wait a while to see what some other people have to say about it?

CLANCY: Wellington—the good quote on this comes from Wellington— where he said the history of a battle is like the history of a ball. And what he meant by that is with a large formal dance you have an immense room and a whole lot of people running around. And the perspectives of the individual dancers will be limited to the areas in which they happen to be at the time. Whereas, if you want to understand what really happened, you have to have somebody up hanging on the chandelier watching the way everybody is moving around. And that's one of the fundamental problems of history written by participants—very rarely does a participant have a complete picture of what happened. Whereas a historian, who has access to records, the interviews, and a great deal more time in which to conduct his analysis, can draw a much more accurate overall picture.

GREENBERG: I would also observe that military memoirs are slightly more reliable than the memoirs of political figures.

CLANCY: Military people are much more honorable than politicians. They have to be. They're in a very tough profession. It's a life-and-death profession, and dishonesty is something that is simply not tolerated. And the ultimate sin in the military is to lie. You get caught lying, you're gone. It's like doctors lying to other doctors. If you are found out, nobody will ever do business with you again.

GREENBERG: Some people think that your novels have helped to change the way people feel toward the military.

CLANCY: I've been widely credited with that, but I think it's false and I'll tell you why. Every year a very large number of kids enlist in the U.S. military. Where do they come from? They come from regular American families. And if the American people did not have a fairly warm and fuzzy feeling toward the military, they would not let their sons and daughters enlist, but they do. So I think the respect for the military has always been out there. I'm simply one of the people in literature that acknowledges the fact.

• • •

GREENBERG: Would you comment on the latest round of nuclear-force reductions and stand-downs?

CLANCY: I just like the zero option—take them all down to zero if possible. I have never liked ballistic launchers. I would be perfectly content to see a world free of them.

GREENBERG: That's why I said we'll have to keep our fingers crossed. Did you feel—pick your date here, five years ago, ten years ago, twenty years ago—that communism would perish so spectacularly and so quickly?

CLANCY: Nobody did. I always figured it was a dead horse, but nobody really dreamed it would come apart as rapidly as it did.

GREENBERG: And that it would dismantle itself without foreign intervention.

CLANCY: Fifty years from now, historians are going to start admitting it was that when Reagan took over, he decided, there's an arms race going on in the world, but only one side was running, and it might be a hell of a lot more fun if both sides were running. So we built up the military. And more important, buying the hardware was the step that nobody really thinks about. A lot more funding went into training to get the military fine-tuned, so that the people could practice with their tools. And as a result of that, by 1985 we had a really lean, mean, hard, tough military structure. When I was researching *Red Storm Rising,* I was very soon convinced that we could in fact defeat the Soviets if we had to. For a variety of reasons the U.S. military had transformed itself into the most formidable institution in the history of the world, as we just demonstrated in Iraq, where we did things that never had been done before. And, God willing, never have to be done again. The Russians looked at that and realized that they just couldn't beat us. The United States won one of the most important wars in its history and did so without firing a shot.

GREENBERG: On the fall of communism—I don't think that it was so surprising that people would chuck it at the first opportunity. But being given the opportunity—that was the surprise.

CLANCY: Remember what Napoleon said: there are two forces in the world, the sword and the spirit, and ultimately the spirit is stronger than the sword. He was right. Napoleon was a pretty perceptive gent. And what happened was that the people in the Soviet Union and elsewhere start getting access to information from other places in the world. In Poland, for example, for years a very popular TV show has been *Kojak.* And what did they see? They saw that as tawdry as America can be—and you know a crime story about New York is not exactly the best advertisement for life in the United States of America—but as crummy as it looked, there were people who had lots of automobiles, who lived in their own individual houses. You could move from one house to another at will. There was a police force that was compelled by law to give people instructions on their legal rights even after they were arrested for committing a crime. And all this information trickled into their society and they knew that we lived better than they did and they knew that we were freer than they are or were. They knew that we had a better system over here, and that just started a grumble underneath and eventually the grumble made it all the way to the top.

The other problem was, from a strategic point of view, quite simply, that the communist system as an economic engine simply doesn't work. And they had to face the fact. They were in an increasingly disadvantageous strategic situation vis-à-vis the West because the ultimate strength of any nation is in its economy. It is the economy that makes the weapons and trains the people, and since our system is stronger than theirs, we turned out better arms and better soldiers.

GREENBERG: And they saw the handwriting on the wall.

CLANCY: And Mikhail Gorbachev took the very courageous action of saying that we're not going to impose communism from without and Eastern European countries are just going to have to make it on their own. And the Eastern European communist governments were dumb enough to think the people loved them because they came to all the parades and waved their flowers and banners and things. And they were just as surprised as hell when they were gone five months later. And Nicolae Ceauşescu, looking at those guns—the look on his face said it all. Like he just didn't have a clue of what was going on. He died not understanding. They lived by the dumb and they died by the dumb.

GREENBERG: The lesson seems to have been learned with the Soviet leadership, at least.

CLANCY: I would disagree with that: if the Soviet leadership really learned a lesson. Well, it depends on what you mean by leadership. If the Communist Party of the Soviet Union had really learned a lesson, they wouldn't have had that idiot coup, but they did. And they paid for it.

GREENBERG: Do you think it was a threshold event—that it's unlikely to be repeated?

CLANCY: I think it's very unlikely to be repeated. Who's going to try? Particularly if the people who are brought to trial for executing the coup are executed for high treason—and treason is something which, historically, the Russians take very, very seriously indeed. I think it is well within the realm of possibility that the people responsible for initiating the coup are going to get lined up against a wall and get Excedrin headache number 762.

GREENBERG: Do you have some views on the future of the so-called Third World? Do you see problems and threats there?

CLANCY: What will happen, what must happen, very simply is that democracy is going to spread itself across the world. And the reason democracy is going to spread itself across the world is that it works. Over the last 200 years, representative democracy and the free-enterprise system have proven to be extraordinarily effective at giving people the things they want—justice and prosperity. Now, I do not claim that it is a perfect system—merely that it works better than everything else. And the world is gradually coming to understand this, and as it does come to understand this, the people are going to get democracy and the world is going to settle down. This is probably the best time in all of human history. For the first time in all the history that I know—and I read quite a lot—there is not an existing dispute between major powers. Now, you can go all the way back to Troy and the Greek city-states, at the end of the second millennium B.C., and take it forward to Rome and Carthage, or Egypt and Assyria, or Rome and Gaul. Gaul wasn't really a superpower, but France and Germany, England and France, England and Spain, various permutations thereof, up until the present time. And the last great confrontation between major powers was the United States and the Soviet Union. Well, that now seems to be a thing of the past. It's not completely gone yet, but it's on the way to being gone. And if this in fact comes to pass, and I believe it will, then there is no major source of conflict in the world. Now, that's kind of remarkable. Nobody's really thinking or writing about it. I've been doing so for quite a while, but this is something that is really happening. Now, regional conflict, remember, has always been fueled by superpower conflict. Either one side or the other pumps weapons into an area to preserve its surrogates and to protect its perceived vital interests. That too is becoming a thing of the past, so both bases for the continuation of large-scale conflict are going away. In the absence of conflict, these little countries can start devoting their energy toward doing important stuff, like maybe getting their countries running and setting up democracies and free enterprise and jobs and prosperity for everyone. Frankly, I think that's Ronald Reagan's legacy to the world— and it is one hell of a legacy.

GREENBERG: Do you take issue with people who would argue that a certain kind of civic or political culture has to be present for democracy to flourish and that say if you installed it in, say, Algeria, the most extreme and fanatical elements in the society, or those embracing the most popular slogans, would win?

CLANCY: I don't know whether to call that view merely stupid or outright racist. It presupposes there are people in the world who are not as smart as Americans or Europeans. Or do not have the ability to act in their own best interest. I find that at the very least to be stupid, at worst, to be arrogant and racist. Why do we assume that Black Africans can't decide for themselves how to manage their own lives? Why do we think that Chinese cannot do this? If you look at America, which has elements of every culture in the world, if you bring these people to America and turn them loose in a free, representative democracy, in a free-market economic system, they do reasonably well. Now, if they can do it here, why can't their cousins do it in the home countries? Since there's obviously not a genetic difference between these people and the rest of us, and there's not a difference in intelligence between these people and the rest of us, then why do we assume they can't do everything we can do, given the proper opportunities? If a person states that position how can you say it is anything other than stupid and/or racist? Yes, there are differences in cultures, but the human spirit is the same all over the world. A human being craves justice and opportunity and a good life—in Iran or in Iowa.

GREENBERG: Have you been surprised by the persistence of rather narrowly based nationalisms in a world so well connected electronically, where lots of people—the majority of people perhaps—see the same images on television, yet there is a persistence of these very deeply held nationalistic-ethnic-religious loyalties?

CLANCY: The factors to which you refer have been around for all of human history. Let's say twenty thousand years. We've only had one generation of communication satellites. They've been around for, say, twenty-five years . . . communication satellites that transfer ideas back and forth. Now it's going to take more than one generation to eliminate something that's been around for a thousand times that long, but it's going away. And democracy is spreading around, and people do have more contact from one nation to another, and the jet airplane has made it easier for people to get around and share ideas and see the way things are in other places. And, in what in historical terms is a very brief period of time, but in day-to-day terms may seem an awfully long period of time, these things are going to change. It may not be as fast as many of us would like, but things take time. For example, I mean, the people running a country—say the people in the fifty-five-to-seventy-five age bracket—are very unlikely to change the views they have felt since childhood. On the other hand, people, say, from five years old to thirty years old, are much more malleable in their thinking processes. And as they gradually get older, these countries are going to change. It's not going to happen overnight. And one of the really disappointing things about commentary you get, particularly in the media, is both the impatience and the absolutism that things can't happen overnight. Well, in reality, the world doesn't change overnight; it takes time. Democracy, as it is currently understood in the world, is an American invention. We've only been running it here for 200 years. But if you look at the way the world was 200 years ago, for the most part things were being run by kings, and the way the world is today, where the only major country being run by a king is, I believe, Saudi Arabia, and even that is a much more democratic sort of monarchy than, say, was common in France two or three hundred years ago. We've made a hell of a lot of progress. It will take time. But the rate of progress is faster now than it has ever been.

• • •

GREENBERG: Do you have some views on economics in this country at the present time and in terms of America's capacity to compete with a global and financial empire like Japan and with a united Europe?

CLANCY: The Japanese have a demographic bomb in their country that is going to go off sooner or later. The racism. They're going to have to grow out of that. If they don't, it's really going to hurt them. But look, a few hundred years ago America was a strip of dirt that did not extend as far west as Wisconsin. That belonged to the Indians—assuming there were any Indians there 200 years ago. In those 200 years we have settled a continental land mass, created the most powerful economy in the world. America is the country that people from all over the world fight to get into. I would suggest, sir, that the same thing that got us here is going to sustain us. Now, there's going to be ups and downs. There always are. There always will be. But the trend line has always been in our favor and will probably continue to be so. What got us here was a political and economic system that encourages people to do well. And as long as that system is in place, people will continue to do well.

GREENBERG: There has been a lot of discussion and some debate about immigration into the United States. Do you have some views on that?

CLANCY: As a descendant of immigrants, I thoroughly approve. The people who come to the United States are people who come here looking for freedom. Two years ago I was the national chairman for the 175th anniversary of the Battle of Baltimore. The "Star-Spangled Banner," the Battle of Fort McHenry, and all that stuff. One of the things I got to do was address-in 175 brand-new citizens. And with approximately two minutes' notice I was told that I had to give a little speech to them. And I wish I had a tape of it because what I think I remember of it, it was a pretty good speech. That may be one of the neatest things I've ever had an opportunity to do. These guys weren't born in America. They looked around the world and they made a conscious choice to come here. And if you want a validation of what America is all about, ask them. A good friend of mine, General Colin Powell—maybe the most impressive fellow I've ever met—we had lunch a couple of days ago. We were talking about a whole lot of stuff. One of the things he pointed out to me was that his family, his parents, were immigrants from Jamaica. And one branch of his family emigrated to England and another branch of his family emigrated to the United States. The family that went to England produced an assistant conductor on British Rail. The family that came to the United States produced an ambassador, a self-made millionaire, and the most senior military officer in the United States. Now what does that tell you about America? It tells you a lot about Colin Powell too. Maybe one of the most attractive things about the man is he really understands; he understands America in a way that few people do. And among his many stellar qualities, I think that's the finest.

GREENBERG: Do you feel that Americans are naive about the world? If so, is that necessarily a bad thing?

CLANCY: A lot of Europeans say Americans suffer from terminal naiveté. Yeah, we were naive enough to go over and save Europe twice. Three times if you count the Russians. If that's naiveté, I can live with it.

GREENBERG: Which brings me to the general strategic world situation of intense nationalism.

CLANCY: What intense nationalism?

GREENBERG: The Balkans.

CLANCY: That's not nationalism, that's tribalism.

GREENBERG: Well, whatever name it goes under, there seem to be a lot of folks that don't like a lot of other folks.

CLANCY: Well, what we're dealing with now are echoes from both the First and Second World Wars. Take a look at a map of the world in 1915 and a map of the world in 1939 and a map of the world today. Just talking about Europe for the moment, you'll see that a lot of borders have been moved around, and in the same sense when the European colonial powers went into Africa in the nineteenth century and they just drew lines on maps without regard to what people lived where, whether the line intersected a tribe or put one hostile tribe with another. Essentially the same was done in Europe. And countries were created and people were thrown together who really didn't like each other very much. And that's going to take a while to settle out. I think it will happen fairly rapidly, at least in historical terms, but it's going to be a little nasty. I understand the death count in Yugoslavia today is something on the order of a thousand, the total number of people killed between the Serbs on one hand and the Croatians on the other. That's an awful lot of people, but in historical terms it's a fairly low casualty count—which, I'm sure, has very little comfort for the families of those thousand people who were killed. That's going to settle out. It will happen one way or another. Frankly, a year ago, in Atlanta, I proposed a model by which we could, the United States alone, or preferably with the UN or other countries, could put an end to those conflicts fairly rapidly—just a matter of developing a political will to do so. We could do so rapidly and bloodlessly if we really wanted. And the model for doing this is actually a very simple one. There's scarcely a country in the world that can live without maritime trade. The United States Navy has the ability to cut off the maritime trade of any country in the world. And to do so without serious challenge. Because there is not a navy in the world that can dispute control over the seas with the U.S. Navy. Nobody. No other navy has the ability even to make the U.S. Navy work up a good sweat. We could today, for example, simply declare that all the Yugoslavian ports are closed and nobody goes in or out until they stop fighting. Just tell them, until you guys stop fighting, no more ships come in or out. And if you don't like it, you'll just have to lump it. Or send your navy to do business with, do battle with ours, and a half hour later we'll repeat the same charge to you that your ports are closed. And by the way, we sank your navy. Today we could move a carrier battle group into the Adriatic and simply tell the Yugoslavians, put your air force on the ground and leave it there, because if it flies, it dies. That your ports are shut down, your air force is out of business, and no commercial air traffic comes in or out of your airport until we decide otherwise. And our sole criterion for deciding otherwise is we want you people to work out a peaceful solution to your problems. We are aesthetically offended by what you're doing. And we want it settled. And we're going to make life real horrible for you guys until you start acting civilized. Now, we have the physical ability to do this. I'm not necessarily saying it's politically or morally correct. I'm simply saying at this point that we have the physical ability to do so. That is a very interesting possibility that I think deserves serious attention. That the U.S. Navy alone could bring most countries in the world to their knees simply by ending their maritime trade, and nobody has the physical ability to dispute the U.S. Navy's ability to do just that.

• • •

GREENBERG: Were you surprised at the efficiency of men and weapons during Desert Storm?

CLANCY: Yes and no. I was not surprised at the overall effect. In fact, the weapons proved even more effective and reliable than I had anticipated. Of course they turned out to be more effective and reliable than the contractors said they would be. It turns out my predictions were somewhat conservative.

GREENBERG: Which weapons impressed you the most, if that's a fair question?

CLANCY: The weapons impressed me a lot less than the people did. Impressed me the most? Hell, everything worked! Patriot—I guess if I had to pick one thing, it probably would be the Patriot missile because it really wasn't designed for the purpose of being an antiballistic missile system and turned out to be very adaptable for that purpose.

GREENBERG: It was largely a software adaptation—more than—

CLANCY: Well, yes, and also the one problem they had with Patriot was a software problem. The detonation sequence proved just a microsecond too slow in some cases, as a result of which the Patriot actually exploded behind the nose, in front of the tail of the inbound Scuds, and the software fix arrived right after the war ended. At least that's what I heard.

GREENBERG: Did the war highlight any important lessons or flaws in doctrine? Combined arms seemed to be tested successfully there.

CLANCY: GPS System turned out to be even more valuable than people thought—the Global Positioning Satellite for navigation turned out to be wonderfully effective. That was somewhat anticipated by its application in the Afghan War, which was something that's never really been written about. On the whole—of course, we evaluated the Stealth technology—we proved that that works. And God, did it ever work! Lessons learned in terms of doctrine—it proved our doctrine is pretty damn effective. That Americans knew how to fight in large numbers and fight global combat just as well as I believed we could. So, on the whole, what we did was validate everything that was out there.

GREENBERG: What about the area of sealift and airlift? We had a lot of time to do this.

CLANCY: We have the best airlift capability in the world. There's room for improvement and we will improve it. But it's already the best. Sealift capability was probably the one real problem. And what we do about that is we build some new ships.

GREENBERG: I know you have expressed concern about the shipbuilding industry in the United States.

CLANCY: We have no shipbuilding in the United States. They're all out of work right now.

GREENBERG: I think everyone was impressed with the level of leadership during the war. Do you have any comments on that beyond the fact that it was excellent?

CLANCY: Well, the people on the political left have been saying . . . one of their favorite lines was, America hasn't done anything right since the Inchon Landing in 1950. Well, I guess they won't be able to say dumb stuff like that anymore. We put an army in the field. The theater commander was Norm Schwarzkopf, the ground commander was John Yeosock. And they knew their jobs. And they weren't stupid at all. They were pretty damn smart. And along the way they accomplished something with few, if any, precedents in military history. They defeated a well-equipped army of 400,000 people, and in the process took less than 200 fatalities in doing so. You're going to have to look pretty hard in military history to find something that worked that well.

GREENBERG: I want to ask you about the extent of the Iraq nuclear and, apparently, thermonuclear effort. I know you're not surprised by the fact that they were trying. Were you surprised by the extent and the variety of the effort?

CLANCY: Before the war even got started, I had learned from a friend of mine that they were about two years away from nuclear capability. Of course, like most people I thought their initial capability would be a simple fission device—Hiroshima or Nagasaki–type weapon. Probably Nagasaki type. I was, but I should not have been surprised that they were going for a multistaged thermonuclear device. I guess it illustrates the fact I wrote the right book at the right time.

GREENBERG: Do you think we'll be able to control that situation?

CLANCY: I think it's something we'd better jump on in a big hurry. There are forty-three countries out there with either power or research nuclear reactors that are capable of turning out bomb-grade material, and that's something that we need to take a hard, fast, serious look at. And we're going to have to go to these countries and take them in the corner and be very serious and say, you will not under any circumstances manufacture fissionable material, because if you do you will offend us. And you do not want to offend us. Ask Saddam Hussein.

GREENBERG: Is a near-boycott mode of operation necessary?

CLANCY: It is in the interest of the United States and the world as a whole to make damn sure that people do not produce weapons-grade material.

• • •

GREENBERG: Finally, Tom: is there anything you'd like to say to the readers of this book?

CLANCY: Well, I suppose I ought to thank them for their support. Beyond that, no. I'll leave the preaching to priests, ministers, and rabbis. If they want to know what I think, it's in my books and my newspaper columns, and I am flattered by the degree of support I do have. I would encourage my readers also to read other people and people with views different from my own. Because I may not always be right about stuff. And I think it's an intellectual duty for a person who lives in a free society to read material not only with which you agree but with which you disagree. Because every so often somebody you think is wrong will actually turn out to be right.

3. Tom Clancy in His Own Words

Before Anyone Gets Carried Away

OLIVER STONE, NEVER one to let facts get in the way of his peculiar ideas, has yet again graced our country with his commercial mendacity. In this case, he has collected a number of hoary tales and transformed them into a lengthy, malignant, and flatulent fantasy on celluloid.

John Fitzgerald Kennedy was done to death by the military-industrial complex, aided and abetted by the Federal Bureau of Investigation, United States Secret Service, and the Central Intelligence Agency. Why the Roman Catholic Church was left out of this I know not. Possibly it was an oversight. After all, we're politically incorrect as well.

Let's apply a little bit of logic, shall we?

The basic question in the investigation of any crime follows the Latin dictum, *cui bon* which roughly means: Who benefits from the enterprise? Prosecutor Stone would have us believe that the "complex" and various nefarious government agencies were greatly concerned that Kennedy would *not* commit our country to the Vietnam War, causing them untold losses. (Might one also note that Kennedy would have denied Stone his blockbuster *Platoon*? Does this make Prosecutor Stone a possible conspirator?)

Frightened to death by this dreadful prospect, the "complex" let their fingers do the walking through the Yellow Pages, presumably until stopping at Assassins 'R Us. It is well known, of course, that all major corporations have access to highly skilled professional assassins. Some, one supposes, even keep a few on staff, probably in their labor-relations offices, so they never, ever have to worry about union problems. (Ask General Electric.) The corporations, all of them competitors for government and other sources of funds, acted in selfless cooperation to eliminate JFK, and have since kept their word faithfully despite such things as, for example, the bankruptcy of LTV Corporation. (*Hey, Charlie, you let me share in this defense contract, or else I'll . . .*) Not a whisper. Remarkable.

Let's next examine a few facts.

The phrase "military-industrial complex" comes to us from President Eisenhower's valedictory address. He was, in fact, expressing concern with possible defense increases to be made by President Kennedy, who had run for the presidency proclaiming a nonexistent "missile gap." One must remember that 1960 was part of an era in which Democrats still supported national defense.

In fact, President John F. Kennedy was arguably the best friend the "complex" ever had. I invite the reader to examine a copy of *Jane's Fighting Ships.* Just as one example, the entire "Lafayette" class of missile submarines— *thirty-one* of them—was authorized and/or built during his administration.[1] That's only one class of one type of ship in one military service. We were building tanks, guns, and airplanes, too. Lots of them. Toss in *one thousand* Minuteman ICBMs.

And it wasn't just defense. Remember that Kennedy was the man who initiated Project Apollo, the funds for which did not go to the Sierra Club, but rather to Boeing, Lockheed, Grumman, General Dynamics, and the other members of the club. Lots of bucks.

The plain truth of the matter is that the "complex" never had it so good as it did under Kennedy. Killing him would not only have been bad for business, but damned ungrateful as well.

Next, one must assume that the Federal Bureau of Investigation and the United States Secret Service cooperated to cover up the facts of the case, and since numerous agents were involved in the investigation (what about the Dallas police detectives, and all the others?), quite a few people were part of the process, and must necessarily have been part of the conspiracy also. For the moment, just consider the institutional issue. FBI and Secret

---

[1] By contrast, in the first four years of the Reagan Administration, only *THREE* missile submarines were authorized. Might we believe that the "military-industrial complex" was behind John Hinckley? Certainly it would seem to make more sense.

Service cooperated in the cover-up. This assumption overlooks a few basic truths. Both are federal agencies which compete for the same federal budget dollars. There's never enough to go around. Never. They're rivals, and they don't always agree on issues and procedures. It would, therefore, be in the interest of either agency to let it be known that its rival may not have performed in a professional manner, and so take some of its money for one's own pet projects. Do you suppose federal agencies play nasty bureaucratic games to get funding? Stone would have us believe that they do not in order that they can. Or that they do in order that they can't. Or something like that. Classical logic at work.

Next, who were the agents of the FBI and USSS in 1963? They were, for the most part, Irish-Catholic Americans. Kennedy was also an Irish-Catholic American, the first Catholic president. I remember how my parents felt about that. For the agents to have covered up the methodology of his death would of necessity have been an explicit betrayal of one of their own *in addition to* being a violation of professional ethics and training—toss in the religious aspects of the crime, since a lot of these people go to church every week—and yet in the subsequent thirty years not a single special agent of the FBI or Secret Service has found himself approaching death and needful of expunging this crime from his conscience. Perhaps Oliver Stone is unaware of this, but Catholics, like Jews, know about guilt. It's just that Jews are born with guilt, whereas we fish-eaters learn it in school. It is inconceivable that one of these people would not have felt the need to clear his conscience. It simply does not coincide with human nature.

There's a saying in Washington: If two people know it, it's not a secret. To believe that a relatively large number of people (say 50 or so as a minimum) could pull this off without a single leak simply applies a fictional (not to say fantasy) standard to the real world. People feel guilt. People brag. People change allegiances and then want to get even. Someone would write a book. Someone surely would have kept notes just as life insurance— *If you kill me, there's a letter that tells it all, Charlie*—but where is it?

There *was* one thing about the assassination that troubled me. It was the question of the rifle. As the Warren Commission noted, the telescopic sight on the Model 1891 Mannlicher-Carcano 6.5×52 mm rifle[2] was not properly sighted in and had to be adjusted before firearms tests could be conducted. Then in October, 1990, I spent a day with the Secret Service at their Beltsville, Maryland, academy. In the basement there is a rather complete

---

[2]Which is not much of a rifle, and not much of a cartridge. Oswald was doubtless shooting old, European-made military ammunition. But, as we will see, he only had a 50-yard shot.

collection of assassination weapons. Included is an exact duplicate of the Oswald rifle. I got to handle it.

Things were instantly clear. The mount for the telescopic sight is of the military type. It is offset high and to the left of the axis of the "iron" sights (that is, the simple metallic notch-and-post sights that you find on the single-shot .22 many of us learned to use at Boy Scout camp), allowing the shooter to use either. *Oswald never used the 'scope.* He didn't have to. The engagement range to his target—President Kennedy—was roughly 50 yards. The target was moving slowly away from him, with a slight left-to-right drift. It was, in fact, an easy shot, all the more so because Oswald was firing from a rest (that is, the front end of the rifle was probably resting on a solid object—a box of books in all likelihood—instead of a standing, unsupported "off-hand" shot). I, too, am a shooter. It was an easy shot.[3] Contrary to popular belief, Oswald's supposed miraculous performance has been duplicated time and again, and was not the least bit remarkable. One of my friends is the FBI's premiere weapons expert—like me, he was in high school at the time of the assassination. He is satisfied with the single-assassin theory. I believe my friend.

I could go on at length, but suffice it to say that my own misgivings were eliminated when I handled that rifle. I commented on this to agents of the Secret Service. None of them thinks that there was a conspiracy. Do remember that these are men who practice shielding the President with their own bodies (as Special Agent McCarthy did, probably saving Ronald Reagan's life), in a maneuver they sardonically call "catching the bullet." Is it likely that such people would betray their President? Could one do so and not be torn apart by guilt?

Could you, reader, keep such a secret for thirty years? Might you dream about a youthful president's brains being splattered on his young, attractive wife? Would your eyes linger on photographs of the orphaned children? For how long could anyone other than a true psychopath contain such infamy in his soul?

I trust the reader will consider this, most particularly the human factors involved. If Richard Nixon could not conceal a "two-bit burglary" perpetrated by a handful of conspirators, is it plausible that after thirty years there is no credible evidence—the sort a jury might believe, something Jim Garrison singularly failed to produce (oh, sure, someone fixed the jury . . .)—of the murder of a popular president through a conspiracy that

---

[3]Hitting a half-silhouette target at 50 yards is easy enough with a pistol.

could not have included less than fifty people? No names? No notes? No nothing?

I think not.

On the other hand, it's surely the stuff of Hollywood.

Five Minutes Past Midnight—
and Welcome to the Age of Proliferation*

An H-bomb in Iraq? Chinese uranium-enrichment hardware in Iran? It's just not the same world as that in which the study of disarmament and proliferation began. Generations have passed since the completion of the Manhattan Project—generations not just of people but technologies. Progress, a concept that generally resolves us to endure the terrors that the future holds, is upon us, and with its arrival we find ourselves confronted with that most ancient and malevolent curse: "May you live in interesting times."

In the decade after Hiroshima, the yield of nuclear weapons increased a thousandfold, and today, seventeen years after India proved equal to the task of building a nuclear device using its own technical resources, the threat from weapons of mass destruction continues to grow. Nevertheless, there persists the naive belief that began with the Manhattan Project—that secrets can be kept. Secrecy, however, is incompatible with scientific success. Although a whole generation of world-class scientists—a traitor or

*By Tom Clancy and Russell Seitz, an associate of Harvard University's John M. Olin Institute for Strategic Studies. This paper draws on a longer one written under the auspices of the Institute's Changing International Security Needs and America's National Interests Program.

92

two excepted—kept their oaths as to the technical details of the first generations of nuclear and thermonuclear weapons, they also helped raise up a new generation of graduate students and post-doctoral fellows who, by the time they matured, collectively knew more than their masters did. What took the Allies 40,000 man-years to do in the 1940s took India perhaps 2,500 in the 1970s.

A generation later still, much that is unspeakably classified in the context of weapons design and fabrication is merely the common knowledge of other disciplines that have undergone a separate evolution in the unclassified world of international scientific endeavor. And circulating today within the scientific community is a wealth of expertise that dwarfs the amount of intellectual currency that existed in the 1940s and 1950s. The number of newly minted Ph.Ds and Sc.Ds entering the marketplace each year is transforming the global R&D scene in ways difficult to comprehend and impossible to reverse.

In the two generations that have grown to adulthood since World War II, the sociology of science and technology has been transformed. A once Eurocentric enterprise has become a global one. In 1939, German was the *lingua franca* of science—of physics in particular. Scientists were far fewer than today. Apart from America, Europe, Japan, and the USSR, few nations could boast of dozens, let alone hundreds, of Ph.Ds in the pure or applied sciences. Whenever individuals of scientific promise arose in the British or French colonies, they tended to be educated at those empires' hearts, there to spend their careers rather than return to the impoverished or nonexistent technical cultures of their homelands.

The intervening years have witnessed a transformation of the world of technology. What was extremely demanding then—building a few bombs stretched the "high technology" of World War II to its limits, and beyond—has ceased to be state-of-the-art or even demanding. In the 1940s, the Third Reich's atomic weapons program barely got off the drawing board. Its experimental program ended before a chain reaction was achieved. Yet today, little of the equipment, instruments, and materials (fissionables and explosives excepted) needed to develop the first generation of atomic weapons is alien to the research establishments of a large university or a Fortune 500 company. High technology has become a global enterprise and the scientific database that underlies it has become almost universally accessible.

With the advent of this burgeoning free trade in technical ideas and the people who think about them, we have entered a new era in the history of proliferation. It is cautionary to note that what the Germans could and did accomplish at the limits of their wartime high-technology binge—the V-2 rocket—has been successfully emulated by Iraq and North Korea. Perhaps the most fitting adjective to apply to the scientific and technical resources of most nations, with or without nuclear ambitions today, is "overqualified."

To be safely ignored in the establishment of an anti-proliferation regime, a nation needs to have rather fewer Ph.Ds and engineering diplomas than Venezuela or Bangladesh, and a technical economy incapable of building a diesel engine from scratch. So excellent an education is being afforded to so many from so far afield in the universities of the First World that technical sophistication has become an increasingly global phenomenon. There is little consolation in demography, for while a bare majority of all foreign graduate students stay on to seek their careers in the nations that educate them, thousands return home annually.*

Warm, Wet, and Gray

For four decades, the United States and Europe have been engaged in exporting to the developing nations the most sensitive of nuclear materials. This uncontrolled trade has grown exponentially, increasing ninefold in the last thirty years and doubling in the last decade. The matter in question is warm, wet, and gray—a small tonnage of human brains freshly armed with doctorates in nuclear physics and all its related disciplines. Most of them go home.

A high-tech cadre of thousands has returned to the Third World with First World advanced degrees. For example, both India and Taiwan now have more than 2,500 American-educated Ph.Ds. Even more remarkable, South Korea is now acquiring more than 1,000 American doctorates *annually*. Similar numbers have stayed behind in the West to participate in state-of-the-art research in disciplines as varied as plasma physics, materials science, chemical engineering, and computer science. The percentage of the world's scientists and engineers resident in developing countries rose from 7.6 percent to 10.2 percent between 1970 and 1980 and today exceeds 13 percent.†

More than mere numbers is at issue. The strength of science has grown

---

*The authors wish to thank Delores H. Thurgood of the Office of Science and Engineering Personnel of the National Research Council for providing *Summary Report 1990: Doctorate Recipients from United States Universities* (Washington: National Academy Press, 1991), as well as tabulations of Ph.Ds on a nation-by-nation basis for the physical sciences and engineering disciplines that have served as the database from which the statistics in this article are derived.

†Jacques Gaillard, *Scientists in the Third World* (University Press of Kentucky, 1991).

to a point where a comparative handful of scientists and engineers can successfully pursue tasks that once required the concerted effort of hordes of the best and brightest. Interdisciplinary areas of research are fertile ground for the rediscovery in the open literature of the technical factors that were originally cultivated in secret and kept thereafter in the well-guarded vaults of the superpowers' weapons establishments. Many, perhaps most, of the concepts, techniques, materials, and machines originally developed to enable the production of the first generation of thermonuclear devices have been reinvented, rediscovered, or spontaneously spun off into the world of civilian R&D and purely scientific endeavor.

A great deal of weapons-related information that is not labeled as such is hidden in plain sight within innocent-sounding subdisciplines that are both unclassified and so widely disseminated as to defy any attempt to return their sensitive content to effective regimes of security and compart-mentalization. The realm of astrophysics, for example, includes all the intellectual underpinnings of nuclear weapons development, and indeed antedates it. The basic principles of how the sun works, set forth by Bethe and von Weizsäcker in the 1930s, gave rise not just to the hydrogen bomb but to the epic task of harvesting fusion as a peaceful source of power.

On the more modest scale of planets, the extreme pressures common to their cores and the ignition of fusion bombs are described by one and the same set of Equations of State—the work of Fermi and Taylor. Static pressures in excess of three million atmospheres, fantasy in 1945, are now reached in diamond anvil cells that fit in a thimble. So today we have robust sub-disciplines of geophysics and astrophysics—the study of the dynamics of asteroid impacts and radiative transport in stars that utilize the liberated (or re-invented) expertise of the weapons laboratories on a daily basis—and those who use such weapons-derived computer codes have at their disposal vastly more computational power than Fermi or Bethe ever dreamed of.

In the aftermath of the information explosion, the component technologies of nuclear proliferation are no longer identifiably labeled as such. What is evolving spans the spectrum of scientific work—but with the advent of computerized databases a macroscope for visualizing such a 360-degree field of view is becoming available on line.

Second-Best Still Works

As high technology ramifies, appropriate technologies multiply: the most engaging illusion of proliferation control arises from the temptation to believe that its central goal is to prevent the duplication of *existing* technology. Before the first prototype of a weapons system comes into existence at the level of conceptual design—before its component technologies have been fabricated—one cannot determine which alternate concept for each component will prevail in the long term. The initial selection between competing prototypes, with the winning concepts going on to participate in the inception of the first generation of fission bombs or ICBMs (or whatever), is a process that does not invalidate the concepts that are discarded at that point. It merely reflects the perceived practicality of a particular, infant technology. The fittest idea for such a time and place gets selected on the spot, on the basis of saving as much time as money can afford. But other concepts may prove as fit or fitter in other times and other places.

Rejecting a technique is not the same as falsifying an hypothesis. Thus, while uranium-isotope separation via gaseous diffusion was the mainstay of the Manhattan Project, what was then an impractical technique of gas-centrifuge separation went on to become a practical source of weapons-grade fissionable materials in the Soviet Union in the 1950s.*

A current example involves the calutron, a bastardized descendant of a Depression-era atom smasher (the original Berkeley cyclotron). Relative inefficiency doomed the early calutrons, and the strength of existing materials limited gas centrifuges in the 1940s. But the Atomic Energy Commission and its successors blithely created a new discipline, materials science, and massively funded it for another half-century. The result: the materials science community naively solved those problems associated with the gas centrifuge and irremediably changed the context of separation technology. This is significant, because such initially dismissed branches of technology as the calutron can take root and flourish in the shadow of their "mature" competitors. Thus the western scientific community was taken by surprise when the calutron, a woefully inefficient device for electromagnetic uranium isotope separation, was reborn in Iraq. This second life testifies to the difference between the undoable and the merely obsolete. At ground zero it matters not if an H-Bomb has fallen from a B-2 or a Zeppelin.

Welcome to the Future

In the near future it will be possible to duplicate almost all past technology in all but the most forlorn of Third World backwaters, and much of the present state-of-the-art will be both intellectually and practically accessible.

---

*The Soviet Union's seizure of German technical personnel after the collapse of the Third Reich led to major improvements in their nuclear program, just as the Manhattan Project benefited from the influx of German refugees in the 1930s. The Nobel laureate Gustav Hertz, who developed the gaseous diffusion process in the 1950s, was taken into custody by Soviet forces in 1945.

It is no longer safe to assume that looking for the paper trail of a nation attempting to emulate the work of the Manhattan Project will lead us to the laboratories of those with nuclear ambitions. The scope of technical enterprise in today's world prevents a rigid definition of what to look for. The motto of today's ambitious bomb-smiths might be, "These are our weapons technologies—if you don't like them, we have others." Teach a man to make microwave ovens and you've opened the door to radar and calutrons alike. COCOM (the Coordinating Committee on Exports Control) can list and monitor trade in "critical" components; but available tools and materials, and the ubiquity of iron, copper, sand, and vacuum, doom the exercise to futility in the not-very-long run.

This applies equally to other information of military value. Witness the publication in the Indian scientific journal *Current Topics* (April 25, 1991, Indian Academy of Sciences, New Delhi) of both low- and high-resolution satellite images of the Gulf War—despite their being withheld by the U.S. for security reasons. Those who did the withholding evidently overlooked India's possession of a downlink to an earthward-looking U.S. weather satellite, and its own high-resolution reconnaissance satellite to boot.*

This is not to suggest that the best efforts of the U.S. or NATO aerospace industries are at risk of obsolescence—India would be hard pressed to deliver a successor to the KH-11 reconnaissance satellite. It does, however, illustrate the already fragile nature of the assumptions that lead to the attempt to deny information to Iraq when satellite data flows unencrypted from orbit twenty-four hours a day. The satellite information could have been had for the asking by anyone on a computer network that, courtesy of DARPA (the Defense Advanced Research Projects Administration) and a host of other federal agencies, has come to span the globe. The new condition of entry to the orbital reconnaissance club is not the capacity to launch a satellite, but access to the Ethernet directory and the necessary subscription fee.

Similarly any effort to keep the microchips vital to *our* technology out of the hands of Iraq and Libya lacks relevance to the question of the evolution of a Third World bomb. The calutron, for example, is nothing more or less than the Mother of All Vacuum Tubes. Any "proliferation-control regime" for calutron-produced U-235 must encompass everything from traffic in vacuum pumps, and wire and sheet metal, to the interdiction of hydrofluoric-acid bootleggers and pick-axe miners of pitchblende. The

---

*India is an illustrative case of a nation whose high-tech sector is sufficiently sophisticated to host an indigenous upgrading of a demonstrated nuclear capability to a thermonuclear one.

prospects for such a regime are poor. Too much may be made out of mere copper, iron, and vacuum.

Centrifuge-enrichment technology is easy to inhibit by denying critical materials exports, but it is impossible to control. Steel is steel; any post–Bronze Age nation that possesses an iron foundry or steel mini-mill can produce a heap of martensitic high-strength metal as good as that embargoed. If high-strength composites—carbon fiber or kevlar—for centrifuge construction should be preferred to maraging steel, the raw material can be obtained by the ton from the stocks kept by any boatyard that builds competitive yachts.

As for the more sophisticated magnetic materials needed for the gas centrifuges, levitated bearings, their embargo can only succeed if accompanied by a product recall encompassing all of the better sort of hi-fi loudspeakers of the last ten years. "Exotic" new materials, whose research is militarily subsidized, very often make their debut not as production-line aerospace components, but as up-scale sporting goods, such as boron fiber fly rods, and carbon fiber skis and tennis rackets. Examples could be multiplied. The point is that expensive materials developed for weapons applications can and do spin off into civilian markets that dwarf their military cousins.

The Russian Yard Sale

We are partly to blame: consider the proliferation risks inherent in our emphasis on classifying data rather than protecting technology from exposure. It is edifying to attend the manufacturers' displays that accompany many large technical meetings sponsored by engineering associations or the Department of Defense. There, proudly displayed, are the first fruit of Pentagon R&D—components whose exotic materials and advanced electronic, thermal, and optical performance seem unparalleled in the civilian sector, and which are very often offered before their end-use systems (the B-2 and SDI, for instance) have even been tested or publicly displayed. Silicon carbide laser mirrors or stealth carbon foam, it's all on offer in the West—albeit without reference to what it has been developed for. And now in the East, even more is on sale.

The Iron Curtain did more than isolate the citizens of the Warsaw Pact nations from the Free World. It also functioned as an impermeable barrier, a containment that kept in a mass of militarily important high technology often rivaling the best in the West. Now that containment has been breached, and the most secretive of military powers is spilling its technology into a new and multi-polar world where nuclear ambitions have multiplied.

Throughout the former Warsaw Pact, we are witnessing the Yard Sale at the End of History. The Soviet Union is selling jewels more precious than the Fabergé eggs of the Romanovs—at distress-sale prices.

To begin with, glasnost is having some curious results. In the course of celebrating the memory of the late Andrei Sakharov, his physicist-colleagues have explicitly revealed some (but not all) of the fundamental tricks of the weapons trade. In *Sakharov Remembered,* V. I. Ritus outlines the foremost of the early breakthroughs on two-stage fission-fusion bombs: the method of increasing the fusion reaction rate by incorporation of depleted uranium into a layered structure containing deuterium and a tritium precursor. When such a composite becomes fully ionized by the X-ray flux of a fast first-stage fission primary (contained in a *holraum* of appropriate geometry made of the right stuff), the radiation pressure is locally amplified by the abundant electrons liberated from the U-238. This increases the concentration of the deuterium nuclei, which increases the fusion reaction rate by an order of magnitude. "Such a method of reaction increase was called 'Sakharization' by our colleagues."

This is not the sort of hoary schematic speculation typical of Howard Morland's decade-old article "The H-Bomb Secret," but straightforward (albeit antique) thermonuclear bomb design information of a quality transcending the fission-bomb secrets that sent the Rosenbergs to the electric chair. It has been on library shelves for over a year. In another paper, A. I. Pavlovski displays some X-ray flash photographs of how to overcome Rayleigh-Taylor instability by an iteration of implosion components. A third, by Yuri A. Romanov, further outlines the similarities and differences of early U.S. and USSR thermonuclear devices and bombs.

This level of candor may be a source of satisfaction to the curious, but while Drell, Teller, and Bethe remain close-lipped, and their protégés safely within the confines of Los Alamos and Lawrence-Livermore national laboratories, one wonders: what is going to become of the corresponding protégés of Sakharov and his contemporaries?

The response of Soviet laboratories to the outbreak of peace has been even more disturbing. Invoking glasnost and perestroika, they are ready and willing to sell off the fruits of decades of innovation and development for hard currency abroad, rather than seeking means of converting it to civilian use in a land where the ruble is despised. Despite the supposedly continuing viligance of both the KGB and the military, a virtual sampler of military technology—some of it arising from nuclear weapons research—has been put on the table for Western entrepreneurs and Third World shoppers.

In the aftermath of Chernobyl, the Soviet nuclear power (and plutonium) industry found itself burdened with a generation of reactors no one wanted to operate and a corps of nuclear engineers and designers whose careers were suddenly jeopardized (along with former counterparts in the defunct Warsaw Pact). In the summer of 1991, the USSR witnessed both a large reduction in the cash flow of many scientific and technical establishments *and* a contraction in many scientists' and engineers' prerogatives: no more cheap cafeterias, company food stores, and free childcare centers. Many institutions seeking to reverse this abrupt decline in the quality of life have established cooperatives to privatize the intellectual property of their researchers, and to seek its practice by joint ventures or licensing abroad. As a result, entities as diverse as national laboratories, military aerospace development centers, organs of the Soviet Academy, biomedical research facilities, and the City Council of St. Petersburg have suddenly circulated reams of abstracts of technical proposals by a variety of channels, ranging from individual scientists turned entrepreneurs to the Minister of Military Conversion.

The consequences of privatizing the component entities of the Soviet military-industrial complex, from basic metallurgical facilities to aerospace centers and nuclear R&D laboratories, may include the proliferation of ideas as well as artifacts and technologies. At one level of the game it is an intelligence windfall, but the de facto declassification of Soviet military high technology will have the effect of making many Western systems comprehensible to outsiders as well. Soviet high technology cannot be compromised without ours falling victim to some extent.

While there is some evidence of restraint concerning state-of-the-art technologies of C³I (command, control, communications, and intelligence), a few of the systems offered are of a sophistication that has the capacity to change radically the correlation of forces among nations used to depending on the generations of technology available on the fringes of the global arms bazaar. These include a variety of dual-use services and information channels—such as image enhancement, and high-resolution satellite optical and radar imaging—that could seriously affect the outcome of conflicts between states otherwise without access to orbital reconnaissance. It would therefore seem prudent for analysts of low-intensity conflict to keep track of more than weapons systems as the 1990s evolve.

Today it costs roughly $100,000 a year, including support personnel and overheads, to employ an American or Japanese scientist. But the institutions employing tens of thousands of displaced Soviet military researchers are growing desperate. The asking price for their services ranges from $500 a month for a group leader with a Ph.D. to $100 for a skilled technician. The liberalization of travel and emigration from Russia might allow weapons scientists, once denied any prospect of leaving, to sell their expertise to the highest bidder. One would expect the bids to be sizable. Pakistan, for example, having purchased a weapon design from China, would clearly benefit from the services of those familiar with the materials and techniques of its manufacture. While a former employee of the now mothballed East German reactors should face a reasonable prospect of gainful employment in a reunited Germany that staunchly supports the International Atomic Energy Agency's anti-proliferation regime, he remains the lawful prey of headhunters in the family of states that seek to circumvent that regime. One truly egregious example of the Soviet crack-up is the International Chetek Corporation—a would-be purveyor of "peaceful nuclear explosives" and *breeder reactors!* This enterprise is a spin-off from the Arzamas-16 nuclear weapons design center.

As glasnost mutates into an unbridled high-tech sell-off, we must revise our perception of how the technologies of mass destruction may soon spread across the globe. For what is on sale is not Manhattan Project surplus, but systems explicitly made for fighting the World War III that never was.

Traffic in Materials

Some of the architects of the present regime of proliferation controls will protest that such speculations are moot. They will argue that, given iron-clad sanctions against trade in ^{235}uranium and ^{239}plutonium and vigilant monitoring of the technological basis for their enrichment and separation, traffic in weapons-building expertise is unlikely to result in anything being built, because of the sheer lack of the critical materials of construction. But such complacency is foolish.

The common wisdom is that, having been stripped of its uranium and plutonium, waste from spent nuclear reactor fuel assemblies poses only the problem of finding a safe means of long-term storage. However, the waste is still pregnant with elements like neptunium which, despite their never having been used in deployed American nuclear weapons, are every bit as fissionable as the better-known trans-uranic elements.*

Thus, by defining the problem exclusively in terms of uranium and plutonium—the historical basis of all past bombs—the IAEA has opened the door to a very curious future. There are no controls on neptunium, tons of

---

*And popular too. The neptunium bomb was first theorized by German President von Weizsäcker's brother, Carl-Friedrich, in a secret report dated July 17, 1940.

which languish in waste repositories around the world. Those repositories are intended to keep humans safe from radiation, rather than radwaste safe from persons bent on mining it for fissionable elements—elements that were originally rejected for weapons use simply because they were uncompetitive with superior fissionable materials, *not* because they will not do the job.

In one of history's more unhappy ironies, those who have objected to international transport of spent fuel for recycling (for fear of putting plutonium at risk of hijacking, or the environment at risk of plutonium contamination) have in fact helped create convenient stockpiles of potentially recoverable weaponizable neptunium and plutonium at sites around the world. Given Iraq's enterprising revival of the uneconomical but viable calutron, perhaps it is time to contemplate anew the Rich Man's Atom Bomb.

Very often we forget how the imperatives of nuclear ambition can warp normative perceptions of safety and cost-effectiveness beyond recognition. Many a terrorist has made his own nitroglycerine. Some of the spent fuel residue is already four decades old and has decayed to a point where its once ferocious radioactivity has fallen nearly a thousandfold. Today, using technologies as diverse as robotics and zeolite ion exchange separation, a group bent on quarrying radwaste for weapons—a patently suicidal notion three decades ago—might live to tell the tale.*

Precisely

More ominous still is the risk of the qualitative escalation of proliferation, of nations following Iraq's example in proceeding directly to the H-bomb. The assumption that "strategic" yield devices are vastly more demanding technically has been undermined by two factors: first, numerically controlled machine tools of optical levels of precision and almost unlimited versatility; second, the availability of computers and attendant software that bridge the gap between the level of sheer genius needed to innovate thermonuclear devices and the less demanding task of getting them built once their operation is understood from its first principles. This hypothesis has been chillingly corroborated by the UN's recent discovery of Iraq's possession of precision machine tools as well as isotopically purified ^{6}lithium, with evident intent to develop a hydrogen bomb.

When the Einstein-Szilard letter brought the possibility of the atomic

---

*Apart from not being, in Oppenheimer's phrase, "technically sweet" in their design philosophy, radwaste bombs repel the mind in terms of their potential fallout. Unfortunately, this may make them all the more attractive to the enthusiastic terrorist.

bomb to President Roosevelt's attention, the American Physical Society had just 4,000 members. About half of this cadre of (mostly) Ph.Ds joined the Manhattan Project, which at its height employed roughly 10,000 scientists with advanced degrees, principally in chemistry and chemical engineering. Some of its veterans have reflected on the acceleration of their research efforts relative to the pace of their pre-war endeavors. They all concur that the program's relatively unlimited budget contributed mightily to its rapid progress. It took a great deal of money, some $2 billion in an era when the largest of industrial research establishments—General Electric or Du Pont, for example—had annual budgets on the order of $10 million. That acceleration has more modern examples, such as the Apollo program in the 1960s and the Iraqi nuclear program of the 1980s. It is a tacit principle of research management that money buys time, and having spent a billion dollars a year for a decade, Iraq's progress should surprise no one.

Technicians are as important to the problem as scientists. Building such devices requires exacting standards of mechanical precision and electronic performance, often reckoned in angstroms and nanoseconds. In the mechanical domain, the advent of digitally controlled machine tools with optical sensors and air bearings has effected a revolution in the quality of precision machining. This has largely trivialized the task of machining components for a first-generation nuclear device. The compatibility of these precision tools with computer-aided design (CAD) and computer-aided manufacture (CAM) software, as well as precision robotic manipulators, substantially lowers the demands on the proficiency and skill of their operators. It also reduces the need for prolonged proximity to potentially dangerous nuclear materials. One built-in deterrent to radwaste bombs—the presumed lethality of the starting material—must be re-examined in the light of machines that produce precision components untouched by human hands. Many Third World nations now produce artifacts as materially diverse as contact lenses and CDs, both of which rival the level of precision of the first generation of thermonuclear devices. Most required manufacturing technology can be had for the asking, and much is in place.

Issues of automation also involve informational components. Linking the output of a hydrodynamical model with the refinement of a mechanical design is a demanding computer-programming task. It has lately been simplified by the advent of sophisticated computer languages that are both mathematically explicit and increasingly user-friendly. Designs in turn must be interfaced with CAM software, but expertise in that area is becoming as widespread as robotics in the Pacific Rim.

While the role of computer science in weapons design led to the installation of formidable cryptographic safeguards to isolate the powerful computers of the weapons labs from the outside world, the advent of highly secure public-key safeguards in unclassified civilian computer networks has serious drawbacks. Provided with almost unbreakable computer security, the international dispersion of the people and hardware necessary to conduct the conceptual design, modelling, and CAD/CAM cycle becomes a possibility. While vigilance might detect the accrual of expertise necessary for realistic nuclear ambition in a single place, the same human assets scattered around the world might go undetected.

Green Hell

Many Third World doctorates are in a discipline that did not even exist in 1945: molecular biology. With its advent, chemical and biological weapons (CBW) have become less the poor man's atom bombs than the lazy one's.

The major substantive advantage nuclear weapons possess as instruments of intimidation or defense arises from the universal realization of just how terrible their effects are. Hiroshima endowed nuclear weapons with status as emblems of national power and as the ultimate talisman of military ambition. It also created a powerful taboo against their further use. Yet the residue of repugnance that led even Adolf Hitler to refrain from risking the use of nerve gas, and a return to the chemical warfare of World War I, has decayed to the extent that Iraq has already ventured into the suburbs of the unthinkable.

Unfortunately, so low is the threshold of technical difficulty and so small the critical mass of men and material within the orbit of whatever fanaticism should find such a deed compelling, that it is hard to imagine a world not at risk once more from chemical and biological weapons. The political and military factors that spared the world a failure of CBW deterrence in the Gulf War and the relative success in interdicting trade in nerve gas precursors are of but little relevance. To build an A-bomb requires a cadre of at least a hundred scientists and a budget of many millions spent in exotic ways. But biotoxins can be obtained by a few, directing the labors of unskilled dozens at a task that might cost less than a pound of gold. As the drug war shows, attempts at interdiction are all but hopeless. Nor are complicated delivery systems necessary; think what Mathias Rust, the young West German who landed a plane in Red Square, could have accomplished with a crop-duster.

Nor is there any need for genetically engineered micro-organisms, produced in high-biotech laboratories. Plants and other organisms containing molecules of intimidating toxicity are both numerous and ubiquitous. For example, ricin, the lectin made infamous by an umbrella-gun wielding

Bulgarian assassin in London, is a potentially abundant byproduct of the production of castor oil. Worse toxins exist. Even in Burundi or Vanuatu, appropriate technologies of mass destruction are at hand in the state of nature. In order not to be eaten, plants have evolved means of producing chemicals of unsurpassable toxicity—one molecule can kill an animal cell. These substances have legitimate uses in biomedical research, and those learning to manipulate them safely in the laboratory can learn to use them as weapons.

Death of the Illusion

Perhaps students of proliferation should begin looking over the shoulders of those who study immunology and oncology, for they too are addressing problems of mutation and metastasis; of constantly changing threats and challenges; and of how to aid the human immune system in rising to meet them. The growth of technology can be as benign as that of any living tissue, or as malignant as the worst of cancers.

The hermetic secrecy of the Manhattan Project gave way in the 1950s to the public emergence of nuclear science and information technology. Half a century later, there are more secrets than ever inside the weapons laboratories, but few that remain novel to the unclassified realm of science and technology that has been burgeoning uncontrollably on the outside. The continuing inflation of an already sprawling high-technology sector that spans the globe is leading us into a future that may be beyond economic repair. It is one in which the growing similarity of civilian and military technologies may lead to the extinction of their meaningful difference.

Information is the universal solvent of secrecy. And secrecy is not to be regarded as a permanent thing. The more that is known, the less remains that can be kept unknown. With the exponential growth of the technologies of information, the pressure of the known can exceed the strength of a secret technology's containment, and secrets can implode into irrelevance. Two thousand years before Columbus, Heraclitus gave us fair warning: *He who does not expect the unexpected cannot detect it.* Contemplating the realm of science and technology today, and considering the prospect of what intelligence, human and artificial, can accomplish in the century to come, we arrive at the depressing conclusion that the present regime of proliferation control may be among that rare set of entities—a fit object for catastrophe theory.

Bibliography

Audouze, Jean, and Vauclair, Sylvie, *An Introduction to Nuclear Astrophysics* (D. Reidel Publishing, 1980).

Bethe, Hans A., *The Road from Los Alamos* (The American Institute of Physics, 1991).

Elton, Raymond C., *X-Ray Lasers* (Academic Press Inc., 1990).

Ginzburg, V.L., *Applications of Electrodynamics in Theoretical Physics and Astrophysics* (Gordon and Breach Science Publishers, 1987).

Herman, Robin, *Fusion* (Cambridge University, 1990).

Kapitza, Peter, *Kapitza in Cambridge and Moscow* (North-Holland, 1990).

Matsuyama, Takashi, and Hwang, Vincent, *SIGMA: A Knowledge-Based Aerial Image Understanding System* (Plenum Press, 1990).

Meyers, Robert A., *Encyclopedia of Lasers and Optical Technology* (Academic Press, 1990).

Miyamoto, Kenro, *Plasma Physics for Nuclear Fusion* (The MIT Press, 1976).

National Research Council, *Materials Science and Engineering for the 1990s* (National Academy Press, 1989).

Parker, Sybil P., *Spectroscopy Source Book* (McGraw-Hill, 1988).

Rosenblum, Arnold, *Relativity, Supersymmetry, and Strings* (Plenum Press, 1990).

Scheindlin, A.E., and Fortov, V.E., *Thermal Physics Review* (Harwood Academic Publishers, 1987).

Weinberg, Steven, *The Discovery of Subatomic Particles* (W.H. Freeman, 1983).

Getting Our Money's Worth

Not long ago I took my family on a European vacation, and while in England I had the opportunity to visit with two good friends. Both are captains in the Royal Navy, both now in their early forties. Both have commanded diesel-powered submarines, nuclear-powered fast-attack submarines, and both went on to command missile-armed frigates. I visited one's ship and found that he had an American midshipman aboard. The young man was looking forward to his final year at the Naval Academy, and I happened to corner him on the train platform before I returned to London. "What do you think of the skipper?" I asked him.

"Hell," the youngster replied, "I wish he was in *our* Navy!"

The sad part is that the earnest young midshipman was wrong. My British friend is better off in the Royal Navy.

That is a strong statement, and not one that I am happy to make. But it is also true. The reason it is true is that the United States Navy does not utilize its officer corps with anything like the efficiency achieved by our British cousins. Twenty years ago, the United States Navy had a force of 980 active ships, roughly 78,000 officers, and about 600,000 enlisted men. Today we have fewer than 600 ships, about 74,000 officers, and 523,000 enlisted men. Moreover, ships now in service are generally less manpower-intensive than they were twenty years ago; yet while the Navy's size has been reduced by about 40 percent, its manpower is effectively unchanged. What has resulted is a personnel system that defeats the reason for having a military in the first place.

My British friend was one week short of forty when I visited his ship. He was into the second year of his third command tour—that is, before turning forty he was into his sixth or seventh year of command at sea when his American counterpart would probably be in Prospective Commanding Officer (PCO) School, or at best in his *first* year of command of an American warship. While touring the ship's Combat Information Center, I found myself wondering if, in the event of war, I would be safer with my British friend or one of his American counterparts. I'd probably be safer there, I concluded reluctantly, for the simple reason that there can be no substitute for command experience. But that's only part of it.

The career track for a British submarine officer is far different from that of his American ally. In an earlier conversation my friend remarked to me that when as a sub skipper he met with an American all the "Yank" wanted to talk about was his reactor plant, invariably drawing the exasperated reply: "I don't want to talk about reactors—I have someone who does that for me. I want to talk *tactics*!"

While American submarine officers must learn all there is to know about their engine plants before having a chance to "drive from the front end," those who aspire to command a submarine in the Royal Navy begin on Day One with navigation and tactics, beginning also a winnowing process far more ruthless than the American way. Part of this results from the all-too-small size of the Royal Navy; it must get maximum performance out of its platforms, and doing that means getting maximum performance from its people—identifying the warriors, training them as hard as possible, then turning them loose. It also means better crew integrity, but I will leave that issue aside for the moment, since the enlisted force is probably the brightest aspect of our submarine service.

Some years ago, when Admiral Sir Sandy Woodward was Flag Officer Submarines, he made an executive policy decision that submarine command was a young man's game. This is also an observation borne out by history. We began the Second World War with submarine commanders in their forties, and ended the war with skippers in their twenties; the same thing happened in most other navies. The stressful tempo of submarine operations, even in peacetime, is better handled by a younger man than an older one. With this objective—war-fighting—in mind, it is not possible to turn out a well-trained generalist officer by age thirty-three (command age for a Royal Navy nuclear sub), much less by twenty-seven (when they get their diesel boats). Those in the command track, therefore, are trained to do one thing: operate the submarine and kill targets. Engineers cannot command; though their career track can lead to flag rank, they must knowingly volunteer for second-class citizenship.

Which is not to say that the choice of the navigating officer's career track guarantees anything: the winnowing-out process is a hard one for would-be COs, ending with "The Perisher," without question the world's toughest PCO school. It has been described to me several times as a course which, if it fails to wash out half of each class, hasn't been properly executed. (I've also been told that the NCOs who work in the PCO school have a betting pool on which officers will pass, and which will not—and that they are rarely wrong. There is a message in that also.)

What does this get the Royal Navy? Ask a Brit skipper, and he'll tell you: Man for man it gets them better COs. It's not hard to get American submariners to say the same thing—in private. "The Brits? They're my heroes," one of our best sub commanders told me over dinner. "I wish I could get away with the things they do." Agreement within the submarine community—in private—is almost universal. Of the numerous American submarine officers with whom I've discussed this issue, only *one* has contended that we have a better system. In public, it's a different matter.

Great Britain is the country which gave the world Drake and Nelson, and most of America's naval traditions were simply stolen from a pre-existing source—but America has given the world more than its share of outstanding naval officers, as a few RN captains learned the hard way. It's not a question of people. it is a question of system.

The American system requires that a submarine officer spend too much time in the engine room. A whole generation's worth of jokes have resulted: *The front end of the boat is the fairing for the reactor plant.* But a submarine is not an excuse to build a nuclear reactor. A submarine is a weapon of war whose only purpose is the destruction of her country's enemies. Any civilian can tell you, if asked, that the reactor plant on a submarine is the motor which drives the submarine through the water so that the submarine can do whatever it is that she does. A reactor is something that boils water. Why doesn't the whole submarine community share this view? Why did one petty officer tell me that his skipper was "a real nuc," while another said, "Are you kidding? I've got the best [deleted] skipper in the whole [deleted] Navy!"? The former skipper never stopped being an engineer; the latter only wanted to be a warrior. But who is in the majority?

The fixation with engineering has had other manifestations which touch upon ship-design philosophy and even upon national strategy. This fixation results from the importance of safety, and the admitted fact that only a few major reactor incidents upon U.S. submarines would result in dire consequences. (Somehow the Brits have avoided a meltdown with their less engineering-oriented system.) Fear of such an incident has enforced on the U.S. Navy the most conservative design philosophy in its history. We are now building one (1) class of attack submarine, the *Los Angeles*es, whose design history dates back to my sophomore year in college (when I was taking Army ROTC). In other words, had I attended the Naval Academy, I would just now be contemplating command of the boat whose design began when I was recovering from my Plebe Year. Something is wrong here.

The Soviets have designed, built, and deployed whole families of attack submarines while we have produced one single class. The *Los Angeles* is probably the best boat in the world, but is she as good as she could be? Isn't she an awfully big platform for carrying twenty-eight weapons internally? Isn't she, in fact, too big, and too expensive? One *Los Angeles* costs about as much as two *Trafalgar*s. Is a 688 twice as good? Probably not, even before you factor in the skill and experience of the COs. She certainly cannot be in two places at once. Also, she is probably not the right boat for every mission, but she's the only one we are building at the moment.

Where are our experimental boats? Why can't we build a single boat to test a new concept—for that matter, why is it that those experiments we have undertaken, a generation ago, led nowhere? Who makes the decisions on submarine design? Warriors? The man who set the Nuclear Navy on its path was an engineering genius, and an administrator of cosmic talents; but a warrior he was not, and the warrior's ethic was foreign to him. This shows in the system he left behind.

What we have gotten from the current system is a community of officers so molded by their training that risk-taking is not rewarded and therefore often avoided; and it shows in a submarine-design process in which risk-taking is scarcely considered. Taking risks means that mistakes are certain—that's why it's called RISK-taking. But you learn from mistakes; in fact you learn more from mistakes than from success. The value of risk-taking in naval history is well known: In the tactical arena, failure to run risks makes for predictable tactics—which can spell death. In the strategic arena, it spells national defeat. Commander Holloway Frost, one of the Navy's leading intellectuals in the interwar period, wrote that the one unforgivable failure in war is the failure to run risks.

This is merely a simple illustration of a serious problem which is not limited to the Navy. In the Army, a captain in his middle twenties will command a company for a brief eighteen months. Do we really expect a young man to learn and master the job of leading over a hundred men in combat in a mere year and a half? Worse: after that, he will not have another operational command for over ten years, when, if he's fortunate, he gets a battalion for two years or so. Throughout the military there are too many officers chasing too few commands. What results is an artificially and unrealistically old group of commanders who shuffle in and out of command billets too rapidly. Command is supposed to be what the career is all about, but it has become a mere adjunct to career advancement—and therefore a place of passage, a place to play safe and make no mistakes. The current system militates toward homogenized mediocrity. That we have any excellent commanders at all—and we do have quite a few—is testimony to the quality of the people who choose this way of life, not to the system that is supposed to support them. To excel one must defeat the system. In historical perspective, this is not unusual. All military forces begin wars with officers and doctrine that are proof-tested by fire, then changed as shortcomings are diagnosed and as the real combat leaders rise to the top. But it is also historically true that the price of that learning curve is the blood of young men—*and that the lessons learned are always the same.*

The difference today is that modern weapons and modern mobility may have eliminated the time in which lessons can be learned and proper changes made. Our military plans to fight a violent, rapid war of maneuver, but may not be providing its commanders with the necessary training to deal with it. There will not be time to create another Arsenal of Democracy. If a war begins, it will be fought by the weapons already in existence, by the men and women already deployed. If there is another learning curve, its slope will probably be too steep for comfortable lessons. We say that we want our commanders to "fight smart," but deny them the experience to get smart. Too many officers; too few commands.

The military is neither a jobs program, nor another federal bureaucracy, though it has become something of both. Its real purpose is not to provide fulfilling careers for people who wish to serve our country. Its purpose is the preservation, protection, and defense of American freedom—by the application of structured violence. The historical paradox, of course, is that readiness to do that grim job is the best protection against being forced into it. Readiness requires that the commanders know their profession. Readiness means every day.

The whole public debate on military appropriations misses the point. The majority of military costs are manpower costs. We speak of our military as though it were a collection of weapons, yet we don't say that hammers build houses; we say that carpenters do. Just as carpenters build houses, warriors fight wars. The foremost "force multiplier" on the battlefield will always be an intelligent commander. It is mainly a question, therefore, of having the right people in place, and getting the wrong people out of the way. There is ample slack in the system to accomplish that, but doing so means a return to fundamentals. Just as surgery is a part of medicine that results most often from failure to take gentler care of one's health, war results from the failures not of soldiers, but of their political leaders. Just as war is a grim, ugly business, unloved even by its best practitioners, so I have never met a surgeon who relishes the mechanics of his profession. But both professions remain necessary, and while we continue to need them, we need the best we can have; and we need them to be ready for emergencies. That means every day.

The military needs to restore the warrior ethic. A warrior is someone who kills his fellow man for a living, and wants to be good at it. Not all officers are or can be warriors, but only those who are deserve to command at any level. The military must change its programs to identify them, to nurture them, to select only the best from their ranks, and then to give them the support and experience they need to fulfill their wartime missions at every level of command responsibility. That will give us the force which will win in war; and recognition of it will go far toward preventing one.

Back to the Frontier

On the evening of July 20 the Arts and Entertainment network ran the complete coverage of the Apollo 11 moon landing and walk. It served only to refresh memories that will remain until death. Who can forget that night? Who can forget the pride of nationhood? Who can forget the excitement and the wonder?

Evidently quite a few people have chosen to do so. The media tell us now that Woodstock, for example, was far more significant—despite the fact that more Americans traveled to Florida to watch Apollo 11 blast off than to have their ears blasted and their minds altered in that muddy New York pasture.

That false impression lingers to this date. It is a routine matter for hundreds of thousands of Americans to drive their cars and campers to the causeways near Cape Canaveral or the desert flatlands of California to watch the Space Shuttle launch and land, and yet, social critics would tell us, the fact that so many American citizens make those pilgrimages is less significant than a shrill demonstration for some social issue or other—in which, of course, the media have greater interest.

Perhaps this fact demonstrates the nature of criticism, that its function is fundamentally negative, limiting—and blind.

Dr. Johnson's most devastating and immortal observation is that it is within the capacity of anyone to do nothing, a fact as true of the eighteenth century as of the twentieth. How easy it is to speak of the worthlessness of a project, how the money might be spent on some present need, how there must be better ways to do things, how we have more immediate concerns. It is the sort of vision that condemns a society to its present forever instead of leading it to the future within its grasp.

It came home to me, watching A&E that night, that the do-nothings have almost won. Watching the tapes of Armstrong and Aldrin, it came home very powerfully indeed that we had wasted twenty complete years. Scarcely had the astronauts returned when NASA's funding was slashed, then slashed again. And why? To help the poor, of course. "A nation that could go to the moon," carped those on the political left who never had any use for Apollo except as a counterpoint for their own arguments, could just as easily take all that money and solve its crushing social problems.

Well, they've had their twenty years to solve their social problems. Vast mountains of funds have been disposed of, whole new bureaucracies created—and those who made it all happen now say that now the problem is worse than ever; that we still cannot afford a space program; that a nation that has gone to the moon can and ought to solve its social problems first.

It was this sort of vision that made Portugal a world power.

Any decent cynic could observe that the social reformers have had their chance, that they've had all their programs and all their funding, and that if the problems are not solved, then their ability to do so is seriously in doubt. An indecent critic might say that the War on Poverty was fought with the same skill as that other war given us by the Johnson Administration. In either case, deducting a few percentage points from twenty years' worth of programs would manifestly have had no effect on the unsolved problem at all.

But it would have given America something that the Soviet Union has—a permanent space station where real people could do real work. What might have come from such a facility? Who can say? You have to go there to find out.

Exploration is part and parcel of American history. It is said that we ought not to go forward with a major space program without assistance from our allies. Lewis and Clark, the first great American explorers, traveled land in which our European friends had little interest—the purchase itself had its detractors, of course; one wonders if some of those who opposed the Louisana Purchase had heard Dr. Johnson's dictum first-hand—and along the way they discovered about a third of what we now call America. The bread we eat comes from the region that was once called The Great American Desert. Now we call it Kansas. Doubtless there were pressing social problems at the time, but it is instructive that those problems are now the subject of dry history, while the subject of the purchase and exploration are a living part of our country.

It is a fact of history that those who press outward always bring home discoveries that are useful. In simple business terms, investment in the future pays better than investment in the past. It is similarly true that you go to strange regions not for what you know is there, but for what you do not know. That's why it's called exploration. And only people can do that, because only people can look about and truly see things. Machines cannot. You can program machines to handle only those functions which you anticipate. Only a human mind can go to a place and see possibilities that were not anticipated, and then act upon them. Machines have their place, but to depend upon them to do creative work is fantasy. Exploration means people.

The one advantage in exploration that did not exist so much in earlier times is that getting there really is half the fun. The home computer industry had as its foundations the need for small, light electronic equipment for missiles and satellites. (Of course, back thirty years ago experts argued that only four—four!—computers would suffice for America's scientific needs. Far more recently than that the purpose of home computers was questioned by a lot of people. More actuarial vision.)

The Space Program is the future. It really is that simple. The poor may always be with us. Certainly the nay-sayers will. And the future will come whether we like it or not. The question is whether or not we will be there to meet and make it. The nay-sayers have had their twenty years, have spent their mountains of funds, and have produced slim results by their own admission. Isn't it time to give somebody else a chance?

But I *Like* to Shoot

Switzerland is a land where crime is virtually unknown, yet most Swiss males are required by law to keep in their homes either a SIG 7.5mm Stgw or the newer 5.56 mm SG550/551. Both can be fired in the semiautomatic (one shot at a time) mode or full-automatic, which makes them portable, personal machine guns. The same situation exists in Israel, whose armed forces are largely based on the Swiss model: many citizens keep their military weapons (the well known Uzi submachine gun, for example) in their coat closets. Street crime in Israel is also very low by American standards. While I do not advocate possession of machine guns, it is plain from this evidence that such possession does not automatically foster crime.

Semiautomatic sporting arms have been available in the United States at least since 1905, when Winchester Repeating Arms introduced their Model '05 rifle. The operating principles for guns of this type are simple. The gun mechanism either uses the recoil energy of the shot that has just been fired, or traps some of the expanding gas from the act of firing; in either case the residual energy operates the bolt mechanism, ejecting the empty cartridge, cocking the hammer, and then loading a new round into the chamber for a rapid second shot. The number of times this act can be repeated is simply a function of magazine size. Nor is this necessarily the quickest way of firing multiple shots. There are many skeet shooters, for example, who contend that a slide-action ("pump") shotgun can be operated more rapidly than an automatic one. Automatics have become more popular as much for their attenuation of recoil energy ("kick") as for rapidity of fire.

I am a gun owner. I was introduced to shooting while a member of Troop 624 of the Boy Scouts of America over thirty years ago, and from the first shooting was something that I have enjoyed. I have shot everything from a .22 long-rifle cartridge to once having "pulled the string" on an eight-inch self-propelled howitzer as a guest of the United States Army. I own a modest number of handguns and long guns, some of which are semiautomatic, and all of which are kept securely out of reach of my children, who know not to touch my guns without my supervision. I have never had so much as a moving violation for driving a car, much less a major felony.

I enjoy shooting. I do not know why this is so, but for me it is enough that it is, in fact, so. Some people play golf, or sail boats, or drive cars at foolish rates of speed, or leap from serviceable aircraft and then wait a while before they open their parachutes. In each case, people get a thrill from their individual hobbies. All can be dangerous. I went to school with a young man who was nearly killed by a golf ball, as testified to by the "L"-shaped scar over his left ear. Boating accidents claim numerous lives each year; the hazards of auto racing and skydiving are self-evident. My hobby is shooting, and I have never come close to injuring anyone, even myself, because I undertake this activity responsibly, as do virtually all of my fellow shooters.

Shooting, like golf, is a discipline in which one must exercise exact control at one point to achieve a goal at a distant point. It requires practice and concentration, and its reward is a puff of smoke where a clay bird ("skeet") used to be, a hole in a paper target, or the knock-down of a steel silhouette target. As with all the sports I have cited above, the reward is really an internal one. One is gratified by his or her own conquest of the laws of physics. Shooting is, in a word, as much fun for me as a good five-iron shot is for someone else; and I find that it is as effective for controlling stress as golf or other hobbies doubtless are for others.

I am not a member of the National Rifle Association. I hunted once, but gave that up years ago.

I live in an area where the great majority of citizens own firearms, mainly shotguns, because it is simply the way things are in the country. (The last animal I killed was a rabid raccoon, about two years ago, which I dispatched with a .22 semiautomatic rifle.) There is little crime where I live, and I can't remember the last time we had a murder in my county. Yet another classic case of many guns but little crime, and less than an hour from D.C., where the reverse is true.

While an insurance agent, I carried the coverage for two separate police forces, and I have numerous friends in the FBI. I have yet to meet a single law-enforcement officer who thinks that confiscating firearms from the general public will do any good at all concerning crime in the United States—*not one*. They all say that gun control has no demonstrable effect on crime—or, that its only effects appear on the surface to be negative, as can be crudely demonstrated in such restrictive cities as Washington, D.C., and New York. Most of the police officers I know, of course, are street cops, not police commissioners, who tend to be political appointees and either have political ambitions of their own or are subject to the whims of those who do.

With the recent slaughter of innocents at Stockton, California, there has come, again, a hue and cry against firearms. But no firearm, nor a knife, nor a club, has ever killed anyone unless directed by a person who acted either from malice, madness, or idiocy. The killer in this case, motivated by malignant racism or mental illness (or a combination thereof), used a cheap semiautomatic firearm to murder children whom he could not even have known. More to the point, this was an individual not unknown to local police agencies. I'll only mention the high points. Purdy had been arrested in March 1982 for selling hashish and cultivating marijuana, both of which offenses, one presumes, are felonies; but evidently nothing happened, since less than a year later he was arrested in Beverly Hills for possession of a dangerous weapon, but his only penalty here was "time served" before trial. Again in 1983 he was arrested for possession of stolen property, and nothing happened; finally, he was arrested in 1984 on robbery and conspiracy charges, but his conviction, despite previous felony arrests, was on the misdemeanor charge of "accessory." How many warnings does the legal system need? Before we start pointing to a gun, we might ask why Mr. Purdy was on the street in the first place.

The weapon in question was a Chinese knock-off of the Russian AK-47. It might as easily have been an automatic (or pump) shotgun, or, for that matter, any of a number of .22-caliber sporting rifles. His choice of weapon was more an indication of his probable mental illness (which might have been recognized and treated, had he been incarcerated for one of his previous crimes) than of considered judgment. He was murdering children of Vietnamese origin with the standard weapon used by the Viet Cong. Perhaps his twisted mind saw poetic justice in that.

I submit, however, that the action of that lunatic is irrelevant to my right to own and use firearms in the pursuit of my personal enjoyment. There are many known cases where maniacs used properly registered automobiles deliberately to run down people on sidewalks. Yet people talk about restricting ownership of firearms, not automobiles.

Why? If we are simply talking about saving lives, the place you go is cars. Do we confiscate the private automobiles of convicted drunken drivers? No. Is the victim of a drunken driver any less dead than the victim of a murder? No.

Clearly, then, the issue is not lives. The issue is something else. Is the issue crime? If so, one could point out that the current pandemic of murders in Washington, D.C., and many other cities is related to the use and sale of drugs, but does anyone propose criminalizing the possession of small amounts of drugs? When was the last time someone was imprisoned for the act of sniffing cocaine? The very idea of mandatory drug testing for people in critical occupations is assailed as an invasion of privacy (often by people who propose invading my privacy to confiscate my firearms). It is clear that the use of drugs creates a market for the sale of drugs, and that the sale of drugs involves so much money that people are willing to kill to do it. But we do not criminalize the *reason* for the killings, we instead criminalize the *means* by which some of the killings are accomplished. Can anyone claim that there is the least chance that such public policy will work? In the event a reminder is necessary, even during Prohibition, neither drinking nor possessing alcohol was ever against the law. Instead, it was illegal to manufacture, import, or sell alcohol. Sound familiar? This example of public policy, carried forward today in the way we attempt to discourage drug use, is doomed to failure.

Personal ownership of firearms has a long history in America. The current use of firearms in hunting and sport shooting merely echoes the time when a gun over the mantel was a means of putting food on the table. Owning a gun meant that a person could protect his (or her) family when the state was unable to do so, a lamentable condition that persists to this day in areas which have large, organized police agencies. Having a gun gives the individual a degree of personal autonomy—the capacity for self-defense—that is not the anachronism many pretend it to be. I do not propose that everyone should own a firearm. A firearm, as with an automobile or any other complex piece of machinery, is something whose use must be learned and should be regularly practiced. Some people are fearful of guns; others are fearful of heights or aircraft. All such fears are irrational, but we live in a free society whose members are allowed to think whatever they care to think. Unfortunately, many people with a morbid fear of firearms seek to expand the scope of their prejudices, enforcing them upon others who do not share them.

This is not a new phenomenon in America. Within living memory there were those so morbidly fearful of blacks that they systematically discriminated against their fellow citizens for no better reason than pigmentation. Earlier, people who disapproved of liquor consumption decided that no one should drink alcoholic beverages. Both prejudices were irrational, but worse, they were fundamentally un-American. Our country, it ought to be remembered, is founded on the idea of individual rights—that a person can manage his or her own life however he or she wishes so long as the exercise of those individual rights does not impinge on the rights of others. To think of making a life-management decision for another individual is something that should trouble all of us, most especially when the proposal is to interfere with another who has shown no sign of being a danger to the rest of society. Often unable to point to a threat, the argument for such interference becomes one of "need." Do I need to own guns? Maybe not. Nor, it might be argued, in an era of crowded streets and polluted air do I need to have more than one automobile. Do I need to consume alcohol? No. Yet I choose to live my life in accordance with my wishes, and so long as I do not trouble others, I expect to be left alone in my personal pursuit of happiness.

And so it is with guns. I choose to own firearms. So long as I act responsibly, what right does anyone have to make my choices for me?

The Federal News Service

It's all about information. Investors read *The Wall Street Journal.* Horse-players stake out tracks at dawn to clock workouts. Football teams have been known to steal other teams' playbooks. Police forces use paid inform-ers to learn what criminals are up to. Reporters guard closely their sources and exclusive stories. Why? Man is alone in nature as the one animal able to absorb, communicate, manipulate, and act upon abstract information. Having the right information is the difference between an "A" and an "F" on a semester exam; between a successful investment and a loss; between being a leader or an also-ran; and for nations, information can be the difference between life and death for its citizens.

Articles on the Pentagon concentrate on weapons systems and what they cost, but what reporters all too often overlook is that modern military systems are not about killing people. Instead they are about getting infor-mation to the local commander just a little more quickly so that he can use the maximum amount of time to decide *how* to use his weapons effectively. The same principle that applies to the captain commanding a company of Marines also applies to the nation which he serves. What you do not know can kill you. What you do know can save your life. More than anything else, we pay our executive leadership to make good decisions. What is the best way to deal with changes in the Soviet Union? How do we respond to terrorism? To make a decision like that, the President must have the best possible information in the shortest possible time. Even if there is no on-going crisis, the more time you have to decide something, the more advice you can get, the more alternatives you can consider, and the more likely you are to guess right on your action.

And that is the business of the Central Intelligence Agency.

There is both a parallel and a stark contrast between news services and intelligence services. While both gather information, the news media generally report on misfortune. When an intelligence service gets information in time, action can be taken to prevent misfortune. The end result of timely intelligence information is most often nothing for the news media to report. Intelligence failures, on the other hand, are tragic bonanzas for the news media. One case in point is the terrorist bombing of PanAm Flight 103. Had the proper information been obtained, the bomb would never have been placed, and the Christmas non-story of 1988 would have been that 272 more citizens had enjoyed the holiday season at home. But the information was not received, or perhaps not recognized, and those citizens died on the cold, wet hills of Scotland. It is rarely possible to determine the importance of intelligence information by its successes, but intelligence failures make landmarks large enough for all to see.

How does it start? That depends on what sort of intelligence it is. Signals intelligence—the sort that comes from breaking someone's codes—is mainly the duty of the National Security Agency. Regarded as the brightest of all jewels in the pantheon of intelligence data, like precious jewels, signals are painstakingly guarded. In an age of increasingly sophisticated computer technology, that protection becomes easier, and, more to the point, NSA operates behind two veils of secrecy. First, it is probably the most security-conscious of all government agencies; second, its work is so narrowly technical that only a gifted few can comprehend how they do what they do.

The next best kind of intelligence is HUMINT: Human Intelligence. This is not the glamorous glitz of satellites, but the intimately dangerous work of a field or "case" officer working for the CIA's Directorate of Operations, the DO. These are the people about whom movies are made, but the movies are rarely accurate. A case officer is a combination of cop and white-collar criminal. He's a criminal because he's trying to steal things that someone else does not want stolen, and is violating the laws of whatever country he happens to be in. He (or quite often, she) is a cop because he deals with people, and that's the art of the business. An "agent"—that's the term for a foreign national employed by a case officer—is a person with a beef, a person angry enough to break his country's laws at the risk of his life. Not every country has America's respect for due process of law, nor the appeals process. Since Mikhail Gorbachev took the reins of the Soviet Union, the Soviet media have cited over thirty individuals executed for espionage. (By contrast, John Walker enjoys a secure if rather circumscribed life in Marion, Illinois.) One of these was TOPHAT. The Soviets have said publicly that TOPHAT—they called him "Donald" in press accounts—was a foreign-service officer. In fact, he was a general officer in the Soviet military-intelligence agency, the GRU, and worked for CIA for over twenty years before his arrest, trial, and execution. The prime item in the CIA's employee-benefit package is survival; not everybody gets to collect.

Recruiting such people to be agents is only the first of many difficult and dangerous hurdles. People bump into one another at receptions. Remarks are exchanged. It's a courtship ritual that can last months, and a field officer must decide whether the prospective recruit is the genuine article or a "dangle," the intelligence version of a police sting. Of course, you can never be really sure. Some recruits are angry with their country's policies; others "just want the mayonnaise jar full of hundred-dollar bills." In either case, once hired, it only gets more dangerous. There are occasional meetings that must take place. Data may be transmitted by low-power "burst" radio equipment, but the other side has detection equipment that can track such devices. It can be a very intellectual exercise, but one in which the players use quite a few sports metaphors. It's a game, the players tell you, the best game in town. Deadly serious, but still a game. You want to keep the "opposition" off balance, never settle into a predictable pattern. You do strange things just to distract them or lead their technical departments into tracking down something that you appear to be doing, but aren't. You can "go long" or "go short." But it's a game where the field officers are "coaches" on the sidelines, while the risks attend mainly to the players actually on the field. If the coach makes a mistake? Case officers are human. What if one is hung over, upset from an argument with a spouse, worried about a sick child, even bored? A single mistake can get someone arrested and executed. The "agents" gathering and transmitting information have been known to die of cockiness and overconfidence. A game, perhaps, but one with stern umpires.

Backing up the field officers is a whole world of gadgets of the Directorate of Science and Technology. What if a case officer is injured or away from his post (it happens) and someone new has to go in? It's very important stuff. But he's never been there. What if he spots a tail—how does he get away?

You can give him a video. DS&T has a computer system that takes satellite photographs* and converts them into a ground-level display that looks and plays like an arcade game that allows you to pre-plan routes into your meeting and away from it—one bizarre aspect to the program is that it doesn't bother converting cars into three-dimensional images, and they come out squashed flat as though in a Roadrunner cartoon. The same system can be used to train a helicopter pilot for a rescue-extraction mission. Sooner or later you have to get your agent out.

That happens, too. Ten years ago, there was a man now living under the name "Victor Orlov." He was an officer in the KGB's communications directorate, and his job was that of watch officer, sending messages to their proper addresses. To do that, he had to read them. He had information that we wanted, and very badly. Badly enough that he and his family were spirited out of Moscow, leaving behind evidence that they had met an accidental death. Exactly how? Nobody talks about that, not even Victor. One of the problems with the intelligence business is that the really good stories rarely get told. In this case, whatever was done might have to be tried again. It was probably successful. Victor didn't surface until this year. One tidbit he brought out was his memorization of an internal KGB communication that the Chairman, Yuri Andropov, was interested in how one might get physically close to Pope John Paul II. Soon thereafter, one recalls, a man named Agca tried to assassinate the Holy Father. Coincidence? I made a trip to Langley in 1986 to give a speech and was told that nobody in the Agency really thought that Agca had decided to attempt this murder entirely on his own.

But intelligence work is rarely that dramatic. As with police work, the good information most often results from the day-to-day grind, painstaking examination of the colossal amounts of data that pour into the Agency; from filing and cross-referencing; from the musings of a single inquisitive mind which spends an hour staring into empty space, chewing on the end of a pen.

If there's one impressive aspect of what the casual observer can see and understand at Langley, it's the Office of Information Technology. They own the computers. At the top of their pyramid is the world's most powerful single unit, a Cray Y-MP, and around it are IBMs, DECs, and custom-built units of all sizes and descriptions. All share a single characteristic—they are not connected to outside phone lines. The Agency probably employs the world's best people in computer security, but the one hundred separate databases in the Agency's two massive computer rooms represent the sum

---

*NASA just spent a great deal of money building and launching the second-best telescope in orbit. The best ones look down, not up.

total of everything the Agency knows. Therefore, the systems are completely isolated. The isolation is even internal to the building. There are two separate networks. Red is "secure" and blue is "general use." Computer-data transmissions are made elsewhere, and what comes in is checked for potential viruses. Backups are kept at a distant, secret location, just in case the central files are contaminated.

How much information is there? The number of characters might interest an astronomer. It's that kind of number. Seven robotic tape racks—Dopey, Sneezy, Grumpy, Doc, Bashful, Happy, and Sleepy, of course—each contain 5,000 tape cassettes, and the tapes pack in data at the rate of 38,000 bytes per inch. The tapes are stored randomly; only a computer knows where they are. The racks are locked, and TV cameras examine the claustrophobic interior of each.

Security is the most obvious and oppressive aspect of the Agency. When you enter some areas, rotating red lights warn the people that the unclean are present. Enter a conference room and note pads are flipped over before people smile at you (if they bother). Entering some parts of the New Headquarters Building, you go through tunnels with several 90-degree turns, as though entering an attraction at Disney World. These are waveguide structures designed to keep electronic emissions inside the building— not unlike what you have on a microwave oven, and with the same purpose, to keep inside things that might cause harm.

The 15,000 or so Agency employees are all carefully recruited and checked. The unofficial motto here is one I first encountered with the Secret Service: IN GOD WE TRUST—EVERYBODY ELSE WE CHECK. I know personally three former foreign intelligence officers who have defected to the West. We try to recruit theirs. It is reasonable to assume that they do the same. Edward Lee Howard, a CIA officer who defected to the Soviet Union, is believed to have taken with him information that resulted in the arrest of an important agent named Tolkachev, "who got about the same appeals process that Nikolae Ceauşescu got," as a senior field officer put it.

The opportunities for a foreign enemy are legion. I played my own mental game while touring the building. If I were able to place a single agent in the building, I'd probably go for "Mercury," the CIA's message center. After all, it worked for us with Victor Orlov. The Agency's own security department *must* assume that the KGB already has such a person in the building. The difference between paranoia and wariness is, after all, merely a sober appreciation of reality. If we do it to them, they must be doing the same to us. That's how the game works. Agency employees are "put on the box"— polygraphed—periodically. Not an especially good tool, it can be beaten, and does give false readings. The real defenses against such an occurrence are subtle but smothering. It's the atmosphere, the day-to-day niggling safeguards on how classified data is handled, how documents must be treated and stored at night, how people are allowed only into "compartments" in which they have direct interest. And here one runs into the fundamental dilemma of intelligence.

The nature of intelligence agencies was determined in another age. Intelligence services began at a time in which it was assumed that some people by virtue of their birth and station simply knew more than anyone else. Intelligence began as the business of the nobility. The first known intelligence mission is described in the writings of Polybius: two Roman officers ostensibly chased a stray horse into the enemy camp. The officers stopped at the entrance, of course, and a "slave" pursued the animal where they, honorable chaps that they were, could not go. The "slave" was another officer of equestrian rank who took the opportunity to examine the encampment, and the information he brought back enabled his commander, Scipio Africanus, to launch a night attack. The interest of the nobility in the great game continued through the ages. Their education (denied the common man) and their mobility (no one trifled with an Earl) allowed them to gather information which they then took home. Thus the cultish nature of intelligence organizations might be seen as much a historical accident as a reasoned decision.

If there is anything troubling about CIA, it is here. Anyone familiar with the sciences knows that the great discoveries are those which cross disciplinary lines. But the internal structure of the Agency is specifically designed to prevent information from spreading too far, lest someone be killed as a result. How does one draw the balance: If the information is so vital that no one can see or use it, what is the point of having it? But if using it compromises the source of the information, then you could lose the source forever. A line must be drawn, but where, and by whom?

There is general agreement, even in CIA, that the government classifies far too many things. America is an open society, and the free flow of information has made us what we are. The Soviets, by contrast, made everything secret, and that was one important reason for their stagnation. Overcompartmentalization of information prevents people from seeing things that could be useful, and overclassification has the even more serious effect of cheapening the currency of secrecy. If things that need not be classified are, then people lose respect for the idea of secrecy—and some things must be secret. Of the many people one can meet at Langley, there are too many who adopt an attitude of, "I'm sorry I can't tell you what I know, because then you'd know just how smart and important I am." Such people are not limited to government service, and they are usually wrong in their self-assessment. That sort of information-elitism ultimately becomes incestuous.

CIA's Directorate of Intelligence is composed of people who try to make sense of what DO and DS&T bring in. One must sympathize with those who must forecast the political future of the Eastern Bloc. Neither CIA nor anyone else predicted the stunning changes of 1989, and at a time when the government's decision makers are crying out for information, DI's analysts are going rapidly mad trying to keep ahead of the headlines—and often failing. Two years ago one very high-ranking "consumer" of intelligence grumbled to me that the stuff the Agency was sending out on the Soviet Union was "crazy." Was this the result of the cultish nature of the analysis crew or simply a comment on how much the Soviets have changed? How can one predict the actions of another when that person or country hasn't a clue where to go? The Soviet Union was once quite predictable, and it was America that drove the KGB's First Chief (Foreign) Directorate's analysts to drink. Now the Russians are taking their poetic revenge on us, giving Western analysts the same chaotic signals that we've given them for two generations.

An outsider is left with many disparate impressions of this organization. Hardly the vast empire of fiction and conventional wisdom—HHS has many more employees and a far larger budget—it contains people of impressive talents, some of whom positively bubble with enthusiasm for what they do.

The technical people operating their computers or one-of-a-kind photographic-interpreting tools operate on discrete engineering problems with straightforward solutions—Edison would be at home here; were he still alive, his research lab would be building some of this special hardware. Does the crate on that ship contain a harvesting machine or a tank? How many mobile missiles do the Soviets have deployed? Was the fire at the Rabta "pharmaceuticals plant" (Eli Lilly sites surface-to-air missile batteries around its penicillin factory, of course) real or fake?

The field spooks on what passes for the front line seem addicted to the job; they are classical romantics, knights-errant on a dark and nasty battlefield who operate within curious but exacting ethical rules. Talking to them reveals a discordant combination of hard-mindedness and whimsy, empathy with and loathing of their enemy. Most of all, they love the action as a gambler loves the craps table, where the action is fast and winning is the only thing.

The Analysts wade through a rising tide of data, making National Intelligence Estimates that can range in accuracy from Holy Writ to uninspired guesswork—and try to tell the difference. They can refer to their work as consulting tea leaves, but it's their reports that find their way onto desks in the White House and State Department, and on that paper foundation are important decisions made. They deal in hard facts and nuance, mind-reading and bean counting. The Directorate of Intelligence must, at this writing, decide whether or not the Russian Federation will seek to secede from the Soviet Union. That is enough to make Solomon himself reach for a bottle.

The Security Officers are required to suspect everyone and everything, to trust no one. Their quarry may or may not exist. If it does, it is clever, crafty, mindful of what the Security Officers do, and tries very hard to be invisible. This must be the most dreary and necessary job of all.

My last impression is of a field officer who worked in Pakistan, supporting the Afghan *mudjaheddin*. A senior man, the Russians knew who he was and what he did. He kept his office lights on the whole time he was there. Easily seen from the Soviet Embassy, he wanted them to know that he was always at work. When General Gromov of the Soviet 40th Army crossed the bridge out of Afghanistan, the light went off.

The Cold War may have ended in the last two years. Certainly it appears to be on its last, wobbly legs. Problems will remain. America has still not decided how to deal with international terrorism, and lack of political will invalidates the best information available, but if the Cold War is really over, and if our side is that which prevailed, one of the battles—perhaps the most important of all—was fought and won in a building off the George Washington Parkway in Langley, Virginia.

Isvestia—1

Just over five years ago I published my first novel, *The Hunt for Red October*. In the brief span of years that has passed, my life has changed remarkably, but the world has changed even more.

In 1984 I owned a small insurance business. I served over 1,100 clients—mainly families—by protecting them against the financial hardship that might result from a fire or an automobile accident. It was a valuable function, and I was good at it. Providing people with the right kind of service requires a certain degree of skill, and I was always in competition with other agents who would take away my business if I did not do my job well. But the insurance business was not intellectually satisfying. All the way back to my days in high school, my dream was to see my name on the cover of a book. For me, that was immortality. And so, taking time away from my work, carrying my typewriter home with me every night, I started work on a book. It was hard. Writing is miserably difficult work. My wife was pregnant with our son, Tommy, and needed a little help around the house. I worked late hours, seven days per week on the book, and necessarily neglected my "real" work of selling insurance.

But writing was my dream, and I decided that my dream had waited long enough. I finished the book on the evening of Sunday, 27 February 1983. It was eventually published in October 1984. When I examined the first copy, Tommy, not yet two years old, came over and pointed to the picture on the cover and said, "Daddy." At that moment, I knew that I had accomplished my dream.

I never expected that my book would be very popular (I didn't put any sex in it, you see), but through a fortuitous series of events, it became a national best-seller, and I was able to build on that success to change my life. *Red October* was followed by four additional books, all of which have been highly successful. The changes in my life? Most importantly, we've been blessed with Katie, our fourth child. The transition from businessman to author has allowed me to meet many new people and to make some wonderful friends. For all my life I dreamed of having a house overlooking the water. Now I have it.

When I wrote *The Hunt for Red October,* the world was a very different place. I was born in 1947, soon after my father returned from service in the U.S. Navy. My father's Uncle Mickey, a merchant captain, had been sunk by the Germans three times while trying to run supplies into Murmansk, but by the time I was born, friends had become enemies. For my whole life I learned that Russia was the source of danger to us. I remember the Cuban Missile Crisis of 1962 (I was a sophomore in high school). Two friends of mine were killed in Vietnam. My best friend and godfather to my youngest child was shot down there three times as a rescue helicopter pilot.

I have no doubt that America looks very threatening to Russian citizens. The sacrifices of your countrymen in war and peace are known to us also. The problem is that your perspective and mine were so different that it was almost impossible to compare the two in order to find points of common understanding. We were enemies, and on several occasions came to the brink of war—but why?

I am a student of history. War is a very simple exercise. A nation declares war for much the same reason that a criminal robs a house—he sees something that his neighbor has, something that he wants but is unwilling to earn honestly. In 1941 Germany invaded your country and Japan attacked my country, in each case for the same reason, to steal land and resources. Both nations failed, but only at enormous cost to everyone.

My point, however, is as follows: there is no reason for your country and mine to be enemies. The Soviet Union is rich in natural resources, and has more land than any other nation on earth. Our country is also rich in size and resources, and there is nothing you have that we would wish to steal. In a historical sense, therefore, our forty-five years of disagreement have been entirely artificial—or less politely, remarkably stupid.

From an American perspective, the problem would seem to lie with Marxism-Leninism. Your country took that path in 1917 as an alternative to the ruin brought about by a bloody war and an inept government. Americans invariably respect people for the courage to try something new and different—that is what progress means. But to us it was clear long ago that the experiment had failed, and we could never understand why you persisted with it. We saw a country full of riches whose people lived in relative poverty. Americans detest standing in line for anything, and when we see pictures of people standing in line for bread, we simply cannot understand how such a thing can be—or, if it were true, then why those people didn't change things.

To change things will not be easy, but the most important thing to remember is that progress begins not with an idea, but with the realization that progress is possible. Once you understand that something is possible, you may then search for a way to make it real. Mikhail Gorbachev is a figure of genuine historical importance because more than any man in my memory he is making possible things that were impossible. He has changed an atmosphere of fear and distrust into something that is beginning to look like an atmosphere of friendship. Because of him we no longer see you as enemies, but as people like ourselves who have experienced bad luck and need a little good luck.

We want to help you. We will not insult you with offers of money, but we can help to teach you to prosper as we have prospered. We are good at that. In 200 years we took a continent of empty land and made it into the world's richest country. You, too, have a continent of land—land even richer than ours. Unlike Americans, who started with only a few million people and no culture at all, you have a hundred times more people and a history rich in literature, the arts, and science. You have the wherewithal to remake your country into the land of your dreams. The most important thing you can do is to recognize that your dreams are within your reach.

What do Americans want for the Soviet Union? That is simple. We want you to succeed. We want you to have everything that we have. A happy neighbor is a good neighbor. We want you to be a good neighbor. You never have enough of those.

Isvestia—2.
Capitalism: The Economic Olympics

Like many Americans, I try rather hard to keep track of what is going on in your country—especially now. I hope I will not offend anyone if I say that we find some of the changes in your country amusing. I mean that in a friendly way. A friend sent me the minutes of your parliament—that is, excerpts of speeches made by members of your parliament; over here we call it *The Congressional Record*—and I found myself rolling with laughter. Why? Because the speeches I read were so much like the speeches I read in school history books from the early years of our own Congress. The giants of my country's early history, Henry Clay, Daniel Webster, John Calhoun, spoke with the same sort of vigor and passion that I see in your representatives. Maybe we are more alike as people than we know. I find that very amusing indeed. Like friends with a new baby, making all the mistakes my wife and I made with our first baby. We smile because there is only one way to learn, and new parents rarely listen to advice.

You are now embarking on what for you is a new economic experiment. You call it a market economy. We call it capitalism—well, that is, we sometimes call it capitalism. That word isn't used as much as you might

132

expect over here. World socialism has worked so hard to give the word a bad name that even capitalists are a little embarrassed to use it.

You are probably very suspicious of capitalism (or whatever you might want to call it). Don't let that worry you. Quite a few people in my country are suspicious of it, too. One reason for this is that the economic system we use in America is a very subtle one. It's so subtle that it is very difficult to explain without using economic jargon. I am one who distrusts economists. They can come up with the strangest ideas, and there are so many of them that you can never tell who's right and who is not. Besides, economists are theorists, and I personally prefer to talk with people who get their hands dirty once in a while.

Well, I am not an economist. I am a writer of books, but before that I owned and operated my own small business. Therefore, I will try to explain what capitalism is in terms that I can understand.

Let's assume that you work hard—as we all do—and each month you earn 100 Stones (or Dollars, or Rubles, or Marks). From that 100 Stones, you have to pay your rent, buy your food, clothing, and whatever else you need to do every month to keep your family happy and secure. Those are the things that you must do. Those are necessities.

The idea is to spend as little as possible on necessities. Why? Well, so you can have a few Stones left over go to a movie once in a while, or the ballet, or a football game. You also want to save a little money so that someday you can buy a house or a car, or take an especially nice vacation with the kids next summer, or buy a special anniversary present for your spouse. For all those reasons, you want to spend your money wisely and efficiently. The more things you can buy with your money, the better off you will be.

That is where capitalism starts to work. But HOW does it work?

Now let us assume that you like to exercise. You're a runner, and your favorite event is the 400 meters. But you don't have a stopwatch. And there's nobody around to tell you how fast you are running. How do you know if you're running well? You cannot tell, can you? At the same time, you won't really run any faster than you have to. Oh, sure, you might work out pretty hard at first, but if nobody else is around to applaud, and you can't even measure your performance yourself, pretty soon you'll just be jogging along enough to keep in decent shape. And maybe not even that much.

Well, you show up at the track one fine day, and surprise! There is someone else there. He's going to race you. He wants to beat you. He wants to be the best runner. Now, you might not be the proudest person in the world, but damned if you're going to watch his backside all around the track, right? So today you really run. The two of you push just as hard as you can, and you finish pretty close to each other, sweating and puffing. You smile at each other, probably shake hands and share a joke.

That goes on for a week, say. But still nobody is in the stands to see you run, and neither one of you has a stopwatch. Pretty soon one of you will say, "Come on, why are we trying to kill each other? Nobody sees but us. Nobody really cares. And, after all, we're friends." Inside of another week, you're both more interested in sharing the latest joke than in working up a good sweat.

But the next day there is a real surprise. Now there are people in the stands. They've come to see you, and measure just how good you and your friend are.

You and your friend shake hands before you start. You are still friends. You have respect for each other as all men should, but today you will have a real race, and the better man will get the cheers. Today, you both will do your best, because each of you wants the cheers. What man doesn't? Maybe you will not win today. No one wins every race—but if you lose, you promise yourself to work out much harder, and maybe the next time the cheers will be for you. If you do win, you know what your friend is thinking—and you have to work out harder also, because you like winning, don't you? And the best thing is, you can still be friends. You are smart enough to understand that the competition is good for both of you. Because there are people to watch and cheer, you will both become better runners.

That is what capitalism is.

You the worker have a limited amount of money to spend. So do all your fellow workers in other jobs. You and they both want to spend as little money as possible on necessities SO THAT you can spend more on the better things in life. That can happen only if all workers do their best. The reason you do better work is a simple one: The better you do your work, the more people will buy your product. The more people buy your product (or service), the more money you make, and the more you have left over to spent on a night at the ballet. So, once you think it over, you want to do better work and get that reward, don't you?

But as with exercise, something is necessary to tell you how well you are doing. The problem with work is that there is no stopwatch that really measures things. You can only measure your performance against the performance of someone else. Economic competition is just as real and just as important as competition on a running track. But instead of cheers, you get paid a little more.

It is also fairer than athletics. Some athletes come along whom no one can defeat. Fortunately, even such people as that finally get old and must step aside. That happens rarely in business. When a business is defeated, it either dies or improves its performance. Most often, it improves. It is not so much a question of working harder as working smarter. Workers and managers look around for a new idea, and make use of it to leapfrog ahead of their competition. The competition then does the same, and the cycle repeats itself.

The subtle thing here is that the process doesn't just happen in your business. At the same time, it is happening everywhere else. Maybe you'll grumble a little at having to do your job a new and different way—but at the same time you'll be glad that someone just made a better TV set to give to your wife for her birthday. Maybe the people who made that TV set grumbled a little, too, but when you bought it for your wife, your money went to those workers.

The problem with capitalism is that it can be terribly subtle and invisible in how it works. People very often think that somewhere, somebody is manipulating things. In fact it has been tried, in my country by robber barons of the last century, and in your country by GOSPLAN. In both cases the manipulators failed miserably. A national economy is too complex for anyone to figure out. It's like trying to decide who's going to win the soccer championship on the day before the season starts. There are simply too many things that can happen, too many surprises out there that you cannot plan for. Even so, here in America, some people talk about "fine-tuning" the economy as though it WERE a TV set. They always fail, but since they are economic theorists, they rarely seem to learn.

What makes capitalism work is greed—everyone's greed. That's an ugly word, of course, but we're all guilty of it. But what does greed mean? It means that you want something you do not have. If you try to steal it, you're a criminal. If you work for it, you have healthy ambition. And when you do better work to earn more money to buy something you want, your work produces something better that someone else wants. And everyone is better off because everyone is manipulating the system. "Profit" is another word that some people think is ugly. But what does "profit" mean? For a company, profit is the money left over after paying all of its expenses. For a worker, profit is the money left over for the good things AFTER he's taken care of all the necessities. "Profit" is the reward for doing your job well; it's the cheers of the crowd for a good race. The Soviet Union has turned out some superb athletes. In that kind of competition you are world-class. I think you can do just as well in economic competition once you understand the playing field a little better, and think hard about the rules of the game.

Isvestia—3.
Principles

Anyone who knows me will tell you that Tom Clancy is no friend of communism. I despise Marxism-Leninism as a political philosophy responsible for millions of deaths and untold misery. My feelings toward socialism are identical—indeed, I think that Marxism-Leninism is merely socialism taken to its logical end. Both political ideas are founded on an absurd and antidemocratic premise, and that premise is held in place by a lie. The premise is that since people can do best when they work together for the common good, they must be organized. Of course, since getting everyone's opinion on every social issue is just not possible, the people must trust a ruling elite to make the correct decisions for them. The lie is twofold—first, that the ruling elite knows what it is doing; second, that the ruling elite cares about the people it is supposed to serve.

Socialism rests on the idea that one person can make a decision for another person—some of us, socialists say, are so wise and so pure of heart that they always know what is good for the rest of us. Communism merely extends that idea—since these wise and pure people are always right, they should have the ability to impose their ideas, by force, on those of us too

136

foolish to see their wisdom. Soviet citizens know the human cost of that misguided idea.

That idea is merely an extension of an older governmental principle that was universally held a few centuries ago—that the King, Prince, or local baron (the guy with the sword) knew what was best for his peasants. Of course, the noblemen of old said that their power came from God, but at least they had the moral authority of the Church both to enforce their power and to keep it within strict guidelines. Even a King feared God. Socialism, in denying God, keeps the bad part of that old social contract while conveniently eliminating the restraint of a higher moral authority.

Now, the Soviet Union is not the only place where this idea has stuck up its head. England is another, and even in the United States there are those who feel this way. I've even heard a man on a radio news show who said, quite seriously, that socialism had failed in the Soviet Union merely because you had not done it right, whereas we Americans could do it properly. It is important that you understand this fact—there are fools everywhere.

In the past week, your people have decided that the rule of the CPSU will no longer be tolerated. My admiration for you is boundless. Your people have displayed a mixture of courage and good sense all too rare in our world. There is not a person in my country who thinks of the Soviet Union as an enemy now. We have seen your people speak clearly and firmly. You are now members of the community of free people. Welcome to the club.

But it is not enough that you have turned away from something evil. It is required of you that you turn toward something good, and that is the hard part.

Your government has taken action to outlaw communism. That is a bad thing, not a good one.

The United States of America has a Communist Party—probably more than one, but I honestly do not know all the details. We always have. Even during the darkest days of the Cold War, we had such a party. When I was a child in school, and we had air-raid-warning drills because we feared nuclear attack from your country, there was a Communist Party of the United States of America (CPUSA) which said things little different from the CPSU. Do you find that strange? There is a good reason for it.

Perhaps the most distinguished judge in my country's history was Justice Oliver Wendell Holmes of the United States Supreme Court. The son of a brilliant poet and thinker, Holmes served with bravery in our Civil War, went on to become a respected attorney, a brilliant professor of law, then took a seat on our highest court, which he held for many years. Perhaps his most important statement as a justice was this one: "The Constitution was written for people of fundamentally differing views."

Just two years ago we celebrated the two hundredth anniversary of our federal Constitution. It has stood in place, with minor changes, longer than any similar government document in the world. The Constitution has served us well, and the reason is that it forces all of us to respect the rights of others. The Constitution sets the rules of our society—most important of all, the Constitution makes it clear what the government may *not* do.

The U.S. government may *not* tell people what they can say or what they can think. The government may *not* tell people what ideas they may hold. We have this rule even though the government is selected by the people and usually does what the people wish.

The point is a subtle one. Democracy is simply the political system in which each citizen may make his or her choice on anything so long as the citizen does not injure another person. The underlying belief here is that a free person will usually make an intelligent choice—that even when the citizen makes a mistake, he or she will learn from that mistake and do better next time. In fact, mistakes are probably the most important aspect of choice. What we call experience is mainly lessons from poor choices. But if you deny choice to a person, how can that person learn? If you allow yourself to make even one choice for that citizen, then why not make another, and another, and another, until you make all of the choices for him?

I am contemptuous of communism and all who believe in it, but neither I nor my government has the right to tell people that they cannot be communists. This is something we have never done. If a person has a brain and chooses to be a communist, then I will be patient and wait for him to learn from his mistake. Most people will see their mistakes, and change, as the Russian people have changed.

My feelings about communism are part of my beliefs. I believe in many things. Beliefs are what form a person's ideology. But there are things more important than ideology, and we call those things principles. Principles are those lines which we may never cross. Principles are what define our character and our worth as a people and as a society. A long-held American principle is that a person has the right to form his own beliefs. To violate that most basic right only begins a process that will ultimately deny freedom for anyone. In our Constitution we agreed that even a government selected by the people might be wrong, and so the people set in place rules which neither they nor the government can ever break. If there is genius in America, it is found in the understanding that even the people may be wrong, and even their government must have rules.

Let people think as they wish. Allow them to make mistakes. Do not impose your personal ideology on others. However foolish another person may seem, remember that it is possible that you are the fool, not he. As citizens of a free society you have a civic duty both to tolerate people whose beliefs are different from your own, and a moral duty to listen to them from time to time, because even a fool has something intelligent to say once in a while.

Above all, remember the words of Justice Holmes. A healthy society allows citizens of different beliefs to speak their mind. The people will decide for themselves what they think is right. This system has served us well in America.

And as far as communism is concerned, why waste a bullet on a dead dog?

Funeral

Some things you remember. The first time I ever went to the White House was in March 1985. It was the day Konstantin Chernenko was buried. My wife and I spoke briefly in the Oval Office with President Reagan, whose kind words had propelled *The Hunt for Red October* onto the national best-seller lists. I was at the time beginning work on *Red Storm Rising,* and a new guy named Gorbachev had just taken over in the Soviet Union. President Reagan was having lunch with Henry Kissinger that day to discuss the new chap. Those were the days of the Evil Empire—a phrase for which Reagan was heavily criticized but which was brutally accurate. For the first time there was a Soviet leader whom President Reagan might meet without attending a séance (remember, the sequence was Brezhnev [in his dotage], Andropov [terminally ill from the day he took over], and Chernenko [who might have been dead the whole time]). Who was this new guy? Hope does spring eternal, and as with every new Soviet leader, there was hope in all camps that this new one might be different. In the meantime I had a book to write.

The thing that got my attention came about twenty months later. Reading my morning *Washington Post,* I spotted an item on page 18 or so: Gorbachev was canceling the nation's high-school history exams. The rea-

140

son? There was no purpose, Gorbachev said, in testing the students' knowledge of lies. Up until that point we'd seen a lot of lip service to new ideas, but this minor news item grabbed me, and so I called a friend, Alex Costa, published author and Soviet emigrée. She has a doctor's degree from Moscow State University and is married to Stan Levchenko, a "retired" KGB major who is also a published author. Both are canny observers of their former country. Yes, Alex confirmed, this is an important step. It's real, we agreed, Gorby's real. He's not kidding.

It may seem like a small thing, but I've always felt that it's the pedestrian things that really matter, and what grabbed me here is that a person will never forget being excused a semester exam, nor the reason why. You simply cannot take back something that finds its way into the human mind. What Gorbachev had done was to announce the moral and ideological bankruptcy of the Soviet Union. And if you're wondering just how important that was, consider this: the soldiers—the kids carrying the guns—who now wear the uniform of the Red Army, are the kids who got a pass on the exam—the timing is just about right. They came to political awareness entirely under a man who had broken them off from the past.

The recent coup in the Soviet Union was bound to fail. That it collapsed so fast came as something of a surprise. In a conversation with a TV-correspondent friend, I gave it until Friday, but this one folded so fast that a column I wrote on Monday outlining its weaknesses didn't have time to run.

One might argue that this resulted from stunning tactical ineptitude—coups have been done far better in Argentina, Chile, and Panama. This Junta of supposedly experienced plotters failed to take Boris Yeltsin out. That is in itself an interesting statement. Perhaps these experienced *apparatchiki* thought that the only part of the government that mattered was its head—Gorbachev. Incredible as it may seem, they might not have realized that the popular election of Yeltsin only a few months ago was something as genuinely important as it was genuinely new. Take out Gorby, they might have thought, and the whole country is in our hands (it worked with Khrushchev, didn't it?). They had the generals—a few of them, anyway—on their side, and that gave them the Soviet Army, right? It seems from the lack of radio intercepts by our intelligence agencies that scant attention was given to sending orders out to the numerous military districts and commands in the country. The Junta had Moscow, and what else mattered, right?

If anything proved that Gorbachev was right when he canceled the exams, this is it. The Communist Party of the Soviet Union was and is intellectually bankrupt. In concentrating on the putative chief of government and the capital city only, they proved unable to break with a past that is—past.

The Soviet Army, I learned a few months ago, was in schism. The junior officers were publishing articles in open-source journals decrying the state of their country and their army. In the Russian Federation election both the rank-and-file conscripts and the company-grade officers had voted for Yelt-sin. I forwarded that tidbit to a Pentagon-reporter friend, who confirmed it with the Defense Intelligence Agency, and by Monday afternoon we were both in agreement that this coup would fail on that basis alone. The histori-cal model here was not Beijing but Bucharest—if the Junta gave orders to shoot people, as Nicolae Ceauşescu did, there was no predicting where the rifles would be pointed. One would like to think that this matter was considered beforehand—after all, there is a universal bias toward having competent enemies—but was it?

I think not. Had the Junta thought about those soldiers and the history exam, and certainly the elections, they would have guessed that Yeltsin—no shrinking violet of a political figure—would climb atop an armored vehicle and give both the confused soldiers and the angry citizens a figure to rally behind. (The people? What do they matter . . . ?) The Junta didn't even think to isolate the Western reporters in their Moscow ghetto—and hasn't *any-body* learned about what CNN can do for world opinion? They didn't take the telephone lines down—how hard can that be?—allowing Yeltsin to communicate with both George Bush and John Major, both of whom did all that they could to lay down the law from the international perspective.

One wonders what the Junta members thought when Gorby canceled the exam for those Red Army soldiers. They were probably appalled. After all, lies were important, and the Junta proved that by their belief in those lies, and they were doubtless surprised when their belief in lies collapsed around them like a demolished building.

For seventy years the Communist Party of the Soviet Union has lived by the lie, by the illusion, by a mind-set that belonged in another century. It believed that people would follow it because they had to, that they would like it because they had to. They believed their army would follow the generals because it had to. They believed a lot of things because illusion had become their reality. How else can one explain their ineptitude? It wasn't lack of intelligence, but blindness.

What we have seen in the past week is the death of communism. The dying has been protracted, and truthfully it is something that ought never to have been born. The home of world socialism has entered the twentieth century only nine years before the end, but it's well and truly here at last.

And world socialism is now confined to Cuba, and North Korea—how long before those infection centers are cleaned up?

Illusions die hard, but when they die, they die loudly. This brutal, bloody illusion that has caused more human misery than any of mankind's mistakes died because one man proclaimed the lie, because its defenders simply did not understand that another man was important, and because the people had had enough of the lie. And the fools never saw it coming, did they? Perhaps that's the epitaph for communism. Even the example of Ceaușescu was lost on the true believers. They never saw reality coming. Having lived by the lie, they will now perish by the lie. Mourn not.

Dinosaurs

There are literally thousands of them. They come in various sizes and shapes. All are flat, or nearly so, at the bottom. Most, but not all, are pointed at the front. The bottom is where the fire comes out. Inside the top are from one to ten (and sometimes more) warheads. They're called ballistic launchers, and the "strategic" ones—that is, the ones made to reshape the enemy's country, not his army—are the scary ones. They're dinosaurs. They're the ultimate blunt instruments. They kill.

Since the Soviets deployed the massive SS-6, and we soon thereafter deployed the first-generation Atlas ICBMs, the world has lived in the shadow of these overgrown skyrockets. Both of these first-generation weapons have entered honorable retirement—both are still used for space exploration. The SS-6 is the Russians' only man-rated launcher, the real purpose for which it may actually have been designed—the "chief designer" of the Soviet rocket industry, Sergey Korolev, seems in retrospect to have been a sensible chap, far more enthusiastic about space than war. The Atlas in expanded configuration still launches satellites. Both of these designs date back to the early 1950s and have long since been superseded. Beginning in the late 1950s and carrying through until today, the United States and the

144

Soviet Union have designed, built, tested, and deployed new variations on these systems for almost two generations.

The mission of these weapons has never quite been understood. Never really tasked to city-smashing, their purpose is roughly the same as that of the strategic bombers of World War II, to eliminate a country's ability to conduct war. They're really designed to eliminate centers of industry, militarily valuable assets, and command-and-control centers. That population centers often find themselves "co-located" with those legitimate targets of war is a regrettable coincidence which the targeteers try—how successfully is anyone's guess—to shut out of their minds. These are the ultimate instruments of war.

But they're a thing of the past.

There is a curious absence of commentary in the American media. We live not merely in exciting times, but in times that are wholly unique. The state of the world today is different from anything in recorded history.

There has always been superpower conflict. You can look as far back in time as the war between Troy and the city-states of Greece—probably it was fought over commercial access through the Hellespont to the Black Sea, not the famous Helen, but even kings need excuses. Rome fought three wars with Carthage for control of the Mediterranean Sea—Hannibal and Scipio Africanus came from the second one. As nation-states matured, so did their wars. England and Spain—Drake, the Armadas, and colonization rights in North America. England and France—over the balance of power in Europe and who would own North America. France and Germany—over who would dominate Europe. Napoleon widened the scope of war around the turn of the nineteenth century—once a fairly civilized affair, the ultimate game of kings, fought by semiprofessional armies for mainly limited objectives. Bonaparte invented the "nation in arms" model for warfare. Now the resources of an entire country would be mobilized, and the goal of war grew also from adjustments of the power balance to physical and political rule over continental landmasses. The growth in scope led to a growth of savagery. While war has ever been a bloody business at the local level, the new Napoleonic rules raised the stakes to national and cultural survival—for which ends one's efforts increased accordingly—and at the same time made the wars far more difficult to win, for a nation-state is a hardy creature, and destroying all its resources is of necessity a protracted business.

Extreme objectives command extreme measures. World War I, fought for both the domination of Europe and by implication the colonial rule of nearly the entire planet, exhausted that continent and upset the pré-existing world order, replacing it with chaos and instability that led inevitably to World War II.

World War II, essentially the second act of the 1914–1918 conflict, was begun to formalize a new but malignant world order, and now the scope was explicitly the political control of the entire world. For these ends new extremes of barbarism were explored, to the point that something as horrific as the Holocaust was merely the political whim of the man who began it all. If one wants to rule the world, why not order it in God-like fashion?

The ultimate confrontation, of course, was the West and Democracy, championed by the United States of America, against the East and Marxism, championed by the Union of Soviet Socialist Republics. The stakes here were not merely the control of the world, but the political philosophy of all mankind. Democracy won. Contemporaneous with the evolution of war was the evolution of human thought—the two are inseparable, of course—and the winning side was that which managed to attract the largest number of adherents and to demonstrate its operational advantages. The good news here—else this column would have been neither written nor read—is that the Final Conflict was won bloodlessly, or nearly so.

And now, for the first time in all of human history, we live in a world where superpower conflict does not exist. There is no historical model for the current world order. None. A world without potential war between major countries was until two years ago the stuff of utopian novels, blue-sky dreams of minds not grounded in reality. But the dream is now real, and we will have to learn to cope with it. The good news is that it seems likely that, even for politicians, adjusting to peace will probably be easier than adjusting to war, just not as exciting.

The world is not yet at peace. There are still regional conflicts. But regional wars are mostly the local echoes of superpower conflict, the current manifestation of the seventeenth-century games, adjusting the balance of power in Africa or Asia, determining spheres of influence with gunfire. Presently, these nasty little conflicts will peter out. Not fast enough. People will continue to die for purposes that will in retrospect seem as meaningful as cancer or heart disease, but it's been a long time coming, and in historical terms the change will appear rapid enough to future spectators.

Still with us, however, are the dinosaurs of this misbegotten age, the ballistic launchers whose warheads were built to keep the peace by the threat of unprecedented destruction. Already people are finding a new reason to worry about them. As the Soviet Union enters its period of decolonization, control of those weapons becomes a very iffy proposition.

I pose a more basic question—why allow them to exist at all?

Perhaps the weapons have served their purpose. Perhaps they really did keep the peace. But the peace appears to have been achieved—or at least that moment of achievement is now in sight. Whatever purpose they may have served is now consigned to the age of Achilles, and Scipio, and Drake, and Napoleon, and all the rest. A new age has begun, and the place for dinosaurs is in museums.

Not all that long ago, President Reagan proposed "The Zero Option" for theater nuclear forces. It proved to be a winning idea. It's time for that idea to be extended. Let's start now to plan an international agreement bringing intercontinental-ballistic weapons down as close to zero as we can. The reason is simple—they are no longer needed. Their existence is itself a danger, however small it might be, that someone with the desire to turn back the clock might have the means to make his perverse dream real. Nuclear weapons will not go away—you cannot revoke the laws of physics—but it should be relatively easy to eliminate the great majority of the launchers. The time to start is now.

Turn Back

How do you talk about the death of a little boy?

In April of 1990, I received a piece of fan mail. There was a little boy in Memorial Sloan-Kettering Cancer Center in New York. His name was Kyle, and at the time he was six years old. His grandfather, I learned, had read one of my books to the little guy, and Kyle enjoyed it. There was more to the letter, some subtextual things, and this one grabbed me rather hard. It gave me an address, from which I got a phone number. So I called, and asked what I might do for Kyle. At the time I had a box full of poster-size aircraft photos, gifts from a major defense contractor, and since little boys usually like pictures of fighter planes, I sent a bunch. Chemotherapy, a form of treatment as thoroughly vile as it is vitally necessary, typically causes a child's hair to fall out. This does give the excuse to wear hats, however, and I sent a few of those as well.

Kyle suffered from Ewing's Sarcoma. There are no good forms of cancer, and this sort is worse than most. I'd later learn that Kyle's personal version of it was mobile, virulent, and unusually resistant to medical science. The odds never looked good, but some chance beats none at all, and this little guy was a fighter. He was also unusually bright, possessed of an active, questing mind. It's a fact that children stricken with serious disease are kicked way up the learning curve. They somehow become adults very quickly, though they never quite lose the child's innocence. The result of this is both immensely sad and wonderfully charming. In any case, keeping the little guy entertained and distracted became a major diversion for me. It was like a little flag on the cardex. Whenever I happened to visit a new place I wondered if Kyle would like a souvenir, which would necessitate a letter explaining where I'd picked up the new gewgaw. Even so, sooner or later you run out of fresh ideas.

At that point I started calling in markers. It has been my privilege to make numerous friends in the U.S. military. These men and women have daily access to the most intricate bits of hardware known to civilized man, and kids invariably find them as interesting as I do. The first such unit I "pinged" was the 37th Tactical Fighter Wing, the people who own and operate the F-117A Stealth fighter. Little prompting was needed. People in uniform live by the warrior's code. Rule Number One: The first duty of the strong is to protect the weak. Our people understand that. The first packet of material was followed by letters of encouragement even after the 37th deployed to fight a war. Kyle got one of the first videos of "my" movie, and just about memorized it. He wanted to see USS *Dallas*. It couldn't be just any submarine—it had to be *Dallas*—but she was away on deployment, the Pentagon told me.

On the Friday before the shooting started in the Persian Gulf, a little light bulb went off in my head, the one you get that says, "Why don't you call . . ." And so I phoned up to Long Island, then to learn that Kyle had just spent his first day in school in a year and a half. It was over, his parents told me. The little guy had lucked out and slain this particular dragon. That was some feeling. I got the word out as quickly as I could, especially to the 37th TFW in Saudi Arabia, and then I got back to work on my new book, secure in the knowledge that the good guys had won a small but important battle. Getting up to see Kyle became a matter of lower priority. Kids have more fun with other kids than they do with stuffy adults.

On a business trip in March, I called home, as usual, for messages, and the news was bad: Mr. Ewing was back. The early return after surgery, CAT scans, and abusive chemotherapy was a particularly evil omen, but the people at Sloan-Kettering did not want to give up on my little friend. He was being blasted with hard gamma-radiation, and if the new growth in his leg was killed, and if the CAT scan showed no additional activity elsewhere, then Kyle would be lucky enough merely to have his left leg surgically removed, followed by another bout of chemotherapy. Otherwise . . . The family hadn't wanted to bother me with the news for fear of interfering with my new book, and Kyle didn't want me to know because, his dad explained,

I might stop liking him if I discovered he was losing a leg. Kids think that way, of course. The emotional impact of this was horrific, but there was work to be done.

The next day I established that USS *Dallas* was finally back in her home port of Groton, Connecticut, and it seemed a good idea to get the little guy aboard while he was still largely intact. The crew of *Dallas* gave my little buddy what was probably the best day of his life. He bubbled about it—*I got to shoot a torpedo, and look out of the periscope, and I ate everything they served for me!* he told me that night. They made him a member of the crew, and presented him with gold dolphins that he still wears. Five days later, his left leg was taken off.

The resilience of these kids is something that confounds reason. Kyle was at this point only seven years old and had already been through an experience to crush the soul of any adult. He sat up on the gurney and steered himself into the operating room. That bit of news reduced a very tough general officer—one of whose legs is still in Vietnam—to an awkward silence. Then began yet another bout of chemotherapy. When "phantom pain" from his amputated leg caused him discomfort, Kyle would say out loud, "I'm sorry, the leg you have reached is no longer in service. Please contact the right leg for further information."

Kyle's parents. It requires no great insight to note that they were living through the ultimate nightmare. Set aside the fact that they faced the death of a child. Consider for the moment only the day-to-day routine. When the child is in the hospital, you live there with him, sleeping in a chair of dubious comfort, eating whatever you might warm in the nearby microwave. Forget your job. Forget your spouse. Forget the rest of your family. Forget sleeping more than four hours at a stretch. You learn a lot of what the medics have to know, and end up as a highly skilled nurse's aide. You get to sit there and watch poisons drip into your child's bloodstream. You are the one who has to be strong for a child who occasionally gets discouraged. You get discouraged when, every time you come back for a new treatment protocol, you learn that a friend's child—*Oh, God, not her—she has the same disease that . . .* You learn to decode what the doctors and nurses tell you, searching for hope among the circumlocutions. And there's always the lingering fear that someday you will leave this place for the last time, and the wrong reason.

Oh, yeah, all this goes on for months—*if you're lucky.*

But, perversely, the parents *are* lucky. Consider the doctors, nurses, and technicians. They are bright, sharp, dedicated, and so fiercely competitive as to make an NFL coach look mellow. Their personal enemy is Death himself, and they fight their nasty little war on many fronts, each one of which is the body of a human child, hairless, pale as parchment, with sunken but twinkling eyes. And they lose a lot. We award medals and honors to professional soldiers who risk their lives in battle, typically for a brief span of hours. These medics put their *souls* at risk, and do it every day, and do you wonder then who are the most courageous people in the world? Kyle's principal physician was a lady named Norma, a Jewish (I think) gal of sixty years and pixieish proportions who started treating kids with cancer when hope was a lie. Professional soldiers would say that she has a clear sense of mission and tenacity of purpose with few parallels except in her own elite community. Norma was the blue-force commander in the war, and she fought valiantly, with consummate skill and obstinate determination.

Unfortunately, the red force won.

I got a call one afternoon in May from Kyle's dad. The little guy was terminal. Make-A-Wish was sending him to Disney World. I was unprepared for this. Probably I am too optimistic, and perhaps the family was overly careful in what they told me. That night I had to travel to Baltimore for a college-trustees meeting. I checked myself into a nice place with a nice bar and proceeded to consume a good deal of alcohol in a puerile and pointless exercise. I had to see Kyle, of course, and I cursed myself for not having taken the time sooner. Since I am something of an expert on Disney World (seven trips), I offered my services as tour guide.

Why did I go? Fear. Everything about this frightened me. I was afraid that I would lose control of myself while with my little buddy. I was afraid that we'd be alone and he would turn to me and ask the question he'd not asked his mom and dad: *When am I going to die?* But most of all I was afraid of living the rest of my life as someone who had failed to stand up for a sick little boy.

We met in the lobby of the Contemporary Resort. Rick and Eileen hadn't told their son that I'd be there. Kyle was easy to spot, the pale little one-legged guy in the wheelchair. I strolled over and dropped my cap on Kyle's head. Rick handled the introduction, and Kyle was incredulous for an instant—and then his eyes lit the room like a strobe. I lifted him up for a rather ferocious hug, my heart already broken. It got immediately worse. His grandfather took me aside a moment later to say that you couldn't hug him like that—*he has a tumor in his chest, Mr. Clancy, and it hurts him when you do that.* I'd never known such horror and shame in my life.

Strangely, that didn't matter to him at all. Kyle, by God, wanted to have fun, and didn't want anything as trivial as cancer to stand in his way. It was an admirably clear mission statement, and with that fixed in my mind I led the family into the Magic Kingdom.

It is good to report that the Disney people have paid systematic and expert attention to their "special" guests. We fast-tracked into every attraction. The costumed characters, Mickey and the rest, single them out for priority attention. The family stayed at Kids' Village in Kissimmee, about half an hour from the park. It's a dedicated facility, superbly designed and executed for its purpose, wonderfully supported by local businesses. Disney (and other) characters come there—the lovely young lady who plays Snow White was particularly angelic in her attention to my little buddy—and they often come on their own time and out of uniform to spell the parents in their duties. Mr. Disney would be proud of them.

Rick and Eileen allowed me to spell them, too. I most often drew the duty of wheeling my little buddy around. I still feel guilty about it, but Rick tells me I'm an idiot to think that way. Not all that guilty. It was a joy beyond words. I quickly learned that my fears on the trip down were even dumber than my usual mistakes. Kids like Kyle, sick as they might be, are more intensely alive than anything on earth. Their eyes glow brightly indeed, and when you see them smile and drink in the wonder of such a place as Disney World, you realize that what you are really seeing is life itself, the entire miracle of existence in one brilliant moment. My little buddy was having a tough time. Every moment drugs were going into his system through a useful obscenity called a broviak that dripped medications into his jugular vein. His thin, abused body was often weak. Eating came hard to him. But he fought back in a way that makes "courage" all too small a word, visibly pushing the discomfort aside and concentrating on the mission at hand, which was having fun.

We were already friends from our letters and conversations, but at this time and in this place, something unexpected happened. Suddenly we were not just friends anymore. As though through some form of divine magic, we were closer still. Kyle trusted me, loved me. He was my son, too.

It wasn't all easy. Every so often reality crashes back into your consciousness. *This little boy is dying, Clancy.* I suppose the one really surprising thing was the rage. You become ferociously protective of a stricken child. Something was killing my little buddy; even as I watched, those misbegotten cells were dividing and spreading. I'm a person who's played with the best killing machines known to man. I've driven and fired tanks, scored a "possible" with a hand-made sniper rifle on a 1,000-yard range, shot pistols with the FBI. You wish cancer really were a dragon, because if it were, you could go after it, hunt the bastard down. You lust for that chance. I know how, and what I cannot do, others of my acquaintance would leap at. All the people in uniform who'd stood up for my little buddy, the world's most effective warriors, and Clancy, the minstrel who writes about them—any of us would have risked it all for Kyle. But cancer is not that kind of enemy. You look around at the passing crowd and start hoping that someone will attack your little buddy so that you might do *something* to protect him. That's how crazy you get, and when you face the fact that there is not a single thing you can do to save him, all you have left is an undirected killing rage that feeds on itself; and then you step away for a moment, and swallow, and take a deep breath, staring off above the heads of passing crowds as though looking for something. In such moments you understand what it's like to be the parent of a critically ill child. So you turn back, smile, and ask your little buddy where he wants to go next. Because even if fate and science have failed him, you can't, not now you can't. And you put it all aside until you get back to your room, because you know when you get there you're going to come apart again.

It was only four days. I was trying to squeeze in a lifetime of friendship in a brief span of hours, doing so with a child whose frail body often twisted with pain. But we did have fun. At the "Indiana Jones Thrill Show" Kyle hopped off his wheelchair and stood on his one leg to get a better view—swallow, deep breath, set it aside! We discussed things mundane and profound. His child's mind wanted to learn, and I dealt with his numerous questions. We talked about the future, what Kyle would do on growing up. A few moments stand out. Holding Kyle in my lap—this required subterfuge since he didn't like that sissy stuff—during the ride through Spaceship Earth. Explaining to him that the hard part about the magic fountains at Journey Through Imagination was training the water to jump repeatedly on command (I almost had him going on that). Having a few pictures taken together. The feel of his arm around my shoulder.

And then it was over. When he hugged me, he must have hurt himself. He went his way. I went mine. From there on we spoke on the phone almost every day.

I saw him again four times, all of them at Sloan-Kettering. The medics gave him one more shot of chemotherapy. What Rick and Eileen didn't tell me was that nobody had ever survived this protocol, and the last time I saw my little buddy, I drew the duty of convincing him to take on one last medication. That wasn't easy. Kyle knew how to resist argumentation, but my last card was to ask him what he would tell me if the situation were reversed. Kyle saw the logic, and took it like a man. All it did was hurt him. It's not the sort of thing you want on your conscience. Sooner or later "right" and "wrong" get muddled, the knowledge of the intellect isn't quite the same as knowledge of the heart, and you wish that there were some agency to tell you that you did the right thing.

Kyle made it to his eighth birthday, had his party, and then Mr. Ewing came back to stay. His last ten days were lost in a cloud of narcotics. In our last conversation, Kyle told me that "When I grow up, I'd like to be like you, but a doctor instead of a writer." I think I left fingerprints on the telephone.

And then he was gone, buried in his treasured USS *Dallas* T-shirt, a custom-made USAF flight suit, with Navy Wings of Gold, and Dolphins, and the unit patch of the 37th TFW. And his parents spent much of their time comforting me. They'd essentially given over their son to a stranger for four days, and they actually thanked *me* for it. Rick and Eileen had made me a part of their family, promoted me to be Kyle's backup dad, and graced me with their friendship. Most of all, I'd received the love of their son. Of all the things I've earned in life, that's the one I'll take beyond the grave.

Life offers few opportunities to do something for which you can be unequivocally proud. It's not very often you can see the person in the mirror and whisper, *Yeah, you really did that one right, pal.* Maybe the price of that is the pain which defines it. What did I learn? I'm no different from the next person, certainly no more courageous, no more decent. When a cousin died of cancer in his teens, I wasn't there. I've always avoided funerals, as though doing so causes their reality to vanish. Kyle's death forced me to face things I'd managed to avoid all my life, and to see things that I'd never before cared to look at.

Perhaps the worst thing that happens to the parents of such a child is that others turn away from them. The unspeakable agony this inflicts can scarcely be described, and the parents view it as a lack of feeling, a lack of caring. I think not. What happens, I think, is denial and rage. When you watch a child suffer, you must accept the fact that it could easily be your own. When you watch a child suffer, every cell of your being wants to do *something* to fix things, and in the understanding that all your money, and skills, and contacts cannot extend his life a single day, you feel singularly useless. Turning away is a defense mechanism, to protect your own feelings, to distance yourself from the rage of the parents which you have no wish to share, from a personal impotence you have no wish to acknowledge.

My own involvement began with the arrogant certainty that luck was transferrable: My just being involved with him could change things. Tom Clancy won't let a little boy die. I can put him in touch with others. I can push buttons. I can *make things happen.* In my blindness I failed to see that I was right after all. In this kind of war the big victories depend on physicians and their skills, but big victories are not the only sort. By turning back, you can give friendship and get friendship in return. Kyle passed by far too quickly, but he was here, for some part of which time he was my friend. That was a victory for both of us. When you see a stricken child having fun, you are watching Death being defeated, and seeing that is a godlike feeling. When he leaves, your heart will be more broken than you ever thought possible. Mine surely was. But even that is a victory, because Kyle might have died without my knowing who and what he was. And then how much poorer would I have been.

Medicine has advanced remarkably in the past century. Louis Pasteur buried half of his children, and it's too easy to forget that there are places still in the world where watching your child die is an all too normal part of life. The very success of medicine has removed from us the understanding that some of the dragons have not yet been defeated. But until the docs get their collective act together, more kids like Kyle will suffer all the pains of hell, and some of them will not survive.

When I went up for the funeral, I took a walk with one of Kyle's nurses. I was in a wretched state. I told her that I was glad for having met and befriended the little guy, but that I'd never be able to do the same thing again. It just hurt too much. I was begging for sympathy, but instead I got what I really deserved. She stopped dead in the street and looked up at me: "What about all the other kids?" Her words had the force of a blow. *What would Kyle think? You're a coward after all, aren't you?*

There are others. Each of them, however ill, is alive and needful of the same things that we all need: love, friendship, conversation. Their parents need to know that they are not alone in their personal hell. Be there for them. Will it hurt? Worse than anything one can imagine. But there are compensations. You will come to know people ennobled by their suffering, and children whose sheer force of being will teach lessons you never dreamed about. You'll learn that Death is ever out there, waiting for his shot, sometimes patiently, sometimes not. But you'll also learn that life is *here* and now, that every moment has meaning, and that even Death cannot take from you the things that others give. You'll rediscover the truth that the love of a child is the truest gift from God, and while the price may be high, the value is higher still.

It's easy to turn away. It's even safe, because doing so is soon forgotten. Turn back anyway. There are children who need us. And along the way, you'll see what life really is.

4. A Tom Clancy Concordance, A to Z

Compiled by Roland J. Green

In this Concordance *Sum = The Sum of All Fears; Danger = Clear and Present Danger; Cardinal = The Cardinal of the Kremlin; Games = Patriot Games; Storm = Red Storm Rising; Hunt = The Hunt for Red October.*

I would also like to pay tribute to the indispensable reference works produced by Norman Polmar and Edward Luttwak. Without them this Concordance would have taken twice as long and been half as good.

—R.J.G.

1 PARA: 1st Battalion of the British Army's Parachute Regiment. In *Games,* Yeoman of the Tower Joseph EVANS is a former sergeant major in the battalion.

11-B: Designation for the Military Occupational Specialty of a Light Infantryman. Domingo Chavez has it in *Danger.*

1ST FORCE RECON: Reconnaissance battalion attached to the First Marine Division in Vietnam. Sergeant Major BRECKENRIDGE in *Games* served as a sniper with the unit.

101ST AIRBORNE: The U.S. Army's 101st Airborne Division, the last command in Vietnam of *Storm's* unnamed SACEUR. Its successor, the 101st Air Assault Division, is the original new assignment for Ding CHAVEZ in *Danger.*

155-MM GUN-HOWITZER: Standard U.S. Army medium-artillery piece. See M-109 and M-198.

173RD AIRBORNE: Independent U.S. Army airborne brigade, which served in the Vietnam War. Robert NEWTON, who discovers the Uzi used in the attack on Cathy RYAN in *Games,* served with the brigade.

175-MM GUN: M-107 self-propelled gun; formerly in service with U.S. Army, still in service with many other countries including NATO countries and Israel. In *Sum,* the Druse farmer who finds the Israeli nuclear bomb lost his wife to a shell from an Israeli 175.

195: Plessey high-frequency dipping sonar, mounted in Royal Navy SEA KING helicopters from *INVINCIBLE* in *Hunt.*

1052-CLASS FRIGATE: U.S. *Knox* (DE 1052)-class, single-screw conventional destroyer escorts. Forty-six built for U.S. Navy, 1966-73. 3,075/ 4,260 tons, 27 knots; one 5″ gun, one PHALANX, four ASW TT, LAMPS, ASROC and HARPOON; crew 280. Largest postwar U.S. class of surface vessels before the *Perry*-class FFGs. They originally had problems with seaworthiness and long-range ASW weapons; these problems have now been solved.

In *Hunt,* three are assigned to the *INVINCIBLE* task force. In *Storm,* Edward MORRIS begins the war as captain of the 1052-class *PHARRIS* on convoy-escort duty. He escorts three convoys and sinks two Soviet submarines before his ship is torpedoed and heavily damaged. She spends the rest of the war awaiting repairs in Boston.

20-MM CANNON: The U.S. Navy Mk. 12 version of this weapon, mounted in the A-4 SKYHAWK. In *Sum,* Lieutenant ZADIN uses it against the Syrian missile battery, just before he is shot down.

2016 SONAR: Long-range hull-mounted sonar of H.M.S. *BATTLEAXE* in *Storm.*

40-MM GUN: Former U.S. Navy Bofors light antiaircraft gun; clip-fed, semiautomatic; range 3,000+ yards, 40+ rounds per minute, shell weight 2 lbs. In *Danger,* one is mounted aboard U.S.C.G. *PANACHE.*

5.56-MM ROUND: Standard round for the U.S. M-16 RIFLE and its variants, developed from the Remington .223 sporting round. The lighter round permits a lighter weapon and a greater ammunition load, valuable in situations like the covert operations in *Danger,* where resupply is difficult.

594-CLASS SUBMARINE: U.S. Navy *Permit* (SSN 594)-class single-screw nuclear attack submarines. Thirteen built for the U.S. Navy 1962-67. Named after fish or sea creatures. In *Sum,* the Soviet VICTOR III submarine is considered the equal of a late-model 594.

637-CLASS SUBMARINE: U.S. *Sturgeon* (SSN 637)-class, single-screw nuclear attack submarines. 4,300/4,800 tons, 30+ knots, four 21″ TT, HARPOON, TOMAHAWK, mines; crew 110. Thirty-seven built for the U.S. Navy, 1967-75. Until the 688s, the largest and highest-performing class of U.S. nuclear submarines. Named after fish or sea creatures.

In *Hunt, POGY,* which helps escort *RED OCTOBER* and participates in the final engagement with *V.K. KONOVOLOV,* is a *Sturgeon.*

688-CLASS SUBMARINE: U.S. *Los Angeles* (SSN 688)-class, single-screw nuclear attack submarines. 6,000/7,000 tons, 30+ knots; four 21″ TT, TOMAHAWK, HARPOON, mines; crew 130. More than fifty built for the U.S. Navy from 1975.

The largest U.S. postwar class of submarines. They are the fastest, quietest, and most capable attack submarines in U.S. service, superior to any Soviet vessel except the *AKULA*-class. The TOMAHAWK missiles are carried in twelve vertical-launch tubes. Named after American cities.

Commander Bart MANCUSO's *DALLAS* in *Hunt* and *Cardinal* is a 688. So is Daniel MCCAFFERTY's *CHICAGO* in *Storm,* as well as the rest of the missile-launching force *(BOSTON, PROVIDENCE, PITTSBURGH, GROTON,* and *KEY WEST)* in Operation DOOLITTLE. 688s in *Sum* include *OMAHA, HONOLULU,* and *KEY WEST.*

76-MM GUN: Main armament of the Soviet World War II T-34 tank. In *Cardinal,* Colonel FILITOV killed a German antitank gun crew with the last shot from his burning tank at the Battle of KURSK.

707: Four-engined jet airliner; Boeing. 150 + passengers, intercontinental range, in service from 1958. The first commercially successful jet airliner.

Basis for the E-3 AWACS, in *Hunt* and *Storm,* and the VC-137 VIP transport, used in *Cardinal.* The 707-320 long-range version is used as AIR FORCE ONE by the President until replaced by 747s in *Sum.*

727: Jet airliner; Boeing. Three rear-mounted engines, 120 + passengers, medium range, in service from 1963. RYAN flies a Pan Am 727 from Moscow to Frankfurt at the end of *Cardinal;* in *Danger* Admiral PAINTER takes one to San Jose.

737: Twin-engined jet airliner; Boeing. 100 + passengers, short range, in service from 1967. In *Storm,* Robert TOLAND flies in one over a blacked-out England; in *Games,* Kevin O'DONNELL flies from London to Cork aboard a Sabena 737.

747: Four-turbofan jet airliner; Boeing. 300 + passengers (depending on version), intercontinental range. In service since 1970. The first of the "jumbo" jets.

In *Hunt,* Jack RYAN flies to London aboard a TWA 747 and for the first time in his life falls asleep aboard an airplane. In *Cardinal,* CIA courier Augie GIANNINI takes 747s from Moscow to London, then from London to Washington. In *Sum,* AIR FORCE ONE is a converted 747, a VC-25A. KNEECAP, with Vice President DURLING aboard, is a conversion of the 747, the E-4B.

7.62-MM: Standard NATO caliber for infantry rifles and light, medium, and general-purpose machine guns. Adopted as NATO standard in late 1940s. The caliber of many weapons, including the helicopter's minigun used by Jack RYAN in *Danger.*

767: Boeing jet airliner. Two turbofans, 200 + passengers, medium to long range, in service since 1982. *COBRA BELLE*, the infrared surveillance aircraft in *Cardinal,* is a converted 767.

82-MM MORTAR: Standard Soviet medium infantry mortar since World War II. 3,000 yards effective range, 15 rounds per minute, shell weight 6-7 lbs. The Soviets use it against EDWARDS's party in *Storm;* in *Cardinal,* captured ones are used by the Afghan guerrillas in the attack on the BRIGHT STAR facility.

88: German World War II antitank gun; also main armament of the Tiger tank. In *Cardinal,* it was the weapon that destroyed FILITOV's tank during the Battle of KURSK.

89TH MILITARY AIRLIFT WING: "The President's Wing." U.S. Air Force unit dedicated to transporting the President and other VIPs. Based at ANDREWS AIR FORCE BASE.

9-MM PISTOL ROUND: The most common pistol and submachine gun round in the Western world; first version developed 1901. The Uzis used against Cathy and Sally RYAN in *Games* are among the many weapons chambered for this round.

A-1 SKYRAIDER: U.S. single-seat, single-engined carrier- and land-based, propeller-driven attack aircraft; Douglas; U.S. Navy, Marines, and Air Force. In *Danger,* Colonel Paul JOHNS was supported by Skyraiders during rescue operations in Vietnam.

A-4 SKYHAWK: U.S. single-engined, single-seat carrier- and land-based light attack aircraft and advanced trainer; McDonnell-Douglas; in service with U.S. Navy, Marine Corps, and many foreign countries, notably Israel and Argentina from 1957. 600 mph; combat radius 300 miles; two 20-mm guns, 5,000+ lbs. of ordnance.

In *Games,* Robby JACKSON has practiced ACM against an A-4 in his F-14. In *Danger,* an A-4 is used as the CHASE PLANE in the live tests of the special light-case bomb at China Lake. In *Sum,* an Israeli Skyhawk flown by Lieutenant Mordecai ZADIN in the Yom Kippur War is accidentally left armed with a nuclear weapon, which is lost when the aircraft is shot down by Syrian antiaircraft missiles.

A-6E INTRUDER: U.S. twin-engined, two-seat all-weather jet carrier- and land-based medium attack aircraft; Grumman; in service with U.S. Navy and Marine Corps from 1970. 600 mph; combat radius 1,000 miles. 10,000+ lbs. of ordnance, with advanced computerized navigation and bombing systems. Variants include the EA-6 PROWLER electronic-warfare version and the KA-6 aerial tanker.

In *Storm,* Prowlers support the second B-52 strike on Iceland. In *Danger,* Intruders carry out the smart-bomb raids on the MEDELLIN drug bosses, refueled in flight by KA-6s. In *Sum,* A-6s from *THEODORE ROOSEVELT* are loaded with B-61 nuclear weapons for strategic strikes as the crisis escalates.

A-7 CORSAIR: U.S. single-engined, single-seat, jet light-attack aircraft; Ling-Temco-Vought; in service with U.S. Navy, U.S. Air Force, Air National Guard, several foreign countries from 1966. 600 mph; combat radius 600 miles. 8,000+ lbs. of ordnance, two 20-mm cannon.

In *Storm,* A-7s fly from *NIMITZ* with "buddy stores" for refueling the F-14s on COMBAT AIR PATROL. A-7s also fly close-support strikes in support of Lieutenant EDWARDS's patrol in Iceland during its final engagement.

A-10 THUNDERBOLT II: U.S. twin-engined, single-seat jet ground-attack aircraft; Fairchild-Republic; in service with U.S. Air Force from 1976. 400 mph; combat radius 300 miles. 8,000+ lbs. of ordnance, including air-to-ground missiles; GAU-8/A AVENGER 30-mm cannon. Nicknamed "Warthog." The A-10 is built around the AVENGER cannon, and is the first dedicated ground-attack aircraft in U.S. service since before World War II.

In *Hunt,* A-10s simulate a low-level attack on the *KIROV,* flagship of the Soviet fleet pursuing *RED OCTOBER.* In *Storm,* A-10s, in their primary antitank role, inflict heavy losses on Soviet armored forces and earn the nickname of "The Devil's Cross" from their victims.

AA: Antiaircraft, either missiles or guns. The Russians use both against the B-52s attacking Iceland in *Storm.*

AA-11:   Short-range Soviet air-to-air missile; highly maneuverable. In service late 1980s. In *Sum,* four are carried by the first MiG-29-N sighted by Robby JACKSON in the Mediterranean.

ABASHIN, "MIRKA," LIEUTENANT: Red Army officer, in Mikhail FILITOV's tank regiment during World War II. In *Cardinal,* FILITOV remembers Abashin being killed in a sacrificial rear-guard action.

ABDUL: In *Cardinal,* an Afghan teenager, orphaned by the war. He becomes a highly skilled spotter and loader for THE ARCHER's STINGER missiles and helps shoot down the AN-26. He survives the Soviet air raid on the Pakistani refugee camp.

ABDULLAH: In *Sum,* one of QATI's bodyguards. He attends the Commander on his visit to the Druse FARMER, and later shoots Manfred FROMM after the East German engineer's work on the bomb is thought to be done.

ABE LINCOLN: *Abraham Lincoln,* U.S. Navy nuclear aircraft carrier, *NIMITZ*-class, in service 1989. In *Danger,* Robby JACKSON learns that he will be commanding the carrier's air wing.

ABM: Antiballistic missile; a form of missle defense mentioned in *Cardinal* as made obsolete by MIRV's.

ABRAMS: See M-1 ABRAMS.

ABU NIDAL: "The Father of Struggle," alias for Sabri el-Banna, dissident Palestinian terrorist leader responsible for up to two hundred terrorist actions in Israel and abroad. In *Games* and *Danger,* he is mentioned as an example of a major terrorist.

ABYSSAL PLAIN: The flat portion of the bottom of the deep ocean, average depth 15-18,000 feet. In *Hunt, RED OCTOBER* will go deeper once the bottom drops off to the abyssal plain.

AC: Aircraft Commander. In *Danger,* Paul JOHNS's title.

ACCELEROMETER: Instrument for measuring the rate of increase in the speed of a vehicle. In *Hunt,* they are safety devices in the arming mechanism of the warheads of *RED OCTOBER's* missiles.

ACHMED: In *Sum,* one of QATI's guards. Too curious for his own good about what is going on in the underground shop, he suffers lethal plutonium exposure. The diagnosis of his condition gives the KGB an important clue, and his deathbed confession reveals the location of the bomb workshop.

ACQUISITION AND GUIDANCE PACKAGE: The portion of a STINGER or other shoulder-fired missile which detects the target and guides the weapon. In *Cardinal,* ABDUL discards the launch tube, then transfers the acquisition and guidance package to a loaded tube.

ACQUISITION OF SIGNAL (AOS):   The moment at which a ground-based station is able to receive signals from a satellite in orbit. In *Cardinal,* Jack RYAN is waiting for AOS at the New Mexico laser-research facility.

ACTION DIRECTE: French terrorist organization which carried out a number of assassinations from early 1980s. In *Games,* their African camp is used for training by the ULA. Acting on CIA intelligence partly supplied by Jack RYAN, the French raid the camp and arrest, try, and execute many of the members of the organization.

ACTIVE MEASURES: Soviet intelligence term for a response to a situation intended to disrupt an opponent's activities, as opposed to mere surveillance. This response can include anything up to assassination. In *Danger,* Colonel CORTEZ thinks the Americans are incapable of using active measures.

ADAIR, RED: Famous American expert in fighting oil-well fires. In *Storm,* the men who detect the oil-field sabotage say that even Red Adair wouldn't tackle this one.

ADAPTIVE OPTICS: Laser mirrors composed of multiple segments, computer-controlled to alter the focus of the laser beam in response to feedback from the target. Essential for ground-based lasers, like the TEA CLIPPER lasers in *Cardinal,* to cope with atmospheric distortion.

ADLER, DEPUTY SECRETARY OF STATE SCOTT: In *Sum,* one of Secretary of State Brent TALBOT's trusted men. Adler approves RYAN's peace plan and participates in the negotiations in Rome. Afterward he pressures the Israeli government with President FOWLER's threat to withhold arms shipments.

ADMIRAL LUNIN: In *Sum,* Soviet submarine, AKULA class.

She is assigned to the Soviet Pacific Fleet. On one patrol in the Gulf of Alaska, she tracks the U.S.S. *MAINE,* one of the super-quiet *OHIO*-class BALLISTIC MISSILE SUBMARINES. She then returns to port for a major refit, in which she receives an improved sonar and a new, quieter FEED-WATER PUMP.

On her second patrol, she again encounters *MAINE,* also on her second patrol. During the crisis she engages the collision-damaged *MAINE,* under the impression that war has broken out, while being in turn engaged by a P-3 ORION. After fatally damaging *MAINE, Lunin* surfaces and rescues eighty-seven of the American crew.

AEGIS: U.S. Navy air-defense system, based on sophisticated phased-array radars controlled by advanced computers. Able to engage numerous targets simultaneously, using STANDARD missiles. Its primary mission is the defense of carrier battle groups.

The major platform for Aegis is the *TICONDEROGA* (CG 47)-class missile cruisers, modified versions of the SPRUANCE (DD 963)-class destroyers. 7,000/9,600 tons; 30+ knots (gas turbine propulsion); 2 5″ guns, STANDARD, ASROC, and TOMAHAWK missiles (later ships have Vertical Launch Systems), LAMPS; crew 360. More than thirty in service from 1983. Aegis is also to be mounted in the *Arleigh Burke* (DDG-51)-class destroyers, entering service from 1991.

Aegis cruisers include *TICONDEROGA* herself in *Storm,* and her sister ships *VINCENNES (Storm)* and *THOMASS. GATES (Sum).*

AEROFLOT: The Soviet state airline. It controls all civil air operations within the Soviet Union as well as operating many foreign routes. Its aircraft are also an airlift reserve for the Soviet Air Force. In *Hunt,* it supplies the IL-62 used to repatriate the survivors of *RED OCTOBER.*

AFTERBURNER: Mechanism in a jet engine which injects additional fuel into the exhaust. Increases thrust, speed, and fuel consumption. In *Storm,* the MiG-29s use afterburners to evade American fighters during the second American air attack on Iceland. The CONCORDE the RYANs take back to the United States in *Games* takes off on afterburners.

AGUSTDOTTIR, VIGDIS: In *Storm,* young Icelandic woman. Extremely attractive and (as it turns out) both physically and morally courageous, she is pregnant out of wedlock at the time of the Soviet invasion.

After a KGB patrol kills her parents and rapes her, Vigdis is rescued by Lieutenant EDWARDS's patrol and travels with them throughout their operations. By the end of the novel, she and EDWARDS are in love and she travels with him to the United States, where they will presumably be married.

AH-1 COBRA: U.S. Army attack helicopter, developed from the UH-1; in service 1968. In *Storm,* Cobras are used in Germany and are compared to the MI-24 HIND seen in Iceland.

AH-64 APACHE: U.S. all-weather attack helicopter; Hughes. 150 mph; 2 hours' endurance; 30-mm gun, rockets, HELLFIRE antitank missiles. In service with U.S. Army from 1983.

In *Hunt,* two Apaches are embarked aboard the U.S.S. *TARAWA,* to support the *NEW JERSEY* task force against the Soviet surface fleet. In *Storm,* they attack Russian tanks in support of the American counterattack near Alfeld, West Germany.

AI: See ARTIFICIAL INTELLIGENCE.

AIM-9 SIDEWINDER: U.S. infrared-homing air-to-air missile. Range 2+ miles, speed Mach 3; in service with U.S. Navy, Air Force, Marines, many other countries, from 1957. Latest versions can home in on a target from any angle.

In *Hunt,* the AIM-9 is carried, along with the PHOENIX, by the F-14s of VF-41 that engage the FORGERs from *KIEV.* In *Storm,* Colonel ELLINGTON's F-19A uses AIM-9s to destroy a Soviet IL-76 MAINSTAY AWACS.

AIM-54 PHOENIX: Radar-guided long-range air-to-air missile; U.S. Navy. Range 25+ miles with semiactive homing, 100+ miles with active homing; speed Mach 4; 130-lb. warhead. The most powerful air-to-air missile in service; main armament of the U.S. Navy's F-14 TOMCAT since 1973.

In *Storm,* Phoenixes are used against the KELT decoy missiles approaching the *NIMITZ* battle group and against Soviet BACKFIRE bombers over the Norwegian Sea. In *Sum,* Robby JACKSON uses them against both Libyan and Soviet MiG-29s over the Mediterranean.

AIR BOSS: Head of the Air Department aboard a U.S. Navy carrier, in charge of the conduct of all air operations. In *Sum, THEODORE ROOSE-VELT's* Air Boss cheerfully informs Robby JACKSON about his less-than-perfect landing.

AIR COMBAT MANEUVERING (ACM):   The tactics employed by fighters to gain a positional advantage over opposing aircraft. Colloquially known as "dogfighting." In *Games,* Robby JACKSON mentions practicing ACM while returning to flight status after his injury.

AIR FORCE: In general, the service controlling a country's land-based military aircraft, except for any operated by the ARMY. In the United States Air Force, the highest combat echelon, usually controlling all combat units assigned to a particular geographical area, as in 8th AIR FORCE. The closest Soviet equivalent is an Air Army.

AIR FORCE ACADEMY: The undergraduate school of the United States Air Force, located in Colorado Springs, Colorado; founded 1958. Lieutenant EDWARDS in *Storm* is an Air Force Academy graduate.

AIR FORCE ONE: Designation of an Air Force plane (usually one of two modified and dedicated 707s or 747s) carrying the President of the United States. In *Sum,* President FOWLER flies to and from Rome aboard Air Force One.

AIR FORCE TWO: Designation of an Air Force plane carrying the Vice President of the United States. In *Sum,* Vice President DURLING's VC-20A is Air Force Two.

AIR-TO-AIR/AIR-TO-GROUND MISSILE: Missile carried by aircraft, respectively designed for engaging other aircraft and for engaging ground targets. The AIM-9 SIDEWINDER is an air-to-air missile; the HAR-POONs carried by the B-52s circling the Soviet task force in *Hunt* are air-to-ground, as are the Soviet missiles launched in *Storm* against Iceland.

AK-47:   *Avtomat Kalashnikov-47.* Standard Soviet infantry assault rifle from late 1940s. 7.62-mm, 30-round magazine, effective range 300 yards, 100+ rounds per minute; loaded weight 11 lbs. Modified lighter version (AKM) introduced late 1950s. The first postwar assault rifle. It is rugged and reliable; thanks to Soviet generosity and licensed production, it is also probably the most widely distributed infantry weapon in modern history.

The saboteurs who strike the oil field in *Storm* carry AK-47s; so does a ULA terrorist in *Games*, the ARCHER in *Cardinal*, and the drug lords' airfield security guards in *Danger*.

AK-74: *Avtomat Kalashnikov-74.* Successor to the AK-47 and AKM as the standard Soviet assault rifle, beginning in the mid-1970s. 5.45-mm, 30-round magazine, effective range 400 yards, 100+ rounds per minute; loaded weight 8.5 lbs. It has most of the virtues of its predecessor, and the lighter round permits the soldier to carry more ammunition.

The ULA terrorist who disabled the Royal limousine in *Games* did so with a rifle grenade launched from an AK-74.

AKULA (NATO code name):   Class of Soviet single-screw nuclear attack submarines. At least five in service with the Soviet Navy, beginning in 1984. 7,500/10,000 tons; 30+ knots; 6 TT; crew 120. They have the most advanced sonar and soundproofing of any Soviet submarines; roughly equivalent to early 688-class boats. The NATO code name is the Russian word for "shark."

In *Sum, ADMIRAL LUNIN* is an Akula of the Soviet Pacific Fleet. Her already impressive capabilities are further increased by a refit.

ALABAMA: U.S. Navy *OHIO*-class submarine, in service 1985. In *Sum,* Captain ROSSELLI mentions unsuccessfully trying to track her while CO of *HONOLULU.*

ALBATROSS 8: Soviet ocean-reconnaissance satellite, the size of a Greyhound bus, which in *Hunt* detects *RED OCTOBER, DALLAS,* and *POGY* in Pamlico Sound.

ALCALDE, REVEREND FRANCISCO: In *Sum,* Father General of the Society of Jesus. A friend of Father Timothy RILEY, he receives the American priest's communication of RYAN's peace proposal and brings it to the attention of the Pope.

ALDEN, DR. CHARLES WINSTON: In *Sum,* the National Security Advisor to President FOWLER. Brilliant, a Yale graduate, a prolific and insightful author, and a notorious ladies' man.

He does indispensable work for RYAN's peace proposal. After being the object of a paternity suit by Marcia BLUM, he is about to be dismissed in disgrace. The stress of this situation as well as high blood pressure brings on a fatal stroke. Replaced as National Security Advisor by Elizabeth ELLIOT and given posthumous credit for RYAN's proposal.

ALEKSEYEV, PAVEL LEONIDOVICH: Soviet general in *Storm,* a gifted, courageous, and brilliant soldier with a background in tanks. As his actions prove, he is also a statesman and a firm opponent of the KGB.

He begins as deputy commander of the Southwest Front, expected to have the main role in seizing the Mideast oil fields after NATO is crippled by RED STORM. He then becomes Deputy CINC-West, briefly commands the 20th Guards Armored Division when its commander is killed, and ends up as CINC-West after the death of one predecessor and the execution of a second. He is wounded in action twice.

Opposed to the use of nuclear weapons, he allies himself with SERGETOV to execute the coup that ends the war. He also orders the execution of KGB Chairman KOSOV, personally negotiates the cease-fire with SACEUR, and takes the posts of Deputy Defense Minister and Chief of the General Staff.

ALEXANDER, MICHAEL "LOBO":   U.S. Navy lieutenant. In *Sum,* he is Commander SANCHEZ's backseater in the engagements with MiG-29-Ns over the Mediterranean.

ALEXANDROV, MIKHAIL: Politburo member. In *Hunt,* he is a leading Party theoretician and self-appointed defender of ideological purity. In *Cardinal,* he is one of KGB Chairman GERASIMOV's firm allies.

ALFA (NATO code name):   A Soviet class of nuclear-powered attack submarines, in service from the early 1970s. 3,000/4,000 tons; 45 knots; 6 TT. The fastest and deepest-diving operational submarines in the world, and the first with titanium hulls. The extremely compact reactor plant operates with very narrow safety margins, and the whole class is referred to in the Soviet Navy as "the golden fish" because of their cost.

E.S. POLITOVKSY, lost in the North Atlantic in *Hunt,* is the first of the class. So is *V.K. KONOVOLOV,* sunk by *RED OCTOBER.* In *Storm,* an unnamed Alfa-class submarine intercepts the retiring Operation DOOLITTLE force and sinks *BOSTON* and *PROVIDENCE;* she is then sunk by H.M.S. *TORBAY.*

"ALLAHU AKHBAR!":   Moslem invocation, "God is great!" The last words of Ibrahim TOLKAZE, leader of the saboteurs in *Storm,* and the words of Ibrahim GHOSN in *Sum* when he knows he has a nuclear weapon in his hands.

ALLEN, ERNEST: In *Cardinal,* chief of the American strategic-arms-limitation negotiating team. He and Jack RYAN have a long conversation on the first flight home from Moscow. He and RYAN do not see eye to eye on how to negotiate with the Soviets; it is a clash of both personalities and principles.

ALLGEMEINE SS: Under the Third Reich, the regular SS, whose duties included guarding concentration camps. In *Danger,* MEDELLIN cartel member Carlos Wagner is the son of a former *Allgemeine SS* guard.

ALPHA STRIKE: A large offensive tactical air operation by one or more CARRIER AIR WINGs. The carrier-based strikes against Iceland in *Storm* are an example.

ALPHAJET: Twin-jet, twin-seat, land-based trainer and light attack aircraft; in service with French and German Air Forces from 1977. In *Storm,* German Alphajets have attacked the Soviet tank formations; one has deliberately crashed into a ZSU-30.

ALTUNIN, EDUARD VASSILYEVICH: In *Cardinal,* attendant at the Sandunovski baths and a courier in the CARDINAL chain. While he was serving in Afghanistan, Soviet tactics alienated him from the regime. He is arrested by Major CHURBANOV and turned into a double agent. He then flees and is murdered by black marketeers; Colonel VATUTIN thinks his death is the result of the CIA violating normal rules against murdering agents.

AMERICA: U.S. aircraft carrier, Kitty Hawk-class; in service 1965. In *Hunt,* she is one of the three U.S. carriers eventually deployed in the North Atlantic against the Soviet fleet. In *Storm,* she operates in support of *REUBEN JAMES's* convoy.

AMERICAN INDIAN MOVEMENT (AIM):   Radical activist Native American political organization. Implicated in terrorist and criminal activities since the 1970s. In *Sum,* both John and Marvin RUSSELL join the AIM while in prison.

AMES, LIEUTENANT (no first name):   In *Hunt,* U.S. Navy officer, in charge of the DSRV *AVALON.* He conducts dives on *Politovsky* and helps take off the crew of *RED OCTOBER.*

AMETIST (AMETHYST):   In *Storm,* KGB-manned GRISHA II corvette, which detects the Operation DOOLITTLE missile launch. She warns of the launch, attacks and damages *PROVIDENCE,* and is sunk by *CHICAGO.*

AN-22 (NATO code name COCK):   Soviet four-turpoprop strategic transport; Antonov Bureau. In service with Soviet Air Force and Aeroflot from 1965, when it was the largest aircraft in the world. In *Storm,* AN-22s fly two MI-24 attack helicopters to Iceland.

AN-26 (NATO code name COKE):   Soviet twin-turboprop land-based light transport; Antonov Bureau. In service with Soviet Air Force and Aeroflot from 1969. In *Cardinal,* an AN-26 shot down by the ARCHER yields major intelligence on the BRIGHT STAR project.

AN/AWG-9 RADAR: Long-range airborne radar, carried by the U.S. Navy F-14 TOMCAT fighter, for operation with the PHOENIX missile. Used against Soviet KELT missiles and BACKFIRE bombers in *Storm.*

ANACOSTIA NAVAL AIR STATION: U.S. Navy facility in S.E. Washington, D.C. Base for Marine helicopters used to transport the Presidential party in *Sum.*

ANATOLIY (no last name):   In *Cardinal,* bodyguard of Andrei Il'ych NARMONOV, who helps bandage Jack RYAN's leg at the General Secretary's dacha. In *Sum,* NARMONOV asks about Anatoliy, to firmly identify RYAN on the hotline during the final crisis.

ANDREWS AIR FORCE BASE: Principal U.S. Air Force facility in the Washington, D.C., area; home of the 89TH MILITARY AIRLIFT WING.

In *Hunt,* the rescued crewmen from *RED OCTOBER* land here, as do the PRINCE AND PRINCESS OF WALES in *Games.* In *Cardinal,* RYAN and his party depart for Moscow from Andrews; so do President FOWLER and Vice President DURLING in *Sum.*

ANDREYEV, GENERAL (no first name):   In *Storm,* commander of the 76th Guards Airborne Division, the Soviet invasion force for Iceland in Operation POLAR GLORY. The best kind of professional soldier, who would be a credit to any army.

He travels to Iceland aboard *JULIUS FUCIK,* survives the air attacks, organizes damage-control efforts, and lands after the ship grounds. Assuming command of the occupation forces, he attempts to maintain good relations with the Icelanders, defend the key air bases, maintain security, and keep the KGB in line (not the easiest job).

In spite of repeated American air attacks, he leads his division in a determined resistance to the Marine landing. Only when his division has suffered heavy casualties and the tactical situation is impossible does he ask for a cease-fire.

ANDROPOV, YURI (1914-84):   Historical figure. Head of the KGB, 1969-84; General Secretary of the Communist Party, 1982-84. Mentioned in *Hunt* as having reduced influence of KGB; in *Storm* as an example of the new kind of Soviet leader who did not rule alone.

ANECHOIC TILE: Tile made of rubber or other sound-absorbing material, applied to the exterior of a submarine's hull (U.S.S. *CHICAGO* in *Storm*). It reduces the amount of reflected sound and therefore the range at which the submarine is detectable by active sonar.

ANGEL: U.S. air services term indicating height in thousands of feet. "Angels three" would be 3,000 feet, the altitude of *INVINCIBLE's* HARRIER in *Hunt* as it heads for its rendezvous with the CH-53 SUPERSTALLION helicopter.

ANNAPOLIS: City, capital of the State of Maryland. Also site of the U.S. Naval Academy; founded 1845.

In *Hunt* and *Games,* Jack RYAN teaches naval history at the Academy. In *Games,* the ULA's terrorists pursue RYAN and the PRINCE AND PRINCESS OF WALES to the Academy's waterfront on the Severn River.

ANTITAMPER DEVICE: Mechanism fitted to a bomb, booby trap, mine, or other explosive device, intended to detonate it in the event of any attempt to penetrate or disarm it. The bomb in *Sum* has only crude antitamper devices.

APACHE: U.S. attack helicopter. See AH-64.

APC: See ARMORED PERSONNEL CARRIER.

APPARATCHIK: Russian term for members of the *apparat* or bureaucracy. In *Cardinal,* KGB Chairman GERASIMOV uses the term to imply stolid, unimaginative reliability in half the POLITBURO.

ARABOV, MAJOR PYOTR: In *Sum,* a Russian instructor pilot assigned to teaching Libyan pilots to fly the MiG-29. As a result of being mistaken for a hostile force, his training flight is shot down by Robby JACKSON. Arabov survives to be rescued by the Americans.

ARBATOV, ALEXEI: In *Hunt,* the Soviet Ambassador to the United States. He frequently meets with both the President and with National Security Advisor Dr. Jeffrey PELT. His position becomes more and more embarrassing as one Soviet cover story after another is overtaken by events.

ARCHDUKE, THE: Archduke Franz Ferdinand (1863-1914), heir to the throne of the Austro-Hungarian Empire. His assassination by Bosnian terrorists led to an international crisis and eventually to World War I—mentioned in *Sum* by Vice President DURLING as a classic example of accidents leading to disaster.

ARCHER, THE: In *Cardinal,* Afghan guerrilla leader with the courage of a man of faith and also of a man with nothing to lose.

Originally a mathematics teacher, he loses his whole family when the Russians destroy their village. He then returns to the practice of Islam. His work with captured SA-7 missiles earns him his name; he later becomes equally expert with the superior American STINGER missile. Using it to shoot down a Soviet AN-26, he acquires major intelligence on BRIGHT STAR for the Americans.

To avenge a Soviet air attack on a refugee camp and help his American allies, the Archer eventually leads his guerrillas north across the Soviet border, to attack the BRIGHT STAR facility. After initial surprise and some success, the attack is repulsed; the Archer himself is killed by Colonel BONDARENKO.

ARK ROYAL: The last conventional aircraft carrier in service with the British Royal Navy; scrapped 1979. In *Storm,* Admiral Sir Charles BEATTIE was *Ark Royal's* last captain.

ARLINGTON NATIONAL CEMETERY: The U.S. Military Cemetery in Arlington, Virginia, across the Potomac from Washington, D.C. Location of the Tomb of the Unknown Soldier. In *Danger,* Admiral James GREER is buried there beside the grave of his son, a Marine lieutenant killed in Vietnam.

ARM: Anti-Radiation Missile. Air-to-ground missile, homing on the emissions of ground-based air-defense radars, forcing them to either turn off (depriving missiles and guns of guidance) or risk destruction. In *Storm,* the F-4 PHANTOM WILD WEASELs launch STANDARD ARMs—15 mi. range, speed Mach 2.5, 200-lb. warhead.

ARMALITES: Simplified versions of the M-16 assault rifles. In *Games,* they are mentioned as easily obtained by terrorists.

ARMORED PERSONNEL CARRIER (APC):   Wheeled or tracked vehicle with light armor and automatic weapons, intended to carry one or more squads of infantry into the battle area. The Soviet BMP and the American M-113 and BRADLEY in *Storm* are examples of modern APCs.

ARMOR-PIERCING   FIN-STABILIZED   DISCARDING-SABOT ROUND (APFDS):   Antitank round, consisting of a heavy (tungsten or depleted uranium) penetrator and a surrounding, lighter sabot. Upon firing, the sabot drops off and the round flies to its target at high velocity (up to 5,000 feet per second), stabilized by integral fins and achieving penetration of armored targets by sheer kinetic energy. Developed for use with smooth-bore tank guns.

The American M-1 ABRAMS tanks in *Storm* and *Sum* and the Soviet tanks (T-72 and later) in *Storm* use APFSDS as their primary antitank round.

ARMY: In the broadest sense, the ground forces of a nation, with their supporting air units. Also a formation, in Western usage consisting of two or more CORPS plus attached units. Soviet and Soviet-derived forces have only recently introduced the CORPS level; a Soviet ARMY normally consists of three to five DIVISIONs. The direct Soviet equivalent of a Western ARMY is the front—as in the Southwest Front.

ARMY GROUP: In Western usage, a strategic formation consisting of two or more field ARMIES and supporting units. The Soviet equivalent may be either the front or the Group of Forces.

ARRESTOR WIRE: A wire (one of four, aboard U.S. carriers) stretched across the deck of an aircraft carrier. Engages the tail hook of a landing aircraft and pulls it to a stop. A perfect landing is catching the #3 wire, as Commander SANCHEZ's F-14 does aboard *THEODORE ROOSEVELT* in *Sum.*

ARTICLE 15:   In the U.S. Army, a nonjudicial disciplinary action used for minor offenses. In *Danger,* a junior enlisted man may receive an Article 15 for his first drug offense.

ARTIFICIAL INTELLIGENCE (AI):   Programs which permit a large computer to simulate some of the functions of the human intellect, including intuition and judgment. In *Cardinal,* an AI program controls the TEA CLIPPER phased-array lasers.

AS-4 (NATO code name KITCHEN):   Long-range air-to-ground missile; in service with Soviet Air Force and Navy from 1962. 2,000 mph; range 200 miles; nuclear or conventional warheads. In *Storm,* they are launched against U.S. bases in Iceland by Soviet BADGERs and BACKFIREs.

AS-5 (NATO code name KELT):   Long-range air-to-ground missile; in service with Soviet Air Force and Navy from 1967. 800 mph; range 150+ miles; conventional warhead. In *Storm,* a force of Soviet BADGERs launches a large number of KELTs against the *NIMITZ* battle group, decoying the CAP away from the real threat, the BACKFIREs with their KINGFISH.

AS-6 (NATO code name KINGFISH):   Long-range rocket-propelled air-to-ground missile; in service with Soviet Air Force and Navy from late 1960s. 2,000 mph; 100+ miles range; nuclear or conventional warheads, highly accurate inertial guidance system. In *Storm,* AS-6s launched from Soviet Navy BACKFIREs inflict major damage on the *NIMITZ* battle group.

ASAT: Anti-Satellite. Missiles designed to destroy hostile satellites in orbit. In *Storm,* Major NAKAMURA launches ASAT missiles from her F-15 EAGLE and destroys two Soviet satellites.

ASHKENAZI, DAVID: In *Sum,* Israeli Foreign Minister. He supports the Fowler Plan, with reservations, and is a political opponent of Defense Minister Ravi MANDEL.

ASROC: RUR-5A Anti-Submarine Rocket. ASW weapons system; U.S. Navy and many other navies. Eight-round box launcher or vertical-launch system. The solid-fuel rocket projects either a homing torpedo or a depth charge to a range of up to 6 miles, aiming at the position indicated by the launching vessel's sonar. In *Storm,* *PHARRIS* both carries and uses ASROC.

ASW: Antisubmarine warfare, the detection and destruction of hostile submarines using surface vessels, submarines, land- and sea-based fixed-wing aircraft and helicopters, satellites, and fixed ocean-bottom sonar arrays. The Soviet task forces in *Hunt,* the convoy escorts in *Storm,* and *ADMIRAL LUNIN, MAINE,* and the P-3 ORION in *Sum* are engaging in ASW.

ATKINSON, CHARLES: In *Games,* British lawyer with a penchant for radical leftist causes. He defends the ULA members on trial for the attempt on the PRINCE AND PRINCESS OF WALES. He aggressively questions Jack RYAN, trying to expose his connections with American intelligence.

ATLANTIC BRIDGE: ·The supply route across the North Atlantic from the United States to Europe, essential to the reinforcement and resupply of NATO forces in any war against the Soviet Union. In *Storm,* the Allied naval and air forces battle to defend the convoys of the Atlantic Bridge against Soviet air and submarine attacks.

ATLANTIC UNDERWATER TEST AND EVALUATION CENTER (AUTEC):   U.S. Navy facility in the Bahamas, testing sonar, antisubmarine weapons, and submarines' silencing. In *Cardinal,* Marko RAMIUS has been there, participating in a variety of training exercises and tests. In *Sum,*

Dr. JONES has been aboard *TENNESSEE*, evaluating a new (presumably sonar) system.

ATOLL (NATO code name):   Soviet K-13 air-to-air missile, used by Soviet Air Force and Navy; both heat-seeking and radar-homing versions exist. In *Hunt*, Lieutenant SHAVROV's FORGER launches four heat-seeking Atolls against Robby JACKSON's F-14 and scores one hit.

AUSTIN, **U.S.S.:**   LPD 4 (Amphibious Transport, Dock). U.S. Navy amphibious vessel; in service 1965, first of a class of eleven. She has a large stern well that can be flooded to launch or dock landing craft.

In *Hunt*, *Austin* carries the deep-diving submarine *SEA CLIFF* into position for her dive to the alleged wreckage of *RED OCTOBER*.

AUTEC: See ATLANTIC UNDERWATER TEST AND EVALUATION CENTER.

AUTHENTICATOR: Communications-security device, consisting of a code word or procedure to establish the identity of the originator of a message. In *Sum*, the authenticator for the Soviet HOT-LINE reply concerning the Denver bomb is the word "TIMETABLE."

AUTOVON: The U.S. Defense Department's main long-distance, nonsecure telephone system. In *Danger*, two Army sergeants talk over it, trying to track down Ding CHAVEZ.

AV-8B HARRIER: U.S.-built version of the British fighter/attack aircraft. See HARRIER.

AVALON, **U.S.S.:**   DSRV 2. Operating from U.S.S. *SCAMP*, she examines the wreck of *Konovolov*. Along with her sister ship *MYSTIC*, she later evacuates from *RED OCTOBER* all officers and men who are not part of Marko RAMIUS's defection plan.

AVENGER CANNON: GAU-8 seven-barreled rotary 30-mm cannon. It is intended to fire depleted-uranium rounds into the thin top armor of tanks; the main armament of the A-10 THUNDERBOLT II.

In *Hunt*, the A-10 pilots imagine what the Avenger would do to unarmored portions of *KIROV* or any stray FORGERs. In *Storm*, it is devastatingly effective against Soviet tanks.

AVGAS: Volatile high-octane gasoline, intended for use in reciprocating aircraft engines. It can be used in turbines in an emergency, as in *Danger* when CLARK and LARSON arrange to refuel the PAVE LOW helicopter from a small private field's avgas supply.

AVRORA   (Aurora): Soviet cruiser from which the first shots of the October Revolution were allegedly fired against the Winter Palace in 1917. She is now moored in Leningrad, a historical monument. The fisherman Sasha who taught Marko RAMIUS about the sea was an officer aboard *Avrora* who took the side of the Revolution.

AWACS: Airborne Warning and Control System. An aircraft equipped with long-range radars to detect hostile aircraft, particularly at low altitude, and the communications facilities for guiding fighters to attack these hostiles. AWACS aircraft in service today include the E-3A SENTRY, IL-76 MAINSTAY, and E-2 HAWKEYE.

B-1B: U.S. four-turbofan strategic bomber; Rockwell International. 800 mph; combat radius 3,000 miles; up to 80,000 lbs. ordnance, including SRAM, cruise missiles, free-fall nuclear and conventional weapons. In service with U.S. Air Force from 1986. Intended as a replacement for the B-52, it has advanced electronics, a low radar signature, and improved low-altitude performance.

In *Hunt,* a B-52 electronic-warfare officer hopes to be assigned to the more modern B-1B. In *Sum,* an alert wing of B-1Bs is scrambled after the nuclear explosion in Denver.

B-17:   Four-engined propeller-driven heavy bomber; U.S. and Allied air forces in World War II. In *Sum,* a preserved B-17 sits outside SAC headquarters at OFFUTT AIR FORCE BASE in Omaha, Nebraska.

B-52:   U.S. eight-engined strategic bomber; Boeing. 600 mph; combat radius 6,000 miles; up to 70,000 lbs. of ordnance, including SRAMS, cruise missiles, free-fall nuclear and conventional bombs, mines. Current models, B-52G and H, in service with U.S. Air Force from 1958-62. The mainstay of the U.S. strategic bomber force since the 1950s, the venerable B-52 is expected to remain effective and in service past the year 2000.

B-52s are deployed against the Soviet task forces in *Hunt.* In *Storm,* they fly a near-suicidal mission against the Soviet air bases in Iceland and suffer heavy losses. A second mission, with fighter escort, is less costly and more effective. An alert wing of B-52s is scrambled during the crisis in *Sum.*

B-61 NUCLEAR GRAVITY BOMB: In *Sum,* U.S. free-falling nuclear weapon; Air Force and Navy. 700 lbs.; yield adjustable from 10 to 500 + kilotons.

They are deployed aboard *THEODORE ROOSEVELT* for strategic missions, to be carried by A-6s. The Soviets suspect that the F-117s at Ramstein may be carrying them for a surprise attack on Moscow.

BAADER-MEINHOF GANG: Prominent West German terrorist organization in the 1970s, named after its two leaders, both of whom committed suicide in prison. Günther BOCK is a former unit leader in the organization.

BACKFIRE (NATO code name): Soviet long-range bomber. See TU-22M/TU-26.

BADGER (NATO code name): Soviet medium bomber; see TU-16.

BAIKONOR COSMODROME: Soviet military facility in the Kazakh S.S.R., the major Soviet base for both manned and unmanned space launches. In *Storm,* a Soviet ASAT launched from Baikonor destroys an American KH-11 reconnaissance satellite.

BAINBRIDGE: U.S. nuclear guided-missile cruiser; in service 1962. Originally classified as a frigate, she was the first nuclear-powered destroyer/frigate type in the world. In *Hunt, Bainbridge* escorts *NIMITZ* as the carrier steams north to join the U.S. forces in the North Atlantic.

BAKER, REAR ADMIRAL SAMUEL B., JR.: In *Storm,* commander of the *NIMITZ* battle group. An abrasive and authoritarian officer, he ignores Robert TOLAND's estimates of the threat presented by the Soviet capture of Iceland added to their satellite capabilities. He is killed in the Soviet missile strike on *NIMITZ.*

BAKUNIN, MIKHAIL: Historical character (1814-76); most famous 19th-century Russian anarchist. In *Sum,* FBI agent PAULSON thinks John RUSSELL's notion of a Native American resembles Bakunin.

BALLISTIC INBOUND TRACK: Radar indication of the reentry of a BALLISTIC MISSILE warhead. In *Sum,* NORAD did *not* have any ballistic inbound track before the nuclear explosion in Denver, one reason to suspect something other than a Russian attack.

BALLISTIC MISSILE: A missile which, after launching, follows a parabolic trajectory to its target without further guidance. Examples are the SS-20-Ns aboard *RED OCTOBER* in *Hunt* or the SS-18 in *Sum.*

BALLISTIC MISSILE SUBMARINE: A submarine (usually nuclear-powered) capable of launching ballistic missiles. They are a major portion of the strategic forces of the United States, the Soviet Union, Great Britain, and France; China has them under development. *RED OCTOBER* and (in *Sum*), the *OHIO*-class *MAINE* are examples of the most advanced classes of ballistic missile submarines.

BANCROFT HALL: The midshipmen's quarters at the U.S. Naval Academy, Annapolis. In *Games,* motorcycle gang members invade the hall in retaliation for midshipmen informants breaking up a drug deal. This leads to the arrest of the bikers and improved security for the Academy.

BANDITS: U.S. air services term for air contacts clearly identified as hostile. In *Sum,* the Libyan MiG-29s are referred to as "bandits" after they are identified and believed to be carrying weapons.

BAOR: British Army of the Rhine, the major British ground force assigned to NATO in Germany. In *Games,* British intelligence interviews one of WATKINS's former messmates, whose regiment is now assigned to the BAOR.

BARBAROSSA: Historical character. Friedrich Barbarossa (1123-90), Holy Roman Emperor and a leader of the Third Crusade. In *Sum,* the ecological crusade of the Greens in East Germany is compared to Barbarossa's crusading in the Holy Land.

BARCAP: See Barrier Combat Air Patrol.

BARCLAY, COMMANDER: In *Hunt,* R.N. officer, Admiral WHITE's fleet intelligence officer. He works with RYAN in deploying the *INVINCIBLE* task force to intercept *RED OCTOBER.*

BAR-LEV LINE: The Israeli defense system in the Sinai Peninsula in the Yom Kippur War (1973). *Sum* mentions its breaching by the Egyptian assault crossing of the Suez Canal.

BARNES, LIEUTENANT COLONEL RICHARD "ROCKY":   In *Sum,* John ROSSELLI's XO in the NMCC. An Air Force F-15 pilot who shot down two MiGs during the Persian Gulf War, he is on duty during the crisis.

BARRIER COMBAT AIR PATROL (BARCAP):   Deployment of a carrier's fighters to prevent hostile aircraft from crossing a specific line. In *Sum,* Robby JACKSON takes part in a BARCAP exercise against Marine F/A-18s.

BATTALION: Ground-forces unit, consisting of three or more COMPANIES (in infantry or armored units) or BATTERIES (in artillery units). The echelon below BRIGADE or REGIMENT and the basic fire and maneuver units in most ground forces.

BATTERY: Artillery unit, equivalent to a COMPANY in infantry or armored formations. Normally consists of four to eight guns, depending on caliber. The basic fire unit for both tube and Rocket Artillery.

BATTLE DRESS UNIFORM (BDU) or FATIGUES: U.S. ground forces basic combat uniform, in various camouflage patterns. In *Danger,* CHAVEZ reports at Ford Ord in his best BDUs.

BATTLEAXE, **H.M.S.:**   British Royal Navy ASW frigate. 3,900/4,400 tons; 29 knots; Exocet missiles, ASW TT, LYNX helicopter; crew 250. In service 1980. *Brazen* is a sister ship.
    In *Storm,* she operates with *REUBEN JAMES,* against the Soviet VIC-TOR, using the wreck of *Andrea Doria* for cover. Her helicopter drops the final, fatal depth charge. She then serves with the American frigate while escorting an Atlantic convoy.

BDRM: See BRDM.

BEAM ASPECT/BEAM-ON: The appearance of a submarine on sonar when she has her side toward the sonar transmitter. In *Sum, MAINE* identifies *ADMIRAL LUNIN* as an AKULA when *LUNIN* is beam-on.

BEAM/BOW SEA: Waves striking the side rather than the ends of a ship, making her roll. In *Storm, JULIUS FUCIK* encounters a beam sea on her way to Iceland. The opposite is a bow sea, which causes a ship to pitch, like *PHARRIS* with her convoy, also in *Storm.*

BEAR (NATO code name):   Soviet bomber and maritime reconnaissance aircraft. See TU-95/TU-142.

BEATRIX: In *Games,* young woman, daughter of a retired RAF sergeant. The bookkeeper and assistant in Dennis COOLEY's bookstore, she does not suspect his activities for the ULA. She is interrogated by British intelligence about her boss after he discovers the bug and flees.

BEATTIE, ADMIRAL SIR CHARLES: In *Storm,* British Royal Navy admiral, COMEASTLANT (Commander, Eastern Atlantic). Robert TO-LAND serves on his staff after being detached from *NIMITZ.* Forces under Beattie's command launch the first Allied counteroffensive against the So-viet attacks on the ATLANTIC BRIDGE.

BEECH KING AIR: Twin-turboprop light passenger aircraft. 6 seats or cargo. Beechcraft (U.S.) but widely exported. In *Danger,* a King Air used by drug smugglers is the first "kill" for Bronco WINTERS and his F-15.

BELKNAP, **U.S.S.:** U.S. conventional guided-missile cruiser. In service 1964; rebuilt after being severely damaged in collision with *JOHN F. KENNEDY* (1975). Lead ship of a class of nine. She was a former command of Admiral CUTTER in *Danger.*

BELL JETRANGER: Turbine-engined light helicopter; Bell (U.S.), widely exported. A civilian version of the OH-58 Kiowa. In *Games,* a JetRanger (call sign "Trooper 1") of the Maryland State Police with a paramedic aboard lifts Cathy and Sally RYAN to the Shock-Trauma Center in Baltimore.

BEN JAKOB, GENERAL ABRAHAM (AVI): In *Sum,* assistant director of the Mossad, Israel's foreign-intelligence agency. A former career soldier, he works closely with Jack RYAN in securing Israeli support for the peace proposal and helps implement it afterward. He also plays an active role in the final location of the terrorists' nuclear-weapons facility and the punishment of the surviving terrorists.

BEREGOVOY, LIEUTENANT GENERAL VIKTOR: In *Storm,* Soviet general, deputy commander of the 8th Guards Tank Army. He relieves General ALEXSEYEV in command of the 20th Guards Tank Division and the Soviet armored spearhead near Alfeld.

BERETTA 92-F: 9-mm automatic pistol; 15-round magazine (9-mm Parabellum); empty weight 2+ lbs. Modification of the Beretta 92SB, adopted by the U.S. armed forces in 1985 as their standard sidearm, replacing the COLT .45. In *Danger,* RYAN's driver is armed with a 92-F in a shoulder holster; John CLARK carries one in Colombia.

BERETTA 10-MM PISTOL: Automatic pistol, model unspecified, chambered for the new 10-mm round. In *Sum,* John CLARK carries one in a hip holster while acting as RYAN's driver and bodyguard.

BERIA: Historical character (1899-1953). Lavrenti Beria, STALIN's head of the state security apparatus. A notoriously ruthless man, he was deposed and executed after Stalin's death—mentioned in *Hunt* as an example in which the Army supported the Party against the KGB.

BERLIN BRIGADE: The U.S. Army ground unit in the American Zone of Berlin. In *Sum,* it becomes heavily engaged with its Soviet counterpart as a result of Günther BOCK's and Erwin KEITEL's terrorist provocation. This deepens the crisis, particularly when U.S. aircraft flying on a reconnaissance mission are shot down by the Soviets.

BERNARDI, CHUCK: In *Danger,* senior FBI agent on duty in Bern, Switzerland. As part of Operation TARPON, he begins the process of freezing and confiscating Swiss bank accounts used for the drug cartel's money-laundering operations.

BETHESDA NAVAL MEDICAL CENTER: The premier U.S. Navy medical facility, in a Maryland suburb of Washington, D.C. In *Hunt,* Captain TAIT is detached from it to treat the survivor of *E.S. POLI-TOVSKY* in Norfolk. In *Games,* RYAN mentions having been hospitalized there after his helicopter crash in Crete, and overdosed with pain medications. In *Danger,* Admiral GREER is treated at Bethesda for pancreatic cancer and finally dies there.

BF-109:   Also known as the Me-109. German World War II single-engined propeller-driven fighter. Czech-modified version used by Israeli Air Force during the War of Independence. In *Sum,* the young Motti ZADIN wants to fly after seeing a Bf-109 trainer.

BIDDLE, U.S.S.:   *BELKNAP*-class missile cruiser; in service 1967. In *Hunt,* she is one of *NEW JERSEY's* radar pickets.

BIG BIRD: U.S. strategic reconnaissance satellite, featuring advanced high-resolution cameras. Launched by Titan IIIs beginning in 1971. In *Hunt,* one of them detects many surface vessels of the Soviet Northern Fleet getting up steam.

"BIGEYE":   U.S. Air Force BLU-80/B bomb, for dispensing binary nerve gasses. In *Storm,* word of their deployment by NATO strengthens East German opposition to Soviet plans for chemical warfare.

BILL: In *Danger,* the detective lieutenant who learns from the CLERK OF THE COURTS that the drug pirates are getting a plea-bargain. He suggests that the PATTERSON twins be used to "send a message" to the druggies by disposing of the pirates.

BILLINGS SENATOR, (no first name):   In *Danger,* senior U.S. Senator from Oregon. He advances the career of Red WEGENER, who rescued Billings's nephew from the *MARY KAT.* Formerly head of the Transportation Committee, he is now head of the Judiciary Committee, which oversees the FBI and lets Billings influence any investigation of WEGENER.

BIRD-COLONELS: Colloquial U.S. military term for full (as opposed to lieutenant) colonels. Their emblem of rank is an eagle. In *Danger,* CHAVEZ knows that sergeants do not ask questions of bird colonels, like "Colonel Smith."

BIRDS: In many countries, a colloquial term for either aircraft or missiles. An example in *Storm:* the KELT missiles launched by the TU-16 BADGERs against the *NIMITZ* battle group.

BISMARCK: Historical character (1815-98). Otto von Bismarck, Chancellor of Prussia and leader in the unification of Germany. Like Cardinal D'ANTONIO in *Sum,* he worked better with a cigar in his hand.

BISYARINA, CAPTAIN TANIA: Female KGB field operative, reporting to Directorate T (scientific espionage); cover name "Ann." In *Cardinal,* she is the control for only one agent, Bea TAUSSIG. On orders from Chairman GERASIMOV, Bisyarina eventually organizes the kidnapping of Major GREGORY. She is killed by FBI sniper PAULSON during the rescue operation in New Mexico. A highly competent agent, who is forced to carry out a major operation on little notice.

BITNER, JOHANNES: In *Storm,* chief of the Communist Party of the German Democratic Republic (East Germany). He is persuaded by his military advisers to oppose Soviet use of chemical weapons.

"BLACK":   U.S. intelligence term describing an operation or project so secret that even the appropriations for it are not recorded in the budget. In *Cardinal,* the TEA CLIPPER project is "black." So is the antidrug Operation SHOWBOAT in *Danger.*

BLACK, SUPERVISORY SPECIAL AGENT DENNIS: In *Sum,* FBI agent in command of the ten agents of the Hostage Rescue Team sent to the confrontation with John RUSSELL. He does not approve of Walter HOSKINS's handling of the affair.

BLACK, GUNNERY SERGEANT (GUNNY):   In *Danger,* Recon Marine NCO, assigned to Special Operations at MacDill Air Force Base in Florida. He leads the Marines who capture and interrogate the crew of the forced-down DC-7B drug-smuggling plane.

BLACK HUNDREDS: Anti-Semitic terrorist bands in Czarist Russia, frequently covertly sponsored by the secret police. In *Sum,* a Jewish paramilitary leader recalls them as an example of the long history of anti-Semitism.

BLACKBEARD: Nickname of Edward Teach, notorious early-18th-century pirate. Killed in battle by British Royal Navy, 1718; his crew was tried and hanged in Williamsburg, Virginia. In *Danger,* WEGENER's XO mentions this when defending his C.O. against the charge of hanging one of the drug pirates captured by *PANACHE.*

BLACKBIRD: U.S. strategic reconnaissance aircraft. See SR-71.

BLACKHAWK: U.S. helicopter. See UH-60/VH-60.

BLINDER: Soviet bomber. See TU-22.

"BLUE"/"GOLD" CREWS: U.S. Navy BALLISTIC MISSILE SUB-MARINES each have two complete crews, "Blue" and "Gold," to increase the submarines' time at sea without straining crew endurance. In *Sum,* Captain ROSSELLI has commanded the "Gold" crews of both *TECUM-SEH* and *MAINE.*

BLUM, MARSHA: In *Sum,* doctoral candidate in Russian history at Yale; a former student (and mistress) of Charles ALDEN. She files a paternity suit against him, leading the FOWLER administration to plan his dismissal.

BMD: *Boeyevaya mashina desantnaya* (Airborne Fighting Vehicle). Soviet lightweight infantry fighting vehicle, equipping Airborne Troops and Air Assault Brigades; in service 1970. 7 tons; 40 mph (road); 73-mm gun, antitank missiles, machine gun; 3 crew, 6 infantry. Amphibious, air-transportable, air-droppable.
  In *Storm,* BMDs come ashore in Iceland aboard the LEBED hovercraft. Later, General ALEXSEYEV rides in one during the battle around Alfeld.

BMP: *Boeyevaya mashina pekhoty* (Armored Vehicle, Infantry). Soviet infantry fighting vehicle. 13 tons; 50 mph (road); 73-mm gun (30-mm in BMP-2), antitank missiles, machine guns; 3 crew, 8 infantry; amphibious. In service with Soviet Army from 1967; widely exported. The first true infantry fighting vehicle, able to provide fire support to its troops, who could also use their personal weapons while mounted in the vehicle.
  Soviet forces use BMPs extensively in *Storm.* In the fighting around Alfeld, General ALEXSEYEV and Captain SERGETOV ride in the command version of the BMP, with extra communications gear. In *Cardinal,* the ARCHER sees a column of Soviet troops riding in BMPs during his march to the raid on BRIGHT STAR.

BOCK, GÜNTHER: In *Sum,* German terrorist and ally of GHOSN and QATI. A former BAADER-MEINHOF and RED ARMY member, he is driven to desperation by the collapse of Marxism, flight from Bulgaria, and the arrest of his wife, Petra HASSLER-BOCK.
  Contacting GHOSN and QATI, he becomes indispensable to the bomb-building project. He brings in Manfred FROMM, while his colleague Erwin KEITEL covers their tracks in Germany. Returning to Berlin after the

bomb is completed, he organizes and carries out a terrorist operation in Berlin. This provokes major combat between American and Soviet forces. Bock is killed by American forces during the fighting and afterward identified by the Germans.

BOGIES: U.S. air services term for unidentified aerial contacts. In *Sum,* the MiG-29s detected by the *THEODORE ROOSEVELT* battle group are first called bogies.

BOMBARDIER/NAVIGATOR (B/N):   The second crewman of an A-6 INTRUDER, controlling the complex on-board electronics. In *Danger,* Commander JENSEN flies with a B/N on his missions against the MEDELLIN drug leaders.

BONDARENKO, COLONEL OF SIGNAL TROOPS GENNADY IOSIFOVICH: A highly competent and professional Soviet officer. In *Cardinal,* his technical expertise leads to his being sent by Colonel FILITOV to evaluate the BRIGHT STAR project. By making his report, he inadvertently provides the colonel with crucial information about it to transmit to the CIA. Bondarenko is not implicated in the breakup of the CARDINAL line.

During the Afghan attack on the base, Bondarkenko assumes command of the defense forces and beats off the attack, personally killing the ARCHER. Although unable to prevent heavy damage, he succeeds in saving most of the key personnel. At the end of the book, he has been placed permanently in command of the facility and is anticipating promotion to general.

BOOMER: Colloquial U.S. Navy term for a BALLISTIC MISSILE SUBMARINE. Used to refer to American vessels in *Hunt* and *Sum,* and Soviet ones in *Hunt* and *Storm.*

BOOTNECKS: Colloquial British term for Marines, U.S. or British. In *Games,* Captain GREVILLE uses it when he hopes the SAS can entertain the RYANs before the U.S. Marines do.

BOQ: Bachelor Officer's Quarters. In the U.S. forces, on-post housing for officers unaccompanied by their families. In *Storm,* Commander TOLAND stays at the Norfolk BOQ before going aboard *NIMITZ.*

BORESIGHTED: In *Sum,* a term used by JACKSON's RIO, to indicate that the Libyan MiG-29s are centered in his sights.

An air-to-air left-side view of a Fighter Squadron 143 (VF-143) F-14A Tomcat aircraft.
Credit: Official U.S. Navy photo, 1987

Pease Air Force Base, New Hampshire. A view of a B-61 nuclear bomb trainer, centre, being shown at a static display of a 509th Bomb Group FB-111 aircraft.
Credit: Official U.S. Air Force photo, 1989, by Master Sgt. Ken Hammond

A bow view of the nuclear-powered aircraft carrier USS *Nimitz* (CVN-68)
underway in the Bermuda operating area.

Aerial starboard quarter view of a Soviet Alfa-class fleet submarine underway.

Nevada. An air-to-air right-side view of an F-15C Eagle aircraft from the
422nd Test and Evaluation Squadron.
Credit: U.S. Air Force photo, 1988, by Ken Hackman

Far East. An air-to-air left-side view of an E-3A Sentry aircraft, one of many aircraft
that flew in support of Operation Kangaroo '81.
Credit: Official U.S. Air Force photo, 1982

Atlantic Ocean. An aerial starboard beam-view of the nuclear-powered
attack submarine USS *Memphis* (SSN-691) underway.
Credit: Official U.S. Navy photo, 1977, by Lloyd Everton

Fort Hunter Liggett, California. A left-underside view of a C-130 Hercules aircraft en
route to Marine Corps Air Station, El Toro, California, after dropping off troops of the
7th Marines during Operation Wild Boar.
Credit: Official U.S. Marine Corps photo, 1987, by PFC. Haynes

Guantánamo Bay, Cuba. A CH-53 Sea Stallion helicopter hovers over the flight deck
of the aircraft carrier USS *Independence* (CV-62). The *Independence* is conducting
post-Service Life Extension Program (SLEP) operations at Guantánamo Bay.
Credit: Official U.S. Navy photo, 1988, by PH3 Tony Cornell

A stern view of a Soviet Typhoon class nuclear-powered fleet ballistic missile submarine underway.

Credit: Official Department of Defense photo, 1987

An air-to-air right-side view of a Soviet Tu-95 Bear aircraft.
Credit: Official U.S. Navy photo, 1989

An air-to-air view of a Soviet Navy Tu-22M Backfire B aircraft.
Credit: Official U.S. Navy photo, 1990

Wertheim, West Germany. An M-1 Abrams tank assigned to the 2nd Bn., 64th Armor, 3rd Infantry Division, Schweinfurt, West Germany, moves out during Carbine Fortress, part of exercise Reforger 82. The tank is part of the 'Friendly Forces', on the defensive.

Credit: Official U.S. Army photo, 1982, by Spec.4 Buck Brignano

BORODIN, CAPTAIN SECOND RANK VASILY: In *Hunt, starpom* or Executive Officer of *RED OCTOBER*. Trained and handpicked by RAMIUS, he is one of the most important members of the plot. He ably assists his captain throughout the voyage, and temporarily assumes command of the submarine after RAMIUS is wounded in the shoot-out in the missile compartment.

BORSTEIN, MAJOR GENERAL JOE: In *Sum,* senior NORAD watch officer at the time of the Denver nuclear explosion. He acts as CINC-NORAD during the crisis, as the CINC is dead at the Super Bowl and the deputy is traveling. He is increasingly aware that President FOWLER is "losing it." After the Soviet SS-18 accident, he informs the President that there has been no launch detected.

BOSTON, **U.S.S.:**   U.S. Navy 688-class nuclear attack submarine; in service 1982. In *Storm,* one of the Operation DOOLITTLE task force; she joins *CHICAGO* in escorting the damaged *PROVIDENCE* and is sunk along with the latter in the final engagement with the Soviet ALFA.

BOSTON WHALER: American line of small boats, known for their rugged fiberglass construction. The "Outrage" used in *Storm* by Robert TOLAND and his father-in-law, Edward KEEGAN, is the largest model.

BQR-5:   U.S. Navy passive sonar system, installed in 688-class submarines such as *DALLAS* in *Hunt* and *CHICAGO* in *STORM.* In *Hunt,* Sonarman JONES aboard *DALLAS* first detects *RED OCTOBER's* CATERPILLAR drive using the BQR-5.

BQR-15:   U.S. Navy towed array SONAR, fitted aboard U.S.S. *DALLAS* in *Hunt.* In *Hunt, DALLAS* uses it off the Grand Banks, detecting the Soviet submarines heading for the American coast.

BRADEN, ERNIE: In *Danger,* a corrupt Alabama police sergeant, taking bribes from the drug cartel. He also coaches Little League. To silence him, cartel assassins kill both him and Mrs. Braden.

BRADLEY: U.S. Army infantry fighting vehicle. See M-2/M-3 BRADLEY.

BRDM: Referred to as BDRM in *Sum.* Soviet armored car; 6 tons; 50 mph; MG and antitank missiles; amphibious and lightly armored. In *Sum,* three of these appear to be part of a Soviet counterattack in Berlin and are destroyed by American M-2 BRADLEYs.

BRECKENRIDGE, SERGEANT MAJOR NOAH:　In *Games,* Sergeant Major of the Marine detail at Annapolis. A highly decorated combat veteran (a sniper in Vietnam), small-arms expert (particularly the Colt .45), and model of a Marine NCO.

He gives Jack RYAN extensive and invaluable pistol training and general advice about self-defense. He helps arrest Ned CLARK outside the Academy, foiling a ULA attempt on RYAN's life. After the RYANs' escape from the second ULA attack with the PRINCE AND PRINCESS OF WALES, Breckenridge organizes the defense of the Academy's waterfront and details Marines to join in the pursuit of the terrorists.

BREEZE OF EVENING:　In *Sum,* antique Arab sword used to execute QATI. Afterward it is presented by Prince Ali bin Sheik to Jack RYAN.

BREMERTON, **U.S.S.:**　U.S. Navy 688-class submarine; in service 1981. In *Hunt,* she is operating off the KOLA PENINSULA when she detects, then loses *RED OCTOBER* after the Soviet submarine engages her CATERPILLAR drive.

BREZHNEV:　Historical figure (1906-82). Leonid Brezhnev, Secretary of the CPSU, 1964-82. He is mentioned in *Storm* as an example of the new kind of Soviet leader, not allowed to control all the reins of power for fear of another Stalin.

BRICK-AGENT:　Colloquial FBI term for an agent with extensive field experience. In *Danger,* Agent MURRAY calls himself one in a conversation with Bill SHAW and Director JACOBS.

BRIGADE:　In Western ground forces, a unit consisting of three or more BATTALIONs, operating either independently or under the control of a DIVISION. Usually organized on a combined-arms basis, mixing infantry and armor battalions depending on assigned mission. Soviet equivalent is the REGIMENT.

In the terminology of the PIRA, a "Brigade" is the IRA forces operating in a particular city or area. In *Games,* it was the head of the Belfast Brigade who put a price on Kevin O'DONNELL's head.

BRIGHT, SUPERVISORY SPECIAL AGENT MARK:　In *Danger,* assistant special-agent-in-charge of the FBI Mobile office. He helps Dan MURRAY handle the *EMPIRE BUILDER* drug piracy case and discovers in her deceased owner's home the crucial data concerning the cartel's money-laundering operations. He and his wife, Marianne, have just had a baby, Sandra. He later carries vital intelligence to Jack RYAN about Admiral CUTTER's betrayal of the covert-action troops in Colombia. This leads directly to mounting the rescue operation.

BRIGHT STAR: In *Cardinal,* Soviet code name for the antimissile laser-research project and its facilities.

***BRISTOL,* H.M.S.:**   British Royal Navy conventional guided-missile destroyer; in service 1973. In *Hunt,* she is one of *INVINCIBLE's* escorts and the first one to detect *RED OCTOBER.*

BROACH: A submerged submarine or torpedo partially breaking the surface of the water. In *Sum, ADMIRAL LUNIN* is broaching in the heavy seas, confusing the homing mechanism of the American MARK 50 TORPEDO.

BROMKOVSKIY, PYOTR: In *Storm,* the oldest member of the Politburo, with serious doubts about the war. In World War II, he was an Army political commissar who saw a good deal of combat. He is opposed to the use of nuclear weapons. After the Kremlin coup that ends the war, he becomes Defense Minister and holds high rank in the Party apparatus as well.

BROW: Portable, usually wheeled, ramp between a ship in port and the wharf, quay, or pier to which she is moored. In *Hunt,* Drydock Eight-Ten's overhead crane places a brow for Admiral FOSTER to board *RED OCTOBER.* In *Sum,* John ROSSELLI walks down one when leaving *MAINE.*

BROWNING HI-POWER: Officially the "Browning GP Mle 35." 9-mm automatic pistol. 13-round magazine; empty weight 2+ lbs. Famous for reliability and accuracy, it is the official sidearm of the British and many other armies. In *Games,* Eamon CLARK is carrying an FN version of the Hi-Power when he is arrested in ANNAPOLIS.

BROWNING, SCOTT: In *Cardinal,* Chicago *Tribune* reporter who witnesses Jack RYAN's "quarrel" with Congressman Al TRENT at the Kennedy Center reception. By publicizing it, he gives credibility to the CIA's cover story about RYAN's being under investigation for insider trading.

BRUSH-PASS: Espionage technique, used in *Sum* to transmit KADISHEV's messages. The cloakroom attendant appears to brush against the CIA agent, the closeness of the two bodies concealing the passing of the message.

BTR-60:   *Bronetransporter* (Armored Transporter). Soviet eight-wheeled ARMORED PERSONNEL CARRIER. 10 tons; 50 mph; machine guns; driver and 13 infantry; amphibious. In service with Soviet Army from 1961, widely exported.

In *Storm,* the 77th Motor-Rifle Division, rerouted through Moscow to support the coup, has to unload its BTR-60s from their railroad flatcars. In *Cardinal,* the ARCHER sends his wounded to Pakistan in two BTR-60s captured by another guerrilla band. In *Sum,* the Druse FARMER's son is wounded when his Syrian BTR-60 is hit by an Israeli tank during the Yom Kippur War.

BUCKEYE: U.S. Navy jet trainer.

BUDDY-STORE TANKS: Self-contained U.S. Navy aerial-refueling device, consisting of an underwing fuel tank and retractable hose. In *Storm,* the A-7s from the *NIMITZ* battle group are launched with buddy stores, to clear the carriers' decks and provide refueling for the F-14s on CAP as the battle group awaits the Soviet missile strike.

BUENTE, HECTOR: In *Danger,* Colombian terrorist, employed by the MEDELLIN cartel in the assassination of FBI Director JACOBS. He is the only member of the assassination squad to be captured.

BUGAYEV (no first name or rank):   In *Hunt,* officer aboard *RED OCTOBER,* one of the defectors. Apparently trained as an engineer, and knowledgeable about diesel engines, he can also handle the ship's sonar. He suffers ear damage in the final battle, trying to jam KONOVOLOV's torpedo until it hits before he can remove his earphones. He is given asylum in the United States.

BUKHARIN, MARSHAL FYODOR BORISSOVICH: In *Storm,* an ambitious Soviet officer with political connections, a possible Chief of the General Staff, but blamed for Soviet strategy in Afghanistan. One of the hard-liners, he briefs the Politburo as the war situation deteriorates, recommending a wholesale purge of the Army staff.

BUNDESKRIMINALAMT: The West German national criminal police, roughly corresponding to the American FBI but with more limited jurisdiction compared to the state and local forces. In *Sum,* the BOCKS' two daughters have been adopted by a childless captain in the Bundeskriminalamt and his wife, and are growing up without any memory of their real parents.

BUNDESNACHRICHTENDIENST: The West German foreign intelligence service. In *Storm* it is the alleged employer of the alleged agent responsible for the Kremlin bombing. In *Sum,* it had many agents among the rioters who raided the East German secret police headquarters before the files could be destroyed—Günther BOCK's included.

BUNDESWEHR: The West German Army. Heavily engaged throughout *Storm,* it retains the traditional German mastery of the art of the counterattack.

BUNKER, G. DENNIS: In *Sum,* the Secretary of Defense. He is a decorated Air Force F-105 pilot in Vietnam, self-made aerospace billionaire, and owner of the San Diego Chargers football team. His combination of wealth and combat experience lets him talk to both civilian and uniformed policymakers on an equal basis. He is basically a supporter of RYAN, and not sympathetic to Elizabeth ELLIOT. He is killed in the Denver explosion while watching his team play in the Super Bowl.

His wife, Charlotte, meets Cathy RYAN at the Kennedy Center party where Cathy has her confrontation with Elizabeth ELLIOT.

BUNKER HILL, U.S.S.:   U.S. AEGIS cruiser; in service 1986. In *Storm,* she is brand-new and escorts the *REUBEN JAMES* convoy.

BURN BAG: Receptacle for classified material which is to be destroyed, used in every novel by both Western and Soviet intelligence and military agencies. In *Danger,* Chuck BERNARDI uses the burn bag for the magnetically erased cassette carrying the encrypted message about the money-laundering operation. A Marine guard takes the burn bag to the incinerator, under supervision.

C-2A GREYHOUND: U.S. twin-turboprop COD transport, version of the Grumman E2-C HAWKEYE; in service with U.S. Navy (improved version) from 1985. In *Danger,* Robby JACKSON flies in one from *RANGER* to Panama; Jack RYAN flew in an earlier version in *Hunt,* on his nerve-wracking ride out to *JOHN F. KENNEDY.*

C-5 GALAXY: U.S. four-turbofan strategic transport; Lockheed. 500 mph; intercontinental range; 150,000 + lbs. payload, including tanks, helicopters, etc. In service with U.S. MILITARY AIRLIFT COMMAND from 1968; strengthened and otherwise improved C-5B from 1986.

In *Hunt,* a C-5 carries the DSRV *AVALON* from California to the East Coast. In *Storm,* C-5s carry the TOMAHAWK missiles for Operation

DOOLITTLE from DOVER AIR FORCE BASE to Scotland. In *Danger,* a CIA courier with the tapes of the first MEDELLIN air strike rides in a C-5. In *Sum,* C-5Bs fly TV equipment to Rome for the signing of the Mideast peace agreement.

C-9 NIGHTINGALE: Aerial-ambulance version of the DC-9 airliner; in service with U.S. Air Force from 1988. At the end of *Storm,* Lieutenant EDWARDS and Vigdis AGUSTDOTTIR leave Iceland aboard one.

C-21 LEARJET: U.S. Air Force version of the light executive jet transport. In *Cardinal,* RYAN flies to New Mexico aboard one.

C-130 HERCULES: U.S. four-turpoprop tactical transport; Lockheed. 300 mph; 2,500+ miles range with 27,000 lbs./64 paratroops. In service with U.S. Air Force from 1956; subsequently in service with many other air forces, including the RAF, and sold on the civilian market as well. Probably the most versatile tactical transport aircraft of the postwar era, it has been adapted to many uses, including the EC-130 electronic warfare aircraft, HC-130 SAR aircraft, and KC-130 aerial tanker. The AC-130 gunship (mounting a 105-mm howitzer among other weapons) and the MC-130 COMBAT TALON version are used by U.S. Air Force Special Warfare units.

In *Storm,* a C-130 drops the Royal Marine team to support EDWARDS in Iceland. *Danger* features the COMBAT TALON HERCULES, modified with special navigation, communications, and detection gear and equipment for the aerial refueling of helicopters. An MC-130E supports the covert operations in Colombia throughout, including numerous aerial refuelings of the PAVE LOW helicopter.

C-141 STARLIFTER: U.S. four-jet strategic transport; Lockheed. 550 mph; 4,000 miles range with 75,000 lbs./120-150 troops or passengers. In service with U.S. Air Force MILITARY AIRLIFT COMMAND from 1965; lengthened C-141B in service from 1979.

In *Danger,* Starlifters carry CHAVEZ and his comrades within the United States and return the bodies of Emil JACOBS and his fellow victims to the United States from Colombia. In *Sum,* one C-141 carries the President's limousine to Rome; another is carrying Marcus CABOT home from Japan at the time of the crisis.

CABOT, MARCUS: In *Sum,* the Director of the CIA, RYAN's immediate superior. A political appointee who likes to use intelligence jargon and smoke cigars, he does not stand up for RYAN in the face of President FOWLER's hostility. Out of the country at the time of the crisis, he plays no real part in dealing with it.

CAG: Commander, Air Group. The CO of a U.S. Navy CARRIER AIR WING (formerly air group; old title for the CO still used). In *Sum,* Robby JACKSON is CAG aboard *THEODORE ROOSEVELT.*

CALIFORNIA, **U.S.S.:**   U.S. nuclear guided-missile cruiser: in service 1974. In *Hunt,* she is one of *NIMITZ's* escorts. In *Storm,* she is also one of *NIMITZ's* escorts during the Soviet BACKFIRE attack.

CALLAGHAN, BATTALION CHIEF MIKE: In *Sum,* an officer of the Denver Fire Department. Commander of the first units on the scene after the nuclear explosion, he is a leader in the rescue and intelligence-gathering efforts.

CALLAGHAN, **U.S.S.:**   U.S. World War II destroyer, sunk by Japanese kamikazes off Okinawa in 1945. In *Storm,* the Boston Harbor pilot who guides *PHARRIS* into port was a survivor.

CALLOWAY, WILLIAM: In *Storm,* British Reuters correspondent. He covers the initial Soviet disarmament activities, including the dismantling of a *YANKEE*-class missile submarine. After evacuation from the Soviet Union, he goes to sea aboard *REUBEN JAMES* under Commander MORRIS, adapts well to the war at sea, and remains with the ship for the rest of the war.

CAMILLE: Hurricane which struck the U.S. Gulf Coast in 1969, causing major loss of life; mentioned in *Danger.*

CAMP DAVID: Weekend country residence of the President of the United States, in northern Maryland. In *Danger,* the President is spending a weekend there when Emil JACOBS is assassinated. In *Sum,* President FOWLER remains there during the crisis, to the concern of his military commanders who know he is better off mobile, safe, and aboard NEACAP.

CAMP PEARY: CIA facility in Virginia, for training field agents. The FOLEYs and CLARK trained there.

'CAN: U.S. Navy slang, short for "tin can," a destroyer-type vessel. In *Hunt,* this term is used for one of the Soviet surface vessels conducting ASW exercises, detected by *DALLAS.*

CANARY TRAP: In *Games,* method developed by Jack RYAN for tracing intelligence leaks through identifying the word processor on which the data was prepared.

CANDID: Soviet jet transport. See IL-76.

CANTOR, MARTY: In *Games,* executive assistant to Admiral GREER at the CIA. He helps train and recruit Jack RYAN and works with him on tracking the ULA. He later retires from CIA due to ulcers and is replaced by RYAN.

CAP: See COMBAT AIR PATROL.

CAPATI, RAMÓN JOSÉ: "John Doe." One of the *EMPIRE BUILDER* gunman-rapist/murderers arrested by *PANACHE* and intimidated into confessions by WEGENER's scheme of a mock execution. After the intimidation is exposed, he is the subject of a plea-bargain, but is murdered in prison, with police cooperation, by the PATTERSON brothers.

CAPTAIN'S MAST: Disciplinary session aboard a naval or Coast Guard vessel, at which the captain administers nonjudicial punishments or commends outstanding performance. In *Danger,* the XO of *PANACHE* calls it the only remaining disciplinary procedure that can be carried out aboard ship.

CARDINAL: CIA code name for Colonel Mikhail FILITOV, in *Sum* and *Cardinal.*

CARL GUSTAV M-2:   Swedish shoulder-fired 84-mm recoilless rifle, firing a rocket-assisted shell. In *Sum,* they are carried by the emergency response teams of the Swiss Guards patrolling Jerusalem.

CARMEN VITA: Greek-registered twin-screw container ship. In *Sum,* she carries QATI's and GHOSN's nuclear device from Piraeus to Hampton Roads in eleven days.

CARON, **U.S.S.:**   U.S. SPRUANCE-class destroyer; in service 1977. In *Hunt,* she is one of *NEW JERSEY's* escorts; in *Storm,* flagship of the ASW commander for the *NIMITZ* battle group.

CARRIER AIR WING: The basic combat aviation unit of the United States Navy, consisting of fighter, attack, early-warning, and ASW SQUADRONs. Permanently organized; shifts from carrier to carrier. In *Sum,* Robby JACKSON commands one aboard *THEODORE ROOSEVELT.*

CARRIER BATTLE GROUP: The most powerful tactical unit of the United States Navy, consisting of one or more aircraft carriers with antiair and ASW escorts. In *Storm, NIMITZ* is flagship of a three-carrier battle group when she is damaged. In *Sum,* it is planned to base such a group permanently at Haifa, as a security guarantee for Israel.

CASE OFFICER: Operative who controls an agent or operation on behalf of an intelligence agency. In *Cardinal,* the FOLEYs are the case officers for CARDINAL; Tania BISYARINA is the same for Bea TAUSSIG.

CASSIUS: In *Hunt* and *Cardinal,* the Soviet code name for Peter HENDERSON.

CASTILLO, JESÚS: "James Doe." The other *EMPIRE BUILDER* murderer. See CAPATI.

CATEGORY: Soviet term indicating the combat readiness of a DIVISION. Category-A divisions are at full strength and have the most modern equipment; Categories B and C have second-line equipment and are filled out on mobilization with reservists. The Soviet forces in East Germany at the beginning of *Storm* are mostly Category-A.

CAVU: Ceiling and Visibility Unlimited. Ideal flying conditions. In *Danger,* Commander JENSEN encounters these conditions on the inbound leg of the first MEDELLIN raid.

CENLAC: In *Games,* Isle of Wight ferry carrying Sean MILLER and his police escort to prison. She is hijacked by ULA and MILLER is rescued, with heavy civilian casualties.

CENTER FOR STRATEGIC AND INTERNATIONAL STUDIES: Highly respected defense/foreign policy "think tank," associated with Georgetown University in Washington, D.C. Jack RYAN had a fellowship there, mentioned in *Games,* and in *Sum* thinks of going back there to teach.

CENTRAL COMMITTEE: The nominally representative national assembly of the Communist Party of the Soviet Union, consisting of delegates elected on a regional basis. Technically, it elects the POLITBURO. At the opening of *Storm,* the Central Committee has been discussing shortfalls in oil production.

CENTRAL INTELLIGENCE AGENCY (CIA):   Principal U.S. foreign-intelligence agency, although sharing that role with the NATIONAL SECURITY AGENCY and the DEFENSE INTELLIGENCE AGENCY. Headquarters in Langley, Virginia, a suburb of Washington, D.C. Nicknamed "The Company." Jack RYAN rises during his career from consultant to Deputy Director of the CIA.

CENTURION: British-built main battle tank, extensively used by the Israelis in the June War of 1967 and the Yom Kippur War of 1973. In *Sum,* ZADIN sights some in action on the Golan Heights during his last mission.

CEP: Circular Error Probability. The radius of a circle within which half of the bombs, missile warheads, etc., are expected to fall. A measure of the accuracy of a delivery system; the "zero CEP" attained by the first A-6 strike in *Danger* means perfect accuracy with all bombs on target. In *Sum,* the warheads of *MAINE's* TRIDENT missiles have a CEP of 165 *feet,* at a range of 4,000 miles!

CH-46 SEA KNIGHT: U.S. twin-turbine medium transport helicopter; Boeing-Vertol. In service with U.S. Navy and Marines from 1961. Jack RYAN had to leave the Marines because of back injuries received in a CH-46 crash in Crete. In *Danger,* one is used in Panama to support the troop-insertion operation.

CH-53/HH-53 STALLION/SUPER-STALLION: U.S. heavy-lift turbine helicopter; Sikorsky. 170 mph; combat radius 200 miles; 15-30,000 lbs. payload. The original H-53 model had twin engines and entered service as a transport helicopter with the U.S. Marines in 1966, as a SAR machine (the "Super Jolly Green Giant" flown by Colonel JOHNS in Vietnam) with the U.S. Air Force in 1967. The CH-53E version entered service with the Marines (transport) and Navy (minesweeper) in 1974; it has three engines and a much heavier payload than the earlier models.

A number of early CH-53s were converted into PAVE LOW special-warfare helicopters, such as the one flown in *Danger.* Modifications included equipment for aerial refueling, sophisticated navigation and communications gear, stealth features, and minigun armament.

In *Hunt,* a hard-used Super Stallion carrying an intelligence team out to *INVINCIBLE* crashes with the loss of all but one man. In *Storm,* one lifts a radar station into position during the Marine assault on Iceland. In *Danger,* another carries cargoes in Panama to support the insertion of the covert-operations party.

CHAFF: Metallic-foil strips, giving false targets to deceive hostile radar or missiles. In *Storm,* dropped by WILD WEASEL PHANTOMs over Iceland and launched by rockets from the *NIMITZ* battle group during the missile attack. In *Danger,* the PAVE TALON helicopter carries chaff in external pods.

CHAIN GUN: The U.S. Bushmaster M242 25-mm cannon, mounted in the M-2 BRADLEY. Weight 230 lbs; rate of fire up to 200 rounds per minute; breech mechanism actuated by an electrically powered chain drive. In *Sum,* during the fighting in Berlin, a 25-mm burst kills Günther BOCK.

CHALLENGER: British main battle tank, improved version of the CHIEFTAIN (bigger engine, tougher armor). In *Storm,* seen on transporters near the Belgian border.

CHAMBERS, WALLY (no rank given): In *Hunt,* executive officer of *DALLAS.* He assumes command when MANCUSO boards *RED OCTOBER* and very ably conns *DALLAS* to help the Soviet submarine during and after the engagement with *KONOVOLOV.* In *Sum,* he is a commander, participates in a war game under MANCUSO, and is about to take command of the attack submarine *KEY WEST.*

CHAPAYEV, MAJOR ALEXANDR GEORGIYEVICH: In *Storm,* Soviet Air Force pilot; son of a general and son-in-law of a CENTRAL COMMITTEE member.

His MiG-29 runs out of fuel while shooting down an American F-18 over Iceland. Rescued by the Americans, he is interrogated by Robert TOLAND and reveals vital information about the Soviet mistakes concerning oil production which helped bring about the war.

CHARLESTON, SIR BASIL: Elderly but still robust and formidable head of the British Secret Intelligence Service, the British equivalent of the CIA. Nicknamed "Bas"; presumably a retired vice admiral of the British Royal Navy.

In *Hunt,* he provides the CIA with its first photographs of *RED OCTOBER.* In *Games,* he meets RYAN at the reception at Buckingham Palace and subsequently cooperates with the CIA and FBI to track the ULA. In *Cardinal,* he has plans to fly to Washington. In *Danger,* he congratulates RYAN on his promotion. In *Sum* he provides intelligence on Soviet code-breaking and the East German nuclear program and warns RYAN about his health.

CHARLESTON, U.S.S.: U.S. amphibious transport; in service 1968. In *Storm,* she is sunk by Soviet missiles during the Marine landings on Iceland, with heavy loss of life.

CHARLIE: Soviet nuclear cruise-missile submarines; first class able to launch missiles while submerged. 4,000/5,000 tons; 25+ knots; 8 missiles, 6 TT; crew 80+. Nineteen in service from 1967.

In *Hunt,* some are detected during ASW exercises by *DALLAS;* others join the pursuit of *RED OCTOBER.* In *Storm,* they are deployed against the Atlantic convoys. *PHARRIS* sinks one and captures eleven of her crew.

CHASE PLANE: Aircraft assigned to fly in company with another aircraft under observation or being tested. In *Sum,* the chase plane can pick up the transmissions from the bugs aboard the Japanese Prime Minister's 747 at thirty miles.

CHAVEZ, STAFF SERGEANT DOMINGO (DING):   U.S. Army NCO, later CIA operative. Of Hispanic descent and a gang member in Los Angeles, he learns discipline in the Army and becomes an outstanding Light Infantryman, with a fine career ahead of him. Small but in top shape, he speaks three languages.

In *Danger* he was recruited for the covert operations in Colombia, and did a superior job throughout, particularly in the final extraction. He was WIA during the operation.

John CLARK then recruited him for the CIA. In *Sum,* he became CLARK's partner as Jack RYAN's bodyguard and helped with the RYANs' reconciliation. He also worked with CLARK to bug the Japanese Prime Minister's plane and helped him arrest and interrogate the terrorists QATI and GHOSN.

CHECKRIDE: Flight to familiarize a pilot with a new type of aircraft or evaluate his proficiency with it. In *Games,* Robby JACKSON promises Dr. SHAPIRO a checkride in a T-38 if he saves Sally RYAN.

CHEKA/CHEKIST: Soviet slang terms for the KGB and its agents, from the original name for the secret police. In *Storm,* General ALEXSEYEV uses it as an epithet after Major SOROKIN shoots KGB Chief KOSOV.

CHERNENKO: Historical character. General Secretary of the CPSU, 1984-85. In *Storm,* he is mentioned as an example of a leader who did not dominate the Party (due largely to age and ill health).

CHERNYAVIN, MAJOR ANDRE: Soviet *SPETSNAZ* officer. In *Storm,* he leads a covert-action team assigned to sabotage the NATO command post at Lammersdorf. Under the cover name "Siegfried Blum," he is the victim of an auto accident and his cover is exposed. Wounded and interrogated, he confesses, then persuades the rest of his team to surrender when surrounded by NATO security forces at their objective.

CHEYENNE MOUNTAIN: A granite mountain near Colorado Springs, Colorado, site of NORAD headquarters. In *Sum,* the people on duty know that the Soviets have an SS-18 targeted on them, to turn Cheyenne Mountain into Cheyenne Lake with a 25-megaton warhead.

CHICAGO, **U.S.S.:**   688-class submarine; in service 1986. In *Storm,* she is commanded throughout the war by Commander Bart MCCAFFERTY. Before her first patrol, she is visited by the Mayor of Chicago. On that patrol, she detects the Soviet withdrawal of missile submarines into a protected enclave. After the war begins, she engages a Soviet amphibious task force, launching HARPOONs before being forced to evade by Soviet ASW forces. Her attack sinks a Soviet destroyer and saves the Norwegian submarine *KOBBEN.*

On her second patrol, *Chicago* leads Operation DOOLITTLE and escorts the damaged *PROVIDENCE.* Near the polar ice cap, she engages a Soviet ALFA which sinks the latter boat.

CHIEF OF THE BOAT: In U.S. Navy, senior enlisted man aboard a submarine. In *Cardinal, DALLAS's* Chief of the Boat is also the diving officer, and so is *MAINE's* in *Sum.*

CHIEF OF STATION: Senior intelligence operative in charge of the agents in a particular area. In *Cardinal,* Bob RITTER complains that they don't have a Soviet one to trade for FILITOV. In *Danger,* the CIA chief of station cannot help CLARK's mission in Colombia.

CHIEF'S SPECIAL: Five-shot .38 Smith & Wesson revolver, short-barreled, handy for quick draws, but not particularly accurate. In *Danger,* Ernie BRADEN uses his ineffectively against his murderers.

CHIEFTAIN: British main battle tank. 55 tons; 25 mph; 120-mm gun; in service from 1963. In *Storm,* General ALEXSEYEV sees them engaging his 20th Guards Tank Division.

CHOPPER: Slang term for helicopter, used in *Storm* when GARCIA sights a Soviet HIP.

CHRISTIANSEN, LIEUTENANT COMMANDER: U.S. Navy. In *Hunt,* Robby JACKSON's RIO. In *Hunt,* he is severely wounded in the head when the F-14 is attacked by SHAVROV's FORGER, but survives after brain surgery and three weeks in the hospital.

CHURBANOV, MAJOR BORIS: In *Cardinal,* former KGB field agent (Spain), now serving in Moscow for health reasons. He detects Eduard ALTUNIN's contact with Ed FOLEY and arrests ALTUNIN.

CHURCH COMMITTEE: U.S. Senate committee, chaired by Senator Frank Church (D. Idaho). Investigation of CIA covert operations in the mid-1970s led to laws against the CIA carrying out assassinations. In *Danger,* LARSON wonders how the CIA still has people like CLARK, after the Church Committee's work.

CHURKIN, CAPTAIN VALERIY MIKHAILOVICH: In *Cardinal,* KGB captain assigned to BRIGHT STAR. Married, with a son who died of cancer at the age of four.

A passenger in the AN-26 shot down by the ARCHER, he is severely wounded and captured by the Afghans. The ARCHER spares him because of the death of Churkin's son from cancer. Churkin dies after being turned over to the American advisory mission in Pakistan. His documents provide major intelligence on BRIGHT STAR and his disappearance is a source of concern to the Soviets.

CIC: See COMBAT INFORMATION CENTER.

CINC: Acronym for "Commander in Chief," as in CINCLANT: Commander in Chief, Atlantic (Admiral PAINTER's position in *Sum*) or CINC-WEST, the post eventually held in *Storm* by General ALEXSEYEV.

CIPHER LOCK: Lock that can be opened only by a coded command sequence, as opposed to a key or combination. In *Danger,* RYAN's briefcase has one.

CLAGGETT, LIEUTENANT COMMANDER WALLY MARTIN "DUTCH": In *Sum,* XO of *MAINE;* Black Annapolis graduate, twice divorced, a dedicated professional. He cannot stand Captain RICKS's martinet style of command and tries to protect the crew from RICKS's whims. He also informs Bart MANCUSO about the captain's poor leadership. In the final confrontation with *ADMIRAL LUNIN* he countermands RICKS's orders and probably saves *MAINE* from being lost with all hands.

CLARK, EAMON "NED": In *Games,* ULA assassin. Sent to intercept RYAN at the Naval Academy, he is suspected and arrested by BRECKEN-RIDGE and CUMMINGS.

CLARK, JOHN TERENCE: Former SEAL and Vietnam veteran, born John Terence Kelly. He served nineteen months in Vietnam, including many covert operations. Recruited by the CIA after vigilante actions against a drug gang who murdered his fiancée, he has been given a new name and identification. He lives in Virginia and has a wife, Sandy, and two daughters, Maggie (seventeen) and Patricia (fourteen). He is over six feet, in top physical condition, speaks six languages, and can pass for a native in three of them including Spanish.

In *Games,* he is off-stage, a field officer in Chad who goes in with the French paras in their raid on the *ACTION DIRECTE* camp. In *Cardinal,* he is still with the Operations Division. He embarks aboard *DALLAS,* goes ashore in Talinn, Estonia, and extracts Maria and Katryn GERASIMOV by small boat after killing their KGB bodyguard.

In *Danger,* he operates covertly in Colombia, partnered with LARSON, providing laser illumination for the A-6 strikes on the cartel leaders. He later provides fuel for the PAVE LOW helicopter and kidnaps ES- COBEDO, who is then turned over to his suspicious colleagues. Knowing that Admiral CUTTER is beyond the reach of conventional justice, Clark uses the Admiral's meeting with Colonel CORTEZ to blackmail the Admiral into committing suicide.

In *Sum* he has transferred from Operations to Security and Protection, and is Ding CHAVEZ's mentor. As RYAN's senior bodyguard, he becomes concerned about his boss's health and strained marriage. He informs Cathy RYAN about Carol ZIMMER, bringing about the RYANs' reconciliation, and learns from Bob HOLTZMAN that Elizabeth ELLIOT has been behind the campaign to discredit RYAN. He also leads the operation to bug the Japanese Prime Minister's plane, and finally helps arrest and interrogate QATI and GHOSN.

CLARKE, CHIEF BOATSWAIN'S MATE: In *Storm, PHARRIS's* bosun. He is put in charge of Soviet prisoners from the sunken CHARLIE. Later he pulls MORRIS to safety before the Soviet torpedo hits and leads the damage-control efforts that save the ship.

CLERK OF THE COURT: In *Danger,* an unnamed civil servant. A devout Baptist outraged that the *EMPIRE BUILDER* murderers will escape execution by a plea-bargain, he leaks this information to the police.

CLINTON, SPECIAL AGENT BILL: In *Sum,* FBI agent in Denver. He interviews Pete DAWKINS after the nuclear explosion and obtains information leading to the identification of Marvin RUSSELL. This reinforces the case for the explosion being terrorism.

CLOSE-IN WEAPONS-SYSTEM (CIWS): U.S. Navy AA weapon. See PHALANX.

CLUSTER MUNITIONS: Aerial bomb consisting of a thin casing holding many bomblets; an area weapon. In *Storm,* Colonel ELLINGTON uses his ROCKEYE cluster bombs to kill the Soviet CINC-West.

CNO: Chief of Naval Operations, highest-ranking officer in the U.S. Navy. Represents Navy on JOINT CHIEFS OF STAFF.

CO: Commanding Officer of a warship: in *Storm,* Commander Morris is CO of *PHARRIS.*

COAMING: Raised area around an opening in a ship's deck or bulkhead. In *Hunt,* a signal light is stowed under *RED OCTOBER's* bridge coaming.

COBRA: U.S. attack helicopter. See AH-1.

COBRA BELLE: In *Cardinal,* U.S. Air Force aircraft, a converted Boeing 767, equipped with a high-powered telescope for observation of Soviet satellites. Observes the destruction of Cosmos 1810 by the BRIGHT STAR laser.

COBRA DANE/COBRA JUDY: Large U.S. phased-array missile tracking radars, used to monitor Soviet missile tests and satellites in *Cardinal.* The first is based in Alaska; the second is mounted aboard U.S.S. *OBSERVATION ISLAND.*

COD: Carrier Onboard Delivery, a cargo plane able to land passengers and high-priority cargo aboard an aircraft carrier. In *Hunt,* RYAN rides a COD to *KENNEDY.* See C-2A GREYHOUND.

COLEMAN, CAPTAIN JOHN: U.S. Navy submariner. In *Hunt,* he is a friend of Skip TYLER and chief of staff to Admiral DODGE; he helps arrange U.S. submarine operations in support of *RED OCTOBER.*

COLLATERAL DAMAGE: Damage to persons and property in the area around a target resulting from misses. In *Danger,* a concern in mounting the MEDELLIN strike; the amount of it causes the President to become alarmed and Admiral CUTTER to begin covering his tracks even at the price of abandoning the covert-action troops.

COLLECTIVE: The control of a helicopter which adjusts the throttle and the angle of attack of the main rotor blades. In *Danger,* Colonel JOHNS uses it at the end of an aerial refueling, to keep the rotors clear of the refueling hose.

COLT PYTHON .357:   High-quality revolver, chambered for .357 Magnum, six rounds, empty weight 2 + lbs. In *Danger,* Dan MURRAY regrets having to retire his "beloved" stainless-steel Python in favor of an automatic.

COM: Abbreviation for "Commander," as in COMSUBLANT, Commander, Submarines, Atlantic, Admiral Vincent GALLERY, in *Hunt.*

COMBAT AIR PATROL (CAP):   Fighters airborne to protect ships from hostile aircraft. In *Storm,* F-14s flying CAP engage the KELT decoy missiles fired at the *NIMITZ* battle group. In *Sum,* Robby JACKSON is flying CAP when he splashes the Libyan MiGs.

COMBAT ENGINEERS: Specially equipped, infantry-trained troops attached to a combat unit, responsible for demolitions, minefields, bridges, and obstacle-clearing. In *Sum,* the Druse FARMER's son was wounded in the Yom Kippur War while serving with this branch of the Syrian Army.

COMBAT INFORMATION CENTER (CIC):   Aboard modern U.S. warships, the compartment where the primary sensor displays and fire controls are located. In *Storm,* the CIC aboard *NIMITZ* is destroyed by a Soviet missile hit and most of the people in it killed; aboard *PHARRIS,* it is Commander MORRIS's post in action.

COMBAT TALON: U.S. Air Force special-operations version of the C-130 HERCULES, used in *Danger.*

COMMAND DUTY OFFICER: In the U.S. armed forces, a qualified officer on duty in place of the commanding officer of a ship or unit. In *Sum,* when the alert is signaled, most of the "boomers" go to sea under their CDOs.

COMMODORE: A U.S. Navy courtesy title for a captain commanding a squadron, task group, or other substantial unit: in *Hunt,* Zachary EATON aboard *NEW JERSEY;* in *Sum,* Bart MANCUSO in command of the missile-submarine squadron.

COMPANY: Ground forces (armor or infantry) unit consisting of two or more platoons; 120-200 men depending on type. The equivalent of a BATTERY in the artillery; usually commanded by a captain or senior lieutenant.

COMPROMISE AUTHORITY: Authorization to an FBI agent to use deadly force in a confrontation situation. In *Sum,* the Special-Agent-in-Charge receives it in the farmhouse shoot-out.

CONCORDE: Anglo-French four-jet supersonic airliner; 100+ passengers. Cruises at 1300+ mph; in service from 1976. In *Games,* the RYANs are flown home on a British Airways Concorde, courtesy of the British Crown and much to RYAN's distress.

CONDOR: World War II German maritime-reconnaissance aircraft, used against Allied convoys. In *Storm,* Soviet BEARs perform the same role: guiding in submarines.

CONE OF SILENCE or BAFFLES: Area behind a submarine where her sonar cannot detect, due to her own propeller noises. It is reduced by towed-array sonars, such as *DALLAS's* BQR-15 in *Hunt.*

CONFORMAL FUEL CELLS: Streamlined fuel tanks, attached to the fuselage of a jet aircraft; offer less air resistance than wing tanks. F-15s carry them in *Hunt,* intercepting the FORGER; in *Storm,* when Amy NAKAMURA engages the BADGERs; in *Sum,* when they escort the F-16s to Berlin.

CONGRESS OF PEOPLE'S DEPUTIES: The "bumptious new parliament" of the Soviet Union. In *Sum,* Oleg KADISHEV believes he has forty percent of the votes there—which feeds his ambition.

CONN: Control of a ship's movements. In *Storm,* Robert TOLAND takes the conn of *NIMITZ* after the missile strike because senior officers are disabled or busy with damage control.

CONNOR, SPECIAL AGENT PETE: Secret Service Agent, assigned to the White House. In *Danger,* he escorts Admiral CUTTER into the President's office. In *Sum,* he is Helen D'AGOSTINO's partner and one of the President's personal bodyguards. He helps D'AGOSTINO deal with Charles ALDEN's death, accompanies FOWLER to Rome, is at CAMP DAVID during the crisis, and does not approve of Elizabeth ELLIOT.

CONTACT FUSE: Mechanical fuse, designed to detonate a warhead on impact. In *Sum,* the MARK 50 torpedo dropped against *ADMIRAL LUNIN* is contact-fused and detonates when it strikes a wave hard enough.

CONTAINER SHIP: The most common kind of modern merchant vessel, carrying her cargo in standardized containers. *COSTANZA* in *Games* and the Maersk Line vessel sighted by *DALLAS* in *Cardinal* are both of this type.

CONVENTIONAL-THEATER FORCE: U.S. ground, air, or sea unit intended to use conventional weapons in a particular area. In *Sum,* the *THEODORE ROOSEVELT* battle group is one for the Mediterranean.

COOLEY, DENNIS: In *Games,* Irish-born London bookseller. ULA agent and contact man for Geoffrey WATKINS. Physically unimpressive, he has a vicious and sadistic streak.

Cooley learns that he is under suspicion when a repairman detects a police bug in the electrical wiring, flees to Ireland, and joins Kevin O'DON-NELL. He participates in the second kidnap attempt on the PRINCE AND PRINCESS OF WALES at the RYANs' house. He is captured by RYAN and JACKSON, induced to show them the ULA escape boats, and is shot by his own side while boarding the boat.

CORAL SEA, U.S.S.: U.S. conventional aircraft carrier; in service 1945. In *Storm,* she supports the Marine landing on Iceland.

CORPS: A body of specialized troops, as in Medical Corps or Marine Corps. Also, a unit of ground forces in Western armies, consisting of two or more DIVISIONs with supporting units, operating either independently or as part of an ARMY.

CORSAIR: U.S. attack aircraft. See A-7.

CORTEZ, COLONEL FELIX: In *Danger,* a former Cuban intelligence officer, he defected to the MEDELLIN cartel after the breakup of a Puerto Rican terrorist organization he was aiding. ESCOBEDO's chief security and intelligence officer, he penetrates American security by seducing Moira WOLFE, Secretary of FBI Director Emil JACOBS, using the cover of a Colombian businessman named Juan Diaz.

He provides essential intelligence for the assassination of JACOBS but is not consulted otherwise and does not approve. He attempts to defuse the escalating crisis and protect his own position by negotiating a truce with Admiral CUTTER, involving the abandonment of the American covert-operations teams in Colombia to the mercy of Cortez's own troops.

Cortez capably leads cartel soldiers against the Americans but fails to prevent the rescue. Afterward, Cortez is captured. In the absence of evidence for an indictment, he is turned over to the Cubans at GUAN-TÁNAMO BAY.

CORVETTE: Small, short-range antisubmarine vessel, usually employed in coastal waters: *AMETIST* in *Storm.*

COSTANZA: In *Games,* Cypriot-registered freighter, intended escape route for the ULA terrorists after the kidnapping at the RYANs'. She is cordoned off, boarded, and cleared by the Maryland State Police, U.S. Marines, and FBI.

COUNCIL OF MINISTERS: Highest-ranking body in the Soviet government (as opposed to Party), nominally elected by the SUPREME SOVIET. In *Storm,* SERGETOV considers its bureaucracy a handicap.

COUNTERBATTERY: Tactic of suppressing hostile artillery or missile fire by targeting the guns/launchers with one's own weapons. In *Cardinal,* Marco RAMIUS mentions the Soviets testing this tactic against submarine-launched missiles, using obsolete land-based missiles.

"COUNTERFORCE" ATTACK: A strategic nuclear attack aimed at destroying the opponent's strategic nuclear forces rather than his population centers. In *Cardinal,* the Soviets are believed to have this capability; the U.S. does not.

COVERT: Intelligence term: clandestine, hidden, or disguised so as to be unrecognizable. In *Danger,* the insertion of U.S. ground troops into Colombia with Operation SHOWBOAT is a classic covert operation.

COXSWAIN: Person in charge of a small boat. In *Danger,* the coxswain of *PANACHE's* Zodiac pulls it clear after the boarding party is aboard *EMPIRE BUILDER.*

CRASH STATUS: The highest priority for a weapons or other defense project. In *Cardinal,* FILITOV asks if BRIGHT STAR should be given this status.

CRAZY IVAN: Russian submarine maneuver, used by *RED OCTOBER* in *Hunt.* The submarine turns a complete circle, allowing the bow sonar to detect any trailing vessel.

CREW CHIEF: Senior enlisted man aboard a U.S. Air Force cargo or passenger aircraft. In *Cardinal,* the VC-137 RYAN takes to Moscow has one.

CROFTER, GENERAL BEN: In *Cardinal,* Chief of Staff, United States Army. He escorts Soviet Defense Attaché DALMATOV to FILITOV's secret funeral at Antietam.

CRUISE MISSILE: Jet-propelled unmanned aircraft, able to deliver conventional or nuclear warheads over long ranges, such as the TOMAHAWK used in *Storm.* Can be launched from submarines, surface ships, aircraft, or mobile land-based launchers.

CRUSADERS: U.S.-built French fighter. See F-8.

CRYOGENIC FUELS: Missile fuels requiring storage at extremely low temperatures. In *Sum,* the toxic propellants of the SS-18 are described as an *improvement* on cryogenic ones.

CUMMINGS, NANCY: Secretary to nine successive Deputy Directors of Intelligence at the CIA, including Admiral GREER and Jack RYAN. She first meets RYAN during the antiterrorist investigation in *Games.* In *Danger,* she no longer considers him an outsider, and in *Sum* is sympathetic and supportive during RYAN's problems. She is so trusted that only RYAN's most secure telephone line bypasses her.

CUMMINGS, SERGEANT TOM: In *Games,* U.S. Marine NCO on duty with Sergeant Major BRECKENRIDGE at the Naval Academy. He helps arrest Ned CLARK and later organizes defense against ULA pursuit of the RYANs and Their Royal Highnesses.

CUTOUT: A person or device separating one agent from another. In *Games,* a ULA cutout informs O'DONNELL that COOLEY is on the run; in *Cardinal,* FILITOV plans to get the BRIGHT STAR data to his cutout.

CUTTER, VICE ADMIRAL JAMES A., JR.:   In *Danger,* the President's Special Assistant for National Security Affairs. He was once CO of U.S.S. *BELKNAP,* but has more staff and Pentagon experience than time at sea, and seems to lack both moral courage and any sense of responsibility or loyalty to anybody but himself.

Initially a strong supporter of the drug offensive, he begins to lose his nerve after the PRESIDENT grows concerned over "collateral damage" from the air raids. Increasingly desperate to save his own position, he negotiates a truce with CORTEZ, involving the abandonment of the American covert-operations troops. He fails to prevent their rescue and afterwards is blackmailed by John CLARK into committing suicide (an apparent traffic accident).

CYCLIC CONTROL: The control of a helicopter that controls the tilt of the main rotor blades. In *Cardinal,* a Soviet MI-24 pilot uses this trying to evade one of the ARCHER's missiles.

DACHA: Russian country retreat. In *Storm,* Petroleum Minister SERGETOV is summoned from his, near Moscow, after the Nizhnevartovsk sabotage.

DAGGER: Argentine single-seat, single-engined jet fighter, Israeli-built version of the French Mirage 5. RYAN's HARRIER pilot in *Hunt,* Lieutenant PARKER, shot one down during the Falklands War.

D'AGOSTINO, HELEN "DAGA": Secret Service agent, on White House duty in *Danger* and *Sum*. Of Italian descent, divorced, she won her nickname by shooting a counterfeiter. She is an outstanding pistol shot, a member of the Secret Service team that defeated the DELTA FORCE team.

In *Sum* she is Peter CONNOR's partner, investigates the death of Charles ALDEN, accompanies President FOWLER to Rome, and is present at CAMP DAVID during the final crisis. She does not like Elizabeth ELLIOT.

DALLAS, U.S.S.: 688-class submarine; in service 1981.

In *Hunt*, under the command of Bart MANCUSO, she is detects *RED OCTOBER* at sea. Thanks to MANCUSO's tactical sense and Ronald JONES's superb ear on the sonar, she is able to regain contact in the open Atlantic.

Dallas participates in the deception operation for removing *RED OCTO-BER's* crew and gaining control of her. She then escorts the Soviet submarine to the coast of Maine, where MANCUSO, JONES, food, medicine, and videotapes are transferred. Continuing her mission under command of Wally CHAMBERS, *Dallas* escorts *RED OCTOBER* south and partici-pates in the engagement with *V.K. KONOVOLOV*.

In *Cardinal*, still under MANCUSCO's command, *Dallas* penetrates the Baltic, with Marko RAMIUS and John CLARK aboard. Her original assignment: to extract Mikhail FILITOV. In the end, CLARK lands in Estonia and instead extracts the wife and daughter of KGB Chairman GERASIMOV, while RAMIUS convinces the Soviet authorities that *Dallas* is a Soviet submarine long enough to permit her to reach international waters.

DALMATOV, MAJOR GENERAL GRIGORY: In *Cardinal*, Soviet De-fense Attaché in Moscow; a tank officer, like Mikhail FILITOV. He is invited by the Chief of Staff of the U.S. Army, he attends what turns out to be FILITOV's secret funeral at Antietam.

D'ANTONIO, GIOVANNI CARDINAL: In *Sum*, Vatican diplomat; the son of a Sicilian fisherman, a linguist, and a heavy smoker. He meets Jack RYAN and Scott ADLER in Rome, supports the idea of Papal mediation in the Middle East, and plays a valuable role in working out the peace plan.

DARYEI, AYATOLLA MAHMOUD HAJI: In *Sum*, Iranian religious leader. Fanatically anti-American and opposed to the peace settlement; sympathizes with anti-American, anti-Israeli terrorist efforts. President FOWLER is ready to destroy his home city of QUM with a nuclear war-head after the crisis, and RYAN confronts the man on the way to attend the terrorists' execution.

DAVENPORT, REAR ADMIRAL CHARLES: In *Hunt*, U.S. Navy officer and director of naval intelligence. A former naval aviator grounded after a barrier crash, he is initially stubborn about working with RYAN until GREER convinces him to cooperate. After that his assistance is valuable.

DAVIDOFF, ERNIE: In *Danger*, United States Attorney in Mobile, Alabama. Because of the irregular interrogation aboard *PANACHE*, he is reluctantly obliged to accept a plea-bargain for the *EMPIRE BUILDER* drug killers, instead of getting the death penalty.

DAVIES, COMMANDER GUS: U.S. Navy F-18 pilot. In *Storm*, he is shot down by Major CHAPAYEV over Iceland. The two pilots find themselves close to each other in the water, and are picked up together.

DAVITS: Fixed or movable cranes projecting over the side of a ship, for lifting heavy objects, especially small boats. In *Storm*, *PHARRIS's* boat with the Russian submarine survivors is lifted out of the water by davits.

DAWKINS, OFFICER PETER: In *Sum*, a Denver police officer. He becomes suspicious of the parked van with a faked ABC logo on it, and passes this on to his superiors. He survives the nuclear explosion, although badly wounded, and provides critical intelligence for proving the bomb was a terrorist attack.

DC-4: Four-engined propeller-driven commercial airliner; Douglas. In service (with airlines) 1946. In *Games*, an engineless one is used for FBI training in assaults on hijacked aircraft. In *Danger*, DC-4s and a later development, the DC-6, are common drug-running planes.

DC-7: Four-engined propeller-driven commercial airliner; in service from 1954, but had a short career due to the coming of jet airliners. In *Danger*, Bronco WINTERS intercepts a drug-running DC-7B and forces it to land. The crew is then captured and intimidated into confessing by the ready force of U.S. Marines.

DC-9: Twin-engined jet airliner; McDonnell-Douglas. 120 + passengers; short to medium range; rear-mounted engines; in service 1965.
 In *Hunt*, Major RICHARDSON normally flies a DC-9 for Allegheny Airlines. In *Danger*, RYAN is aboard one over West Virginia during the first raid of MEDELLIN leaders. Also see C-9A NIGHTINGALE.

DC-10: Three-turbofan wide-bodied commercial airliner; McDonnell-Douglas. 300 + passengers; intercontinental range; in service from 1971.
 In *Storm*, chartered DC-10s carrying American troops to Europe are

warned clear of the air battle around the *NIMITZ* group. In *Sum,* QATI and GHOSN fly in one from Miami to Mexico City after escaping from Denver. See also KC-10 EXTENDER.

DEEP-SUBMERGENCE RESCUE VEHICLE (DSRV):   United States Navy deep-diving submarine, designed to rescue crews of sunken submarines. Air-transportable by C-141 or C-5; crew of 4 plus 24 survivors; able to dive to 5,000 feet; electric motors. In *Hunt,* both U.S. DSRVs, *AVALON* and *MYSTIC,* participate in the *RED OCTOBER* operation and take off the Soviet submarine's crew.

DEFENSE INTELLIGENCE AGENCY (DIA):   The intelligence branch of the Department of Defense, combining most of the work previously done by the separate services and supervising the rest.

In *Cardinal,* it maintains a separate secure photographic laboratory, jointly with the CIA, and provides information on Soviet missile tests to the *COBRA BELLE* commander. In *Sum,* it is skeptical about Soviet claims to be disarming on schedule; President FOWLER thinks it is full of Cold Warriors.

DELTA (NATO code name):   Soviet series of ballistic missile submarines. Forty, in four separate classes (Delta I through IV), in service from 1973 and the backbone of the Soviet BALLISTIC MISSILE SUBMARINE force. The Delta III trailed by *CHICAGO* in *Storm* is 11,000/13,000 tons; 24 knots; 16 missiles and 6 TT. In *Hunt,* an unspecified Delta is tracked in exercises by *V.K. KONOVOLOV,* and Deltas are among the missile submarines recalled after *RED OCTOBER's* defection. In *Cardinal,* Marko RAMIUS mentions commanding one for experimental missile firings.

DELTA FORCE: U.S. Army's elite hostage-rescue and counterterrorist team, first deployed for the abortive hostage rescue in Iran in 1980. In *Storm,* CANTOR's brother-in-law, an Army major with Delta Force, complains of how its operations depend on reliable intelligence. In *Cardinal,* it is considered for use in the rescue of Major GREGORY, in spite of lack of jurisdiction. In *Danger,* CHAVEZ picked up a background knowledge of special operations from a friend in Delta Force.

DELTA-V MANEUVERS: Alteration of the orbital path of a satellite. In *Storm,* CINC-NORAD is advised to permit such maneuvers for an American KH-11 being tracked by a Soviet killer satellite.

DEPTH-BOMB/CHARGE: Antisubmarine weapon consisting of an explosive charge with a hydrostatic fuse that detonates it at a predetermined depth. Against modern high-speed nuclear submarines, it is most useful as an air-dropped weapon. In *Storm, BATTLEAXE's* helicopter uses two to sink the Soviet VICTOR hiding by the wreck of the *Andrea Doria.*

DESTROYER: Type of naval vessel, larger than a frigate. They are usually specialized for either antiaircraft or ASW work. In *Storm, CARON* in the *NIMITZ* group and the *UDALOY* engaged by *CHICAGO* are ASW destroyers; the *SOVREMENIY* in the *KIROV* group is AA.

DEUCE-AND-A-HALF: A two-and-a-half-ton truck, one of the standard U.S. military vehicles. In *Storm,* Sergeant SMITH says that Iceland's winter winds can blow one off the road.

DGSE: *Direction Générale de Sécurité Extérieure* (General Management of Foreign Security)—the French secret intelligence agency, under the Ministry of Defense. In *Storm* a general from the DGSE handles the interrogation of Major CHERNYAVIN. In *Games,* their Washington office works closely with the CIA in tracking the ULA terrorists; they organize the raid on the *ACTION DIRECTE* camp and interrogate the captured terrorists. In *Cardinal,* many of the French doctors in Pakistan are probably DGSE agents. In *Danger,* RYAN knows that DGSE would have immediately avenged something like JACOBS's assassination, with the approval of the French people.

DIEGO GARCIA: Island in the eastern Indian Ocean, site of the major advanced base for the U.S. Rapid Deployment Force. In *Storm,* the Russians fear that nuclear weapons stored there will be used against any Soviet invasion of Middle Eastern oil countries. It is later hit by a submarine-launched missile, but all U.S. ships have already gone to sea.

DIET: The Japanese Parliament. In *Sum,* the Japanese PRIME MINISTER wishes that bribing the opposition there was as easy as bribing the Mexicans.

DIFAR: Directional Low-Frequency Analyzer and Ranging. A type of active sonobuoy. In *Storm,* the ORION working with *PHARRIS* against the FOXTROT drops one. So does the ORION in *Sum,* supporting *MAINE* against *ADMIRAL LUNIN.*

DIOMEDE: British Royal Navy ASW frigate; in service 1971. In *Storm,* she may have sunk a Soviet submarine while escorting a convoy with *BATTLEAXE.*

DIPPING SONAR: A sonar in which the transducer (sound-emitter) is lowered into the water on a cable. The major form of sonar carried by ASW helicopters, such as the SEA KINGS from *INVINCIBLE* in *Hunt* and *REUBEN JAMES's* SEAHAWK in *Storm.*

DISTINGUISHED FLYING CROSS: American medal, awarded for exceptional heroism while engaged in aerial flight. In *Storm,* O'MALLEY has two from Vietnam and is awarded a third for killing the Soviet PAPA while flying a LAMPS from *REUBEN JAMES.* In *Sum,* Secretary of Defense BUNKER also has three, won in Vietnam flying F-105s.

DISTINGUISHED SERVICE CROSS: American medal, the Army's second-highest award; for extraordinary heroism in combat. In *Cardinal,* CIA courier Augie GIANNINI won it as a helicopter pilot in Vietnam.

DISTINGUISHED SERVICE MEDAL: American Army medal, awarded for outstandingly meritorious service. In *Cardinal,* Bart MANCUSO cannot talk about the DSM that he won for his role in securing *RED OCTOBER.*

DIVING OFFICER: Aboard a submarine, the officer or senior enlisted man who controls the flooding and blowing of the ballast tanks. In *Cardinal,* the CHIEF OF THE BOAT acts as diving officer aboard *DALLAS.*

DIVISION: A ground-force unit consisting of two or more BRIGADEs or REGIMENTs, with supporting units. The basic unit of the Soviet and American armies; may be armored, airborne, infantry, light infantry, or amphibious (U.S. Marines). Strength ranges from 6,000+ up to 20,000.

DOBBENS, ALEXANDER CONSTANTINE: In *Games,* Black terrorist and electrical engineer. A disenchanted veteran of earlier Black underground movements, he cooperates with the ULA in their operations in the United States. He provides vehicles, weapons, training facilities, and a safe house, although he disapproves of the attempt on Cathy RYAN.

Using his job as cover, he reconnoiters the RYAN house, arranges for the cutoff of electrical power, and participates in the second attempt on the PRINCE AND PRINCESS OF WALES. After the escape of the RYANs and their guests, he is shot by Sean MILLER.

DODGE, VICE ADMIRAL SAM: U.S. Navy officer. In *Hunt,* he is deputy chief of naval operations for submarine warfare, the senior submariner in the Navy. He was once Skip TYLER's CO, does not like being cut out of TYLER's initial evaluation of the CATERPILLAR drive, but provides extensive support for the *RED OCTOBER* operation after GREER brings him into the picture.

DONALDSON, SENATOR (no first name):   In *Hunt,* Senator from Connecticut, Chairman of the Select Committee on Intelligence. His aide Peter HENDERSON is a Soviet agent, producing major leaks about intelligence sources. After HENDERSON's arrest, CIA Director MOORE and FBI Director JACOBS confront the Senator, inducing him to retire from public office in return for no publicity for his aide's treason.

DONOHO, EDWARD: In *Games,* FBI Special Agent. He reluctantly escorts IRA spokesman Paddy O'NEIL from Boston, then arranges for photographs to be made of Sally RYAN in intensive care.

DONOHO, JOHN: In *Games,* South Boston bartender of Irish descent, former Marine, and IRA sympathizer. Uncle of Edward DONOHO. After his son shows him the pictures of Sally RYAN in intensive care, the elder Donoho bans the local IRA from his bar.

DOOLITTLE, OPERATION: In *Storm,* code name for the submarine-launched TOMAHAWK attack on the air bases of the Soviet Northern Fleet. It destroys a good many of the BACKFIREs that have been decimating the Atlantic convoys, and makes the Politburo aware of how vulnerable the Soviet homeland could be.

DOPPLER: Apparent change in pitch or frequency of a sound or radio source as the listener moves. This effect can be used for navigation, as by Colonel JOHNS's helicopter in *Danger.*

"DOUBLED"/"TURNED":   Intelligence term used in *Sum:* an agent previously working for one side is now working for both. Examples are Eduard ALTUNIN in *Cardinal* and Peter HENDERSON in *Hunt* and *Cardinal.*

DOVER AIR FORCE BASE: U.S. Air Force Base, in central Delaware. Headquarters of the MILITARY AIRLIFT COMMAND. In *Storm,* the TOMAHAWKs for Operation DOOLITTLE are loaded aboard C-5s at Dover. In *Cardinal,* the bodies of the KGB agents killed in New Mexico are flown to Dover.

DRAW-DOWN: In *Sum,* the reduction in U.S. armed forces following the end of the Cold War. It is expected to cause problems in providing the peacekeeping force for the Middle East.

DREADNOUGHT, **H.M.S.:**   The first British nuclear submarine; in service 1961. In *Hunt,* Owen WILLIAMS has served aboard her.

DREAMLAND, OPERATION: In *Storm,* code name for the offensive by Stealth fighters and low-altitude attack aircraft against Soviet air power in Germany, including both the AWACS and bases.

DROGUE: Hose used in aerial refueling, connecting with the PROBE of the receiving aircraft. In *Storm,* drogues are fitted to the BUDDY STORES carried by *NIMITZ's* A-7s, and in *Danger* to the C-130 supporting the covert operations in Colombia.

DRONES: Unmanned aircraft, either specially designed or obsolete aircraft, used as targets. In *Danger,* Robby JACKSON hopes to test the repaired AIM-54s on drones before having to shoot it out with the Iranians.

DUBININ, CAPTAIN FIRST RANK VALENTIN BORISSOVICH: In *Sum,* Soviet naval officer, CO of the *AKULÁ*-class submarine *ADMIRAL LUNIN.* An outstanding officer, who knew Marko RAMIUS and is ambitious to become his successor as mentor and teacher of a whole generation of Soviet submarine captains.

In his first encounter with *MAINE* in the Gulf of Alaska, Dubinin both tracks and is tracked by her. During the submarine's refit, he uses all his influence and all the favors anybody owes him to obtain the best-possible equipment and supplies and speedy, high-quality work.

During the second encounter, she is tracking him when she has her underwater collision with the floating logs. After this he acts in the belief that war is imminent, until he receives the signal to abandon the attack too late to avoid inflicting fatal damage on *MAINE.* He surfaces and conducts successful rescue operations, saving eighty-seven of *MAINE's* crew.

DUKE OF EDINBURGH (not named):   Consort of the QUEEN OF ENGLAND. In *Games,* he and the QUEEN visit RYAN in the hospital to thank him for saving the PRINCE AND PRINCESS OF WALES. He also greets RYAN at the reception at Buckingham Palace.

"DUMB" BOMB: The traditional form of bomb, without any attached special-guidance mechanisms. In *Storm,* the A-7s supporting Lieutenant EDWARDS drop them on the Soviet mortars.

DURANDAL: French-designed runway-cratering bomb, slowed by a parachute and then driven into the runway by a small rocket before exploding. In *Storm,* Colonel ELLINGTON uses them against Soviet underground fuel tanks.

DURLING, ROGER: In *Sum,* Vice President of the United States; Robert FOWLER's running mate. A liberal and veteran of Vietnam. A former governor of California, he carried the state for the ticket.

He has reservations about FOWLER, ELLIOT, and their treatment of RYAN, and wonders if he couldn't have made it to the White House on his own. During the crisis he is evacuated from Washington with his family and is airborne aboard KNEECAP. After RYAN refuses to confirm the President's firing order against QUM, DURLING confers with CINC-SAC and the chairmen and vice-chairmen of the Senate and House Armed Service Committees. He succeeds to the Presidency after FOWLER's (presumed) resignation.

DWYER, MAUREEN: In *Games,* PIRA bomb expert, arrested by the British police on a tip from the ULA. The tip was part of Kevin O'DONNELL's ongoing campaign against his fellow Irishmen.

DZERZHINKSY, FELIX: "Iron Felix." Historical character (1877-1926). First head of the Soviet Secret Police *(Cheka).* In *Games,* Kevin O'DONNELL thinks that Dennis COOLEY is like Dzerzhinsky. 2 Dzerzhinsky Square is the address of KGB headquarters, and at the time of *Sum* still featured a statue of the man.

E-:   U.S. armed forces prefix for grades of enlisted men. At the opening of *Danger,* CHAVEZ is an E-5, or "buck sergeant," but hopes to make E-7, sergeant first class, by volunteering for the covert operations.

E-2 HAWKEYE: U.S. twin-turboprop carrier-based AWACS aircraft; Grumman. 350+ mph; 6 hrs. endurance; sophisticated airborne radar, data-processing, and communications facilities. In service with U.S. Navy (E-2C) from 1971.

In *Hunt,* an E-2 from the *KENNEDY* directs Robby JACKSON's flight of F-14s to their interception of *KIEV's* FORGERS. In *Storm,* the *NIMITZ* group launches four, and they also cover the Marines' landing on Iceland. In *Danger,* one provides Bronco WINTERS with target data, and Robby JACKSON rides in another the night of the MEDELLIN air strike. In *Sum, THEODORE ROOSEVELT* launches them to support her fighters during the crisis.

E-3 SENTRY: U.S. four-turbofan AWACS aircraft, based on the Boeing 707-320B. 500+ mph; 10 hrs. endurance; crew of 20+, manning the most advanced airborne radar, computers, and communications facilities in existence. In service with U.S. Air Force from 1977; also NATO and Saudi Arabia.

In *Hunt,* an E-3 is deployed against the Soviet surface forces. Lieutenant SHAVROV's FORGER attempts to intercept it, but is discouraged by escorting F-15s. In *Storm,* E-3s fly from Iceland before its capture, support NATO interceptors in the battle for air superiority over Germany, and cover the Marines' landing in Iceland.

EC-135:   U.S. Air Force C-135/KC-135 modified for electronic warfare. In *Hunt,* one is deployed against the Soviet fleet, recording the Soviet radars tracking the B-52s. In *Sum,* one is suggested as the CHASE PLANE for the bugging operation against the Japanese Prime Minister.

EF-111:   U.S. Air Force electronic-warfare aircraft. See F-111.

EATON, COMMODORE ZACHARY: In *Hunt,* the commanding officer of the surface-action group deployed against the Soviet surface fleet. His flagship is the battleship *NEW JERSEY,* almost as old as he is; his major opponent is the *KIROV* group.

ECHO (NATO code name):   Soviet class of twin-screw, nuclear cruise-missile submarines; thirty-four in service from 1960. Noisy, unreliable, and need to surface to fire their missiles.

In *Hunt,* RYAN mentions a mutiny aboard an Echo in 1980. Obsolete as they are, Echoes are also deployed in pursuit of *RED OCTOBER.* In *Storm,* one is part of a group rotating out of the Mediterranean Sea just before war begins.

EDWARDS, FIRST LIEUTENANT MICHAEL D., JR.:   In *Storm,* U.S. Air Force officer. An Air Force Academy graduate, he is unable to fly because of deteriorating eyesight. Assigned to Iceland as a weatherman, he survives the Soviet assault, then in company with some Marines escapes and evades the Soviet occupation.

After some difficulties in communication, he reports the Soviet invasion and authenticates his identity, becoming an accepted intelligence source. He reports on the Soviet airlift, warns of the arrival of Soviet fighters and missiles on Iceland, and observes the first, costly B-52 strike.

Moving south, his patrol encounters KGB troops raping Vigdis AGUST-DOTTIR, kills them, and rescues her. (This is against orders, but ED-WARDS's girlfriend was raped and murdered; he cannot let the rapists escape.) The patrol continues to provide invaluable intelligence on Soviet air movements and troop positions around Iceland, and is later reinforced by an air-dropped British SAS detachment.

Finally detected and engaged by the Soviets, Edwards and the survivors of the patrol are rescued at the last minute by Recon Marines spearheading the NATO landing. Wounded in the final action, Edwards receives the Navy Cross, then is medevacked to the United States, intending to marry Vigdis.

EISENHOWER, U.S.S.:   U.S. *NIMITZ*-class carrier; in service 1977. Edward STUART in *Danger* served aboard her as a yeoman and picked up a convincing nautical background there.

EISLY, MAJOR DON: In *Storm,* U.S. Air Force officer, Colonel ELL-INGTON's backseater. He flies numerous F-19 missions with the colonel, including Operation DREAMLAND and the raid that kills the Soviet CINC-West. Wounded when the F-19 is shot down, he is escaping and evading along with ELLINGTON when the war ends.

ELEPHANT, SEEN THE: To have been in combat, a term dating back to the Civil War. In *Sum,* this describes Secretary of Defense BUNKER.

ELLINGTON, COLONEL DOUGLAS "THE DUKE":   In *Storm,* Black U.S. Air Force officer, F-19 pilot, and commander of the F-19 Stealth squadron. A Vietnam veteran and former F-111 pilot. He leads Operation DREAMLAND, shooting down a Soviet AWACS. On another mission he destroys a fuel dump and kills the Soviet CINC-West. He continues to fly until shot down toward the end of the war. He learns of the peace agreement from the Germans, after encountering Soviet troops who send him on his way.

ELLIOT, ELIZABETH (BETH, E.E.):   Professor of Political Science at Bennington, with strongly leftist political views on foreign-policy issues. Attractive, short-tempered, ambitious, and unscrupulous, she is disliked by the Secret Service White House detail.

In *Danger,* she a foreign-policy adviser to Governor FOWLER, and has her first encounter with Jack RYAN. He loses his temper over her views and her threats of his dismissal, and they have a loud confrontation which leaves her holding a grudge.

In *Sum* she succeeds Charles ALDEN, whom she always resented, as National Security Advisor to President FOWLER. Shortly thereafter she and FOWLER become lovers. This begins with ambition on her part and loneliness on his, but develops into real mutual affection.

Elliot is determined to deny RYAN credit for the Mideast peace plan, drive him out of government service, and if possible destroy his personal life. With the help of an unsuspecting journalist, her campaign of misinformation nearly breaks up the RYANs' marriage. Thanks to the RYANs and John CLARK, the campaign fails and leads to a further confrontation, between Elliot and Cathy RYAN.

During the crisis, Elliot's advice tends to make matters worse, as she urges the President to ignore a "Cold Warrior" like RYAN. She also gives undue credibility to KADISHEV/SPINNAKER's implications of lost Soviet bombs and NARMONOV not being fully in control of his armed forces. She eventually becomes completely ineffective, is placed under sedation, and presumably retires from government service after FOWLER's resignation.

EMERSON, MAJOR GENERAL WILLIAM: In *Storm,* U.S. Marine general, commanding the First Marine Amphibious Force landing on Iceland. He cooperates with TOLAND in passing on CHAPAYEV's intelligence about the origins of the war and visits EDWARDS in sick bay, awarding him the Navy Cross.

EMPIRE-BUILDER, MY: In *Danger,* motor yacht owned by a wealthy Southern businessman (unnamed), engaged in a large-scale money-laundering operation for the MEDELLIN cartel. Apparently suspecting that he is growing too independent, the cartel orders his assassination.

Ramón CAPATI and Jesús CASTILLO sign on as crew, murder the owner, and rape and murder his wife and daughter. They are then intercepted by U.S.C.G. *PANACHE. EMPIRE BUILDER* is taken into Mobile by a crew from the cutter.

END-USER CERTIFICATE: Document certifying the intended final recipient of a shipment of arms. Honest governments and legitimate arms dealers are supposed to require them, but not all governments are honest and many arms dealers are like Erik MARTENS in *Games,* who supplied the UZIS that ended up in ULA hands.

***ENTERPRISE,* U.S.S.:** The first U.S. nuclear-powered carrier; in service 1961. In *Danger,* a friend of Robby JACKSON's has just received command of her.

ERNIE: In *Games,* a black Labrador retriever Jack RYAN buys as a protector and pet for his daughter during her convalescence. Although a bit slow to housebreak, he becomes Sally's inseparable companion. He survives the shootout at the RYANs, because he follows outdoors an agent who once gave him half a sandwich.

ERNST, FRANK: In *Storm,* U.S. Navy lieutenant commander. XO of *REUBEN JAMES* and an Annapolis graduate who isn't afraid to get his hands dirty keeping his ship running.

ESCOBEDO, ERNESTO: In *Danger,* one of the leaders of the MEDELLIN cartel targeted as a "clear and present danger." Insanely ambitious, totally ruthless, and personally sadistic, he employs Colonel CORTEZ for security, intelligence, and covert operations. He survives both MEDELLIN air raids, as well as an attempt on his life staged by CORTEZ to give the appearance of an internal power struggle in the cartel. He also uses intelligence supplied by CORTEZ to arrange the assassination of Emil JACOBS.

Evidence is absent for a legal indictment, but CLARK and LARSON are able to exploit the cartel's distrust of him. They kidnap him and plant information suggesting that Escobedo was planning on betraying his surviving colleagues. Before leaving Colombia, the two CIA men turn Escobedo over to those colleagues, after which he is presumably tortured and executed.

E.S. POLITOVSKY: Soviet ALFA-class submarine. The first ALFA, her first captain was Marko RAMIUS. Under his command, she survived a high-speed collision with a whale.

Repaired, she is one of the Northern Fleet submarines sent after *RED OCTOBER.* After an excessive period of continuous high-speed running, she suffers a reactor meltdown due to the rupture of a coolant line, while being tracked by U.S.S. *POGY.* She sinks near the American coast, with the loss of all her crew except one, who is rescued by the Americans. Men who survived in the forward compartments have died from lack of air by the time the DSRV *AVALON* visits the wreck. It is expected by the Soviets that she will be salvaged by the Americans, using the deep-sea salvage ship *GLOMAR EXPLORER.*

ETHAN ALLEN, U.S.S.:   U.S. nuclear ballistic missile submarine, lead ship of a class of five; in service 1961. In *Hunt,* she is obsolete and awaiting scrapping. As part of Skip TYLER's plan for acquiring *RED OCTOBER,* she is taken to sea with a skeleton crew of officers and senior petty officers, into the area of the Soviet submarine, and there scuttled with FUEL-AIR EXPLOSIVE charges. The explosion and debris convincingly simulate the loss of *RED OCTOBER.*

She was Admiral GALLERY's first command, and he pays a final visit to her just before she sails on her last voyage.

EVANS, GUNNER'S MATE SECOND CLASS JEFF: In *Storm,* U.S. Navy petty officer, one of the missing aboard *PHARRIS.* Commander MORRIS visits the Evans home on leave and can't find words to tell four-year-old Ginny Evans why her father is never coming home.

EVANS, JOSEPH: In *Games,* a Yeoman Warder of the Tower, who gives the RYANs a special guided tour of the Tower of London.

F-1/IM BOOSTER: Soviet satellite launchers, three-stage versions of the SS-9 Scarp liquid-fuel ICBM. Payload 5 + tons. Scarp also usable in a FRACTIONAL ORBIT BOMBARDMENT SYSTEM. In *Storm,* F-series boosters launch various Soviet reconnaissance and "killer" satellites.

F-4 PHANTOM: U.S. twin-engined, two-seat jet fighter and fighter-bomber, carrier and land-based; McDonnell-Douglas. 1300 + mph; combat radius 500 miles; M-61 VULCAN cannon, wide variety of missiles and bombs. In service with U.S. Navy and Marines from 1961; widely exported, including Israel, West Germany, and Britain. The outstanding multirole combat aircraft of the postwar era; over 5,000 built and many expected to serve into the 21st century.

In *Hunt,* Dr. NOYES has traded medical care for pilots' families for backseat time in F-4s. In *Storm* they are still in service with many NATO units, including the New York Air National Guard, which sends WILD WEASEL F-4s to escort B-52s against Iceland. In *Games,* the PRINCE OF WALES mentions being rated in the Phantom.

The Phantom was also Robby JACKSON's first fighter, but by *Danger,* when he is CAG aboard *RANGER,* the only F-4 aboard is an engineless one used for training flight-deck crews. CLARK sees it while visiting the ship.

In *Sum,* the crash-landing of an F-4 returning from a mission over Suez distracts the officers watching over the nuclear-armed A-4. Busy rescuing the Phantom's crew, they forget to unload the Skyhawk's bomb before Lieutenant ZADIN takes off on a strike over the Golan Heights.

F-8 CRUSADER: U.S. single-engined, single-seat jet carrier-based fighter; Ling-Temco-Vought. Supersonic speed; four 20-mm cannon, air-to-air missiles. In service with U.S. Navy and Marines from 1957; with French Navy from late 1970s.

In *Storm,* F-8s from *FOCH* are on close-in CAP because of their short range. They are the only fighters of the *NIMITZ* battle group to engage the Soviet BACKFIREs, destroying six and damaging two more.

F-14 TOMCAT: U.S. twin-engined, two-seat carrier-based all-weather fighter; Grumman. 1500 mph; combat radius 800 miles; one 20-mm VULCAN cannon, AIM-54 PHOENIX and AIM-9 missiles. Variable-geometry ("swing") wings, advanced radar and other systems, including a nose-mounted magnifying TV camera for long-range target identification.

The Tomcat was developed as a fleet-defense fighter, defending the carrier battle groups at long ranges with the AIM-54 and at shorter ranges with guns, AIM-9s, or AIM-7 Sparrows. Thanks to the variable-geometry wings and broad fuselage, it is exceptionally maneuverable for a machine of its size, although early versions have proved somewhat underpowered. It entered U.S. Navy service in 1972; some were exported to Iran but are mostly out of service.

In *Hunt,* F-14s fly from most of the carriers deployed in the North

Atlantic. A flight from *KENNEDY's* VF-41 is accidentally engaged by FORGERs from *KIEV.* The Tomcat of the squadron CO, Robby JACK-SON, is hit and damaged; his RIO is seriously wounded.

In *Storm,* Tomcats have a busy war. *NIMITZ's* defend the battle group, although they are decoyed by the Soviet KELT missiles. After the carrier is damaged, they operate from British shore bases against Soviet bombers, using tactics suggested by Commander TOLAND. They also escort the second B-52 strike against Iceland, and provide part of the air cover for the Marine landing.

In *Games,* Robby JACKSON tells the PRINCE OF WALES that his squadron changed from Phantoms to Tomcats just as he was getting used to the older fighter. In *Danger,* JACKSON flies F-14s in support of the MEDELLIN raids and testing the AIM-54 missiles. (He hopes the bugs are out of them before they have to be fired against Iranian Tomcats.)

In *Sum,* JACKSON is still flying Tomcats, this time the improved F-14D. He and his wingmen engage both Libyan and Soviet MiG-29s during the crisis, scoring a total of six kills.

F-15 EAGLE: U.S. twin-engined, single or two-seat land-based air-superi-ority fighter/strike aircraft. 1500+ mph; combat radius 500+ miles (1,500 with CONFORMAL FUEL TANKS); VULCAN cannon, air-to-air mis-siles, wide variety of air-to-ground weapons. In service with U.S. Air Force from 1972; widely exported, including Japan, Israel, Saudi Arabia.

The Eagle was developed on the basis of the air-combat lessons of Viet-nam, and was the finest air-to-air combat machine in the world when it entered service. It was the first fighter in the world with a thrust-to-weight ratio greater than 1:1, thanks to the F100 engine.

The two-seat training versions are as capable as the single-seaters. The F-15 Strike Eagle entered service in 1988; its weapons payload is 15,000+ pounds with no loss of air-to-air capability.

In *Hunt,* F-15s are deployed in the Eastern U.S. against the Soviet fleet in the North Atlantic. Three F-15s carrying FAST CONFORMAL FUEL CELLS intercept Lieutenant SHAVROV's FORGER while he is approach-ing the E-3 AWACS and discourage him from getting any closer.

In *Storm,* Eagles are initially based on Iceland. Two of these strafe *JULIUS FUCIK* on their way to Britain. They also operate continuously and effectively in the air-superiority role over Germany.

Amy NAKAMURA shoots down three TU-16 BADGERs of the Soviet decoy force while ferrying an F-15 to Europe. She also flies Eagles on several ASAT missions, two of them successful.

In *Danger,* the F-15C is Bronco WINTERS's mount. Flying one, he shoots down a twin-engined Beech King Air drug smuggler, and forces a DC-7B to land. A prototype Strike Eagle flies Mark BRIGHT to Panama with his vital intelligence for rescuing the covert-operations troops; its performance frightens him.

In *Sum,* F-15s from Bitburg escort the F-16s on their reconnaissance mission over Berlin and are caught in the same Soviet missile ambush. Two are shot down.

F-16 FIGHTING FALCON: U.S. single-engined single-seat land-based jet air-superiority fighter; General Dynamics. 1300+ mph; combat radius 500 miles; VULCAN cannon, AIM-9 and similar missiles, 6,000+ pounds of air-to-ground weapons. In service with U.S. Air Force from 1978; widely exported, including Israel and Norway, and built in Europe under license. The first operational "fly-by-wire" (computerized controls) combat aircraft.

In *Hunt,* the Air Force offers a wing of F-16s to support the Navy's operations in the North Atlantic. In *Storm,* they are active with several air forces, including the Norwegian; a Norwegian F-16 shoots down one of the MiG-29s headed for Iceland.

In *Cardinal,* Pakistani F-16s arrive too late to deal with the Soviet SU-24s attacking the Pakistani refugee camp where the ARCHER is resting.

In *Sum,* a wing of F-16s is about to leave Ramstein Air Force Base in Germany when RYAN visits it. Another wing will be deployed in Sicily as part of U.S. support for the Mideast peace settlement. At least four F-16s are still at Ramstein during the crisis; they fly a hasty reconnaissance mission over Berlin and three are shot down by Soviet missiles.

F-19 GHOSTRIDER: In *Storm,* U.S. Air Force Stealth fighter, characteristics unspecified. Able to carry a wide variety of air-to-ground weapons as well as AIM-9 SIDEWINDER missiles. Poor flying characteristics; nickname is "Frisbee."

A squadron of F-19s under Colonel ELLINGTON has been secretly deployed to Germany before the war. It immediately goes into action in Operation DREAMLAND, against Soviet AWACS. The squadron continues in action throughout the war, repeatedly hitting Soviet targets in spite of heavy losses.

F-100:   U.S. single-engined, single-seat fighter and fighter-bomber: North American; in service 1957. The first U.S. combat aircraft supersonic in level flight. General BORSTEIN, acting CINC-NORAD during the crisis in *Sum,* started off flying F-100s.

F-104 STARFIGHTER: U.S. single-seat, single-engined land-based jet fighter; Lockheed. The first Western Mach 2 fighter; in service with U.S. Air Force 1958, but most produced for and served with NATO air forces (especially Germany) and Japan.

In *Storm,* General ALEXSEYEV sees one West German F-104 shot down and is wounded by flying glass after another drops an FAE bomb.

F-105 THUNDERCHIEF: U.S. single-engined single-seat fighter-bomber; Republic; in service 1961. Supersonic speed; 6,000 + lbs. of bombs. Originally intended to deliver nuclear weapons, it was the backbone of the Air Force's war against North Vietnam, 1965-68.

Colonel JOHNS in *Danger* won his MEDAL OF HONOR rescuing the crew of a downed WILD WEASEL F-105 in Laos. Secretary of Defense BUNKER in *Sum* flew three tours on F-105s.

F-111:   U.S. twin-engined, two-seat long-range strike aircraft; General Dynamics. 1400 mph; combat radius 900 miles; up to 20,000 lbs. of ordnance, including both nuclear and conventional bombs; in service with U.S. Air Force from 1969. Nicknamed "Aardvark" from its extended nose.

The result of a program originally intended to develop a common aircraft for the U.S. Navy and Air Force, the F-111 was controversial and suffered major development problems. It subsequently became an exceptionally effective low-altitude strike aircraft. A longer-range version, the FB-111, has served with SAC, and there is an electronic-warfare version, the EF-111 Raven.

In *Storm,* F-111s strike Soviet air bases as part of Operation DREAM-LAND. FB-111s carry out the second NATO strike against Iceland, with EF-111s jamming Soviet radars in support.

F-117 THE BLACK JET: U.S. twin-engined, two-seat Stealth fighter-bomber; Lockheed. 600 mph; combat radius 1,300 miles; 4,000 lbs. bombs; in service with U.S. Air Force from 1981; combat debut in Panama (1990) and Persian Gulf (1991). Unusual arrowhead configuration, extensive use of composite materials, and special engine design give it outstanding Stealth characteristics.

In *Sum,* F-117s are deployed in Germany. Their known ability to reach Moscow undetected, carrying nuclear weapons, increases tension among the Soviet leaders.

F/A-18 HORNET: U.S. twin-engined, single-seat carrier and land-based fighter-bomber; McDonnell-Douglas. 1200 mph; combat radius 500 miles; VULCAN cannon and 12,000 + lbs. ordnance, including air-to-air and air-to-ground missiles. In service with U.S. Navy and Marines from 1983, replacing the F-4 and A-7; exported to Canada and Australia.

In *Hunt, SARATOGA's* F-18s are landed, to give her room for more ASW S-3 VIKINGs. In *Storm,* three squadrons from the *INDEPENDENCE* battle group engage MiG-29s in a wild dogfight over Iceland, winning air superiority for NATO.

In *Games,* an F-18 flight-testing new equipment flies past the RYANs' home while they are entertaining the PRINCE AND PRINCESS OF WALES. In *Sum,* two squadrons of Hornets are part of *THEODORE ROOSEVELT's* air wing during the crisis.

FAIRING: Streamlined enclosure of a projection from the fuselage of an aircraft or the hull of a ship. In *Sum,* the copilot of the Marine VH-3 checks the landing-gear fairing for ice accumulation.

FALKEN, GERHARDT EUGEN: In *Storm,* alleged West German agent behind the Kremlin bombing. Almost certainly a Soviet mole, if not a complete invention.

FARMER, THE (unnamed):   Druse farmer, sixty-six years old, with a small farm near the Syrian-Lebanese border. A widower (wife killed by Israeli artillery in the Yom Kippur War), he has little money, few hopes, and only one surviving child, a one-armed Syrian Army veteran and shopkeeper.

He buries the misdropped A-bomb shortly after its fall. When it is thrust to the surface by years of frost heaves, his son recognizes its importance. Through the son's contacts with QATI, the Palestinians visit the farm, salvage the bomb, and reward father and son.

FEDERAL BUREAU OF INVESTIGATION: The principal U.S. national law-enforcement organization, a branch of the Department of Justice. In *Hunt* and *Cardinal* it handles espionage, in *Games* foreign terrorists operating in the U.S., in *Danger* the drug trade, and in *Sum* terrorism again. It cooperates with the Secret Service (a branch of the Department of the Treasury) and the CIA in security matters.

FEED-WATER PUMP: Aboard a ship, the pump which moves the purified water heated into steam by the boiler or reactor. The single largest source of noise aboard a nuclear submarine. In *Sum,* during her refit between patrols in the Gulf of Alaska, *ADMIRAL LUNIN* receives a new feed-water pump, large, clumsy, hard to maintain, but much quieter than her old one.

"FEET DRY"/"FEET WET":   The condition of an aircraft's passing from over water to over land, and the reverse. In *Danger,* Commander JENSEN's A-6 goes "feet wet" as it leaves Panamanian airspace, "feet dry" as it enters Colombian airspace.

FELLOWS, SAM: Mormon Congressman from Arizona, co-chairman with Al TRENT of the House Select Committee on Intelligence Oversight. In *Danger,* both query the PRESIDENT on the covert antidrug operations. In *Sum,* he is known to think highly of RYAN.

FENCER: Soviet fighter-bomber. See SU-24.

FEODOROV, CAPTAIN YEVGENIY STEPANOVICH: In *Sum,* KGB agent, a promising young officer sent to investigate Manfred FROMM's disappearance. Disguised as a journalist, he is captured, tortured, and executed (along with Traudl FROMM) by Erwin KEITEL. He is the son of a well-known KGB officer, Stepan Feodorov, and leaves a widow, Natalia. His disappearance increases concern among the Soviets investigating the East German nuclear-weapons program.

FFG-7 CLASS: U.S. *PERRY* (FFG-7)-class frigates, or "figs." Single-screw conventional missile frigates. 3,000/3,700 tons; 30 knots; 1 3" gun, HARPOON and STANDARD missiles, PHALANX, LAMPS, ASW TT; crew 220+. Fifty-one built for the U.S. Navy 1977-89, the largest class of postwar U.S. surface vessels. Primarily ASW ships, intended for convoy protection.

In *Hunt,* three *PERRYs* are assigned to support *INVINCIBLE.* In *Storm, REUBEN JAMES,* Commander MORRIS's second ship, is an FFG-7.

FIFE: British Royal Navy conventional guided-missile destroyer; in service early 1960s. In *Hunt,* she is one of *INVINCIBLE's* escorts.

FILITOV, COLONEL MIKHAIL SEMYONOVICH (MISHA):   Soviet Army officer and, under the name of CARDINAL, a CIA agent. A brilliant tank officer with an outstanding combat record in World War II (three times a Hero of the Soviet Union) and several wounds, he thought Soviet losses were excessive due to poor national leadership. He finally became alienated from the Soviet regime after the death of his wife and sons (one in combat in Hungary in 1956, one shortly afterward in a training accident caused by poorly manufactured tank ammunition).

He was recruited for the CIA by Oleg PENKOVSKIY in the early 1960s. At the opening of *Hunt* he has been an invaluable agent for many years and is personal aide to Minister of Defense USTINOV. A heavy drinker, he has also developed a heart condition.

In *Hunt,* he provides critical intelligence about the reason for the Soviet Fleet activities, then alarms the CIA by dropping out of sight for some time. This turns out to be nothing worse than a case of pneumonia, which he survives.

In *Cardinal,* Filitov provides even more critical intelligence, this time about the BRIGHT STAR laser-weapons project. In the process, the KGB is finally able to identify some of his contacts and bring him under suspicion. He is arrested, and subjected to the most severe interrogation his health will permit, including sophisticated psychological manipulation.

Jack RYAN blackmails KGB Chairman GERASIMOV into releasing FILITOV by threatening to expose the Chairman's failure over *RED OC-TOBER.* The colonel is given asylum in the United States, where he dies a few months later.

FILITOVA, ELENA: Wife of Colonel FILITOV. A beautiful and intelligent woman, she was a ballerina when she met young Lieutenant Filitov early in World War II. They had a happy marriage, which ended in the late 1950s when Elena died, essentially of grief at the loss of their sons.

FIT-REP (or FitRep):   Fitness report, U.S. Navy report by a superior officer on a subordinate's performance and suitability for promotion. In *Sum,* MANCUSO says he will ignore any bad FitRep Captain RICKS of *MAINE* may give Wally CLAGGETT for reporting on his skipper's bad habits.

FIVE BY FIVE: The clearest level of radio reception. In *Danger,* Bronco WINTERS receives the transmissions from the AWACS that clearly.

FLAMEOUT: Combustion ceasing in a jet or turbine engine, leading to the loss of all power. It can be caused by too little air or by water ingestion (as in *Danger,* with the rescue helicopter in the hurricane).

FLANKER: Soviet interceptor. See SU-27.

FLAPS: Aerodynamic controls on the wings of an airplane, adjustable to increase or decrease lift. In *Cardinal,* loss of hydraulic power to the AN-26's flaps begins the final loss of control.

FLEET: The highest subordinate command in the U.S., Soviet, and French navies, including ships, land- and sea-based aircraft, and shore facilities. The U.S. has four fleets: Second (Atlantic), Third (Pacific), Sixth

(Mediterranean), and Seventh (Asia and Indian Ocean). The Soviet Union has a Northern Fleet (Arctic), Black Sea Fleet, Baltic Fleet, and Pacific Fleet.

In *Hunt* and *Storm,* the major naval confrontation is between the Soviet Northern Fleet and the U.S. Second Fleet, acting as part of the NATO Atlantic Command. The Second Fleet is heavily reinforced by ships from the Third Fleet, including *REUBEN JAMES.* In *Sum, ADMIRAL LUNIN* is assigned to the Soviet Pacific Fleet.

FLOGGER: Soviet fighter-bomber. See MiG-23/27.

FLYNN, PATRICK: In *Storm,* AP Moscow Bureau chief. He covers the Soviet disarmament proposals, the Kremlin bombing, and the Soviet discovery of a "German spy."

FN: *Fabrique Nationale,* leading Belgian weapons manufacturer. Produces the BROWNING HI-POWER among other popular weapons.

FOCH: French aircraft carrier. 25,000/33,000 tons; 32 knots; 35 aircraft; crew 1,800. In service with French Navy 1963.

In *Storm, Foch* is one of the carriers in the *NIMITZ* battle group. Hit by several Soviet KINGFISH missiles in the BACKFIRE attack, she burns and sinks with the loss of more than half her crew.

FOLEY, EDWARD and **MARY PATRICIA KAMINSKY:**   A husband-and-wife team of CIA agents. In *Cardinal,* they are FILITOV's case officers, and do their best to transmit his data and protect his identity. It is Ed who detects the first KGB penetration of CARDINAL's chain of contacts, after an incident on the Moscow Metro.

Ed is of Irish descent, formerly a reporter for the *New York Times,* and press attaché at the American Embassy in Moscow. Mary is a granddaughter of the riding tutor to the son of NICHOLAS II and spoke Russian from childhood. She is also the aggressive, risk-taking, "cowboy" half of the pair—as witness her trying to contact FILITOV at one of her son's hockey games.

The Foleys have two children and are starting a third at the end of *Cardinal.* The son, Edward Foley II, is a good hockey player, and the children together are an important part of the Foleys' cover.

In *Sum,* we learn that Mary Pat recruited Oleg KADISHEV (SPINNAKER). She is also being considered for Deputy Director of Operations, a first for a woman, even though she has her third child, Emily Sarah Foley, during the course of the book.

FONTANA, LARRY: In *Games,* a Maryland State Police officer who pursues DOBBENS and MILLER after their attempt against Cathy RYAN. The terrorists fire on him as he overtakes the van; he is wounded, loses control, and dies in the ensuing crash.

FORGER: Soviet carrier-based VTOL fighter. See YAK-36/38.

***FORRESTAL,* U.S.S.:** U.S. conventional aircraft carrier. 60/80,000 tons; 33 knots; 70+ aircraft, PHALANX; crew 5,000. Lead ship of a class of four, in service with U.S. Navy 1955-59, the first "super-carriers" designed from the keel up to operate jet aircraft.

In *Cardinal, Forrestal* is "sunk" during fleet exercises by Marko RAMIUS, acting as captain of an American 688-CLASS submarine. Others of the class include *SARATOGA* in *Hunt* and *Storm, INDEPENDENCE* in *Storm,* and *RANGER* in *Danger.*

FORWARD EDGE OF THE BATTLE AREA (FEBA): The most advanced line at which one's major ground units are deployed. In *Storm,* the East Germans realize that even a limited chemical exchange along the FEBA will contaminate large areas of Germany for decades.

FOSTER, ADMIRAL DANIEL: In *Hunt,* U.S. Navy officer, the Chief of Naval Operations. He supports RYAN's hypothesis about *RED OCTOBER* against the PRESIDENT's skepticism. When *RED OCTOBER* reaches NORFOLK, he is one of the welcoming party, and requests RAMIUS's "permission to come aboard."

FOWLER, JONATHAN ROBERT: In *Danger,* candidate for President. In *Sum,* President of the United States. A widower, whose wife, Marian, died of multiple sclerosis while he was Governor of Ohio; lonely and less approachable after her death. Able and ambitious, he wants to leave behind a reputation as a peacemaker, but is not particularly scrupulous about the methods, careful about whose advice he takes, or stable in a crisis.

In *Danger,* he wins the Presidency by a narrow margin. In *Sum,* he is influenced by Elizabeth ELLIOT even before they become lovers, concerning Jack RYAN. He allows ELLIOT's campaign against RYAN to proceed more or less unhampered, up to the moment of the crisis caused by the nuclear explosion in Denver.

After that, Fowler's decision-making deteriorates rapidly. He refuses to leave CAMP DAVID, ignores RYAN's advice, and even goes along with ELLIOT's belief that NARMONOV may have been deposed by a military coup. After RYAN intervenes on the hot line to confirm NARMONOV's identity, he orders RYAN's arrest.

As the crisis ebbs, Fowler is seized with a desire for vengeance, and authorizes a missile strike on the city of QUM, home of the Ayatollah DARYEI. RYAN's refusal to confirm this authorization leads to a confrontation, followed by a constitutional crisis ending in Fowler's resignation in favor of Vice President Roger DURLING.

FOXBAT: Soviet interceptor. See MiG-25.

FOXHOUND: Soviet interceptor. See MiG-31.

FOXTROT: Soviet triple-screw conventional long-range submarine; more than eighty built for the Soviet Navy and friendly countries, 1958-84. The most successful Soviet conventional submarines.

By the time of *Storm,* Foxtrots are obsolete. But they are still deployed against the ATLANTIC BRIDGE, and *PHARRIS,* working with a P-3 ORION, sinks one defending her first convoy.

FRACTIONAL ORBIT BOMBARDMENT SYSTEM (FOBS):   A technique in which an ICBM warhead describes part of an orbit around the Earth before reentering. In *Storm,* a Soviet satellite launch using the same ICBM as the FOBS makes the Americans nervous for some time. In *Sum,* the possibility of an FOBS strike at Denver is considered.

FRAGS: Short for "fragmentation," a type of grenade intended to inflict casualties by disintegrating into small pieces. In *Danger,* CHAVEZ carries four Dutch-made grenades of this type.

FRANKLIN, SENIOR CHIEF OCEANOGRAPHIC TECHNICIAN DUKE: U.S. Navy petty officer. In *Hunt,* he is one of the senior console operators at SOSUS Atlantic Control and nearly the first man in the *RED OCTOBER* crisis to detect unusual behavior by Soviet submarines.

FREMONT, GENERAL PETER: In *Sum,* CINC-SAC (Commander in Chief, Strategic Air Command). President FOWLER tends to ignore his advice before the crisis. During the crisis the General performs outstandingly, opposing impractical suggestions from Elizabeth ELLIOT about partial alerts.

By the time the crisis is over, he has begun to suspect that FOWLER is not quite stable. His insistence on the confirmation of the President's strike order against QUM gives RYAN the chance to intervene by refusing the confirmation. Afterward, it is Fremont who sets up a conference call with the Vice President and relevant Senate and House members to meet the constitutional crisis.

FRENZA, CAPTAIN NIKOLAI: In *Games,* captain of the Cypriot-registered freighter *COSTANZA.* Clearly not an innocent party, he has to be intimidated by the Maryland State Police into letting them search his ship.

FROMM, DOCTOR MANFRED: In *Sum,* German engineer and terrorist. Formerly chief engineer for the East German nuclear-weapons program, Fromm has also provided Günther BOCK and other terrorist groups with technical information. It is BOCK who recruits Fromm for the project of rebuilding and improving the captured Israeli nuclear weapon.

Fromm travels to the Middle East and is indispensable to the whole bomb project, designing the new fusion mechanism, procuring tools, and training key workers. When GHOSN convinces QATI that he, GHOSN, can finish the bomb on his own, Fromm is executed.

FROMM, TRAUDL: In *Sum,* Manfred FROMM's wife. Somewhat estranged from her husband, she is reconciled to his departure (allegedly for Argentina) by the extra income. Under surveillance by Erwin KEITEL's men, she is interrogated and executed along with Captain FEODOROV.

FRONTAL AVIATION: The branch of the Soviet Air Force operating in support of the Soviet Army's ground forces. In *Storm,* CINC-West worries about the readiness of his Frontal Aviation pilots (among other things). In *Cardinal,* its reconnaissance units protect the BRIGHT STAR facilities by conducting training exercises over the valleys in the area.

FUEL AIR EXPLOSIVE (FAE): A weapon which dispenses an aerosol cloud of highly explosive vapor, which is then detonated. Theoretically up to ten times as powerful as TNT.

In *Hunt,* four FAE bombs are loaded aboard *ETHAN ALLEN,* then filled from tank trucks alongside. They are later used to scuttle the ship, simulating a reactor explosion aboard *RED OCTOBER.* In *Storm,* General ALEXSEYEV is wounded by flying glass from the explosion of an FAE bomb dropped by a German F-104.

FUENTES, LUIS: In *Danger,* a MEDELLÍN cartel leader not present for the first bombing. At the time of the second strike he is planning a strategy meeting with ESCOBEDO, who is delayed by an attempt on his life. This delay saves ESCOBEDO's life; Fuentes is not so lucky.

FULCRUM: Soviet interceptor. See MiG-29.

FULDA GAP: The valley of the Fulda River in West Germany, the easiest east-west route for armored forces in otherwise hilly or wooded country. In *Storm,* the Soviets expect that Operation Zhukov would have them hitting this area before NATO was alert.

GALAXY: U.S. strategic transport. See C-5.

GALLERY, **U.S.S.:**   U.S. Navy frigate, FFG-7 class, in service 1981. She is part of *PHARRIS's* escort group on all three of her convoys.

GALLERY, VICE ADMIRAL VINCENT: In *Hunt,* U.S. Navy officer, COMSUBLANT (Commander, Submarine Forces, Atlantic). He provides most of the submarine support for the *RED OCTOBER,* operation. This includes *ETHAN ALLEN,* his first command, which he visits before she leaves on her last voyage. A crusty man and a dedicated professional, he pulled strings to get MANCUSO command of *DALLAS* much younger than usual.

GAME, THE: The annual Army-Navy football game. In *Games,* Jack RYAN describes Navy's victory in loving detail to Skip TYLER, a former Navy fullback.

GARCIA, PRIVATE: In *Storm,* U.S. Marine, one of EDWARDS's patrol throughout. He speaks Spanish, kills one of the KGB rapists, and is wounded in the patrol's final action before rescue.

GAZ-69:   A standard light truck of the Soviet Army from 1950s; payload ¾ ton. In *Sum,* BOCK and KEITEL use one in Berlin when they are impersonating Soviet officers to provoke an incident with the Americans.

GAZELLE: French-built turbine-powered German scout helicopter in service from late 1960s. In *Storm,* they launch antitank missiles at Soviet units in support of Sergeant MACKALL's platoon.

GBU-15 PAVEWAY: U.S. guided bomb, made by attaching optical or infrared guidance packages and fins to a standard 2,000-lb. Mark 84 low-drag bomb. In service with U.S. air arms from 1970s.
    In *Storm,* an F-111 drops a GBU-15 on a bridge laser-illuminated by Colonel ELLINGTON's F-19. In *Danger,* the GBU-15's laser guidance package is attached to the Hush-a-Bomb.

GENERAL SECRETARY: The leader of the Communist Party of the Soviet Union, elected by the Politburo; often de facto ruler of the Soviet Union (as with Joseph STALIN and Nikita KHRUSHCHEV).

In *Storm,* the unnamed incumbent is an elderly compromiser, who successively accepts the need of war, the execution of unsuccessful commanders, and the proposed use of nuclear weapons. He is presumably arrested along with the rest of the Kremlin leadership during the ALEXSEYEV-SERGETOV coup.

GEORGE MCREADY, M.V.: Diesel-propelled cargo vessel. In *Games,* she is in the port of Baltimore at the same time as *Costanza.* In *Sum,* she is carrying as deck cargo four massive Douglas fir logs to Japan to rebuild a temple. During a storm in the Gulf of Alaska, a freak wave washes the logs overboard, where they become a submerged menace to navigation and eventually collide with *MAINE.*

GEORGIA, U.S.S.: *OHIO*-class submarine, in service 1984. In *Hunt,* the cover story for *RED OCTOBER's* escort is that they are protecting the disabled *GEORGIA.* In *Sum,* MANCUSO mentions having failed to track her while he was XO of *HAMMERHEAD.*

GEOSYNCHRONOUS ORBIT: An orbit in which a satellite appears to remain over the same spot on the Earth's surface. In *Storm,* an early-warning satellite in such an orbit is the first to detect the Nizhnevartovsk refinery fire.

GERASIMOV, NIKOLAY: Chairman of the KGB. At the time of *Cardinal,* he is fifty-three, young for the post which he has occupied four years. A tough, ambitious man, a Party rather than an intelligence professional. One of his goals appears to be settling the old conflict between the armed forces and the KGB in favor of the KGB. Another is becoming leader of the Soviet Union. Married to Maria Ivanova Gerasimov; they have one daughter, Katryn. Both ladies are comfortable with the privileges of the Soviet elite.

In *Hunt,* Gerasimov is newly in office and vigorously exploits the *RED OCTOBER* incident. Among other arrangements he makes is turning Yuri PADORIN into a KGB spy in the Navy Ministry.

In *Cardinal,* his ambitions for the top post are open. He plans to use the exposure of CARDINAL as a weapon against his chief rival, NARMONOV, and his supporter VANEYEV. Jack RYAN confronts the KGB chief with evidence that *RED OCTOBER* actually fell into American hands, and that the KGB has been fed incorrect information about the American arms-control proposals.

GERASIMOV's first response is the kidnapping of Major GREGORY, hoping that this intelligence coup will save his position. After GREGORY's rescue and VANEYEV's continued support of NARMONOV, the KGB chief knows he is finished.

RYAN then offers help in defecting in return for the release of Colonel FILITOV. Thanks to some fast footwork, both the KGB chief and FILITOV are able to board the plane carrying the U.S. disarmament negotiating team and fly to safety; John CLARK gets the chairman's family safely aboard *DALLAS*.

GERASIMOV provides invaluable intelligence, but he and his wife have trouble adjusting to their new country. Daughter Katryn does not; she is last reported to be "working on a tan."

GHOSN, IBRAHIM: In *Sum,* Palestinian terrorist, one of the two leaders of the plot behind the Denver nuclear explosion. The youthful-looking, fair-skinned child of Palestinians who left Israel when the country was founded, he is one of the Popular Front for the Liberation of Palestine's experts on explosives and electronics. He is also an expert at technical reconnaissance, but is too valuable to risk in front-line combat. He nearly earned an engineering degree at the American University of Beruit, and has gone on teaching himself engineering in his own laboratories. Although an observant Moslem, he is more tolerant than QATI, and better able to work with non-Moslems like Marvin RUSSELL.

QATI sends him to identify the bomb mentioned by the FARMER's son, and recognizes it as a nuclear weapon. He persuades QATI to make the full-scale effort involved in repairing and improving the bomb, and works with Manfred FROMM in obtaining tools, training workers, and performing delicate operations. Ghosn's belief that he can finish the last stages of the work himself is the signal for FROMM's death. (In fact, he is responsible for the contamination of the tritium in the bomb that limits its yield and makes it possible to suspect a terrorist device rather than a Soviet attack.)

After the completion of the bomb, he arranges for its transportation by sea to the United States, and with Marvin RUSSELL, for its transportation to Denver by long-distance truck. He and QATI together kill RUSSELL, fuse the bomb, and leave Denver. Arrested in Mexico City by CLARK and CHAVEZ, he is interrogated on the flight home.

In the absence of a Federal death penalty, he is turned over to the Saudi Arabian government. He is ceremonially beheaded, with RYAN, GOLOVKO, and BEN JACOB as witnesses.

Like his partner QATI, a dangerous opponent and an able man—but not quite as good as he thinks he is.

GIANNINI, AUGIE: In *Cardinal,* diplomatic courier bringing CARDINAL data from Moscow to Washington. A retired Army warrant officer who won the DSC and four Purple Hearts as a medevac helicopter pilot in Vietnam.

GLOMAR EXPLORER: U.S. Salvage ship. 63,000 tons; 11 knots; in service with CIA 1974. Built to salvage a Soviet *GOLF*-class missile submarine from more than three miles down in the Pacific, and succeeded in salvaging part of her. In reserve at the time of *Hunt,* but the Russians expect that she will be recommissioned to salvage the *E.S. POLITOVSKY.*

GOLDMARK, RABBI ELEAZAR: In *Sum,* Israeli religious militant. A survivor of Auschwitz, he is one of the leaders of the march to the Temple Mount that leads to the shooting incident with the Palestinian demonstrators.

GOLF CLASS: Soviet conventional ballistic missile submarine. Three missiles; twenty-one built 1958-62. Based on the FOXTROT class. One lost in the Pacific 1968; partly salvaged 1974 by *GLOMAR EXPLORER.*

GOLOVKO, SERGEY NIKOLAYEVICH: Soviet intelligence officer, later second-in-command of the KGB.

In *Cardinal,* he is a colonel; one of his assignments is surveillance of the U.S. arms-control team. Here he meets Jack RYAN. He is also brought in on the investigation of FILITOV, eventually realizing what GERASIMOV is planning after comparing notes with Colonel VATUTIN. Golovko's desperate effort to stop the plane are foiled by RYAN.

In *Sum,* Golovko is First Deputy Chairman of the KGB. He makes a well-publicized visit to RYAN at CIA headquarters to obtain information about parliamentary oversight of intelligence operations. Returning to Russia, he learns of Captain FEODOROV's disappearance and begins investigation of a possible link between the East German nuclear-weapons program and the international terrorist underground.

During the crisis he provides invaluable moderating advice to NARMONOV and helps identify RYAN when the American breaks into the hot line. He also cooperates with the CIA and the Israelis in locating the secret bomb laboratory, and is a witness at GHOSN's execution.

GOODLEY, BEN: In *Sum,* one of Jack RYAN's assistants. A postdoctoral fellow at Harvard's Kennedy School of Government, he has done impressive analyses of the Cuban missile crisis.

Although brilliant, he is not a "Cold Warrior" and somewhat naive about government operations. This makes him susceptible to Elizabeth

ELLIOT's manipulation; he provides some of the classified information about RYAN's activities which she uses in her campaign against him.

By the time of the crisis, however, Goodley has realized his mistake and his loyalty to RYAN. He remains at his post, tries to calm his boss, and eventually drives him to the Pentagon for his intervention on the hot line.

GORSHKOV, ADMIRAL SERGEY GEORGIYEVICH: Historical character, 1910-1988. After a distinguished wartime career commanding Navy units supporting the Red Army, he was the Commander in Chief of the Soviet Navy from 1956 to 1985. Under his leadership the Soviet Navy expanded enormously in size and capabilities. One of the major postwar world naval leaders and one of the major figures in Russian naval history. A prolific author; one of his books mentions using lighter ships like *JULIUS FUCIK* in *Storm* for amphibious landings.

In *Hunt,* the *RED OCTOBER* defection places Gorshkov (one of RAMIUS's patrons) in an embarrassing position before the Politburo, most of whom have no use for the Navy anyway. In spite of his best efforts to track the errant submarine, in the end he fails, and internal security for the Navy is transferred to the KGB under GERASIMOV. Gorshkov remains in office strictly on the KGB man's suffrance, and is eventually dismissed when no longer useful.

GRAYSON, DOREEN and **NOREEN:** In *Danger,* eighteen-year-old identical twin prostitutes in Mobile, Alabama. Their lovers, the PATTERSON brothers, killed their pimp after he beat them, and are in jail for that death when recruited by the police to dispose of the *EMPIRE BUILDER* murderers.

GREAT MOTHERLAND WAR: Also translated "Great Patriotic War." The Soviet name for World War II, used several times by Colonel FILITOV in *Hunt* and *Cardinal.*

GREENLAND–ICELAND–UNITED KINGDOM GAP (G.I. UK.):   The line extending from Greenland to the northern tip of the British Isles. NATO strategy calls for defending it against Soviet attempts to reach the North Atlantic, by air, submarine, or surface vessel. In *Hunt,* the Soviets develop their submarine tactics of running the underwater canyons in the area as one way of countering NATO defenses. In *Storm,* they breach the defenses directly by seizing Iceland.

GREER, VICE ADMIRAL JAMES: Deputy Director (Intelligence) at the CIA. Sixty-six at the time of *Hunt.* He began his naval service aboard the battleship *TEXAS,* then went to Annapolis. He later served in submarines, then specialized in intelligence, going to the CIA after retirement. A widower; one son, Robert White Greer, graduated from Annapolis and was killed in Vietnam as a Marine lieutenant. Jack RYAN's recruiter, mentor, and second father. Lonely, brilliant, indefatigable, with a strong moral sense and a diplomatic streak, he does his best to discourage RYAN's sharp tongue and Irish temper.

In *Hunt,* he receives RYAN's British-supplied intelligence about *RED OCTOBER,* then backs his evaluation of the situation. With Judge MOORE, he directs the CIA's contribution to the *RED OCTOBER* crisis. At the end, he reluctantly goes against the code of the sea by refusing for security reasons to consider rescuing possible survivors of *V.K. KONOVO-LOV.*

In *Games,* he quickly recognizes RYAN's aptitude for a more active role with the CIA than consultant. He skillfully appeals to RYAN's concern for his family's safety to involve him progressively deeper in CIA work.

In *Cardinal,* he authorizes RYAN's blackmail of GERASIMOV as a last-ditch effort to save FILITOV. By the time of *Danger,* he is hospitalized with terminal pancreatic cancer. He dies while RYAN is on the rescue mission in Colombia, and is buried at ARLINGTON NATIONAL CEMETERY.

GREGORY, MAJOR ALAN: In *Cardinal,* U.S. scientist. Twenty-nine years old, apparently a complete nerd, short, thin, and acne-pocked, he is actually a West Pointer and a brilliant theoretical physicist. He is engaged to Candi LONG, who forgives him many things, including his appetite for junk food.

Gregory is indispensable to the American SDI program. So he is kidnapped by KGB agents under Tania BISYARINA, on orders from Chairman GERASIMOV, who hopes to save his position by this intelligence coup. He is rescued by the FBI, whose snipers have unusual orders to shoot the KGB agents on sight, regardless of danger to Gregory.

He finally meets FILITOV after the Colonel's rescue. After hearing of FILITOV's death, Gregory and Candi plan to name their first child "Michael" after him.

GREVILLE, CAPTAIN WILLIAM: In *Games,* SAS officer, the son of a peer, assigned as bodyguard and escort to the RYANs during their travels in England after Jack gets out of the hospital.

GREYHOUND: U.S. COD transport. See C-2A.

GRIGGS, MAJOR: In *Sum,* U.S. Army officer from the Rocky Mountain Arsenal, first military man on the scene of the Denver nuclear explosion. A weapons specialist, he brings in a Nuclear Emergency Search team (NEST) to begin the investigation of the explosion.

GRISHA (NATO code name):   Soviet conventional corvettes. 850/1150 tons; 30 knots; light guns and ASW weapons, including rocket launchers. Sixty-plus built from 1968 on, many for KGB Maritime Border Guard.

AMETIST in *Storm* is a KGB-manned Grisha II. Aboard *DALLAS* in *Cardinal,* Marko RAMIUS expects to meet Grishas patrolling the Estonian coast. On the way out from picking up CLARK and GERASIMOV's family, they do meet one, but RAMIUS convinces the captain that *DALLAS* is Russian.

GROTON, **U.S.S.:**   688-class submarine, in service 1978. She participates in Operation DOOLITTLE.

GROUND-BURST: Detonation of a nuclear weapon at ground level, like the Denver explosion in *Sum.* Usually less effective than an air burst.

GROVES, **U.S.S.:**   In *Storm,* U.S. missile frigate, escorting the *REUBEN JAMES* convoy, probably an FFG-7. She fires a missile at a reconnaissance BEAR during one of the BACKFIRE raids.

GRU: *Glavnoe Razvedyvatelnoe Upravlanie* (Main Intelligence Organization). The Soviet military-intelligence organization, controlled by the Soviet General Staff and roughly corresponding to the U.S. DEFENSE INTELLIGENCE AGENCY. It has no internal-security functions but a great many activities in foreign areas, where it is an unfriendly rival of the KGB. Among its other resources is control of the *SPETSNAZ* troops and their COVERT operations, such as the abortive sabotage at the opening of *Storm.*

GSG-9:   *Grenzschutzgruppe* (Border Police Group) 9. Elite German counterterrorist unit, formed 1972 after the Munich Olympics terrorist attack. In *Storm,* they are considered as a counter to *SPETSNAZ* operations. A team of five arrested Günther BOCK's wife, Petra, before the opening of *Sum.*

GUADALCANAL, **U.S.S.:**   U.S. Navy conventional helicopter carrier, sister ship of *Guam,* in service 1963. In *Danger,* a CH-53E from this ship lifts the communications van for the covert-operations troops to its site in Panama.

GUAM, **U.S.S.:** U.S. Navy conventional carrier, lead ship of a class of seven; in service 1965. 19,000 tons; 20 knots; carries a battalion of Marines and 25+ helicopters to land them.

Jack RYAN served aboard her during his brief career as a Marine officer. In *Storm,* she participates in the Marine landing in Iceland.

GUANTÁNAMO: U.S. Navy and Marine base at the eastern end of Cuba. Nickname "Gitmo." In *Danger,* Colonel CORTEZ is turned over to the Cubans there.

GUARDS: Soviet designation for an elite unit (ARMY, DIVISION, or REGIMENT). Usually conferred for outstanding performance in combat. Guards units formerly received extra pay and priority on new equipment. All Soviet paratroop units (including the 76th Guards Airborne, which seizes Iceland in *Storm*) are Guards units.

GULFSTREAM: U.S. twin-turboprop/jet executive transport; Grumman, later Gulfstream America. Four models, introduced successively from 1959 through 1980s; later ones are the only business jets with intercontinental range.

In *Games,* South African arms dealer Erik MARTENS has a G-3. At the end of *Cardinal,* FILITOV and GERASIMOV fly from Ireland to the U.S. aboard a VC-20A, a converted Gulfstream 3. In *Games,* Emil JACOBS flies to Colombia aboard another VC-20A.

GUTTA-PERCHA: A substance made from the dehydrated sap of certain trees found in the Malay peninsula. Used for insulating electrical wires before the development of plastics. In *Games,* it is the plastic insulation the wires of a bug found among older wiring that tips off COOLEY.

HALLSTON, BOB: In *Games,* Yeoman Warder of the Tower and former SAS sergeant. With Joseph EVANS, he gives the RYANs a private tour of the Tower of London.

HAMMERHEAD, **U.S.S.:** U.S. nuclear attack submarine, in service 1968. In *Sum,* Bart MANCUSO remembers being XO of the submarine when she failed to track an *OHIO.*

HARD-TARGET-KILL CAPABILITY: The ability of a missile, through CEP and warhead yield, to destroy protected ("hard" or "hardened") targets. In *Cardinal,* the Soviets are worried that the Global Positioning Satellites may give the U.S. Navy's TRIDENT D-5 missiles that power against Soviet ICBM silos.

HARPOON: U.S. antiship missile. 1,200-1,500 lbs.; 570 mph; 60-80 miles range; 480-lb. conventional warhead. Exists in air, ship, and submarine-launched versions; in service with U.S. forces from 1976, and widely exported.

In *Hunt,* the B-52s orbiting the Soviet surface forces carry the air-to-ground Harpoon. In the final engagement around *RED OCTOBER, POGY* has two of her tubes loaded with the submarine-launched version.

In *Storm,* a P-3 ORION launches Harpoons against *JULIUS FUCIK.* One fails to ignite; the other hits, inflicting serious but not fatal damage. *CHICAGO* carries a mixed load of Harpoons, MARK 48 torpedoes, and TOMAHAWKs; in her engagement with the Soviet amphibious group she sinks a Soviet destroyer with the missiles.

HARRIER: U.S. and British Vertical Takeoff and Landing (VTOL) fighter and attack aircraft; McDonnell-Douglas/BAC. 700+ mph; combat radius 300-700 miles; cannon and 5,000-9,000 pounds of ordnance, including air-to-air missiles. In service with British RAF and Fleet Air Arm from 1969; U.S. Marines from 1971. AV-8B (built by McDonnell-Douglas) with higher performance in service with Marines from 1985. The world's first operational VTOL combat aircraft, the first one to see combat (the Falklands War, where it was indispensable), and still the best of its kind.

In *Hunt,* AV-8Bs are based aboard *TARAWA* to give her some attack capability as well as ASW. Jack RYAN flies in a Royal Navy Harrier from *KENNEDY* to *INVINCIBLE,* having his second hair-raising airplane flight within days.

In *Storm,* Marine Harriers provide close air support for the Marine landing on Iceland.

HARRIS, LIEUTENANT GENERAL EDWIN: In *Hunt,* U.S. Marine general, Director of Operations for the Joint Chiefs of Staff. An ex-football player, he plays peacemaker among the brass and pushes Skip TYLER's proposal for acquiring *RED OCTOBER* without her crew knowing about it.

HASSLER-BOCK, PETRA: In *Sum,* wife of Günther BOCK and his partner in their terrorist activities. Fanatical and ruthless, she is personally responsible for at least three murders, including one by castration, and has had an affair with Ismael QATI.

Arrested by GSG-9 and convicted with the help of material from East German files, she is sentenced to life imprisonment. Her twin daughters, Erika and Ursel, are adopted by a Federal German police officer and his wife. After seeing a film of the girls with their new parents, she is deliberately left unsupervised, and in a fit of depression commits suicide. Her well-publicized suicide helps push Günther BOCK into his alliance with the Palestinians.

H-BLOCKS: The maximum-security areas of regular British prisons, holding the IRA prisoners Kevin O'DONNELL in *Games* plans to free by kidnapping the PRINCE AND PRINCESS OF WALES.

HEAT: High-Explosive Anti-Tank. A type of tank-gun ammunition relying on a shaped charge, which projects a thin jet of hot gas through the target's armor. In *Storm,* Sergeant MACKALL's tank disables a Soviet commander's T-80 with a HEAT round that wrecks the engine.

HELIX: Soviet Navy ASW helicopter. See KA-27.

HELLFIRE: U.S. AGM-114 antitank guided missile; Rockwell. Laser-guided; the main armament of the AH-64 APACHE attack helicopter; in service with U.S. Army from 1986.

In *Storm,* APACHEs supporting Lieutenant MACKALL's counterattacking tanks use Hellfires against Soviet armored forces. In *Sum,* the U.S. agrees to supply Hellfires to Israel as part of the peace agreement.

HENDERSON, PETER: Chief aide to Senator DONALDSON and Soviet agent. He began dealing with the Soviets after the Kent State shootings in 1969 and was eventually entrapped into becoming a full-scale agent under the code name CASSIUS. He was responsible for the betrayal and execution of at least one major CIA agent in the Soviet armed forces.

In *Hunt,* he passes on the CIA's cover story about *RED OCTOBER* to the Soviets, thereby exposing himself. Arrested by the FBI soon afterward, he is offered the choice of life imprisonment or turning double agent, and accepts the latter. His treason is used to induce Senator DONALDSON, a longtime critic of the CIA, to retire from public life.

In *Cardinal,* Henderson is used to feed the KGB the cover story about RYAN being under investigation for insider trading. His case officer, FBI Special Agent Helen LOOMIS, says he may earn his way out of his suspended life sentence if this works.

HERO OF THE SOVIET UNION: The highest combat award of the Soviet armed forces, equivalent to the MEDAL OF HONOR. Its emblem is a large gold star.

Colonel FILITOV in *Hunt* and *Cardinal* has three Gold Stars, one of the few Soviet soldiers ever to win so many. This is one of the main reasons his superiors are slow to suspect him of treason. In *Storm,* General ALEX-

SEYEV awards the Gold Star to the engineer major responsible for the bridge at Alfeld.

HEZBOLLAH: Extreme Shiite group in Lebanon, considered pro-Iranian and claiming to hold many Western hostages. In *Sum,* the bomb workshop is established in what used to be one of Hezbollah's underground command posts.

HIGHLAND, SERGEANT BOB: In *Games,* British police officer, from the antiterrorist branch of the Metropolitan Police, C-13. Married, with four children.

He takes Maureen DWYER into custody and helps investigate the origins of the tip that led to her arrest. At Brixton Prison, he breaks up the rape of Sean MILLER by two non-political criminals. Escorting MILLER from Brixton Prison to the maximum-security facility on the Isle of Wight, he is severely wounded by the man he rescued. First-aid by the veterinarian and the timely arrival of the Royal Navy surgeon by helicopter save his life. Although still walking with difficulty, he has returned to duty in time to help discover Geoffrey WATKINS's body after the man's suicide.

HIGH-MOBILITY MULTI-WHEEL VEHICLE: HMMWV or Hummer/Humm-Vee, U.S. all-wheel-drive utility vehicle, able to carry troops, cargo, or antitank and antiaircraft weapons; in service 1980s.

In *Danger,* one is used in the final training exercise of the covert-action troops. In *Sum,* they are used by the Swiss Guard peacekeeping force in Jerusalem.

HIND: Soviet attack helicopter. See MI-24.

HIP: Soviet transport helicopter. See MI-8/17.

HOLTZMAN, BOB: Senior White House correspondent for one of the Washington papers. He has the good journalist's eye for a hot story, but also an honest man's distaste for being manipulated for somebody else's gain.

In *Danger,* he has an off-the-record background interview with Admiral CUTTER, who is trying to strengthen the cover story and reassure the public after the first MEDELLIN bombing.

In *Sum,* Elizabeth ELLIOT's leaks give him the story of RYAN's being suspected of both financial and sexual irregularities. Confronted by CLARK with evidence that the charges are false, Holtzman realizes that he has been manipulated. In return for CLARK's promise to give him an exclusive on the Colombian rescue mission in five years, Holtzman tracks down the source of the leaks he used and exposes ELLIOT's part in the whole affair.

His wife, Libby, has a spectacular figure, which Cathy RYAN notes when they meet at the party where Cathy has her confrontation with ELLIOT.

HONOLULU, U.S.S.:   U.S. nuclear attack submarine, 688-class, in service 1985. In *Sum,* Captain ROSSELLI was her CO for two and a half years, and upheld her high reputation.

HOSKINS, SPECIAL-AGENT-IN-CHARGE WALTER "WALT":   In *Sum,* senior FBI agent. He is in charge at the farmhouse confrontation in which John RUSSELL is killed. Inept at field work, he allows the affair to become a media circus, then further mishandles the situation so that sniper PAULSON has to go into action.

After this, retiring him is considered. But Hoskins is brilliant at handling fraud and financial crimes, and is transferred to the Denver office. He is in the middle of several successful investigations when the nuclear incident takes place. He survives, although badly shaken, and his report of being alive when he ought to be dead reinforces suspicions about the bomb's yield.

HOT: French-German wire-guided antitank missile; vehicle and helicopter mounted; in service 1977. Equivalent to the U.S. TOW. In *Storm,* Sergeant MACKALL sees the Germans using them in the fighting around Bieben.

HOT LZ: A landing area for helicopters that has come under hostile fire. In *Games,* the ULA creates one at the RYANs' house for the FBI Hostage Rescue Team helicopter, using automatic weapons and a REDEYE missile.

HUEY: U.S. utility helicopter. See UH-1.

HUNTER, CAPTAIN (no first name):   In *Hunt,* Royal Navy officer, Admiral WHITE's fleet operations officer. He works with RYAN in arranging for interception and contact with *RED OCTOBER.*

IDENTIFICATION, FRIEND/FOE (IFF):   A transponder mounted aboard aircraft which automatically sends a coded authentication when interrogated by the appropriate radar.

In *Hunt,* a B-52 pilot switches his IFF from military to commercial, to make his plane appear to be an airliner on the radars of the Soviet ships. In *Storm,* Major NAKAMURA's IFF interrogates the Soviet BADGERS and proves they aren't friendly.

In *Danger,* Commander JENSEN flips on his IFF transponder when his A-6 enters Colombian air space on the first raid. In *Sum,* ZADIN is warned about checking his IFF before he takes off on his last flight.

IGNATIEV, GENERAL YEVGENIY: In *Cardinal,* Soviet officer, chief of the GRU counterespionage branch. He tries to discourage Colonel VATU-TIN from pursuing the investigation of FILITOV, to avoid embarrassing the Army by the exposure of such a hero's treason.

IL-38 (NATO codename MAY):   Soviet four-turboprop land-based ASW aircraft, based on the Il-18 airliner; in service with Soviet Navy from 1970. Resembles the P-3 ORION but is less capable. In *Storm,* Il-38s are part of the Soviet ASW effort in the opening stages of the war; *CHICAGO* is forced to dive by one.

IL-62 (NATO code name CLASSIC):   Soviet four-engined jet airliner; Ilyushin Bureau. Rear-mounted engines, 150+ passengers, intercontinental range. In service with AEROFLOT and other Soviet-bloc airlines since 1967. In *Hunt,* an Il-62 is sent to Dulles International Airport to fly home the returning survivors of *RED OCTOBER.*

IL-76 (NATO code names CANDID/MAINSTAY):   Soviet four-engine strategic jet transport/AWACS aircraft. 500 mph; range 3,000 miles; 75,000+ lbs. cargo/120+ troops or paratroops. In service with Soviet Air Force, AEROFLOT, allied countries from 1975. Strongly resembles the C-141 STARLIFTER, as EDWARDS points out in *Storm,* but has better rough-field and takeoff performance.

The MAINSTAY AWACS entered service in the early 1980s but is inferior to the E-3 SENTRY. There is also an aerial-refueling version, the Il-78 Midas.

In *Storm,* CANDIDs do the major work in the airlift of the 76th Guards Airborne Division into Iceland. The MAINSTAY AWACS are a major target of Operation DREAMLAND; five are shot down by F-19s (including one by Colonel ELLINGTON), severely crippling Soviet air defense and allowing heavy attacks on Soviet air bases.

IL-86 (NATO code name CAMBER):   Soviet jet airliner; Ilyushin Bureau; in service with AEROFLOT 1980. The first Soviet wide-bodied, turbofan-powered airliner.

In *Storm,* Mikhail SERGETOV flies in one from Nizhnevartovsk to Moscow to make his report on the oil field disaster.

ILLUSTRIOUS, **H.M.S.:**   British Royal Navy conventional aircraft carrier, *INVINCIBLE* class; in service 1982. In *Storm,* she is part of the escort for the Marine landing in Iceland, and works with the AEGIS cruiser *Bunker Hill.* She is damaged by an SS-N-19 missile fired by the OSCAR, which is subsequently attacked and forced to the surface by *REUBEN JAMES* and *BATTLEAXE.*

IMAM: Islamic religious teacher. In *Cardinal,* an unnamed imam is a major inspiration to the ARCHER. In *Sum,* the imam of the principal mosque in Jerusalem is one of the religious triumvirate supervising the peace settlement.

INCHON, **U.S.S.:**   U.S. Navy conventional helicopter carrier, sister ship of *GUAM;* in service 1970. In *Storm,* she is part of the amphibious force retaking Iceland.

INDEPENDENCE, **U.S.S.:**   U.S. conventional aircraft carrier, *FORRESTAL* class; in service 1959. In *Storm,* she operates in the Atlantic in defense of the Atlantic convoys. She is then the flagship of Strike Fleet Atlantic, defending the landing in Iceland while continuing to oppose Soviet attacks on the convoys.

Her fighters engage Soviet bombers and help win air superiority over the MiG-29s based on Iceland. Her attack aircraft support the Marines. Robert TOLAND goes to sea aboard her, serving on Admiral JACOBSEN's staff for the balance of the war. He has his revealing interview with the captured Major CHERNYAVIN aboard the carrier.

In *Danger,* she is going in for an overhaul.

INGRAM MAC-10:   U.S. submachine gun; empty weight 3+ lbs, 20-round magazine. Can be chambered for 9-mm or .45 rounds. Its small size makes it easily concealable and highly inaccurate. In *Danger,* it is used by drug-cartel assassins in the murder of the BRADENs.

INTERCONTINENTAL BALLISTIC MISSILE (ICBM):   A land-based BALLISTIC MISSILE with a range of more than 5,000 miles. First operational with Soviet and U.S. forces in the late 1950s, they have become steadily more accurate and reliable, and have largely replaced bombers as the main land-based strategic weapon. A classic ICBM is the SS-18 SATAN, which explodes at the wrong moment in *Sum.*

INTERMEDIATE RANGE BALLISTIC MISSILE (IRBM):   A land-based BALLISTIC MISSILE with a range of 1,500-3,300 miles. They are theater weapons for the U.S. and Soviet Union, strategic ones for France and China. The best known IRBMs are the SS-20; also the earlier missiles the Soviets placed in Cuba, mentioned in *Sum.*

INTRUDER: U.S. attack aircraft. See A-6E.

INVINCIBLE, **H.M.S.:**   British Royal Navy conventional aircraft carrier. 16,000/19,500 tons; 28 knots; AA missiles and guns, 20 aircraft, including HARRIERS and ASW helicopters; 900 crew. In service 1980; distinguished record in the Falklands War. "Ski-jump" flight deck to improve performance of the HARRIERs.

In *Hunt, Invincible* is the flagship of Admiral WHITE and of the Anglo-American squadron that ends up being the primary protection for the American coast. Once Jack RYAN has boarded her, she is also intended as the main contact ship for *RED OCTOBER.* Thanks to RYAN's and WHITE's improvisation after the original contact party dies in a helicopter crash, *Invincible* carries out her mission.

IOWA, **U.S.S.:**   U.S. battleship. 45/54,000 tons; 33 knots; 9 16", 12 5" guns, TOMAHAWK and HARPOON; crew 1,700. In service 1942, the lead ship of a class of the four finest battleships ever built.

In *Storm, Iowa* and her sister ship, *NEW JERSEY,* support the Marine landing in Iceland. With RPV spotting, their heavy guns are devastatingly effective against Soviet artillery positions.

IRISH NATIONAL LIBERATION ARMY (INLA):   Extreme Marxist–Irish terrorist organization, responsible for Lord MOUNTBATTEN's assassination. In *Games,* the loss of American support from that event is mentioned as a reason why the IRA wouldn't have attempted the kidnapping of Their Royal Highnesses.

IRISH REPUBLICAN ARMY (IRA):   The oldest Irish resistance organization, dating back to World War I. At the opening of *Games,* RYAN at first thinks they are responsible for the attempted kidnapping.

ISLAMIC JIHAD: Coalition of Shiite groups, initially based in Lebanon, and with an extensive record of terrorist incidents, most notably the hijacking of a TWA airliner over Greece in 1985. In *Games* they are one of the "high-profile" groups everyone in the intelligence business is trying to crack.

ITHACA 12-GAUGE SHOTGUN: Any one of several models of repeating shotguns manufactured for police use. In *Games,* Sergeant Powers boards *COSTANZA* with one and threatens Captain FRENZA with it.

IVAN EMMETOVICH: In *Cardinal,* GOLOVKO refers to Jack RYAN in the Russian style: given name and patronymic. In *Sum,* he greets RYAN with the same form while visiting CIA headquarters. Translates as "John, son of Emmet."

IVANOV, DR. (no first name):   In *Hunt,* physician to the Soviet Embassy. He accompanies KGB agent PETCHKIN to the Norfolk Naval Medical Center to watch *POLITOVSKY's* sole survivor. He harshly criticizes PETCHKIN after the cigarette incident that leads to the confrontation with Captain TAIT.

IVANOV, LIEUTENANT PAVEL ILYCH: In *Hunt,* the greenest officer aboard *RED OCTOBER,* and apparently a junior navigator. Not one of RAMIUS's party, he abandons ship with the crew and returns to the Soviet Union after KGB interrogation. In that interrogation he strongly defends RAMIUS.

JACKSON, CECILIA: Robby JACKSON's wife. Unable to have children of her own, she is fond of the RYANs' Sally. She is wounded in the foot during the second ULA kidnapping attempt at the RYANs' house, but recovers completely.

JACKSON, ROBERT "ROBBY" JEFFERSON: U.S. Navy officer and F-14 pilot. A Black Annapolis graduate, the son of the Reverend Hosiah JACKSON by his first wife. Married to Cecilia JACKSON; no children. Timothy JACKSON is his younger half-brother. Below medium height, stocky, aggressive in the air and forceful on the ground. A good friend and a bad enemy.

In *Hunt,* he is a commander, flying from *KENNEDY* as CO of Fighter Squadron 41 (VF-41). With his wingman, Bud SANCHEZ, he is involved in an accidental engagement with FORGERs flying from *KIEV.* His F-14 is hit and damaged, but he lands back aboard *KENNEDY* with his wounded RIO.

In *Games,* we learn that he has been a friend of the RYANs for some time, after meeting Jack at Annapolis. He is teaching there while recovering from a flying accident. He is an indispensable help to the RYANs, driving Jack to the hospital after the attempt on Cathy and Sally, restraining him from assaulting the IRA spokesman, and offering the doctor a check ride in a T-38 if he saves Sally.

Back on flying status and promised the command of VF-41, he is invited to the RYANs' to meet the PRINCE AND PRINCESS OF WALES, and talks flying with the PRINCE. He is out of the living room when the ULA breaks into the house. He finds RYAN's shotgun, and kills two of the terrorists with it. This allows RYAN and the PRINCE to subdue COOLEY and the survivors, and the whole party to escape in one of the ULA boats.

In *Danger,* he is serving aboard U.S.S. *RANGER,* but is not informed of the role of the ship's A-6s in the covert operations against the drug cartel. In spite of this, he compares notes with his brother, Timothy, and comes to the appropriate conclusion after the raids. He lays this evidence before Admiral Joshua PAINTER, who is *not* happy. While aboard *RANGER,* Jackson is informed of his promotion to captain, and his prospect of being a CAG.

In *Sum,* Jackson is CAG of *THEODORE ROOSEVELT,* doing his best to make maturity and experience take the place of youth and reflexes. He has one kill, an MiG-29, in the Persian Gulf, and adds to his score during the crisis, shooting down both Libyan and Soviet planes.

JACKSON, LIEUTENANT TIMOTHY WASHINGTON: In *Danger,* U.S. Army officer, half-brother to Robby JACKSON. A West Pointer and regarded as a highly promising young infantry officer, he is no longer the runt of the family.

Originally Ding CHAVEZ's platoon commander, he is concerned about the sergeant's mysterious disappearance. Pressing his inquiry in the face of official discouragement, he helps his older brother learn about the covert operations.

JACKSTAFF: A flagpole mounted at the bow of a ship. In *Storm, FUCIK's* captain conns his battered ship to her final landing in Iceland by lining up the jackstaff with the quay.

JACOBS, EMIL: Director of the FBI, apparently the first person of Jewish faith to hold the position. A former Federal prosecutor, who has no use for druggies (or most other criminals), he is respected by everyone and loved by many, particularly the field agents.

In *Hunt* he and Judge MOORE confront Senator DONALDSON over Peter HENDERSON's treason and induce the Senator to plan retirement from public life. In *Games,* he works with the CIA's Judge MOORE to coordinate intelligence-gathering on the ULA. This cooperation continues in *Cardinal,* with the assignment of top-quality people to key jobs like the surveillance of Peter HENDERSON and the rescue of Major GREGORY.

In *Danger,* he has lost his wife, Ruth, to cancer some nine months ago. He is opposed to any plea-bargain for the *EMPIRE BUILDER* killers. Although the FBI is not the primary agency for the drug crackdown, Jacobs flies to Colombia to coordinate activities with their national police. On his way in from the Bogota airport, he is murdered by cartel assassins, terrorists hired by ESCOBEDO.

His body is flown home; Jack RYAN attends his funeral. Jacobs's death escalates the war with the drug cartel.

JACOBSEN, REAR ADMIRAL SCOTT: In *Storm,* U.S. Navy officer, commanding Strike Fleet Atlantic, replacing Admiral BAKER. He flies his flag in *INDEPENDENCE,* with Robert TOLAND serving on his staff. Unlike BAKER, Jacobsen is willing to take advice from subordinates, and listens to TOLAND as the carriers defend the ATLANTIC BRIDGE and cover the landing in Iceland.

JAGUAR: Anglo-French twin-engined, single- or two-seat supersonic fighter-bomber and advanced trainer; in service with British RAF, French Air Force, some foreign countries from 1972. In *Storm,* an RAF photo-reconnaissance Jaguar flies over Iceland and is promptly shot down by the newly established Soviet missile batteries—an event witnessed by Michael EDWARDS.

JAMESON, DOCTOR (LIEUTENANT) ALBERT: In *Hunt,* U.S. Navy medical officer at the Norfolk Naval Medical Center. A graduate of Harvard Medical School, he is the physician in charge of Andre KATYSKIN, the sole survivor of *E.S. POLITOVSKY.*

JARHEAD: U.S. Navy term for U.S. Marines, used by Robert TOLAND in *Hunt.* He also refers to himself as a "squid," the Marine term for naval personnel.

JEAN-CLAUDE: In *Games,* a senior French intelligence officer, presumably from DGSE. He is introduced to Jack RYAN by Marty CANTOR, and shows RYAN a tape of the DGSE-organized para assault on the *ACTION DIRECTE* camp.

JEFE: As CORTEZ uses it to ESCOBEDO in *Danger,* a rather obsequious form of "boss."

JEFFRIES, EDGAR: In *Danger,* a former Army officer now working for the CIA. Under the name of "Colonel Smith," he helps recruit and train light infantrymen for the covert operations in Colombia and discourages inquiries about them.

JENNINGS, MARGARET "PEGGY":   In *Cardinal,* FBI agent assigned to the security of the TEA CLIPPER project. She has Beatrice TAUSSIG under surveillance and suspects her of being both a lesbian and a security risk. She later interrogates TAUSSIG, after the woman's confrontation with Candi LONG.

JENSEN, COMMANDER ROY: U.S. Navy officer and A-6 pilot, a thoroughgoing professional. In *Danger,* he commands the A-6 squadron aboard *RANGER.* The only man to know that the "Drop-Ex" is actually part of the war on drugs, he flies both missions against cartel chiefs, dropping the light-case "smart" bombs precisely on targets illuminated from the ground by CLARK and LARSON.

JINK: Evasive maneuvering by an aircraft, involving rapid changes of altitude and course. In *Storm,* a B-52 of the first strike against Iceland loses too much altitude on one jink and crashes north of Keflavik.

JOHANNSEN, CAPTAIN BJORN: In *Storm,* Royal Norwegian Navy officer, CO of the submarine *KOBBEN.* He engages the *KIROV* battle group, sinking the battle cruiser with three hits from MARK 37 torpedoes. He is in serious danger from the Soviet counterattack when *CHICAGO's* engaging the Soviets provides an essential diversion. He later meets MCCAFFERTY at a cheerful party ashore and thanks him for saving his ship.

JOHN F. KENNEDY, U.S.S.: U.S. conventional aircraft carrier; in service 1968. Modified *KITTY HAWK*-class, originally intended to be nuclear-powered.

In *Hunt,* she is the flagship of Admiral PAINTER, and the only American carrier available at first. RYAN flies to her via COD and briefs the Admiral and the carrier's CO on the *RED OCTOBER* situation. He then flies on to *INVINCIBLE,* after the HARRIER sent for him is refueled aboard *Kennedy.*

Robby JACKSON's VF-41 is also flying from *Kennedy,* but he does not meet RYAN, presumably for security reasons. JACKSON lands his battered F-14 aboard the carrier after the incident with the FORGERs, and the fire and rescue crews extract his wounded RIO.

JOHN RODGERS, U.S.S.: *SPRUANCE*-class destroyer, in service 1979. In *Hunt,* Edward MORRIS mentions being her tactical action officer when O'MALLEY was doing system qualification aboard *MOOSBRUGGER.*

JOHNS, COLONEL PAUL (PJ): In *Danger,* U.S. Air Force officer. His distinguished career as a helicopter pilot goes back to the Vietnam War, where he flew both covert operations and SAR missions. He won the Medal of Honor rescuing a downed F-105 crew in Laos. A consummate pilot, who can obviously get more out of a helicopter than one would expect was humanly possible.

In *Danger,* he is assigned to the 1st Special Operations Wing in Florida, in charge of the PAVE LOW covert-operations helicopters. He flies the mission to insert the troops, and is more than willing to fly an illegal but thoroughly honorable mission to extract them after CUTTER's betrayal. Thanks largely to his superb flying skill, the helicopter is able to reach CLARK's fueling point, then fly on out to sea in the teeth of a hurricane to land at the last possible minute aboard *PANACHE.*

JOHNSON, LIEUTENANT SVEN: In *Hunt,* U.S. Navy officer. In charge of the deep-diving submarine *SEA CLIFF,* he takes Captain KAGANOVICH down to view the alleged wreckage of *RED OCTOBER.* He "finds" a Soviet depth gauge (provided by *RED OCTOBER)*—and also the ejected SS-N-20, which leads to a near-confrontation with his Soviet passenger.

JOINT CHIEFS OF STAFF (JCS):   The highest body for planning and coordination in the U.S. armed forces, consisting of the senior officer of the Army, Navy, Air Force, and Marines, with a chairman (who is appointed in rotation from each service) and an extensive staff. In 1986 the chairman was given actual command authority.

The Joint Chiefs listen to Jack RYAN's briefing in *Hunt;* they attend the signing ceremonies of the peace agreement in *Sum.*

JONES, RONALD: Sonarman aboard *DALLAS,* and later civilian consultant to the Navy. A technical genius but like many good sonarmen, slightly weird. (He joined the Navy from Caltech after getting top grades for five semesters; a practical joke destroyed too much equipment.) Physically nondescript, he manages to be extremely attractive to women.

In *Hunt,* he is a Sonarman Second Class aboard *DALLAS.* The new computer linked to the BQR-5 sonar, his own acute hearing and experience, and an illegal map of Soviet submarine routes help him decide that the sound of *RED OCTOBER's* CATERPILLAR drive is not "magma displacement," as higher authority would have it. MANCUSO's acting on this evaluation keeps *DALLAS* on the trail of the Soviet submarine. It also earns Jones a promotion to Sonarman First Class.

Jones goes aboard *RED OCTOBER* when the submarines reach the Maine coast. He doesn't think too highly of Soviet electronics, but with BUGAYEV's help he quickly learns to handle the sonar. He is invaluable in tracking *V.K. KONOVOLOV* during the final underwater confrontation.

In *Cardinal,* Jones is called back as a civilian technical representative (the alternative was going back on active duty). He is working on his master's degree and engaged to a library clerk named Kim. He is aboard *DALLAS* when she enters the Baltic on her covert mission, and does his usual superb job.

By *Sum,* Jones has a doctorate, a family, a lucrative job with Sonosystems, and periodic rides aboard submarines testing out new sonar systems. Bart MANCUSO consults him about Harry RICKS's performance aboard *MAINE* on her first patrol, and Jones has nothing good to say about the martinet skipper.

JO'S: Junior officers of the U.S. Navy—ensigns and lieutenants. In *Sum,* Harry RICKS is extremely harsh toward those aboard *MAINE.*

JULIET (NATO code name):   Soviet class of conventional cruise-missile submarines; sixteen in service 1962-69. In *Storm,* one is on her way home from the Mediterranean. She or another one later hits the Panamanian cruise ship *OCEAN STAR* with a missile; the ship burns, with heavy casualties.

JULIUS FUCIK, **MV:**   In *Storm,* a Finnish-built Soviet cargo vessel used in Operation POLAR GLORY. Diesel engines; 35,000 + tons of cargo. Her design permits her to carry loads in barges floated in through a stern door.

Carrying a battalion of the 234th Guards Air Assault regiment and their equipment, including LEBED hovercraft, she sails from Leningrad before the war begins. Her disguise as a U.S. Lykes Lines vessel allows her to approach Iceland and launch her hovercraft simultaneously with the missile strike.

Identified as hostile, *Fucik* is attacked with HARPOON missiles by a P-3 and strafed by F-15s. She suffers major damage and casualties, but she remains afloat and her mortally wounded captain is able to ground her so that the remaining troops and equipment can be safely landed.

KA-27 (NATO code name HELIX):   Soviet twin-turbine antisubmarine helicopter; Kamov Bureau. ASW weapons, airborne radar for targeting cruise missiles.

In *Hunt,* Captain KAGANOVICH flies off *KIEV* in one. In *Storm,* they are active around the Soviet force attacked by *CHICAGO.*

KADISHEV, OLEG KIRILOVICH: In *Sum,* Soviet political leader and American agent. An effective and popular leader with a large bloc of votes in the CONGRESS OF PEOPLE'S DEPUTIES and enough influence to bother NARMONOV, he is also a CIA agent, code name SPINNAKER, recruited by Mary Pat FOLEY.

In his position, he is able to provide a continuous flow of intelligence about the most secret and high-level activities in the Soviet Union. Unfortunately, he interprets the investigation of the East German nuclear weapons program and its possible terrorist links as a search for missing nuclear weapons. This in turn implies less than complete control of the military by NARMONOV—which implies an opportunity for Kadishev to become the Soviet leader with the support of the CIA.

During the crisis, Kadishev's interpretation tends to reinforce the conviction of FOWLER and ELLIOT that NARMONOV may have been the victim of a military coup. This conviction progressively worsens their judgment, their morale, and the crisis in general, until RYAN's intervention.

After the crisis, both NARMONOV and RYAN are more than somewhat unhappy with Kadishev, who committed treason, provided inaccurate intelligence, and nearly caused a nuclear war. RYAN persuades NARMONOV that Kadishev should be removed from public life rather than shot, tempting as the thought may be.

KAGANOVICH, CAPTAIN IGOR: In *Hunt*, Soviet Navy officer. He is flown in stages from *KIEV* to *AUSTIN* and from her goes down in *SEA CLIFF* to view and authenticate the "wreckage" of *RED OCTOBER*. He does not seem to understand the American style of naval discipline.

KAGANOVICH, LAZAR: Historical character (1893-1991). Of Jewish origin, he was one of STALIN's most ruthless henchmen and the last survivor of that gang. In *Sum*, it is mentioned that he was in charge of the building of the Moscow subway line leading to the shelter where NARMONOV spends the crisis.

KALASHNIKOV: General term for Soviet assault rifles, both the AK-47 and -74 and their variants. In *Games*, RYAN refers to their easy availability to terrorists when talking with Marty CANTOR. In *Cardinal*, the term is used for the weapons of the ARCHER's guerrilla band.

KAMAROV, CAPTAIN LIEUTENANT GRIGORIY: In *Hunt*, Soviet Navy officer, *RED OCTOBER's* navigator. His previous post was as a pilot for large surface vessels entering and leaving the KOLA Inlet. He is one of RAMIUS's party and is invaluable throughout the voyage, particularly in evading Soviet ASW forces and concealing the ship's position from suspicious members of the crew. After RYAN boards the ship, Kamarov goes to search the ship with Lieutenant WILLIAMS; he is surprised, shot, and killed by GRU agent Igor LOGINOV.

KAMINSKY, DR. VLADIMIR MOISEYVICH: In *Sum,* Soviet physician teaching in Syria. The dying ACHMED is referred to him by a Syrian colleague, and his diagnosis of a nuclear-related condition is an important clue for the KGB in their search for the East German/terrorist connection.

KARA (NATO code name):   Soviet class of conventional missile cruisers. 8,200/9,700 tons; 34 knots; cruise missiles, heavy AA and ASW armament; crew 500 + . Seven in service 1973-80.

In *Hunt,* three Karas, including *NIKOLAYEV,* are among the Soviet Northern Fleet ships detected getting ready for sea.

KASHIN (NATO code name):   Soviet class of conventional guided-missile destroyers. The first gas-turbine-powered warships in the world. Twenty-three in service, 1963-82. In *Storm, CHICAGO's* sonar detects a Kashin as one of *KIROV's* escorts.

KATYSKIN, ANDRE: In *Hunt,* cook aboard the ill-fated *E.S. POLITOVSKY;* young, fit, and good-looking. When the doomed submarine broaches briefly, he is able to get through an escape hatch according to the drill, but the ship sinks before anyone can follow him.

Thanks to his excellent physical condition, an immersion suit, and courageous rescue work by U.S. forces, he is picked up and taken to Norfolk Navy Medical Center. He is suffering from exposure, hypothermia, frostbite, and pneumonia, but receives excellent care and presumably survives. He is the object of great concern by the Soviets, and stringent security precautions by the U.S.

KATZ, DR. BERNIE: Ophthalmological surgeon at the Wilmer Eye Institute of Johns Hopkins and one of Cathy RYAN's most valued friends and colleagues. In *Games,* he assists at a cornea replacement, then takes the lead in emergency surgery on a child's glass-damaged eye because Cathy hasn't handled such a case for a while.

In *Sum,* he inadvertently provides information for ELLIOT's campaign against the RYANs to a supposed government investigator. He is furious with Jack until he learns the truth, and meanwhile offers a sympathetic ear to Cathy RYAN over her marital troubles.

KC-10 EXTENDER: Military version of the DC-10. It can carry cargo and passengers as well as fuel; equipped with both flying-boom and drogue refueling equipment. In service with U.S. Air Force from 1980. In *Sum,* KNEECAP with DURLING aboard tops off from a KC-10.

KC-135:   Aerial-tanker version of the C-135. The most numerous version of the C-135, and the basis for many of the conversions (EC-135, etc.). In service with the U.S. Air Force from 1957.

In *Storm,* the F-14 escorts of the second B-52 strike against Iceland refuel from KC-135s. In *Danger,* Bronco WINTERS tops off his F-15 from a KC-135 before his first drug shootdown. In *Sum,* "Looking Glass," the airborne SAC command post in the crisis, is a converted KC-135.

KEEGAN, EDWARD: In *Storm,* Robert TOLAND's father-in-law. He is a retired naval officer, now working for NSA. While fishing on Chesapeake Bay, he and TOLAND compare notes on suspicious events in the Soviet Union.

KEITEL, ERWIN: In *Sum,* former lieutenant colonel of the East German STASI. Refusing to work for capitalists, he was pensioned off, and is now unemployed and embittered. Like Günther BOCK, he thinks the Russians have betrayed everything he worked for.

He retains some intelligence contacts and is able to tell BOCK exactly how his wife, Petra, died. With other associates he keeps an eye on Traudl FROMM and when Captain FEODOROV contacts her, Keitel is in charge of their interrogation and murder.

After BOCK's return from the Middle East, Keitel works closely with the man in setting up the incident in Berlin. Disguised as a Soviet officer, he is the key man in killing the Soviet vehicle crews and acquiring the vehicles for the incident. He is killed in the fighting in Berlin.

KELT: Soviet air-launched cruise missile. See AS-5.

KEY WEST, U.S.S.:   U.S. nuclear attack submarine, 688-class; in service 1987. In *Storm,* she participates in Operation DOOLITTLE and survives. In *Sum,* Wally CHAMBERS, *DALLAS's* former XO, is about to take command of her.

KGB: *Komitet gosudarstvenny bezopasnosti* (Committee for State Security). The principal Soviet security and intelligence organization, divided into a number of specialized Chief Directorates, Directorates, Divisions, and other subordinate bodies. It has a long-standing rivalry with the armed forces for control of intelligence and is much disliked by Soviet military professionals because of its function of surveillance over them.

Among its responsibilities are control of the nuclear warheads of Soviet delivery vehicles—a problem in the case of missile submarines like *RED OCTOBER.* Another responsibility is border security, and the KGB Border Guards Directorate has several hundred thousand troops under its control, armed with tanks, helicopters, and seagoing ships (which U.S. submarines encounter in both *Storm* and *Cardinal*).

In *Hunt,* an ambitious KGB Chairman, GERASIMOV, tries to use the *RED OCTOBER* incident to extend KGB influence over Navy security. The KGB also interrogates and presumably executes the Commander of the Northern Fleet.

In *Storm,* the KGB is virtually responsible for the war to begin with, because of an ambitious official's presenting the worst-case scenario for oil supplies. They then carry out the *maskirovka* Kremlin bombing, with a ruthless disregard for innocent lives.

Once the shooting starts, they seem to be more trouble than they are worth. A KGB patrol rapes Vigdis AGUSTDOTTIR and is deservedly executed by EDWARDS and his men. The senior KGB officer on Iceland is a thorn in General ANDREYEV's side. Two KGB colonels arrest Pavel ALEXEYEV's predecessor as CINC-West; they later execute him and six other generals for the crime of not winning on schedule. More KGB field police confront Major SERGETOV as he tries to return to his post. A KGB-manned corvette attacks the Operation DOOLITTLE submarines and inflicts major damage on *PROVIDENCE.*

Toward the end, KGB Chairman KOSOV supports the SERGETOV/ALEXEYEV coup, but for his own reasons. He is shot the moment the coup is successful.

In *Games,* RYAN suspects that Sergei PLATONOV, who deplores the attack on the RYAN family, is actually KGB, or at least some sort of intelligence officer masquerading as a diplomat.

Much of *Cardinal* is a duel over Mikhail FILITOV between the KGB and the CIA. Colonel VATUTIN and Major CHUBANOV represent the old type of KGB officer, GOLOVKO the new. Tania BISYARINA is as good a field agent as any intelligence agency could wish, even when she is given a nearly impossible job. Captain CHURKIN is another professional, but unlucky enough to be shot down by the ARCHER while carrying vital intelligence about BRIGHT STAR.

As for Chairman GERASIMOV, he is on the verge of turning control of the KGB into leadership of the Soviet Union. But he is aware that the Soviet system cannot tolerate failure, and when RYAN informs him of the size of his failure over *RED OCTOBER,* not even trying to kidnap Major GREGORY can save him.

In *Danger,* Colonel CORTEZ thinks of a typical response of the KGB First Directorate (foreign operations) to the taking of Soviet hostages: they took their own hostages off the streets and returned them much the worse for wear. Such "ACTIVE MEASURES" are crude but formidable.

In *Sum,* the KGB is the main Soviet organ investigating the East German nuclear-weapons program and its possible links to terrorist groups. Captain FEODOROV, son of a distinguished KGB officer, is murdered by Erwin KEITEL when he gets too close to the trail of Manfred FROMM.

KH-11:   U.S. reconnaissance satellite, with a computerized digital imaging system capable of giving real-time images. 11 tons; launched by Titan IIIs beginning in 1976.

In *Hunt,* a KH-11 photographs ships of the Soviet Northern Fleet getting up steam. In *Storm,* one detects the Nizhnevartovsk refinery fire; it or another is later destroyed by a Soviet antisatellite weapon. In *Sum,* a KH-11 photographs the site of the Denver nuclear explosion; another records suspicious activity at Soviet missile sites and the SS-18 explosion, inadvertently contributing to the tension.

KH-12:   U.S. reconnaissance satellite, with radar-imaging and electronic-intelligence capabilities, designed to be launched by the Space Shuttle. In *Sum,* two are in orbit during the crisis.

KHEROV, CAPTAIN (no first name):   In *Storm,* captain of M.V. *JULIUS FUCIK,* the key to the amphibious phase of Operation POLAR GLORY. He disguises his ship, both visually and over the radio, to deceive U.S. air patrols all the way to Iceland.

When the war starts, he adopts effective damage-control measures after the ship is hit by a HARPOON missile, and although severely wounded in the F-15 strafing he remains at his post. He does not accept medical attention until he has successfully grounded his ship so that her remaining troops and cargo can be unloaded, and by then it is probably too late.

KHRUSHCHEV, NIKITA: Historical character (1894-1971). Premier and General Secretary, 1957-64; denounced STALIN in 1956 and began post-Stalin reforms.

In *Hunt,* he is mentioned as having been responsible for the Moscow subway being deep enough to serve as bomb shelters. In *Storm,* he is described as the last example of one-man rule in the Soviet Union.

KIA/MIA: Killed in Action/Missing in Action. In *Danger,* Ding CHAVEZ and his covert-action comrades would all have suffered one or the other fate without the rescue mission.

KIDD, CAPTAIN: Historical figure (1645-1701). William Kidd, executed on a charge of piracy in 1701.

KIDD, U.S.S.: Leadship, *Kidd*-class. (Modified *SPRUANCE*-class destroyers with additional AA suite including STANDARD missiles.) In service 1981. One of four originally built for Iran and modified to carry guided missiles.

In *Storm,* she is in Norfolk, severely damaged; the admiral commanding U.S. surface forces in the Atlantic visits her after dropping Edward MORRIS off at Morris's new command, *REUBEN JAMES.* In *Sum,* she has a role in one of the White House CAMELOT war games, reporting the loss of the AEGIS cruiser *VALLEY FORGE.*

KIEV: Soviet conventional aircraft carrier. 36,000/43,000 tons; 32 knots; 30 aircraft (FORGERs and ASW helicopters); AA and cruise missiles, guns, ASW weapons; crew 1,200. The lead ship of a class of four, in service 1975. The first Soviet ship able to operate fixed-wing aircraft, but with more surface and ASW capabilities than Western carriers.

In *Hunt, Kiev* is part of the Soviet Northern Fleet. She is detected getting up steam. Later, her FORGERs are involved in the attempted E-3 SENTRY interception and the shooting incident with Robby JACKSON's F-14.

In *Storm,* she is with the Soviet amphibious group bound for northern Norway, reported to *CHICAGO* and later attacked by her. Later she is reported as the flagship of one of the Soviet ASW groups operating in the Barents Sea, in the path of the Operation DOOLITTLE submarines.

KILOTON/MEGATON: Measurements of the yield of a nuclear/thermonuclear weapon. One kiloton = 1,000 tons of TNT. One megaton = 1,000,000 tons. The terrorist bomb in *Sum* was intended to be several hundred kilotons but barely exceeded eleven thanks to impure tritium. The warhead intended for CHEYENNE MOUNTAIN is expected to be twenty-five megatons.

KINDER-KIRCHE-KÜCHE: "Children-Church-Kitchen"—the legitimate role of women, according to the traditional German male (and the Nazis). The *BUNDESKRIMINALAMT* detective who interrogates Petra HASSLER-BOCK wonders if her extremism isn't a reaction to that philosophy.

KING, GUNNERY SERGEANT WILLIE: Black U.S. Marine NCO, Jack RYAN's Drill Instructor at Quantico. In *Games,* RYAN describes him to the PRINCE OF WALES as a "humongous black guy, we called him Son of Kong." BRECKENRIDGE later tells RYAN that King has retired and runs a sporting goods store in Roanoke.

KINGFISH: Soviet air-launched cruise missile. See AS-6.

KIROV: Soviet nuclear battlecruiser. 24/28,000 tons; 32 knots; AA and cruise missiles, guns, ASW weapons (including helicopters); crew 800. Lead ship of a class projected at five, in service 1980. The largest surface-warfare vessel built since World War II and the first warship ever to combine nuclear and steam propulsion.

In *Hunt,* she is one of the Northern Fleet ships detected getting up steam, and is the flagship of the Soviet surface forces pursuing *RED OCTOBER.* A simulated low-altitude attack by A-10s on *Kirov,* which would have been fatal if real, persuades the Soviet admiral to avoid any provocative behavior that might lead to more incidents like the FORGER shooting. She is also Commodore EATON's intended target for *NEW JERSEY's* guns with their rocket-assisted shells.

In *Storm* she is with the Soviet amphibious force bound for northern Norway. She is *CHICAGO's* intended target for HARPOON missiles, but before the American submarine can launch, the Norwegian submarine *KOBBEN* hits *Kirov* with three MARK 37 torpedoes. Fatally damaged, *Kirov* quickly blows up and sinks.

KITTIWAKE, NURSE: In *Games,* one of Jack RYAN's nurses in the surgical recovery unit of St. Thomas's Hospital, London. Young and pretty, she is quite accomplished at dealing with difficult patients like RYAN.

KLICK: Military slang for a kilometer. In *Storm,* the collective farm where satellites detect expanded private plots is described as "two hundred klicks northwest of Moscow." In *Cardinal,* CHAVEZ says the covert-action troops have covered two miles—roughly three klicks.

KNEECAP: See NATIONAL EMERGENCY AIRBORNE COMMAND POST (NEACAP).

KOBBEN: In *Storm,* Royal Norwegian Navy conventional submarine. 370/480 tons; 13/17 knots; 8 TT; in service 1964, German-built. She engages the Soviet amphibious task force being trailed by *CHICAGO,* sinks *KIROV,* is nearly lost in the Soviet counterattack, but evades in the confusion caused by *CHICAGO's* HARPOONs sinking a Soviet destroyer.

KOHN, RABBI ISRAEL: In *Sum,* American-born Israeli religious leader and combat veteran of the Middle Eastern wars. He helps make Benjamin ZADIN once more an observant, believing Jew. Along with Rabbi GOLD-MARK, he leads the march to the Wailing Wall that turns into a confrontation with the peaceful Palestinian demonstration.

KOLA PENINSULA: Peninsula in the NW Soviet Union, projecting east. The site of the city of Murmansk and one of the largest complex of air, naval, and missile bases in the Soviet Union. These include *RED OCTO-BER's* base at Polyarny and the Soviet Northern Fleet air bases used in *Storm* to attack the convoys, and attacked in turn by TOMAHAWK missiles in Operation DOOLITTLE.

KOMSOMOL: The youth group of the Communist Party of the Soviet Union. Membership is virtually a requirement for career advancement or Party membership. In *Hunt,* most of the young officers of Marko RAMIUS's "family" are Komsomol members. In *Cardinal,* more Komsomol members, including graduate students, are helping build the BRIGHT STAR complex at Dushanbe.

KOREAN AIRLINES 747:   Incident in 1983 in which Soviet air-defense forces failed to properly identify a commercial 747 and shot it down over the Soviet Far East. Over 200 people died, and in *Sum* Captain ROSSELLI remembers that it nearly provoked a crisis.

KOROV, ADMIRAL (no first name):   In *Hunt,* Soviet naval officer, commander of the Northern Fleet. He is arrested after Moscow learns of *RED OCTOBER's* defection and interrogated by the KGB. He is either executed or dies under interrogation.

KOSOV, BORIS GEORGIYEVICH: In *Storm,* Chairman of the KGB. Short, stocky, and superficially jolly, he is quite as ruthless as his post demands or maybe a little more so.

At the opening of the war, he was in poor health and not fully in control of his own organization. As the Soviet situation deteriorates and the threat of nuclear war increases, he has a confidential meeting with SERGETOV. He agrees to provide essential support for SERGETOV and ALEXSEYEV, less out of patriotism than to save himself from being discredited for his role in bringing about the war.

He keeps his promise of support through to the success of the coup. However, ALEXSEYEV knows that the Army will refuse to obey Kosov as part of a troika and has him summarily shot by Major SOROKIN.

KREPKIY: In *Cardinal,* KGB-manned GRISHA corvette, which encounters *DALLAS* on the way out from the pickup at Talinn. Marko RAMIUS persuades the suspicious KGB skipper that *DALLAS* is actually the Soviet submarine *Novosibirsk Komsomolets,* on a secret *SPETSNAZ* exercise.

KRESTA (NATO code name):   Soviet class of conventional guided-missile cruisers. 6,200/7,700 tons; 34 knots; AA and cruise missiles, ASW weapons, 1 helicopter; crew 380. Fourteen in service 1967-78.

In *Hunt,* five Krestas are detected getting ready to go to sea with the Northern Fleet surface forces pursuing *RED OCTOBER.* In *Storm,* one is flagship of an ASW group facing the Operation DOOLITTLE submarines in the Barents Sea; another is one of *KIROV's* escorts when *CHICAGO* attacks.

KRETCHMER, OTTO: Historical character, the highest-scoring German submarine captain of World War II. In *Storm, CHICAGO's* XO jokingly refers to him after the successful mock-attack on the supertanker *UNIVERSE IRELAND.*

KRIVAK (NATO code name):   Soviet class of conventional ASW frigates. 3,100/3,700 tons; 30 knots; AA and cruise missiles, guns, ASW TT; crew 200 +. More than thirty in service, 1975-82; more constructed for KGB Border Guards.

In *Hunt,* the Northern Fleet sends four Krivaks after *RED OCTOBER.* In his briefing of the President and JCS, Jack RYAN mentions the nearly successful mutiny in 1975 aboard a Baltic Fleet Krivak, *STOROZHEVOY.*

In *Hunt,* several Krivaks are part of the Soviet ASW forces hunting *CHICAGO* after the Operation DOOLITTLE missile launch. She has damaged one of them.

In *Cardinal,* JONES tracks and identifies a Krivak while aboard *DALLAS* in the Baltic Sea. This impresses MANCUSO and even more so, the sonarman JONES is training.

KRYLOV, FILIP MOISEYEVICH: In *Storm,* the Soviet Minister of Agriculture. He takes seriously his responsibilities for feeding the people and is confident about the food supply, less confident about the fuel for transporting it.

He eventually becomes a supporter of SERGETOV and ALEXSEYEV. After their takeover, he retains Agriculture and takes over as Minister of Internal Affairs as well.

KUROPATKIN, LIEUTENANT GENERAL IVAN GRIGORYEVICH: In *Sum,* Soviet Air Force officer, a former fighter pilot, the command duty officer in the headquarters bunker of Soviet air defense at the time of the Denver explosion. He is a thorough professional, as he proves by obtaining and passing on to NARMONOV continuous intelligence about the location and yield of the explosion.

KURSK: World War II battle on the Russian Front, summer, 1943. The Germans attempted to destroy major Soviet forces by attacking the Kursk Bulge, a Soviet salient. They failed, and the losses crippled German armored forces for the rest of the war. The largest armored engagement in history. Mikhail FILITOV won his third Gold Star there, as well as receiving the wounds that kept him out of combat afterward.

KUZNETZOV: Soviet conventional aircraft carrier. Originally named *Tbilisi*. 65,000 tons; 30+ knots; 30 aircraft (MiG-29s) and AA missiles; crew 2,000+; ski-jump bow. In service late 1980s; the first "real" (capable of operating conventional aircraft) Soviet carrier.

In *Sum,* she and her escorts enter the Mediterranean some 240 miles behind *THEODORE ROOSEVELT's* battle group. Robby JACKSON overflies her as she passes through the Strait of Gibraltar. Later, during the crisis, she maneuvers so as to give the impression of being a threat to the American carrier, and JACKSON's F-14s shoot down two of *Kuznetzov's* MiG-29s.

L-1011:   U.S. three-engined wide-bodied jet airliner; Lockheed. Intercontinental range; 300+ passengers; in service 1972. In *Games,* the RYANs were originally planning to fly home on an L-1011.

LARIONOV, JOSEF: In *Storm,* leader of a faction within the KGB, who has the ear of the General Secretary and Defense Minister. Ambitious to replace KOSOV, he submits the pessimistic estimate of oil production which heavily influences the decision to go to war, while his superior is recovering from heart surgery.

LARSON, CARLOS: In *Games,* CIA field agent in Colombia. Actually named Larson, his cover is that of a general-aviation pilot and flight instructor, of mixed Danish and Hispanic descent, who has established himself financially by a few illegal flights. He is thirty years old, fluent in Spanish, an excellent pilot, and enjoys as a fringe benefit a stewardess who really *is* his lover.

He receives CLARK on the latter's arrival in Colombia and provides valuable intelligence on drug flights. After the cartel begins to suspect the interceptions, Larson's cover is blown and he and his lover have to move fast. The woman leaves Colombia; Larson accompanies CLARK into the field.

Although CLARK thinks Larson may be a bit young and romantic, the man earns his pay during the rest of the mission. He is CLARK's partner in the laser-targeting for the two air strikes, the emergency avgas refueling of the rescue-mission helicopter, and the kidnapping of ESCOBEDO. After extraction from Colombia, he leaves the CIA, intelligence work, and presumably government service.

LASER: Device projecting an intense beam of coherent, monochromatic light. Their principal uses are for rangefinding and target designation, but in *Cardinal* they are being developed by both the U.S. and the Soviet Union as strategic defense weapons against ICBM warheads and satellites.

LASER DESIGNATOR: Device which projects a laser beam at a target, causing a reflection detectable by the guidance mechanism of a "smart" bomb, which then homes in on the reflection.

In *Storm,* Colonel ELLINGTON uses one mounted in his Ghostrider to illuminate a bridge span for an F-111's bombs. In *Cardinal,* laser-designators have become standard equipment in Soviet MI-24 HINDs. In *Danger,* CLARK and LARSON use a manportable laser-designator to illuminate both targets for Commander JENSEN's A-6.

LAVAL, CHIEF SONARMAN "FRENCHIE":   In *Hunt,* senior petty officer of *DALLAS's* sound department and Ronald JONES's immediate superior. He loyally supports JONES and MANCUSO, although he thinks his skipper is running enormous risks. He remains aboard *DALLAS* during the voyage south from Maine, and skillfully runs the sonar during the final battle with *KONOVOLOV.*

LEARJET: U.S. twin-jet executive transport; Lear/Gates. In service 1964. U.S. Air Force version is the C-21/VC-21.

In *Storm,* an Air Force Learjet acts as chase plane for Amy NAKAMURA's F-15 on her first successful ASAT mission. In *Cardinal,* Jack RYAN flies out to New Mexico for the TEA CLIPPER test in one with a female pilot; Major GREGORY returns to Washington in another after the Soviet BRIGHT STAR test destroys Cosmos 1801. In *Sum,* Marvin RUSSELL explains that the "tape machine" (the bomb) in the van was too big to fit through the door of a Learjet.

LEBED: Soviet turbine-powered assault hovercraft. 85 tons; 60+ mph; 120 troops or 2+ tanks. In service with the Soviet Navy from 1976. In *Storm, JULIUS FUCIK* carries four to Iceland; they are essential for achieving surprise (as Michael EDWARDS discovers) and unloading armored vehicles.

LEFORTOVO PRISON: The principal operational KGB facility in Moscow. In *Storm,* the generals conferring in the bath are aware that it is only a mile away. In *Cardinal,* Edouard ALTUNIN, Svetlana VANEYEVA, and Mikhail FILITOV are all interrogated there.

LENIN: Soviet nuclear icebreaker; in service 1959. The world's first nuclear-powered surface vessel. In *Hunt,* she is described as having suffered a major nuclear accident due to poorly trained personnel, and has been out of service for some time.

LENIN, V. I.: Historical character (1870-1924). Vladimir Ilych Lenin, (born V. I. Ulyanov). Founder of the Soviet Union. In *Hunt,* his cult is described as the Soviet substitute for religion, along with love of the *rodina.* In *Storm,* SERGETOV wonders what has become of the dreams of Lenin's Revolution.

LENNER, LIEUTENANT COMMANDER: In *Storm,* combat systems officer aboard *REUBEN JAMES.* He has trained his men well and mans the CIC during most of the ship's battles.

LEONID: In *Cardinal,* Soviet KGB agent, Tania BISYARINA's chief assistant in the kidnapping of Major GREGORY. Like his chief, he is an able field man, determined to carry out nearly impossible orders; he is wounded in the arm and captured by the FBI during GREGORY's rescue in New Mexico.

LEONID BREZHNEV: Soviet nuclear icebreaker, the first surface ship to reach the North Pole; in service 1975. In *Storm,* she was the previous assignment of the Soviet captain guiding William CALLOWAY on his tour of the Polyarny submarine base.

LEOPARD: West German main battle tank. Leopard 1: 40 tons; 40 mph; 105-mm gun; in service 1965. Leopard 2: 60 tons; 45 mph; 120-mm gun; in service 1979. The first postwar German-designed tank and the most widely used NATO main battle tank.

In *Storm,* a *SPETSNAZ* driver on his way to a sabotage mission doesn't see any Leopards on the Belgian border. His Soviet Army comrades see many, however, during the fighting in Germany, where they are involved in every *BUNDESWEHR* armored action.

LGB: Laser Guided Bomb, a type of "smart" bomb which homes in on the reflection from a target illuminated by a LASER-DESIGNATOR. In *Danger,* one is being tested at the opening of the book; two are later used in the MEDELLIN raids.

LINEBACKER II: U.S. strategic bombing campaign against North Vietnam in 1972; the first combat use of "smart" bombs, as Colonel CORTEZ recalls in *Danger.*

LOADMASTER: NCO member of the crew of a U.S. air services transport aircraft, in charge of loading, distributing, and securing cargo or passengers for flight. In *Danger,* the loadmaster of the C-141 carrying CHAVEZ makes sure that all the troops riding in the unsoundproofed cargo hold have ear protectors.

LOGINOV, IGOR: In *Hunt,* GRU intelligence officer, on duty aboard *RED OCTOBER.* Son of industrial manager Arkady Loginov and a graduate of several advanced schools although only twenty-four. Highly trusted by Yuri PADORIN.

He is aboard the submarine with the cover identity of a cook; his mission is to prevent the defection or capture of the vessel by igniting a missile specially fitted with a self-destruct mechanism, then escaping. He nearly succeeds, too, being surprised by KAMAROV and WILLIAMS in their search of the ship. He kills the former and wounds the latter.

Suspicious, RYAN leads Marko RAMIUS into the missile compartment and discovers the casualties. Loginov then wounds RAMIUS in the leg, but is tracked down, confronted, and killed by RYAN before he can complete setting the igniter.

LONG, DR. CANDACE (CANDI):   In *Cardinal,* an expert in ADAPTIVE OPTICS and Major GREGORY's fiancée. She is taller than he is (five ten), dark-haired, and thin because she forgets to eat; her lifelong hobby is astronomy.

Like Gregory, she considers herself something of a nerd, but she and her fiancé are intellectually equal, sexually compatible to a high degree, and in general a fine, happy couple. Long keeps her head and provides useful intelligence to the FBI after GREGORY's kidnapping.

Long is also the object of an unrequited lesbian passion in Bea TAUSSIG, which is one of Bea's major motives for treason. Candi's unambiguous rejection of TAUSSIG is so traumatic for the other woman that Bea opens up to FBI interrogators about her role in the kidnapping.

LONG KESH PRISON: British maximum-security facility in Northern Ireland, where a large percentage of IRA prisoners are confined. In *Games,* one of O'DONNELL's men remembers spending eighteen months in the Long Kesh H-BLOCKS.

LONGLEY, BERT: In *Games,* one of the two senior British security men assigned to the PRINCE OF WALES on his American visit. He tours the RYANs' house and is on duty the night of the ULA attack. He courageously leads his men in resisting the terrorists, but is killed by one who catches him by surprise.

LOOMIS, SPECIAL AGENT HAZEL: FBI agent, daughter of a pilot lost over North Vietnam. A veteran field agent, who has shot and killed two men in the line of duty.

In *Hunt,* she acquires the final evidence against Peter HENDERSON and helps arrest him for treason. In *Cardinal* she is "running" HENDERSON, now a double agent, as his case officer. She refuses to show anything more than contempt for him and sometimes reminds him of the life sentence he could be serving. She is unhappy over the possibility that HENDERSON may earn his way clear by passing on the CIA's cover story about the investigation of RYAN.

LORAN: Navigation system which uses the intervals between the receipt of signals sent out by two different shore stations to fix a ship's position. It is one of the modern systems that has largely replaced the celestial navigation Robert TOLAND remembers as he watches the stars aboard *NIMITZ* in *Storm.*

LOS ANGELES: U.S. nuclear attack submarine; in service 1976. Lead ship of the 688-CLASS. Skip TYLER was up for command of her when he lost his leg in the accident with a drunk driver.

LOW-DRAG CASES: Streamlined bomb cases with a high length-to-width ratio, designed to reduce drag when carried externally on attack aircraft. (World War II bombs were designed for carrying internally.) The standard type of bomb aboard *RANGER* in *Danger,* including the special bombs for the drug raids.

LOWE, COLONEL CHARLES DEWINTER: In *Storm,* U.S. Marine officer. He begins the war in the Intentions office of CINCLANT headquarters, with his leg in a cast from a skiing accident. He works closely with Robert TOLAND, interpreting a mass of data about Soviet plans (including a showing of Eisenstein's *Aleksandr Nevsky,* a paean of praise to Russian nationalism). He comes to share TOLAND's suspicions of Russian intentions.

Lowe afterwards recovers in time to take command of a regiment in the Marine Amphibious Force landing on Iceland. He again works with TO-LAND, interpreting and passing on Major CHAPAYEV's invaluable intelligence about the origins of the war.

LUBYANKA: The Lubyanka Prison, 2 Dzerzhinsky Square, Moscow, KGB headquarters. Once a much-dreaded prison and interrogation center (in *Hunt,* Admiral KOROV dies there), by the time of *Cardinal* the accumulated mass of paperwork and paperpushers has turned it into an office building.

LUPARA: Traditional large-bore Sicilian shotgun, a favorite weapon in the island's blood feuds and Mafia activities. In *Sum,* Bart MANCUSO thinks that his great-great-great grandfather would have used a *lupara* on the rude and defiant Captain RICKS.

LYALIN, OLEG YUREVICH: In *Sum,* KGB "illegal" operating in Japan. His cover is representative of a Soviet industrial concern; his well-developed network of agents is code-named THISTLE. He offers its services to the CIA, which accepts him (under the code-name MUSAHASHI) and uses his intelligence to launch Operation NIITAKA, aimed at exposing the Japanese Prime Minister's undercover dealings with the Mexicans over trade agreements. Lyalin's intelligence is essential to the eventual success of the operation—which also provides the basis for blackmailing the PRESI-DENT OF MEXICO into allowing the summary arrest of QATI and GHOSN after the Denver bombing.

After the crisis, NARMONOV wants to charge Lyalin with treason. RYAN points out that the man gave away no *Soviet* secrets, and in fact helped prevent a nuclear war.

LYNX: British Royal Navy twin-turbine light antisubmarine helicopter; Westland-Aerospatiale. 170 mph; 2 + hours' endurance; ASW torpedoes, depth charges. In service with Royal Navy 1978.

In *Storm,* H.M.S. *BATTLEAXE* carries a Lynx, code-named "Hatchet." "Hatchet" is homed in on the VICTOR hiding by the wreck of *Andrea Doria* and destroys it with two Mark-11 depth charges. The helicopter continues ASW operations as the *REUBEN JAMES* convoy crosses the Atlantic.

LZ: Landing Zone, a cleared area used for the landing and takeoff of helicopters. Examples: the FBI Hostage Rescue helicopter in *Games;* the PAVE LOW helicopter in *Danger* inserting CHAVEZ and his comrades— and later extracting them under fire (see HOT LZ).

M-1 ABRAMS: U.S. main battle tank. 55 tons; 45 + mph; 105-mm gun, M-2 heavy machine gun; crew of four (commander, gunner, loader, driver); in service 1982. M1A1 with 120-mm gun, 57 tons, 40 + mph, in service from 1986.

Developed during the 1970s as a conservative effort to produce a long-overdue successor to the M-60, the Abrams has highly sophisticated computerized fire control, anti–gas pressurization, ammunition protection, composite armor, and a 1500-hp turbine engine which gives it a high power-to-weight ratio and great agility. In spite of early problems with reliability, it has emerged as the world's best all-around main battle tank.

In *Storm,* U.S. armored units in Germany are equipped with M-1 model Abrams. These include B Troop, 1st Squadron, 11th Cavalry Regiment, where Sergeant MACKALL begins the war as a tank commander, rises to platoon leader, and receives a field commission. He is still riding an Abrams at the end of the war, rolling at freeway speeds in the vanguard of the NATO counterattack around Alfeld.

In *Sum,* they equip the BERLIN BRIGADE; many are engaged and some destroyed in the terrorist-provoked fighting with the Soviets. They will also equip the peacekeeping 10th Armored Cavalry Regiment in Israel.

M-2 .50-CALIBER MACHINE GUN: U.S. heavy machine gun, in service in both ground and aircraft versions from 1921. The secondary armament of the ABRAMS tank and primary armament of the M-113 APC in *Storm.* In *Danger, PANACHE* mounts one, and its gunner keeps it trained on *EMPIRE BUILDER* a little too long.

M-2/M-3 BRADLEY: U.S.-infantry fighting vehicle. 22 tons; 40 mph; 25-mm CHAIN GUN (or TOW in M-3); 3 crew, 7 infantry; amphibious and pressurized against gas. In service with U.S. Army from 1982. Designed to replace the M-113, it can keep up with the ABRAMS and has more firepower than its predecessor, including the personal weapons of the infantry inside.

In *Storm,* a company of Bradley-mounted infantry crosses two of the Russian bridges during the NATO counterattack near Alfeld; Ivan SERGETOV is cut off and has to swim for his life.

In *Sum,* they will equip the 10th Armored Cavalry Regiment in Israel. As part of the BERLIN BRIGADE, they engage Soviet forces; a gunner in one Bradley also kills Günther BOCK.

M-14 RIFLE: U.S. semiautomatic 7.62-mm rifle, standard U.S. infantry rifle late 1950s–mid-1960s. By the time of *Storm* it has been replaced with ground forces by the M-16, but it still arms the *PHARRIS* sailors who receive the survivors of the Soviet CHARLIE.

M-16 RIFLE: U.S. assault rifle, standard with U.S. ground forces from mid-1960s. 5.56-mm; 20/30-round magazine; 100+ rounds per minute; effective range 400 yards; loaded weight 8 lbs. The M16A2 (in service from 1985) has greater range and cannot be fired on full automatic. Early versions had reliability problems in Vietnam, largely remedied in the A1 model.

In *Storm,* Air Force police on guard duty and EDWARDS's Marines carry M-16s, as do U.S. infantrymen in Germany. In *Games,* we learn that RYAN qualified with it at Quantico, when he was in the Marines. In *Danger,* they are the main weapon of the covert-action troops inserted into Colombia. In *Sum,* the Marine sentries at CAMP DAVID carry M-16s with white camouflage covers for snowy conditions.

M-19: Colombian terrorist organization, founded with Castro's support in 1970s and allied with the MEDELLIN cartel from the 1980s. In *Danger,* ESCOBEDO recruits from their ranks for the assassination of JACOBS.

M-60 MACHINE GUN: U.S. general-purpose machine gun, standard with U.S. ground forces from early 1960s. 7.62-mm; belt-fed; 200+ rounds per minute; effective range 700+ yards; loaded weight 23 lbs. It draws heavily on the design of the German World War II MG42 and has been widely exported.

In *Games,* RYAN learns that some stolen from U.S. Army arsenals have turned up in the hands of Irish terrorists in Ireland. One of them also turns up in the U.S., when the ULA safe house is raided just before the attack at the RYANs' house.

In *Cardinal,* the FBI Hostage Rescue Team uses one for heavy firepower to back up the snipers while rescuing Major GREGORY.

M-60 TANK: U.S. main battle tank; in service from 1960. The standard U.S. tank until replaced by the ABRAMS in the 1980s. In *Storm,* MACK-ALL's gunner misses one of the M-60's conveniences, a hatch in the bottom of the hull that lets a man eliminate without leaving the tank.

M-72:   U.S. Light Antitank Weapon. Shoulder-fired antitank rocket, in service from mid-1960s; copied by the Soviets for their RPG-18, which replaced the RPG-7 used in *Danger* to assassinate JACOBS.

M-109:   U.S. 155-mm self-propelled gun-howitzer; in service with U.S. Army from 1961 (longer-ranged version from 1973), and widely exported. They are the principal self-propelled guns used by NATO forces in *Storm.*

M-198:   U.S. 155-mm towed gun-howitzer; in service with U.S. Army from 1979 and widely exported. Nuclear-capable, it is the principal U.S. towed medium gun in *Storm.*

M-203 GRENADE LAUNCHER: U.S. infantry weapons system, consisting of an M-16 rifle with a tubular launcher for 40-mm grenades mounted under the barrel. Maximum range 400+ yards; in service 1970s. In *Danger,* M-203s are the heaviest firepower the covert-action teams carry.

M-728 ENGINEER TANK: U.S. combat engineer vehicle, conversion of the M-60 tank; in service from 1966. In *Sum,* three are used in Denver after the nuclear explosion, for clearance and rescue work at the stadium.

MACH: The speed of an object in relation to the speed of sound. Frequently used to express the speed of aircraft: Mach Two for the Soviet missiles launched at Iceland in *Storm.*

MACKALL, SERGEANT FIRST CLASS TERRY: In *Storm,* U.S. Army tank commander, later platoon leader, in B Troop, 1st Squadron, 11th Cavalry Regiment. He is a thoroughly competent NCO and tanker, who richly deserves his field commission as second lieutenant (even if he doesn't bother to put up the appropriate insignia).

He appears near Bieben, leading a platoon of the truncated troop (the platoon leader was KIA) in support of German *Landwehr.* After being forced to withdraw by the pressure of the Soviet attack led by General ALEXSEYEV, Mackall is promoted to second lieutenant.

As NATO goes over to a desperate offensive, he is in the vanguard of the counterattack near Alfeld. Using the high road-speed (governor removed) and silent turbine propulsion of the Abrams, he is able to penetrate the Soviet rear and wreak havoc.

MAGNETIC ANOMALY DETECTOR (MAD):   Airborne ASW detection device, registering any changes in the local magnetic field caused by large metallic masses (such as the hull of a submarine). Carried in most ASW aircraft and some helicopters.

In *Storm, CHICAGO* is nearly detected by a MAD-equipped Soviet ASW MAY. Later, in the North Atlantic, *PHARRIS's* helicopter makes a MAD contact on a Soviet NOVEMBER, and a P-3 ORION drops a torpedo for a kill. The Soviet VICTOR hiding near *Andrea Doria* presumably hopes that the larger magnetic signature of the hull of the sunken liner will mask the submarine's smaller one.

In *Sum,* another P-3 uses its MAD to detect *ADMIRAL LUNIN* and drop a MARK 50 ASW torpedo on her.

MAGNETIC EXPLODER: Device which detonates a torpedo warhead by detecting a strong magnetic field, such as generated by the hull of a ship. In *Sum, ADMIRAL LUNIN* fires a torpedo so equipped at one of *MAINE's* decoys, which is too small to set it off.

MAINE, U.S.S.:   *OHIO*-class BALLISTIC MISSILE SUBMARINE. Assigned to Captain MANCUSO's squadron, she is based at Bangor, Washington, and carries a full load of TRIDENT D-5 missiles. Commissioned and shaken down by a "GOLD" crew under Captain ROSSELLI, she and the crew are taken over by the martinet Captain Harry RICKS. Under his command the crew remains highly efficient but ceases to be happy, as he drives rather than leads.

On RICKS's first patrol she is detected by *ADMIRAL LUNIN,* while testing the captain's theory that boomers can track attack boats. On RICKS's next patrol, she is close to *ADMIRAL LUNIN* during the escalating crisis when she strikes submerged logs, deck cargo washed overboard from *GEORGE MCREADY.* She suffers major damage to her propellers, sonar, and silencing, and becomes a detectable and vulnerable target. In spite of the help of a P-3, *ADMIRAL LUNIN* is able to hit *MAINE* with a torpedo that inflicts fatal damage.

RICKS is able to surface his boat, and with the resolution of the crisis *ADMIRAL LUNIN* rescues eighty-seven survivors.

MAINSTAY: Soviet AWACS aircraft. See IL-76.

MAJOR OF THE AFGHAN ARMY (no name):   In *Cardinal,* a competent officer of the Russian-sponsored Afghan Army who defects and joins the ARCHER's band. He is enthusiastic about the cross-border raid on the BRIGHT STAR facility and throughout the mission provides invaluable intelligence on Russian communications procedures, positions, and tactics.

Although not entirely trusted by the ARCHER and his band, the Major also proves himself in combat at the site. After the death of the ARCHER and the repulse of the assault, the Major assumes command of the survivors of the ARCHER's company and leads them in their escape and evasion.

MAKAROV: Soviet 9-mm automatic pistol based on the German Walther PP; empty weight 1.5 lbs. A standard Soviet Bloc military sidearm.

In *Games,* the first assassin RYAN tackles is carrying one. Jack takes it away, shoots the man in the hip with it, and uses the Makarov for the rest of the fight.

In *Sum,* Erwin KEITEL buys ten to help disguise his Berlin terrorists as Soviet troops. He later uses one to shoot a Soviet tank-regiment commander, while opening fire on the Americans to provoke the Berlin incident.

MAMALUKE SWORD: U.S. Marine officer's dress sword, said to be based on the sword of an Arab governor won by a Marine officer in the Barbary Wars, 1803-5. In *Games,* the picture of Jack RYAN in the London *Daily Mirror* shows him graduating from Quantico, in full-dress uniform complete with sword.

MAN, THE: Term used in *Hunt, Cardinal,* and *Danger* for the PRESIDENT.

MANCUSO, BARTOLOMEO VITO: U.S. Navy officer, an Annapolis graduate and first-class submariner. Of Sicilian descent, the son of a barber in Cicero (a suburb of Chicago), he learned the pleasures of hunting on fall trips with his father. Commanding an attack submarine gives him the same challenge (whereas commanding a BOOMER is "about as interesting as watching paint dry"). He received his first command, U.S.S. *DALLAS,* unusually early, thanks to the influence of Admiral GALLERY and probably also due to his already having one DSM.

He is married and the father of two sons, Mike and Dominic, eight and four respectively at the time of *Hunt.* He is also the archetype of the daring submarine tactician and naval professional, both demanding and receiving high performance from his subordinates but also giving them that loyalty in return and listening to what they have to say. His recognition of Ronald JONES's skill and judgment is an example.

In *Hunt,* he commands *DALLAS,* trailing *RED OCTOBER* across the North Atlantic until the deception operation removes her crew, then escorting the Soviet vessel to the Maine coast. After the rendezvous, he leads a team of ten men from *DALLAS* aboard *RED OCTOBER.* He is aboard the Soviet submarine throughout her trip to Norfolk, and makes RAMIUS an excellent XO and adviser during the battle against *KONOVOLOV.*

For his part in the hunt for *RED OCTOBER,* Mancuso receives a second DSM—which he can't talk about.

In *Cardinal,* Mancuso is nearing the end of his service aboard *DALLAS.* With his usual skill and the help of Marko RAMIUS, he takes his submarine into the Baltic, lands CLARK for his covert mission, and escapes with GERASIMOV's wife and daughter.

In *Sum,* Mancuso has done his time commanding a BOOMER, and is a full captain (selected for rear admiral). He commands a Pacific Fleet squadron of seven boomers, including *MAINE* with her "GOLD" crew under the martinet Captain RICKS. Mancuso does his best to change RICKS's methods without undercutting his authority, and finally resigns himself to writing the man an efficiency report that will end his chances of promotion beyond captain.

MANDEL, RAFI: In *Sum,* Israeli Defense Minister. A hard-liner, he is violently opposed to the peace settlement, but lacks the support to make that opposition effective.

MANDOLIN, OPERATION: In *Hunt,* the code name Judge MOORE gives to the operation for contacting *RED OCTOBER.*

MANNION, LIEUTENANT PAT: In *Hunt,* U.S. Navy officer, *DALLAS's* navigator and a qualified OOD. Black and from the South Bronx, he is one of the party boarding *RED OCTOBER,* where he raises Soviet eyebrows. He is one of the control-room party during the battle with *KONOVOLOV.*

MAO, CHAIRMAN: Historical character (1893-1976). Mao Tse-Tung, leader of the Chinese Communist Party from 1934 and leader of the People's Republic of China from 1949. In *Sum,* his theories of revolutionary tactics and guerrilla warfare have influenced Ismael QATI.

MARINE ONE/MARINE TWO: In *Sum,* U.S. Marine VH-3 helicopters with picked crews, based at ANACOSTIA NAVAL AIR STATION and transporting the President and Vice President. A weather-related accident to Marine One helps persuade FOWLER to remain at CAMP DAVID.

MARINE UNITS: In *Storm,* a U.S. Marine Amphibious Unit (MAU; a reinforced BATTALION) is overwhelmed by the Soviet attack on Iceland. A Marine Amphibious Brigade (MAB; a reinforced REGIMENT) is on the way, but is too late and suffers heavy losses when *SAIPAN* is sunk in the attack on the *NIMITZ* battle group. Iceland is finally retaken by a Marine Amphibious Force (MAF; the reinforced First Marine DIVISION).

MARK 12 FISSION BOMB: U.S. tactical nuclear weapon; in service from 1956. The first really compact nuclear weapon. The Israeli bomb turned into a terrorist weapon in *Sum* is an Israeli copy (with improvements) of the Mark 12.

MARK 32: U.S. triple-tube torpedo launcher, for 12.75" ASW torpedoes (MARK 46 or MARK 50). In service from 1960s aboard most U.S. ships with any ASW capability. In *Storm, PHARRIS's* Mark 32s survive the torpedo hit that blows off her bow.

MARK 37: U.S. heavy submarine-launched homing torpedo; no longer in U.S. Navy service but widely exported to NATO navies. In *Storm, KOBBEN* uses Mark 37s to sink *KIROV* with three hits.

MARK 46 TORPEDO: U.S. lightweight ASW torpedo, air-dropped or launched from surface ships by MARK 32 tubes or ASROC. Diameter 12.75 inches; speed 40+ knots; range 6+ miles; 500 lbs. (100-lb. warhead); operates down to 1,500 feet. In service with U.S. Navy, many other navies from 1963.

In *Hunt,* the P-3s hunting the deployed Soviet submarines carry Mark 46s. In *Storm,* P-3s with *PHARRIS's* first convoy use them to kill a NOVEMBER and a FOXTROT; *PHARRIS's* ASROC hits a CHARLIE with a third. They are also standard equipment for O'MALLEY's helicopter from *REUBEN JAMES,* accounting for a PAPA and an OSCAR.

MARK 48 TORPEDO: U.S. heavy submarine-launched wire-guided or acoustic-homing antiship torpedo. Diameter 21 inches; speed 50+ knots; range 20 miles; 1.75 tons (1,000-lb. warhead); operates down to 3,000 feet. In service with U.S. Navy from 1972; through successively improved models it has remained the standard U.S. submarine torpedo.

In *Hunt,* both *DALLAS* and *POGY* carry Mark 48s; *POGY* has two of them loaded and ready to launch during the final battle with *KONOVOLOV.* In *Storm, CHICAGO* engages the *KIROV* force with a mix of HARPOONS and Mark 48s in her tubes, and later uses a Mark 48 to sink *AMETIST.* The torpedo is not fast enough to overtake the Soviet ALFA which sinks *BOSTON* and *PROVIDENCE.*

In *Cardinal, DALLAS* faces a problem in the Baltic: when aimed at surface targets, Mark 48s can be confused by floating ice.

In *Sum,* they are carried by American BOOMERs, and loaded when Soviet submarines are trying to track them. *MAINE* fires one in her final engagement with *ADMIRAL LUNIN,* but it fortunately misses.

MARK 50 TORPEDO (BARRACUDA): U.S. ASW torpedo, intended to replace the MARK 46 for air and surface-ship launch. Faster (unique chemical-propulsion system), deeper-diving, and with a more powerful shaped-charge warhead. In *Sum,* a P-3 supporting *MAINE* drops a Mark 50 on *ADMIRAL LUNIN,* but in the rough seas the torpedo BROACHES and explodes when it hits a wave.

MARK IV: Standard German World War II medium tank. In *Cardinal,* we learn that Corporal ROMANOV sacrificed his life to save FILITOV's in an engagement with a Mark IV.

MARK C TORPEDO: Soviet heavy submarine-launched wire-guided or acoustic-homing antiship torpedo. Diameter 21 inches (533 millimeters); range up to 10 miles; 500-lb. high-explosive warhead.

In *Hunt, V.K. KONOVOLOV* has all tubes loaded with Mark Cs. She fires three at *RED OCTOBER.* One hits and explodes, causing significant damage; a second misses; the third hits before the warhead is armed—a dud.

MARLIN '39:   Lever-action small-game and target rifle; .22 caliber; 14-round tubular magazine. In *Danger,* Erik SANDERSON uses it against BRADEN's killers and makes a lethal hit on one.

MARSHAL USTINOV: Soviet conventional missile cruiser; in service 1986. In *Sum,* she is one of the carrier *KUZNETSOV's* escorts.

MARTENS, ERIK: In *Games,* a wealthy South African arms dealer, with some CIA contacts but not too fussy about "end-user certificates." He trades in intelligence as well as weapons, and probably was involved in the supply of the UZIs used against Cathy and Sally RYAN. Unfortunately, Martens has too many intermediaries and too much influence with his own government for anything to be done against him.

MARX, KARL: Historical character (1818-93). The founder of dialectical materialism, the theoretical basis for Communism. In *Sum,* KADISHEV thinks Western leftists are idiots for believing Marx's teachings that advanced countries are a more favorable climate for socialism.

MARY-KAT: In *Danger,* Oregon fishing boat. The rescue of her crew by Senior Chief Boatswain WEGENER was publicized by a reporter aboard the rescue vessel *POINT GABRIEL* under the title "The Angel of the Bar," and helped win WEGENER his commission.

MASADA: Fortified hill in Israel, besieged by the Romans at the end of the Jewish Rebellion, A.D. 72-73. The defenders preferred to kill themselves and their families rather than surrender. Now part of Israel's tradition of resisting to the last. In *Sum,* Jack RYAN thinks of its influence on Israeli foreign and defense policies.

MASLOV, ADMIRAL ANDREY PETRAVICH: In *Storm,* Commander in Chief of the Soviet Navy. He strongly advocates Operation POLAR GLORY and afterward conducts a skillful air and sea campaign against the ATLANTIC BRIDGE.

MASTER SHIPWRIGHT (no name given):   In *Sum,* Superintendent of the shipyard where *ADMIRAL LUNIN* was built, who prefers this more traditional title. A former submarine officer, he works closely with Captain DUBNIN on the submarine's refit. He is responsible for obtaining the new FEEDWATER PUMP, improving the ship's sonar, and making many other minor improvements.

MASTIFF: U.S.–Israeli-built REMOTELY PILOTED VEHICLE. In *Storm,* one is used to spot the fire of battleships *IOWA* and *NEW JERSEY* against Soviet artillery positions in Iceland.

MAY: Soviet antisubmarine aircraft. See IL-38.

MCCAFFERTY, COMMANDER DANIEL M.:   In *Storm,* U.S. Navy officer, first CO of U.S.S. *CHICAGO* and her captain throughout the war. Formerly served aboard *WILL ROGERS.* Clearly an outstandingly able and professional officer, able to get the best out of an equally good crew. Married (wife Celia) and a friend of Robert TOLAND and Edward MORRIS, who have dinner with him at the NORFOLK O-CLUB before they all go to sea; his friends note that with his new responsibilities he has cut back on his drinking.

After receiving the Mayor of Chicago aboard his ship, he takes her north to the Barents Sea, where he detects the Soviet efforts to get their BOOMERS into a protected sanctuary and is engaged by (probably) Soviet ASW forces. After the war starts, he engages the *KIROV* amphibious force on his first patrol, then participates in Operation DOOLITTLE as his second.

MCCLINTOCK, COLIN: In *Cardinal,* British commercial attaché in Moscow, actually an officer of the Secret Intelligence Service. Seconded to the CIA, he is Svetlana VANEYEVA's case officer and a crucial Western link in the CARDINAL chain.

MD-80:   U.S. jet airliner, development of the DC-9; in service 1980. In *Sum,* QATI and GHOSN take one from Denver to Miami.

MECHANICAL TRANSIENT: Underwater noise of short duration and artificial origin; to a submarine's passive sonar it indicates human activity. In *Sum, MAINE's* collision with the floating logs registers as one on *ADMIRAL LUNIN's* sonar.

MEDAL OF HONOR: The highest U.S. military award, given for extraordinary heroism in combat, above and beyond the call of duty. Its Soviet equivalent is the Gold Star of a HERO OF THE SOVIET UNION. In *Danger,* Colonel JOHNS has the Medal of Honor.

MEDELLIN: City in NW Colombia, the second-largest in the country. Founded in 1675, it has become the capital of the Colombian cocaine cartel and the residence of the leaders targeted in *Danger.* Both air raids against the leaders take place in the region of the city.

MELEKHIN, CAPTAIN FIRST RANK (no first name):   In *Hunt,* chief engineer of *RED OCTOBER.* One of RAMIUS's allies, his first job is to systematically fake radiation leaks (which he is handy enough with tools to fix himself). After establishing the suspicion of "sabotage," his next job is to simulate a reactor accident well enough to persuade the non-defectors to abandon ship. This he also does with consummate skill that even leaves KGB interrogators of the returnees convinced that Melekhin was telling the truth.

After the rendezvous off the Maine coast, Melekhin has his hands full, being practically a whole engineering department by himself. He works well with the Americans and does a skilled job of damage control after the torpedo hit.

MELLON, U.S.C.G.:   U.S. Coast Guard high-endurance cutter; in service 1967. In *Danger,* we learn that Chief RILEY served aboard her, when Edward STUART pretends to have been a shipmate.

MEMPHIS, U.S.S.:   688-class submarine; in service 1977. In *Hunt,* she is tracking a Soviet DELTA, which takes off for home when all the Soviet BOOMERS are ordered back to port.

MENDELEV, RABBI SOLOMAN: In *Sum,* elderly New York Jewish leader, militantly pro-Israel and opposed to the peace settlement. Elizabeth ELLIOT thinks out loud about doing something to him, which ignites RYAN's Irish temper and sense of ethics and provokes yet another fight between them.

MENDEZ, OFFICER PETE: In *Cardinal,* New Mexico State Police officer. He pulls Major GREGORY and his KGB kidnappers over for improper lane changing, recognizes a signal for help from GREGORY, but is shot by the kidnappers before he can act. Although wounded, he survives and gives a description of GREGORY and the KGB people that is valuable to the FBI.

MG-3:   West German machine gun, based on the MG-42. In *Danger,* five, acquired from the Colombian Army, are used in the attempted assassination of ESCOBEDO.

MG-42: World War II German machine gun, noted for its simplicity, reliability, and high rate of fire (1,200 rounds per minute). The basis for the MG-3 used in *Danger,* as well as the U.S. M-60.

MI-8/17 (NATO code name HIP):   Soviet twin-turbine medium transport helicopter; Mil Bureau. 150+ mph; range 250 miles; machine guns and rockets; 32 troops/6,000+ lbs. cargo. In service with all Soviet air services from 1966, and widely exported; the most widely used helicopter in the world other than the Bell HUEY series.

In *Storm,* Hips are carried to Iceland aboard *JULIUS FUCIK* and afterward used for the assault landing, troop movements, and carrying General ANDREYEV. They are also used (with heavy losses) in air-assault operations in Germany, and as VIP transports.

MI-24 (NATO code name HIND):   Soviet twin-engined turbine-powered attack helicopter; Mil Bureau. 200 mph; combat radius 100 miles; air-to-ground rockets, machine guns, 23-mm cannon; crew of 2 plus a squad of infantry. Heavily armored, with sophisticated detection and fire-control electronics in later versions. In service with Soviet Army from 1973; widely exported.

In *Storm,* two MI-24s are airlifted to Iceland, where Sergeant SMITH warns EDWARDS about firing at one. The HINDs go out to hunt ED-WARDS after the KGB patrol turns up missing, but only bring back a deer. They are also used in Germany, with limited success due to NATO air superiority; General ALEXSEYEV travels in them several times; he and Ivan SERGETOV are shot down over East Germany in one.

In *Cardinal,* the ARCHER uses a STINGER to shoot down an MI-24 supporting Soviet ground troops, and kills the wounded pilot. The HIND is the major Soviet aerial threat to the Afghan guerrillas, and the STINGER the major Afghan response to it.

MICHELANGELO JUMPSUITS: In *Sum,* Jack Ryan's facetious description (in a conversation with Father RILEY) of the ceremonial dress of the Papal Guards, which was designed by Michelangelo.

MICHMAN: Soviet naval rank equivalent to Warrant Officer or Chief Petty Officer in the U.S. Navy. In *Sum,* two *michmaniy* are assigned during the refit to *ADMIRAL LUNIN's* otherwise all-officer sonar department.

MIDWAY: U.S. conventional aircraft carrier; in service 1945. In *Storm,* she is the only U.S. carrier in the Western Pacific, and not enough to handle Soviet Far East bases by herself.

MiG: A brand name of Soviet fighters—see the description of the results of Operation DREAMLAND in *Storm*—referring to the many products of the Mikoyan and Gurevich (abbreviated MiG) design bureau.

MiG-21 (NATO code name FISHBED):   Soviet single-engined, single-seat supersonic interceptor; in service 1958. The first Soviet Mach Two combat aircraft and the most widely used jet fighter in history.

Although being phased out in favor of the MiG-23/27 by the time of *Storm,* many are still in service; a flight of them escorts General ALEX-SEYEV on one of his helicopter flights. In *Cardinal,* a photoreconnaissance MiG-21 flies over the ARCHER's company on its way to the BRIGHT STAR attack.

MiG-23/27 (NATO code name FLOGGER):   Soviet twin-engined, single-seat jet fighter/attack plane; MiG Bureau. 1,200+ mph; combat radius 500 miles; 23-mm cannon, air-to-air missiles, and in the -27, up to 10,000 lbs. ordnance. In service with Soviet Air Force from 1972; widely exported. Fighter and attack versions of the same airframe; the first operational Soviet aircraft with variable-geometry wings.

In *Hunt,* Lieutenant SHAVROV anticipates with pleasure flying a naval version of the MiG-27 off a real aircraft carrier. In *Storm,* they are known to have rough-field capability (which would let them operate from a disused airstrip in Iceland). Later they escort BLINDERs against England; two are shot down.

MiG-25 (NATO code name FOXBAT):   Soviet twin-engined, single-seat jet interceptor; MiG Bureau. 2,000+ mph; combat radius 700 miles; air-to-air missiles. In service with the Soviet Air Force 1971; exported to several Soviet allies. A pure high-speed interceptor, originally intended to intercept the canceled U.S. B-70; part of the inspiration for the F-15 EAGLE.

In *Hunt,* Skip TYLER refers to an occasion when a defecting Soviet pilot landed a MiG-25 in Japan and it was returned (after examination by Western experts). He says this wouldn't happen in the U.S., so why return *RED OCTOBER*?

In *Storm,* a MiG-25 tries but fails to intercept Colonel ELLINGTON's Stealth fighter before it kills the MAINSTAY AWACS. Many others are destroyed on the ground in Operation DREAMLAND.

In *Cardinal,* MiG-25s are sent up to intercept the VC-137 on which GERASIMOV and FILITOV are escaping. Unable to shoot it down without causing a diplomatic incident, they are baffled by Colonel VON EICH's deceptive tactics and forced to break off their pursuit.

MiG-29 (NATO code name FULCRUM):   Soviet twin-engined, single-seat fighter; MiG Bureau. 1500 mph; combat radius 700 miles; 23-mm cannon, AA missiles, variety of bombs and rockets. In service with the Soviet Air Force from 1985; substantial numbers exported.

The Fulcrum is probably the best all-around combat aircraft yet produced in the Soviet Union, with outstanding maneuverability. It is certainly the first major Soviet type comparable in all respects to its Western counterparts. It is similar in size and overall performance to the F/A-18 HORNET.

In *Storm,* a REGIMENT of MiG-29s is deployed to Iceland, and constitutes the basic air defense of the Soviet forces there. Initially they are highly successful against an unescorted B-52 strike, but better NATO tactics and lack of reinforcements (Fulcrums are badly needed in Germany) progressively reduce their strength. In their final battle, their CO uses the resemblance between the HORNET and the Fulcrum to force an all-out dogfight, with considerable success.

In *Sum,* a flight of four Libyan Fulcrums on a training mission is detected by the *THEODORE ROOSEVELT* battle group during the crisis. When it appears the MiGs are carrying weapons, they are attacked and shot down by Robby JACKSON and his wingman. Two more Fulcrums from the carrier *KUZNETSOV* snoop the battle group later; they also are shot down.

MiG-31 (NATO code name FOXHOUND):   An improved version of the FOXBAT, with better low-altitude performance, maneuverability, and radar. In service 1983. In *Storm,* it is one of the planes the Soviets might have deployed to Iceland.

MIKE (NATO code name):   Soviet nuclear submarine, able to launch cruise missiles; in service at the time of *Storm.* Commander MCCAFFERTY mentions detecting one on *CHICAGO's* prewar patrol in the Barents Sea, when she wandered into a large-scale Soviet Navy live-fire exercise.

MILAN: Franco-German light antitank missile. In *Games,* one of Erik MARTENS's feats was obtaining the plans of this embargoed missile for the South African government.

MILITARY AIRLIFT COMMAND (MAC):   U.S. Air Force command, providing airlift for all U.S. services; headquarters at DOVER AIR FORCE BASE, Delaware.

In *Hunt,* MAC provides the C-5 that flies the DSRV *AVALON* from the West Coast for the *RED OCTOBER* operation. In *Storm,* a flight of MAC

C-141s is turned back from Iceland when the Soviet raid is detected; throughout the war it hauls most of the troops, while the convoys fight their way across with the heavy equipment and supplies.

MILLER, SANDRA: In *Storm,* Lieutenant EDWARDS's girlfriend. In her second year at the University of Connecticut, she was raped and murdered; the culprit got off on an insanity plea. Her memory and fate is EDWARDS's major reason for intervening to save Vigdis AGUSTDOTTIR.

MILLER, SEAN: In *Games,* ULA terrorist, Kevin O'DONNELL's chief of operations and general right-hand man. An physically unimpressive orphan, he looks and is dangerous—at least partly because he doesn't seem to regard anyone else as entirely human.

He is the leader and sole survivor of the first ULA attempt on the PRINCE AND PRINCESS OF WALES, defeated by Jack RYAN. After being sentenced to life imprisonment, he is raped in prison (with the tolerance of a warden). While being transported to a maximum-security facility, he is rescued by O'DONNELL and actively participates in the slaughter of civilians.

He trains in the *ACTION DIRECTE* camp in Chad, then travels to the United States. Working with Alex DOBBENS, he establishes the ULA presence there and carries out the attempt on Caroline and Sally RYAN. After that, RYAN regards him as the family's personal nemesis.

He is at O'DONNELL's side during the second attempt on Their Royal Highnesses, at the RYANs' house. After the escape of the intended victims, MILLER loses his temper and kills DOBBENS and another American ally. He is aboard the ULA boat that pursues the royal party, then tries to reach the escape ship *COSTANZA.* He is captured aboard her, and escapes being killed by RYAN only because Jack can't bring himself to kill even someone like Miller in cold blood.

In *Sum,* Miller is one of the ULA murderers finally executed, after exhausting all appeals.

MINIGUNS: Gatling-type (multiple rotating barrels) 7.62-mm machine guns mounted aboard the PAVE LOW helicopter in *Danger.* Sergeant ZIMMER teaches RYAN to use one on the flight in, and RYAN takes over after ZIMMER is mortally wounded during the extraction of the covert-action troops.

MINUTEMAN: U.S. solid-fuel three-stage fixed-base ICBM, the principal U.S. land-based strategic missile from the early 1960s. Based in complexes of hardened silos in rural areas of the U.S.

In *Cardinal,* the SS-18 gives the Soviets the ability for a "counterforce" attack, destroying the Minuteman bases without damaging American cities.

In *Sum,* the Minutemen are one of the three strategic forces placed on heightened alert during the crisis. President FOWLER plans to use a re-targeted Minuteman to destroy the city of QUM and with it the Ayatollah DARYEI.

MIR: Soviet space station, launched 1986. In *Sum,* a Soviet research ship supporting the station is suspected during the crisis of having used micro-wave beams to knock out communications satellites—a suspicion which further heightens tension.

MIRAGE: In *Storm,* French jet interceptors which, along with U.S. F-15s, engage the Soviet attack against the NATO AWACS. Probably Mirage 2000s, single-engined, single-seat, Mach Two; the standard French Air Force interceptor.

MIRKA (NATO code name):   Soviet class of light ASW frigates; at least twenty in service from 1964. In *Storm,* they are in the four light ASW groups facing the Operation DOOLITTLE submarines.

MIRV: Multiple Independently Targeted Reentry Vehicle. A type of mis-sile payload carrying a number of nuclear/thermonuclear warheads, each capable of hitting a different target. The SS-N-20s aboard *RED OCTOBER* in *Hunt* and the TRIDENTS aboard *MAINE* in *Sum* have these payloads. In *Cardinal,* it is mentioned that the development of these warheads wiped out fifteen years' progress in ABM defenses and made something like the BRIGHT STAR or TEA CLIPPER systems necessary.

MITCHELL, SERGEANT FIRST CLASS BOB (MITCH):   In *Danger,* U.S. Army NCO, CHAVEZ's and Timothy JACKSON's platoon sergeant. He has helped both the promising young NCO and the new lieutenant. When JACKSON is sharply warned not to try finding CHAVEZ, Mitchell uses the NCO's network to obtain information, which helps Robby JACK-SON work out what is going on.

MOLOTOV COCKTAIL: Improvised terrorist or guerrilla weapon, con-sisting of a gasoline-filled bottle equipped with an igniting mechanism. A popular weapon with Palestinians in Israel, as indicated in *Sum.*

MONTAIGNE, CAPTAIN FRANCES (FRANCIE):   In *Danger,* U.S. Air Force officer, pilot of the special-operations COMBAT TALON C-130 that supports Colonel JOHNS's helicopter on all the operations in Colombia. She is short, dark, energetic, has a puckish sense of humor, and is obviously a superb pilot. She also shares with the other people who fly the illegal rescue operation a strong sense of duty to one's comrades.

MOORE, JUDGE ARTHUR: Director of the Central Intelligence Agency. He is a former judge of the Texas Supreme Court, with a Harvard law degree, the façade of a West Texas cowboy, and a great deal of field experience going back to some of the more ruthless CIA operations during the Korean War.

In *Hunt,* he acts on the basis of CARDINAL's information to support Jack RYAN's theory about *RED OCTOBER* and plans for contacting RAMIUS, and later Skip TYLER's scheme for acquiring the submarine sans crew. He also works with Emil JACOBS and the FBI in exposing Peter HENDERSON's treason by feeding Senator DONALDSON a story about the *RED OCTOBER* episode being a Polish intelligence disinformation effort directed at the Soviets. He joins JACOBS in the confrontation that removes DONALDSON from public life.

In *Games,* he is skeptical of RYAN's youth and enthusiasm but agrees he is talented, and is willing to go along with Admiral GREER's serious efforts to recruit the young man. He keeps an eye on Marty CANTOR's work at indoctrinating RYAN, coordinates CIA and FBI activities, and finally accepts GREER's judgment of RYAN.

In *Hunt,* we learn that Moore has successfully fought politicization of the CIA. He is not so successful in getting FILITOV out; the KGB moves first. But Moore has *DALLAS* and CLARK in position, and supports the deception that permits RYAN to blackmail GERASIMOV into arranging FILITOV's escape. He also throws the CIA's resources into full cooperation with the arms negotiations in Moscow and with the FBI in rescuing Major GREGORY.

In *Danger,* he and RITTER insist that CUTTER take full responsibility for the covert operations in Colombia. He does not inform RYAN about those operations, which arouses RYAN's suspicions about the legality of what is going on.

By the opening of *Sum,* he has retired and been replaced by Marcus CABOT.

MOOSBRUGGER, U.S.S.: U.S. *SPRUANCE*-class destroyer; in service 1978. In *Storm,* Commander MORRIS remembers O'MALLEY doing systems qualifications aboard her.

MOROZOV, BORIS FILIPOVICH: In *Cardinal,* young Soviet engineer on the BRIGHT STAR project. A gifted member of the mirror-control team, he becomes a friend of Colonel BONDARENKO, helps evacuate and lead the technical staff during the Afghan attack, and is ready to be a leader in the rebuilding afterward.

MORRIS, COMMANDER EDWARD: In *Storm,* U.S. Navy officer, successively CO of *PHARRIS* and *REUBEN JAMES.* A friend of Robert TOLAND from when they were part of a bridge foursome at Pearl Harbor, he is immensely proud of having a command, to the point of having a personalized license plate with his ship's number (FF-1094) on it. Married.

He is also an entirely competent CO, taking *PHARRIS* on three convoys, assisting in the destruction of two Soviet submarines, and making a solo kill on a third, taking eleven prisoners. He undergoes a personal crisis, however, after *PHARRIS* is torpedoed and put out of service for the rest of the war by a Soviet VICTOR, with fourteen of her crew killed or missing.

He is still in the middle of this crisis when he is called to assume command of *REUBEN JAMES,* whose previous CO has been hospitalized with bleeding ulcers. This does not keep him from working with *BATTLEAXE* to detect and kill the Soviet VICTOR by *Andrea Doria.* After LAMPS pilot and Vietnam veteran O'MALLEY lends a sympathetic ear to his new CO's guilt over *PHARRIS's* dead, Morris returns to his former level of performance. He is again a highly competent skipper, as *REUBEN JAMES* escorts another convoy, then supports the landings on Iceland, in the process accounting for two more Soviet submarines.

MORTON, MUSH: Historical character, KIA 1943. Dudley W. Morton, CO of U.S.S. *WAHOO,* sank twenty-one Japanese ships and was famous for his aggressive tactics and leadership. In *Sum,* MANCUSO knows that not every BOOMER skipper is that kind of man.

MOSKVA: Soviet conventional ASW helicopter carrier; in service 1967. In *Hunt* she is one of the Northern Fleet vessels detected getting up steam to pursue *RED OCTOBER.*

MOSSAD: The Israeli national intelligence agency. In *Hunt,* it is supposed to be excited over the Polish disinformation effort (the CIA cover story).

In *Sum,* Motti ZADIN wonders if the Mossad's failure led to the Arab surprise in 1973. Ari BEN JACOB is head of Mossad, and leads his organization in the hunt for the terrorists and their nuclear connection.

MOTOR RIFLE: Soviet equivalent of U.S. "mechanized infantry"—an infantry division whose troops are entirely mounted in APCs and supported by extra tanks. Many such units are deployed in Germany in *Storm.*

MOUNTBATTEN, LORD LOUIS: Historical character, 1900-79. British World War II hero and statesman; his assassination by the extremist INLA (mentioned in *Games*) cost the Irish resistance movement much American support.

MOUSSA, HASHIMI: In *Sum,* Palestinian student and leader of the peaceful demonstration at the Temple Mount. He refuses to obey Benjamin ZADIN's orders to move and is shot by him—an event captured on TV for the whole world.

MP-5: West German submachine gun; Heckler & Koch. 9-mm; 20/30-round magazines; 100+ rounds per minute; empty weight 5+ lbs. Rugged, reliable, compact, and easily controllable, it is popular with antiterorrist units, including GSG-9, the SAS, and the FBI Hostage Rescue Teams.

In *Games,* the FBI HRTs are carrying MP-5s to the RYANs' house. So do the four HRT members in *Cardinal,* led by WERNER, who rappel from the helicopter during the rescue of GREGORY.

In *Danger,* CHAVEZ is introduced to it during his covert-operations training. It becomes a favorite weapon, and he uses a silenced version in Colombia against sentries.

MULLER, JOE: Cathy RYAN's father. A short, dark, egotistical senior VP at Merrill, Lynch, a widower and veteran of two years in the Army. He wanted Jack to stay in the stockbroking business and quarreled violently with him three years before *Games,* when RYAN left New York.

In *Games,* Muller and RYAN have another violent quarrel, with Joe accusing RYAN of recklessly endangering his daughter. Muller forgets that he is giving Cathy more trouble; RYAN forgets that Muller may be genuinely concerned about his daughter's safety.

MURRAY, SPECIAL AGENT DANIEL E.: FBI agent, a South Boston Irishman and thorough professional, although fond of good beer. His specialty is counterterrorism and he prefers revolvers to automatic pistols. His wife's name is Liz.

In *Games,* he begins as Legal Attaché to the American Embassy, and visits RYAN in the hospital, bringing a CARE package from McDonald's and intelligence on the ULA. He continues to work with British intelligence and law-enforcement officials throughout the battle against the ULA. He is particularly close to Commander OWENS, and is present at the arrest of Maureen DWYER. At the end, he is one of those who find Geoffrey WATKINS's body.

In *Danger,* he has finished four years in London and is now back in

Washington as Deputy Assistant Director of the FBI. With Bill SHAW, he leads the investigation of JACOBS's assassination. He later establishes contact with CLARK and obtains vital intelligence about the abandonment of the troops. Working with Bill SHAW and Pat O'DAY, he launches an investigation of CUTTER and passes along crucial intelligence to RYAN.

In *Sum,* he holds the same post. He arranges Walt HOSKINS's transfer to Denver. After the explosion, he is the senior man on duty at FBI head-quarters. He protests but executes President FOWLER's order to close down the media. He immediately passes on HOSKINS's information about the limited damage in Denver to RYAN, then organizes FBI efforts to track down the terrorists after the identification of Marvin RUSSELL.

MVD: Soviet Ministry of Internal Affairs, with its own national police force for matters not under the jurisdiction of the KGB. One of the Nizh-nevartovsk saboteurs in *Storm* is a former MVD police sergeant.

MYSTIC **(DSRV 2):**   U.S. deep-diving rescue submarine; in service 1977. In *Hunt,* she operates from the submarine rescue vessel *PIGEON* to remove the non-defecting portion of *RED OCTOBER's* crew.

NAKAMURA, MAJOR AMELIA: In *Storm,* U.S. Air Force officer and F-15 pilot. Short and stocky, she is called "Bunny" by her father, "Buns" by her fellow pilots. Proficient, professional, and aggressive.

While leading a ferry flight of F-15s to Europe, she finds some of the decoy BADGERs sent against the *NIMITZ* group and engages them, per-sonally shooting down three. As she was a test pilot for the ASAT rockets, she is then assigned to fly ASAT missions from Langley Air Force Base. She flies several missions, killing two satellites and becoming the first American female ace.

NARMONOV, ANDREY ILY'CH: General Secretary of the Communist Party and President of the Soviet Union. An engineer by training, he began his career as an effective factory manager and rose through the Party ranks by rewarding allies and ignoring enemies as much as possible. His projects included the Moscow radio tower. He has retained an engineer's bias in favor of making things *work right,* whether submarines, navies, or the whole Soviet Union. (This may be why he builds the fires in the fireplace of his dacha himself.)

At the time of *Hunt,* he is the fairly new successor to ANDROPOV, somewhat insecure in his position, and kept in power as much by other men's fear of the KGB as anything else. He is furious with Yuri PADORIN over the defection of *RED OCTOBER,* threatening him with execution in the old style. Along with the rest of the POLITBURO, he is lulled by Operation MANDOLIN into a belief that *RED OCTOBER* is safely disposed of. He does not oppose GERASIMOV's move to extend KGB influence over Navy security.

By the time of *Cardinal,* Narmonov is secure enough in power to be charming to the American arms-control delegation, including RYAN. He genuinely wants to reduce the danger of nuclear war, but American intelligence has justified doubts about his hold on power.

The major threat comes from GERASIMOV, and particularly from the KGB chief's use of the connection between FILITOV and Svetlana VANEYEVA, daughter of one of the President's crucial supporters. Thanks to VANEYEV's courage, RYAN's successful blackmail, and the failure of GREGORY's kidnapping, Narmonov survives. At the end, he personally intervenes to secure RYAN's safety and the secrecy of the whole episode. It also seems likely that he handpicks GOLOVKO for future promotion within the KGB.

In *Sum,* Narmonov is presiding over the post–Cold War Soviet Union, trying to reconcile political factions, national security, and peaceful relations with the United States. He is facing opposition, not from the now-professionalized KGB, but from within the armed forces and also from a leading democratic politician and CIA agent, Oleg KADISHEV.

In the wake of the Denver explosion, he goes to his underground command center and remains there during the crisis. He is increasingly confused, then alarmed, at the American belief that he has been overthrown, and is reassured only by RYAN's desperate break on to the hot line. After the crisis is defused, he is sufficiently furious with the terrorists' backers to consent to FOWLER's nuclear attack on QUM.

NARWHAL, U.S.S.:   U.S. nuclear attack submarine; in service 1969. Exceptionally quiet due to her natural-circulation reactor, she is stationed off the Soviet coast in *Storm.* She intercepts radio conversations among the aircraft of the Soviet strike against the *NIMITZ* group.

NASSAU, U.S.S.:   U.S. *TARAWA*-class amphibious assault ship; in service 1979. In *Storm,* she is the flagship of the amphibious force sent against Iceland and survives the Soviet missile attack. Michael EDWARDS is operated on in her sick bay and receives the Navy Cross after waking up.

NATIONAL EMERGENCY AIRBORNE COMMAND POST (NEACP, pronounced "KNEECAP"):   U.S. Air Force E-4B (a converted Boeing 747), equipped to act as a mobile command post for the President of the

United States during a nuclear exchange or crisis. Extensive communications facilities, living accommodations, and air-to-air refueling capability give it an endurance of several days.

In *Sum,* President FOWLER's military advisers would prefer that he board NEACP instead of remaining at CAMP DAVID. He stays on the ground, however, sending Vice President DURLING in his place. DURLING remains airborne during the crisis, and lands after the conference call set up by General FREMONT.

NATIONAL SECURITY AGENCY (NSA):   Branch of the Defense Department, primarily responsible for electronic intelligence and communications security. Established 1952; headquarters at Fort Meade, Maryland. It is sometimes in conflict with the CIA over U.S. codes and codebreaking (as in *Sum,* where NSA denies RYAN's contention that U.S. diplomatic codes have been compromised).

In *Hunt,* an NSA radio-interception station in China picks up the signals from ALBATROSS 8, with data from its pass over the submerged submarines in Pamlico Sound. In *Storm,* Robert TOLAND is employed at NSA before his recall to active duty.

In *Danger,* NSA handles communications concerning Operation SHOWBOAT; at a remote listening post, its technicians intercept a cartel conversation about missing drug shipments.

In *Sum,* NSA takes a position on codes that gives RYAN one more headache at a time when he really doesn't need it.

NATYA (NATO code name):   Soviet diesel ASW corvette; in service at the time of *Storm.* On her first patrol, *CHICAGO* detects one escorting the DELTA III into the minefield sanctuary.

NAVY CROSS: U.S. Navy and Marine Corps award for extraordinary heroism above and beyond the call of duty. Equivalent to the Army DISTINGUISHED SERVICE CROSS.

In *Storm,* Colonel LOWE has one from Vietnam; Michael EDWARDS wins one for his work on Iceland. In *Games,* Sergeant Major BRECKENRIDGE won it as a sniper in Vietnam.

NCO: Noncommissioned officer: military personnel promoted from the ranks to act as small-unit leaders, technical specialists, or advisers to COs. CLARK in *Storm,* BRECKENRIDGE in *Games,* and CHAVEZ and MITCHELL in *Danger* are all good NCOs.

NEVADA, **U.S.S.:**   U.S. *OHIO*-class submarine; in service 1986. In *Sum,* Captain DUBNIN thinks he might have detected either her or *MAINE* in the Gulf of Alaska.

***NEW JERSEY*, U.S.S.:**   U.S. *IOWA*-class battleship; in service 1942. In *Hunt,* she is the flagship of a surface action group deployed in the Atlantic against the Soviet fleet. Her 16″ guns are equipped with rocket-assisted shells. In *Storm,* she bombards Soviet artillery positions in Iceland.

***NEWPORT*, U.S.S.:**   U.S. landing ship tank; in service 1969. In *Storm,* she is one of the three Marine amphibious ships being escorted by the *NIMITZ* battle group.

NEWTON, ROBERT and **LEON:**   In *Games,* father and son who find the UZI used in the ULA attempt on Cathy and Sally RYAN while fishing in an abandoned quarry. They bring it to FBI headquarters, where it becomes a valuable clue in tracking the ULA's source of arms.

NICHOLAS II: Historical character (1868-1918). The last Czar of Russia, who abdicated after the March Revolution in 1917 and was shot with his family by the Bolsheviks in 1918.

   In *Storm,* Mikhail SERGETOV remembers that the Czar did not know what happens when Russian leaders lose the trust of the *narod* (people). The Politburo does, but is going to go ahead and break faith anyway.

   The grandfather of Mary Pat FOLEY in *Cardinal* was riding teacher to the Czar's hemophiliac son. She has always considered the death of the Czar and his family to be cold-blooded murder.

   In *Sum,* NARMONOV remembers how the Austro-Hungarian note to Serbia was so threatening that it forced the Czar to go to war to defend a people he did not love, setting the world on fire and costing him throne and life.

NICOLS, SERGEANT: In *Storm,* British Royal Marine NCO. He takes command of the Royal Marines dropped on Iceland after their CO is killed and works with EDWARDS for the remainder of the patrol's mission. Politely curious about Vigdis AGUSTDOTTIR, he comes to respect ED-WARDS, and is KIA in the patrol's final action.

***NIKOLAYEV*:**   Soviet *KARA*-class missile cruiser; in service 1973. In *Hunt,* she is in the *KIROV* group and acquired by the B-52s' targeting radars. She returns the compliment, giving an EC-135 with the B-52s a chance to record all her radar emissions.

***NIMITZ*:**   U.S. nuclear aircraft carrier, named for Chester W. NIMITZ. 81/92,000 tons; 35+ knots; 80+ aircraft, PHALANX, AA missiles; crew 6,000. In service 1975. The lead ship of what has become the standard class of U.S. nuclear carriers, she and her sisters are the largest and most formidable warships ever built.

In *Hunt, Nimitz* is in the South Atlantic, on her way to the Pacific, but is temporarily recalled to strengthen U.S. forces in the North Atlantic.

In *Storm,* she is the first flagship of the main NATO carrier battle group in the North Atlantic; Robert TOLAND is assigned to the Admiral's staff. She is also the main target of the Soviet attack; she is hit by two KINGFISH missiles and suffers heavy damage (including the destruction of the CIC) and casualties (five hundred dead, three hundred wounded).

Good damage control and the ship's aircraft being airborne at the time save the carrier. She proceeds at high speed to England, where she is docked at Southampton and receives hasty repairs, enough to make her fit for sea and even for combat again.

NIMITZ, FLEET ADMIRAL CHESTER W.: Historical figure (1885-1966). U.S. naval officer, CINCPAC 1941-45 and CNO 1945-47. One of the outstanding naval leaders of World War II and one of the American military leaders to receive a British knighthood, as RYAN does in *Games.*

NIMROD: British four-jet ASW and maritime reconnaissance aircraft; British Aerospace. 500+ mph; 12 hours' endurance; MAD, ASW torpedoes and depth charges, HARPOON; crew 13. In service with the Royal Air Force from 1969. A development of the DeHaviland Comet, the Nimrod was the first jet-powered maritime patrol aircraft.

In *Hunt,* Nimrods based in Scotland are part of the saturation air effort against the Soviet fleet. In *Storm,* they fly ASW missions; one is stationed north of Iceland to detect Soviet air raids against the ATLANTIC BRIDGE.

NKVD: Designation of the Soviet secret police (later KGB) under STALIN. In *Cardinal,* the theater doorman was glad that Lieutenant FILITOV was not some drunken NKVD officer.

NORFOLK: Seaport city in SE Virginia. With its sister cities of Newport News and Hampton, it accommodates the largest complex of naval bases in the world.

Facilities in the area include the Norfolk Naval Medical Center, Norfolk Naval Shipyard, and Eight-Ten Dock in *Hunt;* CINCLANT headquarters, the Little Creek Amphibious Base, and Langley Air Force Base in *Storm.*

NORFOLK, **U.S.S.:** U.S. 688-class submarine; in service 1983. *MAINE's* XO in *Sum,* Wally CLAGGETT, served aboard her.

NORTH AMERICAN AEROSPACE DEFENSE COMMAND (NORAD): A joint U.S.-Canadian command responsible for the detection of missile attacks on North America and the detection and interception of manned bomber attacks. Its super-hardened headquarters is at CHEY-ENNE MOUNTAIN, Colorado.

In *Hunt,* NORAD goes to a slightly increased alert status in response to the Soviet naval activity. In *Storm* it receives satellite data on the Nizhnevartovsk fire, and later monitors Soviet satellite launches and U.S. and Soviet ASAT operations.

In *Cardinal,* the Soviets are suspected of beaming lasers and microwaves at satellites just to test NORAD's reactions. They certainly get a reaction when the BRIGHT STAR laser destroys Cosmos 1810!

In *Sum,* NORAD loses its CINC in the Denver explosion, and the deputy is traveling. The officers present, however, rise to the occasion, indicating that there has been no inbound missile track and establishing that the SS-18 explosion was not a launch. Both are crucial pieces of evidence in eventually establishing Soviet innocence.

NORTH ATLANTIC TREATY ORGANIZATION (NATO):   The principal U.S.-European mutual-defense organization; established 1949. It maintains an international staff and a series of regional multinational joint commands.

In *Storm,* NATO has the major strategic control of the Allied war effort. SACEUR, although an American general, holds the principal NATO regional command.

NOVEMBER (NATO code name):   Soviet class of nuclear attack submarines. 4,200/5,000 tons; 25+ knots; 8 TT; crew 80. Fifteen built 1958-63. The first Soviet nuclear submarines, they have proved slow, noisy, and dangerously unreliable; now obsolete.

A November was Marko RAMIUS's first nuclear command, when he was in his early thirties; he rescued the crew of another November that suffered a reactor failure, then sank the vessel. In *Hunt,* two of the old boats are stationed off the American coast at the beginning of the *RED OCTOBER* incident.

In *Storm,* one November is exercising with the Cuban Navy. Others are deployed against the Atlantic convoys; a P-3 working with *PHARRIS* sinks one.

NOYES, COMMANDER ED: In *Hunt,* U.S. Navy flight surgeon. He trades medical care for pilots' dependents for flying time and has a glider license.

He is flown by helicopter from North Carolina to Maine and boards *RED OCTOBER.* There he performs emergency chest surgery on the wounded Lieutenant WILLIAMS, treats RAMIUS, and praises the Soviet lieutenant who did first-aid on WILLIAMS.

NR-1: U.S. nuclear deep-diving research submarine; in service 1969. In *Hunt,* Lieutenant AMES of *AVALON* has served aboard all the U.S. deep-submergence vehicles except the NR-1.

NUC: U.S. Navy slang for nuclear-powered vessels or personnel serving aboard them; Skip TYLER (mentioned in *Games*) or Daniel MCCAFFERTY in *Storm.*

NUCLEAR WINTER: Hypothetical condition following a nuclear war, in which smoke and dust in the atmosphere would critically lower mean temperatures worldwide. In *Storm,* the Soviets surprise Patrick FLYNN by acknowledging it in public for the first time.

NUGGET: U.S. Navy term for a newly commissioned ensign (equivalent to other services' second lieutenant), especially a naval aviator. In *Danger,* Robby JACKSON uses the term for his brother Tim. In *Sum,* CAG JACKSON wishes he were one again.

OBERON, H.M.S.: British conventional attack submarine; in service 1961. In *Storm,* her CO introduces Daniel MCCAFFERTY to Captain JOHANNSEN after *CHICAGO's* first patrol.

OBSERVATION ISLAND, U.S.S.: U.S. missile range instrumentation ship; in service 1958. In *Cardinal* she is returning from TRIDENT tests in the South Atlantic and provides both video and radar pictures for the test of the TEA CLIPPER laser that RYAN witnesses. Mounts the COBRA JUDY radar.

OCEAN STAR: In *Storm,* Panamanian cruise liner, hit by a Soviet missile in the early stages of the Atlantic battle. She burns with heavy casualties; Spanish frigates rescue the survivors.

O-CLUB: Officer's Club, social facility for officers at a military installation. In *Storm,* TOLAND, MCCAFFERTY, and MORRIS meet for bridge at the Norfolk O-Club. In *Sum,* the crews of the Japanese PRIME MINISTER's chase planes relax at the ANDREWS AFB officer's club.

O'DAY, INSPECTOR SEAN PATRICK (PAT): FBI agent, trusted by both MURRAY and SHAW. In *Danger,* they send him to ANDREWS AIR FORCE BASE to obtain confidential information on air operations, and assign him to work with the Secret Service.

He later takes charge of the surveillance of Admiral CUTTER, including the search of the man's garbage, and obtains the diskettes with the incriminating evidence against the man. O'Day finally witnesses CUTTER's suicide.

In *Sum,* he is Dan MURRAY's second-in-command at FBI Headquarters during the crisis, and helps identify Marvin RUSSELL and Ibrahim GHOSN.

O'DONNELL, KEVIN JOSEPH: In *Games,* leader of the Ulster Liberation Army. Thirty-four years old, six feet tall, one hundred sixty pounds, unmarried, and a fanatic with a strong Marxist bent and no scruples whatever. He is college educated, with a degree in political science and much exposure to left-wing professors while acquiring it.

He believes that the liberation of Ireland needs ideological commitment, and used his position as chief of security for the PROVOS to purge it of his opponents. He eliminated ten to fifteen before the Brigade Commander caught on and put out a contract on him. Another victim was a man who told the British that O'Donnell had a new source of intelligence. Generally, he is about as unpopular with his own side as he is with the British.

O'Donnell operates with a hard core of dedicated followers. He has many contacts in the international terrorist underground, and enough influence in the Soviet Union to undergo major appearance-altering plastic surgery in a KGB facility in Moscow.

He devises the plan to kidnap the PRINCE AND PRINCESS OF WALES and their son and hold them (especially the baby) hostage for the release of Irish prisoners held in British prisons. After the first failure, he launches the attack on the RYANs partly in retaliation, partly to embarrass the other Irish resistance groups. He also betrays Maureen DWYER for the same reason.

He personally leads the second attempt on Their Royal Highnesses at the RYANs' house, then leads the pursuit to Annapolis. Attempting to escape aboard *COSTANZA,* he is arrested with the remainder of his followers and is one of those executed near the opening of *Sum.*

OFFUTT AIR FORCE BASE: U.S. Air Force Base, Omaha, Nebraska, headquarters of the STRATEGIC AIR COMMAND. In *Sum,* the underground command post shares control of SAC during the crisis with the airborne CINC-SAC.

OHIO: U.S. class of BALLISTIC MISSILE SUBMARINE. 17,000/ 19,000 tons; 25 knots (submerged); 24 TRIDENT missiles, 4 TT; crew 160. Lead ship of the class in service 1981; twenty more built or building.

The *Ohios* are intended to be the major U.S. seaborne strategic launching platforms. They are probably the most advanced and certainly the quietest submarines of their type, with a radiated noise level lower than the background noise of the ocean. Named after states.

GEORGIA (*RED OCTOBER's* cover identity) in *Hunt* and *MAINE* in *Sum* are both *Ohios.* In *Sum, Ohio* herself is loading missiles at Bangor, Washington, and unable to go to sea during the crisis.

OLEG (no other names):   In *Cardinal,* an experienced KGB field agent, assigned to Tania BISYARINA for the kidnapping of Major GREGORY. A Muscovite, he has passed as an American businessman on South American missions. He is killed during GREGORY's rescue by an HRT man with an MP-5.

OLSON, LIEUTENANT GENERAL RONALD: In *Sum,* Director of the National Security Agency. Against RYAN's and the CIA's advice, he maintains that U.S. diplomatic codes have not been compromised—a position which does nothing to ease the burden on RYAN or improve relations within the U.S. intelligence establishment.

OMAHA, **U.S.S.:**   U.S. 688-class submarine; in service 1978. In *Sum,* she attempts to track *MAINE* on her first Gulf of Alaska patrol, but is detected before achieving a firing position.

O'MALLEY, LIEUTENANT COMMANDER JERRY: In *Storm,* U.S. naval officer, pilot of *REUBEN JAMES's* SEAHAWK LAMPS helicopter; nicknamed the Hammer. A decorated veteran of SAR operations in Vietnam, he doesn't care about promotion and prefers to run his department with minimum interference from the captain. Muscular, plainspoken, with a good head for liquor and a keen eye for both superior officers' problems and enemy submariners' tricks. Married, with three sons who aren't going to be sailors if he has anything to say about it.

He comes aboard *REUBEN JAMES* with a test-model SEAHAWK. He works with *BATTLEAXE's* helicopter to detect and kill the Soviet VICTOR hiding by *ANDREA DORIA.* Before the ship sails, he gets Commander MORRIS drunk and lets him talk out his guilt over the dead aboard *PHARRIS.* (That sort of problem from losing people under you is something O'Malley remembers painfully well from Vietnam.)

At sea, O'Malley shows both endurance and skill, scoring one kill in the Atlantic and a second off Iceland. He also acts as an unofficial tactical adviser to MORRIS.

O'NEIL, PADRAIG: In *Games,* spokesman for the Irish resistance movement Sinn Fein in the United States. He visits the Trauma Center in Baltimore after the attack on the RYANs, with an FBI escort who wishes they could get something on the man. He offers sanctimonious sympathy to Jack RYAN, who assaults him and has to be pulled off by Robby JACKSON; O'Neil is thereafter forcibly removed from the hospital.

OOD (OFFICER OF THE DECK):   An officer on duty aboard ship as the commanding officer's representative. In *Hunt,* Lieutenant MANNION is OOD of *DALLAS* when she detects *RED OCTOBER.* In *Sum, OMAHA's* navigator is OOD during his ship's tracking contest with *MAINE.*

OP: Observation Post, a lightly held position to provide surveillance of a target or warning of hostile attack. In *Danger,* the covert troops' OP is always equipped with a heavy weapon, an SAW or grenade launcher.

OPERATIONAL MANEUVER GROUP (OMG):   A Soviet concept: a formation of several mobile DIVISIONs, assigned to penetrate gaps in an opponent's line and carry out attacks in depth. In *Storm,* Moscow orders that the OMGs remain intact until the breakthrough is achieved, although ALEKSEYEV desperately needs reinforcements to make the breakthrough in the first place.

ORDER OF LENIN: Soviet award, for distinguished civilian or military service, comparable to U.S. Legion of Merit. The CHAIRMAN in *Storm* has it.

ORDER OF MERIT: The highest British order of knighthood. In *Sum,* Sir Basil CHARLESTON thinks RYAN deserves it for the Mideast peace settlement, and is afraid the QUEEN would give it to him if she knew about his role.

ORDER OF THE PURPLE TARGET: In *Games,* humorous award given to Jack RYAN as a token of appreciation by his ANNAPOLIS naval history class. It consists of a large brass bull's-eye hung from a purple ribbon, inscribed SHOOT ME.

ORDER OF THE RED BANNER: Soviet award for heroism in combat, comparable to U.S. SILVER STAR. In *Storm,* Major SOROKIN won it, leading his company during Operation POLAR GLORY.

OREZA, CHIEF QUARTERMASTER MANUEL (PORTAGEE):   In *Danger,* boatswain of U.S.C.G. *PANACHE.* The son of a Gloucester fisherman, he makes a fine cup of coffee, has helped educate a whole generation of Coast Guard officers during three tours at the Academy, and is a complete master of practical seamanship.

He also has a daughter in law school, who has told him of cases where people like the *EMPIRE BUILDER* pirates have escaped any punishment. Mentioning this to Red WEGENER gives his CO the idea of the mock execution to frighten the pirates into a confession. Oreza is one of the key people in carrying it out.

He is later one of the men who reveals the execution to the disguised Edward STUART, but escapes without a penalty. As the best seaman aboard, he takes *PANACHE's* wheel during the hurricane landing of the rescue helicopter, and maneuvers the cutter to allow JOHNS to make a safe landing.

ORION: U.S. turboprop ASW and maritime patrol aircraft. See P-3.

ORONTIA, CHIEF PETTY OFFICER PABLO: In *Sum,* U.S. Navy yeoman, operator in charge of the hot line during the crisis. He is a veteran of Vietnam and the Persian Gulf and does his duty in spite of having relatives in Colorado.

ORTIZ, EMILIO: In *Cardinal,* CIA field agent advising the Afghan guerrillas. A sturdy man with a gift for languages, able to pass as any sort of Caucasian, he respects Moslem customs and threatens his Army-captain partner for lacking that respect.

Strongly sympathetic to the Afghan cause, he receives Soviet equipment, prisoners, and intelligence from the ARCHER. He also supplies him with medical care, more STINGER missiles, and intelligence on the BRIGHT STAR project, which the ARCHER uses to mount his cross-border ground attack.

ORTOLAN, **U.S.S.:** U.S. *PIGEON*-class submarine-rescue vessel; in service 1973. In *Hunt,* Lieutenant AMES says that both ships are capable of supporting his DSRV *AVALON*.

OSCAR (NATO code name): Soviet class of nuclear cruise-missile submarines. 14,00/16,000 tons; 30+ knots; 24 missiles, 6 TT; crew 100+. At least five in service from 1982. The largest and most advanced Soviet cruise-missile submarine; improved versions of the PAPA.

In *Hunt,* ETHAN ALLEN has been considered for conversion into something like an Oscar, but the idea proved too expensive.

In *Storm, CHICAGO* was trailing one on her prewar patrol when she ran into the Soviet live-fire exercise. Oscars are deployed against the ATLANTIC BRIDGE and against the Marine landing in Iceland, where one damages the British carrier *ILLUSTRIOUS* with a missile and is then damaged and forced to the surface by *BATTLEAXE.*

OSIRIS, H.M.S.:   British Royal Navy conventional attack submarine; in service 1964. In *Storm* she patrols off Faslane and embarrasses MCCAF-FERTY by gaining a firing position on *CHICAGO* as the American submarine comes in from her first wartime patrol.

OVERHEAD: Naval term for "ceiling."

OVERWATCH: Ground-warfare tactic, in which part of a unit moves and the rest remains stationary, in a position to observe possible threats to the first and bring fire against them. In *Danger,* CHAVEZ suspects that the cartel's mercenaries won't know this technique.

OWENS, COMMANDER JAMES: In *Games,* senior British police officer, a large, burly, plainspoken man who comes across as having much experience as a street cop. He certainly has no use whatever for terrorists.

He is in overall charge of the ULA case and begins by interviewing RYAN in the hospital, after assuring him that he is *not* suspected of anything. He continues the investigation, commanding at the arrest of Maureen DWYER and working closely with Dan MURRAY. He plans to interview Geoffrey WATKINS personally when the man comes under suspicion, but arrives only in time to find the man's body.

P-3 ORION: U.S. four-turboprop ASW and maritime patrol aircraft; Lockheed. 400+ mph; combat radius 1,500 miles; ASW weapons (torpedoes, depth charges), AIM-9, HARPOON, MAD; crew of seven. Based on the Electra commercial airliner; in service with U.S. Navy from 1961; current version (P-3C) from 1969; widely exported.

The Orion is the standard U.S. maritime-patrol aircraft and the most widely used NATO one. It carries HARPOONs for antishipping work and AIM-9s against Soviet FORGERS.

In *Hunt,* P-3s fly from Iceland and many other bases to track the Soviet submarines heading for the American coast. They also "saturate" the air over the Soviet surface forces. Eventually they fly cover for *RED OCTO-BER* on her voyage south from Maine to Norfolk.

In *Storm,* they are active in support of the ATLANTIC BRIDGE; one kills a Soviet submarine detected by *PHARRIS.* Others are not so lucky. One goes missing early in the war, possibly the victim of a submarine-launched AA missile. Another, code-named Penguin 8, is the first NATO observer to identify *JULIUS FUCIK* as hostile, and launches two HAR-

POONs. Only one hits, not enough for a kill, and there is nothing else the Orion can do short of a kamikaze dive.

In *Sum,* P-3s have tried to locate *ADMIRAL LUNIN.* In the final crisis, one supporting the damaged *MAINE* does, and drops a MARK 50 TORPEDO on the Soviet submarine. Fortunately the torpedo explodes upon hitting a wave.

P-51: U.S. single-engined single-seat propeller-driven World War II fighter; North American. In *Danger,* even something that old could kill both the sophisticated covert-mission aircraft.

PADORIN, ADMIRAL YURI ILYCH: Historical character. In *Hunt,* chief political officer for the Soviet Navy. Although now officebound, he won the GOLD STAR commanding gunboats on the Volga in World War II. Well into his sixties, he still smokes in spite of a mild heart attack.

He has been one of RAMIUS's mentors and patrons, as well as a personal friend to the younger man and his late wife. He has even trusted RAMIUS's political reliability enough to allow the Captain to gather a band of followers aboard his new command *RED OCTOBER.* So it is a shock for him to receive RAMIUS's impudent "Dear Uncle Yuri" letter.

The letter places Padorin in a nearly impossible position, responsible for a gross breach of security. NARMONOV even threatens him with execution when informed that the "mole" aboard *RED OCTOBER* is a twenty-four-year-old cook. Neither USTINOV nor FILITOV have much use for Padorin either.

In the end, Padorin's life is saved by the success of Operation MANDOLIN, which leaves the KGB suspecting that *RED OCTOBER* has been destroyed. However, KGB chief GERASIMOV demands that as the price of surviving to draw his pension, Padorin become the KGB's tool for taking over Naval security.

PADUCAH, U.S.S.: U.S. Navy large harbor tug; in service 1961. In *Hunt,* she meets *RED OCTOBER* off Norfolk, leads her to the Eight-Ten Dock, and lines her up with the dock because the submarine's damaged bow makes maneuvering difficult.

PAINTER, JOSHUA: U.S. naval officer and aviator; native of Vermont. A Phantom pilot in Vietnam, he wrote a forthright book about his experience, *Paddystrikes.* He is small (one hundred thirty pounds), a gifted tactician, a man of puritanical integrity, and an ASW expert.

In *Hunt,* he is a rear admiral, commanding the *KENNEDY* battle group in the North Atlantic. He receives RYAN, raises eyebrows at the man's naval uniform, but thoroughly supports Operation MANDOLIN. He is the senior naval officer afloat for both the confrontation with Soviet surface forces and for contacting *RED OCTOBER*, and does a superb job in both roles.

In *Danger*, he is a vice admiral, and Assistant Chief of Naval Operations for Air Warfare. With intelligence provided by the JACKSON brothers, he draws the correct conclusions about the covert operations in which his aircraft have been involved without his knowledge—and is *not* happy. His support makes naval-aviation assets available for missions like flying RYAN down to launch the rescue mission.

In *Sum*, he is a full admiral, holding what he knows will be his last post, CINCLANT. (He has too many rough edges to be CNO.) He talks with Robby JACKSON about the problems the DRAW-DOWN may create for his Air Wing. During the crisis, he alerts all his forces, including BOOMERs and CARRIER BATTLE GROUPs.

PALESTINE LIBERATION ORGANIZATION (PLO):   The oldest and largest Palestinian political/military organization, with a complex history since the late 1960s. In *Sum*, RYAN and BEN JACOB discuss one of its major terrorist actions, in which the Japanese Red Army was hired to shoot up Israel's major international airport. The peculiar conduct of the sole surviving terrorist is evidence that in the world of terrorism almost *anything* can happen.

PANACHE, **U.S.C.G.:**   In *Danger*, a one-of-a-kind U.S. Coast Guard cutter. 280 feet long; 25 knots; 40-mm and .50-caliber guns, helicopter-landing facilities.

Under the command of Red WEGENER, she overcame problems of experimental and unreliable diesel engines, low morale, and a shipbuilder on strike, to become a crack ship. On drug patrol in the Gulf of Mexico, she intercepts *EMPIRE BUILDER*, boards her, and arrests the pirates, who are intimidated into confessing by the mock hanging.

At sea again in the Gulf during the rescue mission, she is the only possible landing site for the PAVE LOW helicopter before it runs out of fuel. Although *PANACHE's* stern helipad is marginal for the big helicopter, Colonel JOHNS's superb piloting and the seamanship of the cutter's crew make a safe landing possible. She then carries the helicopter, the survivors (the wounded in sick bay), and the captured Colonel CORTEZ to GUAN-TÁNAMO BAY.

PANZERFAUST: German World War II shoulder-fired antitank recoilless rifle. The direct ancestor of the RPG-7 used in *Danger* to assassinate JACOBS.

PAPA: Soviet nuclear CRUISE-MISSILE submarine; in service 1970. Distinguished by twin screws and high speed; prototype for the OSCAR class. In *Hunt,* the one Papa is deployed against the ATLANTIC BRIDGE, attacks *REUBEN JAMES's* convoy, and is attacked and sunk by the convoy's escorts.

PAPAGO, U.S.S.:   U.S. oceangoing fleet tug; in service 1970. In *Hunt,* she takes the damaged *PHARRIS* in tow and brings her safely to Boston.

PAPANICOLAOU, SERGEANT SPIRIDON: In *Sum,* a Hellenic National Police officer in Athens, an expert at surveillance thanks to a photographic memory for faces. He recognizes Ibrahim GHOSN as a suspect and trails him and Marvin RUSSELL without alerting help. The terrorists lure the sergeant into a blocked street, where RUSSELL kills him barehanded.

The Greeks, however, record a possible connection between GHOSN and RUSSELL. This helps the FBI, during the crisis, in establishing the terrorist nature of the Denver explosion.

PARKER, LIEUTENANT TONY: In *Hunt,* British Royal Navy officer and HARRIER pilot from *INVINCIBLE.* He shot down an Argentine DAGGER fighter during the Falklands War, and has tested his two-seater HARRIER in ASW exercises.

He flies RYAN from *KENNEDY* to *INVINCIBLE,* giving him a few unexpected thrills on the way. He later flies his HARRIER sent to escort the intelligence team's helicopter and witnesses its crash.

PARSONS, DR. LAWRENCE (LARRY):   In *Sum,* head of the Nuclear Emergency Search Team (NEST) called to Denver after the nuclear explosion. He works with both the Army and the FBI, advising on radiation exposure and helping identify the terrorists. Technicians of his team obtain samples of the radioactive material from the bomb and identify it as American.

PATRIOT: U.S. mobile SAM, with antimissile capabilities; in service 1983. In *Cardinal,* the COBRA BELLE mission commander helped develop the Patriot's antimissile capability and was CO of a Patriot battery in Texas.

PATTERSON, HARVEY and **HENRY:**   In *Danger,* Black twins, twenty-seven years old, and professional criminals (mostly armed robbery) for fourteen years. They finally face a long sentence for murdering Elrod McIlvane, the GRAYSON twins' pimp.

After the police learn that the *EMPIRE BUILDER* pirates will be allowed to plea-bargain, they offer the Patterson brothers a lighter sentence if they will kill the pirates. Using concealed homemade weapons, they carry out the killings in the prison bath.

PAULSON (no first name):   Chief sniper for the FBI Hostage Rescue Teams. A hunter who learned woodscraft in his native Tennessee, he is clearly about as good at the physically and psychologically demanding job of sniping as anyone can be. A member of the "Quarter-Inch Club"—three aimed shots into a half-inch bull's-eye at two hundred yards.

In *Games,* he responds with WERNER's HRT but is unable to engage the ULA terrorists because he cannot positively identify his targets. He witnesses DOBBENS's death and the escape of O'DONNELL and his team in the second boat.

In *Cardinal,* he is a key man in the rescue of Major GREGORY. He initiates the rescue action by killing Tania BISYARINA. After examining her body, he realizes he will not be able to hunt again.

In *Sum,* he is again the key man in a hostage situation. After John RUSSELL tries to take the newsmen hostage, Paulson kills RUSSELL and his companions without injuring either reporter. Afterward he has a confrontation with Walt HOSKINS, whom he correctly blames for letting the situation get out of hand.

PAVE LOW: U.S. covert-operations helicopter. See CH-53.

PEACEKEEPER: U.S. advanced ICBM, also known as the MX; in service from 1986. In *Storm,* the Soviet Foreign Minister calls it a first-strike weapon and considers its development a provocation.

PELT, DR. JEFFREY: In *Hunt,* the PRESIDENT's National Security Advisor. Formerly at Georgetown University's CENTER FOR STRATEGIC AND INTERNATIONAL STUDIES, he there met Jack RYAN, who found him somewhat pompous.

In fact, he does his job extremely well, supporting RYAN and Operation MANDOLIN as appropriate. He also works closely with the PRESIDENT, particularly in dealing with Ambassador ARBATOV, and proves himself a good actor at the time of the rescue of *V.K. KONOVOLOV's* one survivor.

In *Cardinal,* he meets Major GREGORY to discuss the implications of TEA CLIPPER. When CARDINAL is in danger, he warns the PRESI-DENT about the danger of weakening NARMONOV by an open demand for the man's release.

Admiral CUTTER was his deputy and successor.

PELTON: Historical character. Ronald W. Pelton, NSA employee arrested for espionage in 1985. In *Sum,* it is mentioned that he and WALKER compromised NSA codes.

PENKOVSKIY, OLEG: Historical character, executed 1963. A colonel in the GRU, he became a CIA agent in the 1950s and provided vital intelligence during the Cuban Missile Crisis, at the cost of his own exposure. He also recruited CARDINAL (Mikhail FILITOV), and urged the latter to betray him to reinforce his own cover.

In *Hunt,* RYAN learns of Penkovskiy's connection with CARDINAL when he is cleared for WILLOW and reads his first CARDINAL document, containing information on *RED OCTOBER* that FILITOV gained from Defense Minister USTINOV.

In *Cardinal,* FILITOV describes Penkovskiy as a "sad, confused man," and reminds his KGB interrogators that he himself denounced the man.

In *Sum,* RYAN says that the documents on Penkovskiy's intelligence during the Missile Crisis will be classified for another twenty years.

PERKINS, WILL: In *Cardinal,* FBI agent assigned to the security of TEA CLIPPER, partner of Margaret JENNINGS. A Mormon, he initially doubts that Bea TAUSSIG is either a lesbian or a security risk. He works with JENNINGS on the investigation of leaks and afterward on the kidnapping of GREGORY and the interrogation of TAUSSIG.

PERMIT: U.S. class of nuclear attack submarines. See 594-CLASS.

PERRIN, CAPTAIN DOUG: In *Storm,* British Royal Navy officer, CO of *BATTLEAXE.* A former submariner and friend of O'MALLEY. He promptly sends his LYNX to make the kill on the *Andrea Doria* VICTOR. Afterward he holds a party aboard his ship, and at the conclusion warns O'MALLEY that Commander MORRIS is in no shape to go to sea. After the ships put to sea, he commands his damaged frigate with skill and effectiveness.

PERRY: U.S. class of conventional missile frigates. See FFG-7.

PERSHING-2: U.S. medium-range BALLISTIC MISSILE; in service 1983. Developed to counter the Soviet SS-20; deployment opposed by German leftists (mentioned in *Sum*). Withdrawn under the Strategic Arms Limitation Treaty after 1987.

PERSISTENT AGENT: Low-volatility chemical agents which remain lethal for a long time after being delivered. In *Storm*, the East Germans fear they would wreak long-term havoc on Germany.

PETCHKIN, VASILY: In *Hunt*, second secretary at the Soviet Embassy, actually a KGB "legal" under the diplomatic cover. He heads the Soviet team visiting the Norfolk Naval Medical Center to see *V.K. KONOVO-LOV's* survivor, and lights a cigarette in the oxygen-rich environment of the intensive-care unit. As this could cause fatal burns to KATYSKIN, it leads to a confrontation with Captain TAIT, who accuses Petchkin of a murder attempt and has him barred from the floor by armed Marines. It seems that Petchkin was ignorant and arrogant rather than homicidal.

PETCHUKOCOV, CHIEF ENGINEER VLADIMIR: In *Hunt*, chief engineer of the *ALFA*-class submarine *E.S. POLITOVSKY*. A good atheist, he still wishes that he had the help of a few blessings and prayers at the ship's launching, for the temperamental and dangerous power plant.

He diagnoses the plant as in need of minor repairs and urges the captain to slow down, but under the influence of the *zampolit* the captain refuses. This leads to a catastrophic loss-of-coolant accident and a meltdown of the nuclear pile. Petchukocov dies heroically at his post, knowing that he is doomed but vainly hoping that he has saved at least some of his shipmates.

PETROV, DR. YEVGENI KONSTANTINOVICH: In *Hunt*, *RED OC-TOBER's* medical officer. He prefers East German instruments and pharmaceuticals to Soviet ones, and finds submarine duty tedious, surrounded by healthy young men who give him nothing to do unless they have an accident.

Although Marko RAMIUS does not bring him into the defection plot, the Schoolmaster manages to cure Petrov's boredom and make him play a vital role in *RED OCTOBER's* escape. The first step is to secure Petrov's certification that Political Representative PUTIN is dead.

Petrov is then confronted with carefully exposed crew radiation badges as evidence of overdosages from a radiation leak. The doctor becomes and remains a believer in RAMIUS's cover story and is one of the officers evacuated with the returning crew. He continues to support RAMIUS even in his interrogation by the KGB on the flight home.

PHALANX CLOSE-IN-WEAPON-SYSTEM (CIWS): U.S. shipboard AA weapon, consisting of a VULCAN 20-mm cannon in a self-contained mount, with its own radar, power, and ammunition supply (depleted-uranium rounds). In service from 1980; to be installed in over 250 U.S. ships. Nicknamed "R2D2" because of its resemblance to the robot in *Star Wars.*

In *Storm,* many ships carry it and some use it in action. A *NIMITZ* CIWS tries to track two incoming KINGFISH, ends up tracking neither, and allows damaging hits. Aboard *NASSAU* off Iceland, another R2D2 blows up a missile so close that the ship suffers fragment damage.

PHANTOM: U.S. jet fighter. See F-4.

***PHARRIS,* U.S.S.:** 1052-class frigate; in service 1974. In *Storm,* she is commanded by Commander Edward MORRIS, and is clearly his pride and joy. He even exercises a CO's privilege of having his ship's number on his license plate.

Under his command she escorts three Atlantic convoys, engaging Soviet aircraft and submarines. She assists with the kills of a NOVEMBER and a FOXTROT, and scores a solo kill against a CHARLIE, taking eleven Russian survivors prisoner.

However, the skilled captain of a Soviet VICTOR is able to reach a firing position undetected. A torpedo hit blows off *PHARRIS's* bow, leaving her disabled with fourteen of her crew dead or missing, her gun gone, and one boiler inoperable. Heroic damage control and good luck with the weather bring her safely to Boston, where she remains for the rest of the war as the shipyards work on vessels that can be repaired in time to return to combat.

PHILBY, KIM: Historical character. At one time head of British counterintelligence against the Soviet Union, he was also a Soviet agent who fled to Russia in 1963. His recruitment was one of the all-time coups for Soviet intelligence. In *Cardinal,* PLATONOV considers the possibility of recruiting RYAN, which would be nearly as big a victory.

PHOENIX: U.S. air-to-air missile. See AIM-54.

***PIGEON,* U.S.S.:** U.S. submarine-rescue vessel. 3,400/4,500 tons; 15 knots; crew 200. In service 1973. Catamaran (twin-hull) design, with advanced anchoring gear; support DSRV.

In *Hunt,* she is based out of Norfolk and takes the DSRV *AVALON* out to the rendezvous with *RED OCTOBER.* She receives the crew evacuated from the Soviet vessel by both *AVALON* and *MYSTIC,* and gives them a lavish meal before they are evacuated to the mainland by helicopter.

PITTSBURGH, U.S.S.:   U.S. 688-class nuclear attack submarine; in service 1985. In *Storm,* she participates in Operation DOOLITTLE.

PIZARRO: Historical character (1474-1541). Francisco Pizarro, Spanish explorer, who overthrew the Inca Empire and conquered Peru. In *Danger,* CLARK claims to have discovered gold, "the biggest find since Pizarro," to lure out ESCOBEDO.

PLANES: Movable horizontal control surfaces, mounted at the bow (or SAIL) and stern of a submarine. Varying the angle of the planes permits the submarine to rise or dive without the noise of blowing tanks. In *Hunt, E.S. POLITOVSKY's* planes are thrown over to full rise by electrical failure while the submarine is at full speed, and she ends climbing nearly vertically.

PLANKOWNER: Naval personnel who help put a ship in commission; from the tradition that each of them owns a plank of the ship's deck. MCCAFFERTY in *Storm* and ROSSELLI in *Sum* have the best of it, being not only plankowners but COs.

PLATONOV, SERGEY NIKOLAYOVICH: Third Secretary of the Soviet Embassy; in fact, the KGB *rezident* (senior officer) in Washington. Florid, superficially jolly, he is nonetheless a professional and RYAN does not much care for him. He is married, with two sons; he lost his daughter, Nadia, to leukemia at the age of seven.

In *Games,* he meets RYAN at a Georgetown University reception. They exchange barbed pleasantries as Platonov tries to learn more about RYAN and dissociate the Soviet Union from the ULA attack on RYAN's family.

In *Cardinal,* he has a "covert" meeting with RYAN, as part of the CIA's deception plan. The meeting, a study of RYAN's files, and possibly wishful thinking convince him that RYAN is genuinely disaffected—which further reduces Soviet alertness about the CIA's plans for saving FILITOV.

PLIMSOLL MARKS: Lines painted fore and aft on the hull of a ship, indicating her draft; originally devised as a safety measure to prevent overloading. In *Cardinal,* water covers *RED OCTOBER's* Plimsoll marks as the Eight-Ten Dock is flooded before the submarine sets out on her final voyage.

PNG'ED: Declared *persona non grata:* unwelcome in a country and required to leave immediately. In *Cardinal,* the Soviet government declares the FOLEYs PNG after Mary Pat's efforts to warn FILITOV.

POGY, U.S.S.:   U.S. 637-class submarine; in service 1971.

In *Hunt,* she is at sea off the U.S. coast following a refit when the Soviet submarines hunting *RED OCTOBER* begin arriving. She is tracking two

ALFAs, one of them *E.S. POLITOVSKY,* when the Soviet submarine has her fatal accident. *Pogy's* sonar gives her a ringside seat at the other submarine's death and pinpoints the sinking enough to allow for the rescue of a survivor and exploratory dives.

After contact is made with *RED OCTOBER, Pogy* works with *DALLAS* in escorting the Soviet submarine. She supports them in their confrontation with *KONOVOLOV,* using her sonar as a weapon since she cannot legally open fire. She then continues the escort mission all the way south and works with *DALLAS* off the Virginia Capes as the Soviet submarine enters NOR-FOLK.

POINT GABRIEL, U.S.C.G.:   82-foot U.S. Coast Guard patrol vessel. Stationed at the mouth of the Columbia River, she was the flagship of Red WEGENER (in *Danger*) during the *MARY-KAT* SAR operation, although manned by a mixed crew of veterans and volunteers.

POKRYSHKIN, GENERAL: In *Cardinal,* commander of the BRIGHT STAR facility, a former fighter pilot but now primarily an engineer and researcher. Although he has connections in the Ministry of Defense, he remains an able, hardworking leader and cooperates with Colonel BON-DARENKO. He appears to have been somewhat careless about security (no sentry dogs), or else allowed the KGB CO to be so.

In the Afghan attack, POKRYSHKIN effectively turns over command to the Colonel. He remains with the rearguard, fighting a delaying action to protect the staff, and is killed by the Afghan MAJOR.

POLAR GLORY, OPERATION: In *Storm,* Soviet code name for the operation to seize Iceland, a brilliant strategic coup which breaches the G.I. UK GAP and threatens the ATLANTIC BRIDGE.

POLARIS: U.S. SLBM; in service 1960-81. The first SLBM capable of being launched from a submerged submarine. In *Hunt, ETHAN ALLEN* carried Polaris missiles for more than twenty years of patrols.

POLITBURO: The directing body of the Communist Party of the Soviet Union, normally consisting of thirteen full and eight candidate members. It elects the CHAIRMAN, and is nominally elected by the CENTRAL COM-MITTEE. In fact, the full members are the real rulers of the Soviet Union.

Marko RAMIUS's father, Alexsandr, served STALIN so well that he was a candidate member of the Politburo at the time of his death.

In *Storm,* Mikhail SERGETOV is a candidate member, basically an adviser, but plays a key part in all the debates, including the ones to start the war and escalate to nuclear weapons. Most of the Politburo is arrested in SERGETOV's coup.

In *Sum,* reforms have effectively eliminated it, along with the opportunities it gave Soviet statesmen for a high-level apprenticeship in international politics. KADISHEV intends to keep this in mind.

PONCE, U.S.S.:   U.S. *AUSTIN*-class amphibious transport dock; in service 1971. In *Storm,* she is one of the three amphibious vessels with the *NIMITZ* battle group, but survives the Soviet missile attack.

POTI (NATO code name):   Soviet class of conventional ASW corvettes; 70+ built 1961-67. In *Storm, CHICAGO* has a sonar plot on one in the Barents Sea while tracking Soviet BOOMERs before the war.

PPSh SUBMACHINE GUN: Standard Soviet Army World War II SMG, 7.62-mm, noted for its pan-shaped 71-round magazine. In *Hunt,* RAMIUS remembers carrying a deactivated one as a YOUNG PIONEER, standing guard at Soviet war memorials.

PRESIDENT (unnamed):   President of the United States. Formerly a prosecuting attorney, he has sent at least one kidnapper to execution and survived an attempt on his life by the Mafia, which did his career no harm.

In *Hunt,* he has many of the virtues of a good leader, including the willingness to hear and support subordinates like RYAN and PELT. He and PELT make a good team for dealing with Ambassador ARBATOV. He also shows some acting ability as he orders medical care for the *V.K. KONOVOLOV* survivor and indignantly denies the charge of "kidnapping" *RED OCTOBER's* crew.

Jeffrey PELT is right: the man didn't start off knowing much about foreign policy, but picked up a working knowledge of it very quickly.

In *Cardinal,* he is balancing the value of the TEA CLIPPER project, on the verge of success, against its effects on the strategic-arms negotiations with the Soviets. The balancing act becomes even more nerve-racking when the safety of FILITOV, to whom the United States owes so much, becomes a factor. The President is more than ever aware of how acutely painful the ethical dilemmas of power can be.

The President reluctantly refuses to demand FILITOV's release or authorize his extraction. This reluctance fades, however, after GREGORY's kidnapping, when the President authorizes the FBI to use deadly force even if GREGORY is not in danger.

In *Danger,* he appears to be suffering from election-year jitters. Although he sets the actions against the drug cartel in motion by declaring them a "clear and present danger" to the U.S., he is almost obsessively concerned about COLLATERAL DAMAGE. This leads to several key people (such as RYAN) not being adequately informed, and also influences Admiral CUTTER, who lacks the command or combat experience to handle this situation.

After the civilian casualties from the two bombings are revealed, the President's outrage leaves CUTTER fearing for his job. This in turn leads to his negotiations with CORTEZ and the attempted betrayal of the covert-action troops, only prevented by the secret rescue mission.

The President has a disagreeable confrontation with RYAN, whose Irish temper is aroused over what he considers the President's questionable ethics. In the end, the President loses his bid for re-election, being narrowly defeated by Robert FOWLER.

PRESIDENT OF MEXICO (unnamed):   In *Sum,* he has been generously bribed by the Japanese to violate trade treaties. RYAN threatens to expose this bribe during the crisis, to force the Mexican authorities to cooperate with CLARK and CHAVEZ in arresting QATI and GHOSN.

PREVAIL, U.S.N.S.:   U.S. ocean surveillance ship; in service 1986. Civilian-manned, she resembles a large fishing vessel and tows a 6,000-foot sonar array. In *Storm,* she is on station in the North Atlantic during the war and detects Soviet submarines approaching *REUBEN JAMES's* convoy.

PRIME MINISTER OF JAPAN (unnamed):   In *Sum,* head of the Japanese government; fond of luxuries (like a specially fitted 747) and convinced that every man ought to have his price. He has paid a twenty-five-*million*-dollar bribe to the PRESIDENT OF MEXICO to ignore trade treaties.

RYAN obtains his first intelligence about this from LYALIN and seeks confirmation by having the Prime Minister's 747 bugged. This provides the desired confirmation, and also makes CLARK and CHAVEZ available in Mexico during the crisis.

PRINCE OF WALES (not named):   Heir to the British throne; eldest son of the QUEEN OF ENGLAND. He holds the rank of Captain in the Royal Navy and is a rated PHANTOM pilot and parachutist. He has also had Royal Marine training in ground combat and is in good physical condition.

In *Games,* he and the PRINCESS OF WALES and their infant son are saved by RYAN's intervention from a ULA attempt at kidnapping. The Prince throws his family to the floor of the limousine and covers them with his own body.

This is exactly the right thing to do, but he feels guilty about not doing more until he visits RYAN in the hospital. At that point RYAN reads the Prince the riot act, based on his own Marine training, and the police support RYAN's position.

Refusing to be intimidated by the terrorists, the Prince goes ahead with plans for a visit to the United States and dinner with the RYANs. In spite of stringent security precautions, the ULA's second attack is launched and nearly succeeds.

In the fight after Robby JACKSON intervenes with a shotgun, the Prince is valuable in the rough-and-tumble subduing of the remaining terrorists. He helps in the descent of the cliff and in taking care of the women on the way to ANNAPOLIS.

After the women are safe, the Prince remains aboard the pursuit YP boat and mans the radar tracking the terrorists. He is present at the final roundup of the terrorists aboard *COSTANZA*.

In *Sum,* he dines with RYAN, and is concerned about the American's health. The Prince and Sir Basil CHARLESTON are the only two Englishmen who know the truth about RYAN's role in the Mideast peace settlement.

PRINCESS OF WALES (unnamed):   Wife of the PRINCE OF WALES, and with him, object of the ULA's attempts at kidnapping in *Games.*

In the London attempt, her husband protects her with his own body. Although unhurt, she has the driver's brains splattered on her face and is in shock afterward.

At the time of the second attempt, she is pregnant again. She conducts herself with great dignity and courage, helping the wounded Sissy JACKSON.

PROVIDENCE, U.S.S.:   U.S. 688-class submarine; in service 1985. In *Storm,* she participates in Operation DOOLITTLE. Detected and attacked by *AMETIST,* she is severely damaged by an ASW rocket hit. Her CO urges MCCAFFERTY to leave, but the senior officer refuses and sets out to escort *PROVIDENCE* to the safety of the polar ice cap, since she is too badly damaged to return south or proceed unescorted.

With *BOSTON, CHICAGO* successfully escorts the damaged submarine most of the way to the ice, engaging Soviet ASW forces on the way. *PROVIDENCE,* too noisy and too slow to escape, is finally sunk by a lurking ALFA.

PROVISIONAL IRISH REPUBLICAN ARMY (PIRA OR PRO-VOS):   Marxist faction of the IRA, which broke away from the now inactive parent organization in the 1970s. It is responsible for most of the anti-British and anti-Protestant terrorism connected with the Troubles in Northern Ireland. It has received money and weapons from the American Irish community and some from the Soviet-backed international terrorist underground.

In *Games,* Kevin O'DONNELL was their chief of internal security until he eliminated too many of his ideological opponents. Now the PIRA would be as glad as the British to see the end of him, as their representative assures David ASHLEY in Dublin. Maureen DWYER was a Provo bomber for three years before her betrayal and arrest.

PROWLER: U.S. electronic-warfare aircraft, nicknamed "Queer." See A-6.

PURDEY: British brand of high-quality shotguns. In *Hunt,* RYAN mentions using a pair that he couldn't use comfortably when he went shooting with Admiral WHITE.

PURGA: Soviet armed icebreaker, possibly KGB-manned; in service 1955. In *Hunt,* she clears a path through the ice of Polyarny as *RED OCTOBER* puts to sea.

PURPLE HEART: U.S. military award, given to personnel killed, wounded, or dead of wounds. In *Cardinal,* Augie GIANNINI has four of them from Vietnam, which means four combat wounds.

PUTIN, CAPTAIN SECOND RAN IVAN YUREVICH: In *Hunt, RED OCTOBER's* Political Officer *(zampolit).* A loud-mouthed political hack, he knows *RED OCTOBER's* orders and has the other warhead-control key. So he has to be eliminated, which RAMIUS does quickly and effectively, breaking his neck in such a way that the ship's doctor pronounces it an accident.

In *Cardinal,* we learn that Putin was KGB. In his blackmailing GERASIMOV, RYAN tells the man that Putin was part of RAMIUS's plot but died of a heart attack in the U.S.—and that this is a lie, "but try proving it!"

QATI, ISMAEL: In *Sum,* Palestinian terrorist, leader of the bomb plot (although his financial support comes from the Ayatollah DARYEI). An experienced field commander for the Popular Front for the Liberation of Palestine, he has been associated with numerous incidents, including the bombing of the Marine barracks in Beirut, Lebanon, in 1982. He has worked with Günther BOCK, speaks five languages, and is a devout, even fanatical Moslem. He has also had a brief affair with Petra HASSLER-

BOCK (after a successful mission), and is suffering from terminal cancer (which makes him even more willing to die if he can take enough of his enemies with him).

Desperate after the Mideast peace settlement shows signs of success, he is given a new opportunity with the discovery of the Israeli nuclear weapon on the Druse FARMER's land and its identification by Ibrahim GHOSN. Using his contacts with Günther BOCK, he recruits Manfred FROMM for the work on the bomb, while using Marvin RUSSELL for his knowledge of the United States. (He considers RUSSELL an infidel, being generally less tolerant than GHOSN.)

Although the cancer is progressing, Qati is able to carry the project through to the end. He and GHOSN get the bomb to Denver, murder RUSSELL, set the timer, and leave the city safely. He follows the same path as GHOSN, although because of the effect of the cancer on his appearance he is harder to identify. He is arrested with GHOSN in Mexico City, interrogated by CLARK and LARSON on the flight home, confesses, and is executed in Saudi Arabia.

QUANTICO: U.S. Marine base in NE Virginia, site of many Marine schools, including the Basic Officers' Course from which Jack RYAN graduated.

QUEEN OF ENGLAND (Queen Caroline): The constitutional monarch of Great Britain and Northern Ireland. Mother of the PRINCE OF WALES; accomplished at putting people at their ease.

In *Games,* she and her husband, the DUKE OF EDINBURGH, visit Jack RYAN in the hospital after his first encounter with the ULA, to express their gratitude. She also makes him a Knight of the Royal Victorian Order, for service to the Crown. Meanwhile she has ordered Cathy and Sally RYAN to be accommodated in the security of Buckingham Palace, the London royal residence, although RYAN warns her about Sally's tendency to break things.

After RYAN's release from the hospital, the Queen invites the RYANs to a state dinner, accommodates the whole family, and provides Cathy with a tour of castles and Sally with riding lessons. She is much charmed with Sally, who insists on the Queen kissing her goodnight at bedtime.

After the attack on Cathy and Sally RYAN in the United States, the Queen sends a personal message of sympathy, for which RYAN is profoundly grateful.

In *Sum,* both Sir Basil CHARLESTON and the PRINCE OF WALES will keep RYAN's role in the peace settlement secret, or the Queen might honor him so publicly that the secret will be out.

QUEENFISH, U.S.S.:   U.S. 637-class submarine; in service 1966. In *Hunt,* she is tracking a Soviet BOOMER when it is recalled.

QUENTIN, COMMANDER (no first name):   In *Hunt,* U.S. naval officer. On limited duty while recovering from a battle with cancer, he is in charge of the SOSUS operations center, monitoring submarine activity in the North Atlantic. A surface-warfare officer, he has always regarded submarines as the enemy and is frustrated at having so many Soviet boats located without any of them being attacked.

QUM: City in NW-central Iran, a holy city to Shiite Moslems. In *Sum* it is the residence of the Ayatollah DARYEI; he moves around enough to make a normal assassination impossible. This leads President FOWLER to prepare a nuclear strike on the city, whose destruction would have led to a *jihad* against the United States.

RALSTON, ENSIGN WILLY: In *Storm,* U.S. naval officer and helicopter pilot. A non-drinker, he is inexperienced, even naive, but cool-headed and a quick learner. He is O'MALLEY's copilot, monitors the tactical display located between the two pilots' seats, and gets a quick, drastic, and thorough education in ASW while flying from *REUBEN JAMES.*

RAMIREZ, CAPTAIN (no first name):   In *Danger,* U.S. Army officer, a tough, fair leader of the covert-action troops. He trains with them and goes on both missions into Colombia. The senior officer after Captain Rojas's death, he is KIA in a desperate rearguard action against cartel troops.

RAMIUS, ALEXSANDR: The Lithuanian father of Marko RAMIUS. A faithful Stalinist, he helped round up "anti-Soviet elements" after the occupation of his native country in 1940. He later distinguished himself as a political commissar at the Battle of Leningrad and rose steadily through the ranks of the Party *apparat* until he was a candidate member of the POLITBURO at the time of his death. His career made his son's possible—and made that son ashamed of him.

RAMIUS, CAPTAIN FIRST RANK MARKO ALEXANDRO-VICH: Soviet naval officer, CO of *RED OCTOBER,* outstanding submarine tactician, and leader in his ship's successful defection to the United States.

The son of Alexsandr RAMIUS and a Russian mother who died in childbirth during the siege of Leningrad, Ramius learned to love the sea while being raised by his paternal grandfather on the Baltic coast. A major influence there was an old fisherman named Sasha, a veteran of the Russo-Japanese War, who took Marko out in his boat many times and entertained him with stories of seafaring.

Ramius entered naval training at the age of thirteen and rose rapidly thereafter. His career was largely in submarines, and he received his first nuclear command in his early thirties. His record included rescuing the whole crew of a sinking NOVEMBER and tracking U.S.S. *TRITON* so effectively that the American vessel was retired shortly afterward.

In due course, Ramius became known as the "Vilnius Schoolmaster" (from his birthplace and his skill at teaching submarine tactics). He trained many of the Soviet Navy's best submarine captains and commissioned the first ship of each new submarine class, including the *ALFA*-class *E.S. POLITOVSKY* (which he saved when she was severely damaged in a high-speed collision with a whale).

Ramius had always had vague suspicions that Socialism did not meet as many human needs as it claimed. This conviction did not affect his loyalty, although it made him less active politically than needed for promotion to admiral—a promotion he did not in any case want.

Meanwhile Ramius had enjoyed a long and happy marriage to Natalya Bogdanova RAMIUS. Her death crystallized his realization that the Soviet system was a failure. More important, her death was a crime by the system that demanded its punishment.

Thanks to his reputation and reliability, Marko was not suspected of a "cult of personality" when he handpicked certain officers for his new command, the Soviet Navy's latest BALLISTIC MISSILE SUBMARINE. What he was actually doing was assembling his party of defectors, right under Yuri PADORIN's nose.

At the opening of *Hunt,* Ramius is taking his ship to sea. He quickly disposes of the *zampolit,* the loud and useless PUTIN, and tells the crew about a secret change of orders that will take them to Cuba instead of staying in Arctic waters running exercises. Faith in Ramius, reinforced by the engineers' skilled faking of reactor trouble, keep the crew loyal as *RED OCTOBER* is pursued across the Atlantic.

Thanks to the American support mobilized on the basis of Jack RYAN's evaluation of *RED OCTOBER's* behavior (confirmed by CARDINAL), Ramius is able to make contact with the Americans. Ramius's ten-officer party stays behind, with the ironic cover story of making sure the ship will *not* fall into the hands of the Americans, while the remaining officers and crew are evacuated by DSRV for eventual return to the Soviet Union.

This does not save Marko from being wounded in the leg by the GRU agent who remained behind, when he and RYAN search the missile compartment. But the wound, while painful, is not serious, and RYAN kills the agent and administers first aid.

Off the Maine coast Ramius receives medical care from Dr. NOYES, food and reinforcements from *DALLAS*. Under American escort he takes his ship south, to encounter his star pupil, Captain TUPELOV of *V.K. KONOVOLOV,* who recognizes the unique signature of *RED OCTOBER's* CATERPILLAR drive. This leads to a deadly underwater duel in which the American escorts cannot legally intervene.

However, the teacher is still better than the pupil. In spite of his wound, his short and mixed crew, the inability to launch torpedoes, and damage to his vessel, Ramius maneuvers *RED OCTOBER* so as to ram *KONOVOLOV* and sink her. He then takes his vessel to Norfolk, Virginia.

Ramius and his men are given asylum in the United States. By the time of *Cardinal,* he has been working with the United States Navy and the CIA for some time, including cruises aboard 688-class submarines and visits to the AUTEC range. His English is improving, and he is known as "Mark Ramsey."

He first appears in Norfolk, saying farewell to his ship as she heads out to sea on her last voyage, to be scuttled in deep water. He is aboard *DALLAS* when she enters the Baltic on her covert CARDINAL mission. On the way in he advises MANCUSO on Soviet ASW deployments; on the way out, with GERASIMOV's family aboard, he fools a KGB corvette captain into thinking that *DALLAS* is a Soviet vessel.

In *Sum,* Captain DUBININ remembers learning submarining under Ramius. He would like to play the same role for the next generation of Soviet submarine captains.

Ramius, the "New Soviet man," was too much of a man to be content with being merely Soviet, when he saw what that really meant.

RAMIUS, NATALYA BOGDANOVA: Marko RAMIUS's wife. She and Marko had a long and happy marriage, although childless. With her husband, she virtually adopted a number of promising young officers as the sons she never had.

She died of postoperative infection after an appendectomy. The operation was botched by a drunken surgeon, related to a Party mogul and therefore untouchable. The fatal infection developed after the use of unreliable Soviet-made antibiotics. Natalya's death precipitated her husband's decision to break with the Soviet state and to punish it for murdering her.

RANGER: U.S. Army elite reconnaissance/raider troops. Many officers and men now assigned to Ranger BATTALIONs are graduates of the rigorous Ranger School at Fort Benning, Georgia. These include both Ding CHAVEZ and Timothy JACKSON in *Danger*.

***RANGER*, U.S.S.:**   U.S. conventional aircraft carrier, *FORRESTAL* class; in service 1957. In *Danger,* Robby JACKSON is aboard her for bomb and missile tests. She is also the ship assigned to launch the two MEDELLIN raids.

RAPID DEPLOYMENT FORCE: U.S. joint command, intended for intervention in the Middle East; established 1979-80. In *Hunt,* the Russians know that it is largely on paper and no threat to their plans for taking the Mideast oil fields if it is not reinforced with the armored and mechanized units that will be tied up by RED STORM.

RAVEN: U.S. electronic-warfare aircraft. See F-111.

RBU: *Reaktivnaya bombometnaya ustanovka* (Rocket Bombardment Mount). Soviet ASW rocket launcher, firing either contact-fused rockets or rocket-propelled depth charges. Numerous models, in service from 1957.

In *Storm,* Soviet destroyers engage *KOBBEN* with their RBUs. Later, during Operation DOOLITTLE, *AMETIST* hits *PROVIDENCE* with an RBU rocket. In *Cardinal,* MANCUSO knows that RBUs aboard Soviet GRISHAs will be useless over ice.

REAR ADMIRAL (LOWER HALF):   In *Sum,* the rank for which Bart MANCUSO has been selected. The U.S. Navy has no peacetime one-star rank, so the two-star rear admirals are divided into two halves. MANCUSO would be equivalent to a brigadier general; PAINTER in *Hunt* to a major general.

RECON MARINES: U.S. Marines trained for amphibious reconnaissance operations and raids, analogous to the Army RANGERS. The Marines who rescue EDWARDS in *Storm* and capture and interrogate the crew of the drug-running DC-7 in *Danger* are Recon Marines.

RED ARMY FACTION: West German terrorist organization, which evolved from the BAADER-MEINHOF GANG in the 1970s; assassinated a German businessman in 1985. Has cooperated with *ACTION DIRECTE.*

In *Games,* it is one of the groups whose captured members often refuse to confess, knowing they will not be tortured. Dan MURRAY knows this is exploiting a weakness of democracies that the democracies cannot change.

In *Sum,* both Günther BOCK and his wife were active in the group. Petra was caught by GSG-9, and many other RAF people were rounded up on the basis of intelligence obtained from East German files after the unification of Germany. Günther BOCK was one of those who escaped to the temporary safety of Bulgaria.

RED BRIGADE(S): Italian terrorist organization, best known for the kidnapping and murder of statesman Aldo Moro in 1979. In *Games,* RYAN thinks that they may be using the suspected terrorist camp along with the ULA and *ACTION DIRECTE.* In *Sum,* their resurgence produces heavy security precautions at the Rome peace conference.

RED OCTOBER: Soviet BALLISTIC MISSILE SUBMARINE, a development of the TYPHOON class. 32,000 tons (submerged); 650 feet long, 85-foot beam; crew up to 200. In addition to being larger, she differs from the original TYPHOONs in carrying twenty-six (instead of twenty) missiles. Like the standard TYPHOONs, she has a double-pressure hull, with a seven-foot space between the inner and outer hulls to absorb torpedo explosions.

In *Hunt,* she is under the command of Marko RAMIUS, and is his vehicle for defecting to the United States. She survives all the dangers of her passage to American waters, including a hit by a MARK C torpedo from *V.K. KONOVOLOV.* This inflicts considerable damage forward, but even the heavy Soviet warhead cannot make a fatal penetration of the inner hull. Battered but triumphant, *Red October* reaches Norfolk and the Eight-Ten Dock in safety.

Red October is subjected to a minute examination by U.S. authorities, including the removal of her missiles, reactor, sonar, and everything else of possible interest. The reactor plant is tested in Idaho and at least two of the missiles are secretly launched from Vandenberg Air Force Base in California.

At the opening of *Cardinal, Red October* is making her last voyage. With a skeleton crew aboard, she is heading out under diesel power, her passage cleared by large-scale ASW exercises off the Virginia coast. She will be scuttled in the Caribbean, in 25,000 feet of water.

Although the submarine is gone, one of her warhead-control keys survives. RYAN uses it in his confrontation with GERASIMOV over FILITOV, as evidence that a major breach of Soviet security took place after all—with the cooperation of a KGB agent.

Marko RAMIUS says it well: "He was good ship."

REDEYE: U.S. shoulder-fired SAM. 1,000 mph; range 2 miles; infrared homing. In service with U.S. and allies from 1968. The first shoulder-fired SAM, now replaced by the more advanced STINGER, it has turned up in the hands of terrorists, such as the ULA in *Games,* when they use it to shoot down an FBI helicopter during the battle at the RYANs'.

REFORGER: Return of Forces to Germany. U.S. plan to deploy up to six divisions' worth of reinforcements to Germany in the first week of a war. In *Storm,* Reforger is authorized before the shooting starts and the Allied commanders know this will force the Russians' hand.

REGIMENT: In Soviet and Soviet-bloc forces, the basic tactical unit, consisting of three or more BATTALIONs (ground forces) or SQUAD-RONs (air and missile units). In the U.S. forces, regiments exist only in the armored cavalry, such as the 10th Armored Cavalry Regiment reactivated as the Mideast peacekeeping force in *Sum* or the 11th Armored Cavalry, Sergeant MACKALL's unit in *Storm.*

***REUBEN JAMES,* U.S.S.:** U.S. FFG-7-class frigate (FFG-57); in service 1986.

In *Storm,* she is originally in the Pacific, and is one of the ships redeployed through the Panama Canal to reinforce the Atlantic convoy escorts. On the way to Norfolk, her captain collapses from a bleeding ulcer brought on by overwork in getting his ship fully operational.

Edward MORRIS is given command of *REUBEN JAMES.* He has little experience with the FFG-class vessels and has heard rumors about the laid-back California Navy, but keeps an open mind and is willing to learn. Also, he has inherited a good ship and a good crew, and has the help of Jerry O'MALLEY with more than the ship's helicopter.

Under MORRIS's command, *REUBEN JAMES* is involved in the destruction of four Soviet submarines and the escort of the crucial Atlantic convoy as well as the Marine landing on Iceland. She suffers no damage or casualties.

RF-5: U.S.-built Norwegian twin-engined, single-seat supersonic jet reconnaissance plane; Northrop. In *Hunt,* the last Norwegian RF-5 is sent to Bodo (where the Soviets may have landed) and disappears.

RICHARDS, CAPTAIN ERNIE: In *Sum,* U.S. naval officer, CO of *THEODORE ROOSEVELT.* A friend of Robby JACKSON, he uses *Star Wars* music to signal alerts and is senior officer of the battle group during the crisis. He authorizes JACKSON's engagements with the MiG-29s and the subsequent SAR for the splashed pilots.

RICHARDSON, MAJOR ANDY: In *Hunt,* Maryland Air National Guard officer and A-10 pilot. Normally he flies DC-9s for USAir, but his 175th Tactical Fighter Group has been called to active duty for the *RED OCTOBER* crisis.

Guided by an E-3 SENTRY, he leads a flight of four A-10s on a low-level approach to the *KIROV* group. Coming in on the deck, the aircraft are difficult radar targets and are able to catch *KIROV* in a box of magnesium flares. This simulates an attack that the Soviets know would have probably sunk *KIROV* for the loss of no more than two A-10s. All four aircraft evade a belated launch of FORGERs from *KIEV.*

RICKOVER, HYMAN G.: Historical character (1900-86). U.S. admiral, a brilliant, bad-tempered technocrat and father of the U.S. nuclear navy. Like James GREER he was so good that he stayed on the job long past retirement age; GREER is much easier to work for.

RICKS, CAPTAIN HARRISON SHARPE (HARRY): In *Sum,* U.S. naval officer, CO of the GOLD CREW of *MAINE* in succession to John ROSSELLI.

Ricks is a technically brilliant officer, an Annapolis graduate with a strong engineering background. He is also extremely aggressive, believing that *OHIOs* can use their quietness to successfully track attack submarines.

Unfortunately, he is also a harsh, authoritarian martinet, in contrast to ROSSELLI. Driving rather than leading his crew, he wants a perfect score on the Operational Reactor Safeguard Examination; minor faults in the sonar and torpedo departments also set him off. (FBI Director Bill SHAW's son, Ensign Ken SHAW, is one of his pet hates.)

During his first patrol in *MAINE* he applies his tactical notions; he tracks *OMAHA* and is detected by *ADMIRAL LUNIN.* He also damages crew morale; there are numerous requests for transfers. Even Ronald JONES, visiting as a civilian technical expert, notices the situation, and RICKS's XO, Wally CLAGGETT, is torn between loyalty to his skipper and loyalty to the crew.

Bart MANCUSO finally confronts Ricks. The Captain is nearly insubordinate, and MANCUSO resolves to give Ricks an efficiency report that will stop him at the rank of captain.

However, Ricks has to take *MAINE* to sea again. This time he is again attempting to track *ADMIRAL LUNIN* when *MAINE* has her underwater collision with the floating logs. Ricks does not handle himself well in this crisis, giving at least one order that CLAGGETT has to countermand. He does get the stricken *MAINE* to the surface and orders "Abandon ship," but does not survive the sinking.

316   R—CONCORDANCE

RILEY, CHIEF BOATSWAIN'S MATE ROBERT TIMOTHY (BOB): In *Danger,* one of the senior petty officers aboard *PANACHE.* Six feet two, two hundred pounds and muscular, he is a classic boatswain's mate and a master of practical deck seamanship. He learned his trade under another classic boatswain's mate, a veteran of Prohibition-era chases after rum-runners.

He commands the boarding party sent to *EMPIRE BUILDER,* arrests the pirates, and prepares the report on what happened aboard. When one of the pirates spits in Captain WEGENER's face, Riley slams him across the bridge railing, hurting and scaring him.

Along with OREZA and WEGENER, Riley is one of the key men in the mock hanging used to intimidate the pirates into confessing. He is also one of the people who reveal what happened to Edward STUART, who poses as an old shipmate of Riley's.

When *PANACHE* makes the life-or-death rendezous with the PAVE LOW helicopter, Riley is in charge of the ten-man crew on the helipad, and his skill and leadership play an important part in the safe landing.

RILEY, FATHER TIMOTHY, S.J.: A short, plump Jesuit priest. He was head of the history department at Georgetown University while RYAN was getting his doctorate, and has a sharp tongue.

In *Games,* he joins RYAN's conversation with PLATONOV and warns him that the Russian is sounding him out because of his prospective CIA connection. He also warns RYAN against being too strongly motivated by hate.

In *Sum,* he has become the President of Georgetown University. He is also one of the first people not to take RYAN's remarks about the Pope's divisions as a joke. Instead he uses the Jesuits' communications network to lay the peace proposal before the Pope and ensure the American negotiating team (with RYAN) a favorable reception.

RITTER, ROBERT: Senior CIA officer. Like Judge MOORE, a Texan. A rather austere man, with a normally harsh manner, his confidence in Jack RYAN grows slowly but surely.

In *Hunt,* he is Deputy Director (Operations), and one of the three WILLOW-cleared men in the Agency. He backs GREER's decision to give RYAN WILLOW-clearance and let him see CARDINAL material. He also accompanies MOORE to the confrontation with Senator DONALDSON over Peter HENDERSON, and is one of the three senior CIA men who congratulate RYAN after *RED OCTOBER* is safe.

In *Cardinal,* he plans to use CLARK to extract FILITOV after it appears that the agent is in danger. After the Colonel's arrest, Ritter is frustrated at the apparent impossibility of doing anything to save him, and takes out his anger on RYAN. After this, however, he uses all his resources and skill to support the deception that will allow RYAN to make his approach to GERASIMOV.

In *Danger*, CLARK and LARSON are under his orders. He goes along with Judge MOORE's idea of not informing RYAN about the covert operations. CLARK confronts him when the danger to the covert-action troops becomes critical. Realizing what is happening, Ritter and MOORE together decide to back up RYAN by investigating (with FBI cooperation) what has gone wrong.

ROACH WAGON: Truck-mounted soft-drink or snack stand, particularly in Latin America, where it is likely to be overrun with cockroaches. In *Danger*, one visits the Special Operations field in Panama; the driver is an aviation buff and collecting intelligence that will end up in the drug cartel's hands.

ROBINSON, EUGENE: In *Storm*, U.S. general, SACEUR. The son and grandson of soldiers, he served four tours in Vietnam, the last in command of the 101ST AIRBORNE. Fifty-nine years old, he has three children, four grandchildren, a reputation for unorthodox tactics, and a speaking knowledge of Russian.

The right man in the right place, he has his forces as ready as possible, keeps his head, and conserves resources as the ATLANTIC BRIDGE shows signs of faltering. He also has reserves ready for the counterattack around Alfeld when the Soviets in turn weaken. After the coup, he personally meets with ALEKSEYEV to negotiate a cease-fire.

ROCKEYE: U.S. cluster bomb. 500 or 750 pounds; 200+ shaped-charge or fragmentation SUBMUNITIONS; in service from 1968.

In *Hunt*, Major RICHARDSON's four A-10s each carry a pair of antitank Rockeyes. In *Storm*, during Operation DREAMLAND, F-111s drop Rockeyes on Soviet bridging equipment, guided by flares from Colonel ELLINGTON's F-19.

ROKOSSOVSKIY: Soviet DELTA-class submarine. In *Hunt*, she is being tracked by *V.K. KONOVOLOV* when *RED OCTOBER* puts to sea.

ROKOSSOVSKIY, KONSTANTIN: Historical figure (1896-1968). Marshal of the Soviet Union, he survived the *gulag* to become a World War II hero; FILITOV was in his Second Tank Army at the Battle of KURSK.

ROMANOV, CORPORAL ALEKSEY IL'YCH: In *Cardinal,* one of Mikhail FILITOV's World War II comrades. A tank commander in FILITOV's company, he was KIA at Vyazma, saving his CO and winning a posthumous ORDER OF THE RED BANNER. Of all FILITOV's old comrades, he is the most affectionately remembered, and the one to whom the Colonel talks most when drunk or dreaming, even in the LEFORTOVO PRISON and in the last moment of his life.

ROSSELLI, CAPTAIN JAMES (JIM, ROSEY):   In *Sum,* U.S. naval officer, Annapolis graduate, friend of Bart MANCUSO, and first CO of the GOLD CREW of *MAINE.*

He is an exceptionally able submarine skipper, commanding both attack and missile boats with success. His third tour of command aboard *MAINE* was just long enough to make him want more, as he leaves with MANCUSO's good wishes and assorted PLANKOWNER souvenirs.

His next post is as a duty officer at the National Military Command Center in the Pentagon. He is the senior officer on duty at the NMCC during the crisis because of blocked roads and accidents to other officers. It is his decision to allow Jack RYAN access to the hot line when confronted with evidence that the crisis is escalating out of control and that the President and his advisers are not handling it well.

ROZHKOV, MARSHAL YURI: In *Storm,* Soviet officer, Commander in Chief of Ground Forces. A World War II veteran, a tanker, and a competent officer who does his best. When that is not good enough, he is executed by the KGB as part of a purge of the Army high command, which helps push ALEXSEYEV and SERGETOV into their planned coup.

RPG-7:   *Reaktivnyy protivotankovyy grantomet* (Rocket-Propelled Antitank Grenade Launcher). Soviet shoulder-fired antitank weapon. Loaded weight 20 lbs; fires a shaped-charge grenade to an effective range of about 100 yards. In service 1962; widely exported to Soviet allies.

The most widely used Soviet light antitank weapon, it has been extensively supplied to terrorists as well as an antivehicle weapon. In *Games,* Irish terrorists have killed a judge's bodyguard with a dud RPG round. In *Cardinal,* one of the ARCHER's men blows up a bus with a captured RPG. In *Danger,* terrorists hired by the cocaine cartel use RPG-7s in the assassination of Emil JACOBS.

RPG-18:   Soviet shoulder-fired antitank weapon; resembles the American LAW in having a disposable tube. In service 1978; supplements the more powerful RPG-7.

RPV: Remotely Piloted Vehicle. In *Storm,* a small unmanned aircraft with a television camera, used for observing Soviet artillery positions for the U.S. battleships supporting the Marine landing on Iceland. In *Sum,* the same term is used for an underwater equivalent, a cable-controlled robot submarine under development by the Russians, able to carry sonar and weapons deeper than any manned vehicle.

RUSSELL, JOHN: In *Sum,* professional criminal, drug dealer, and AIM activist, of Sioux descent. Six feet five inches tall, two hundred and fifty pounds (running to fat), and wears numerous tattoos. Brother of Marvin RUSSELL.

He is tracked down by the FBI to a farmhouse in the Dakotas, but the confrontation comes to the attention of the media through the bungling of Walter HOSKINS. When two reporters attempt to interview RUSSELL, who is aggressively drunk, he attempts to take the female one hostage. He is then promptly shot by HRT chief sniper PAULSON.

RUSSELL, MARVIN: In *Sum,* professional criminal, drug dealer, and AIM activist, of Sioux descent. Brother of John RUSSELL; five feet eight, two hundred pounds, and in top condition thanks to pumping iron. He is a romantic revolutionary, idealizing a mythic Indian past and rationalizing his criminal activities as a means to restoring it.

He has been his brother's partner in AIM activities, crime, and prison. After his brother's death, Marvin uses John's drug profits to flee abroad, in a mood for vengeance.

He makes contact with Ibrahim GHOSN in Athens, in the process killing with his bare hands a Greek policeman who is trailing the Palestinian. Marvin thereafter becomes a valuable member of the bomb plot—although he does not know that the terrorists plan to use a nuclear weapon. His strength, combat skills, and endurance make him useful as an instructor and general strongarm man. GHOSN respects him considerably; QATI tends to dismiss him as a pagan.

After the bomb crosses the Atlantic, Russell's knowledge of America and American business methods is indispensable. Once the bomb has reached Denver, however, he is nothing but a security risk, and QATI and GHOSN murder him in the motel.

His body is found before the bomb explodes, but in the general confusion it is some time before word reaches the FBI. The identification of Russell is an important step toward untangling the mystery of the bomb.

RYAN, CAROLINE MULLER (CATHY), M.D.:   Ophthamological surgeon and wife of Jack RYAN, mother of Sally and John Patrick Jr.; on the faculty of the Wilmer Eye Institute, Johns Hopkins Hospital, Baltimore, Maryland, and in private practice.

Daughter of Joseph MULLER; mother dead. She did her undergraduate work at Bennington, medical school at Johns Hopkins. She is of medium height, with a small, round face, blond hair, and what her husband Jack considers beautiful blue eyes. She considers herself reasonably attractive (and doesn't understand the fetish for large breasts).

Her hobbies are photography and the classical piano; she drives a racing-green Porsche. Her outlook on life is a combination of optimism and fatalism. She decided against going into pediatric oncology (children with terminal cancer) because of the psychological toll it would have taken; with eye surgery there is always life and often hope.

In *Hunt* she and the children are in London during Jack's adventures ashore and afloat.

In *Games,* she is on the scene within minutes of Jack's rescue of the PRINCE and PRINCESS OF WALES. She examines Their Highnesses, administers first aid to her husband, and insists on proper treatment for him. She also views his care in the hospital with a surgeon's critical eye.

She and Sally are guests at Buckingham Palace and receive literally royal treatment, with a castle tour (including the Tower of London) and riding lessons for Sally. She and Sally return to the U.S. with the convalescent Jack aboard the CONCORDE. By then she is carrying Jack, Jr.

At Christmas she receives a magnificent gold necklace, but also the bad news about Sean MILLER's escape. After the ULA sets up operations in the U.S., she is targeted along with her husband for assassination.

The attempt fails only because Cathy hits the Porsche's accelerator just enough to spoil the ULA marksmanship. She is still hit by one bullet and Sally is dangerously hurt. Jack has to help her through serious guilt feelings, and also through a visit from her father that turns into a confrontation between him and Jack.

She makes a complete recovery and is feeling as well as anyone can in the last month of pregnancy when the ULA makes its second attempt. Cathy administers first aid to Sissy JACKSON, then remains behind at ANNAPOLIS when Jack and the Marines chase the terrorists. She goes into labor and Jack Jr. is born shortly after his father's return from Baltimore.

In *Cardinal,* she is a happy wife and mother, as well as earning more than her husband from her private practice. She is also holding the fort during *Danger.*

In *Sum,* she wants a third child. Unfortunately, Jack has started having sexual problems, thanks to stress, insomnia, exhaustion, lack of exercise, and too much cheap Australian wine. His impotence, added to the various bits of evidence put about as part of Elizabeth ELLIOT's disinformation campaign, lead Cathy to suspect that Jack is unfaithful and that their marriage is doomed.

The tension is becoming unbearable when CLARK steps in, arranging for Cathy's meeting with Carol ZIMMER and also finding out who is behind the disinformation campaign. When Cathy learns that it is ELLIOT, she and the National Security Advisor have a sharp public confrontation which Cathy wins hands down. She and Jack have a private and passionate reconciliation, and she remains in Annapolis during the crisis—although one can imagine she is quite happy to see Jack shaking the dust of the CIA from his feet.

RYAN, JOHN PATRICK: CIA officer and patriotic citizen. The son of Emmet William Ryan (a Baltimore policeman) and Catherine Burke Ryan (both killed in a plane crash at O'Hare Airport five years before *Hunt*). One sister, living in Seattle. Married to Catherine Muller RYAN, M.D.; father of Sally and John Jr.

He has an undergraduate degree in economics from Boston College and a doctorate in history from Georgetown University. He was commissioned a second lieutenant in the U.S. Marines but had to retire on medical disability after a helicopter crash in Crete. His Marine training sank deep, however, and has saved both him and others more than once. He is still a reluctant flyer.

He made a modest fortune on Wall Street and has continued to add to it by shrewd dealing, until he is worth about 20 million dollars at the time of *Sum.* Before becoming a full-time CIA employee, he taught naval history at the Naval Academy, and is the author of several books. These include *Fighting Sailor,* a biography of Admiral Halsey, and *Agents and Agencies,* a discussion of intelligence methodology that brought him to the attention of both the CIA and the British Secret Intelligence Service.

He is six feet one, with a long, lantern-jawed face and a tendency to five o'clock shadow. He keeps fit with jogging and is an above-average marksman with a shotgun or pistol. Except when he neglects his health, he is fit and quite formidable in a rough-and-tumble.

He considers himself an heir to the Irish-American tradition of standing on the side of law, order, and loyalty to country. He also has strong principles (marital fidelity is one of them), and an Irish temper that has more than once got him in deep hot water.

In *Hunt,* Ryan has been in England, as CIA liaison with the British SIS, and returns to the U.S. with British-supplied photographs of *RED OCTO-BER*. With Admiral GREER's permission, Ryan takes the photographs to Skip TYLER, who suggests that the mysterious holes in the submarine's hull are a propulsion system. This leads to the discovery of the MAG-NETOHYDRODYNAMIC drive and TYLER's contribution to the hunt.

On the basis of Soviet fleet behavior and a CARDINAL report about the sink-on-sight order, Ryan draws the correct conclusions about *RED OC-TOBER's* intentions. Persuading the PRESIDENT and CNO of this leads to massive American naval operations to support the Soviet submarine.

Part of these operations involves reluctant flyer Ryan taking a COD to *KENNEDY* to brief Admiral PAINTER, then a HARRIER to *INVINCI-BLE* to brief Admiral WHITE. Ryan's role is further enlarged by the helicopter crash that kills the original contact team.

Aboard *RED OCTOBER,* Ryan's Marine Corps training is useful as he shoots it out with GRU agent LOGONOV in *RED OCTOBER's* missile compartment, gives RAMIUS first aid, and helps launch the sabotaged SEAHAWK missile. He remains aboard the Soviet submarine on her voyage south, acting as emergency helmsman through the duel with *KONOVO-LOV.*

He returns at last to CIA headquarters with a warhead-control key, and between good bourbon and exhaustion ends up in no shape to see the President. He falls asleep on the return flight to London, the first time in his life he has ever fallen asleep on an airplane.

In *Games* we return to a period when Ryan had done only consulting work for the CIA, and learn why he has so many connections in England. In a London street he sees what he thinks is IRA terrorists at work and ends up saving the PRINCE and PRINCESS OF WALES and their baby from ULA kidnapping. He also ends up in the hospital with a bullet in one shoulder.

He is well cared for, and visited not only by the police but by the Royal Family; he gives the PRINCE OF WALES a lecture on firefight tactics that eases the man's guilt over not tackling the ULA barehanded. He and his family thereafter receive royal treatment. In their first lovemaking after Jack gets out of the hospital, they start John Jr., and return home on the CONCORDE.

In due course, Jack returns to teaching, to the pleasure of his students. After the ULA escape over Christmas, he begins to become more involved in the combined SIS-CIA-FBI effort to track down the terrorists. He also starts keeping a shotgun ready and takes pistol instruction from BRECK-ENRIDGE.

This involvement becomes total after the attempt on Cathy and Sally

(Jack's would-be assassin, Ned CLARK, is rounded up at the Academy gate). He learns the fine art of photointerpretation as well as analysis, and helps set up the French elimination of the *ACTION DIRECTE* camp. The more he becomes involved, the more talent he shows for intelligence work, and the more GREER and MOORE want to have him working for them on a regular basis.

The PRINCE and PRINCESS OF WALES visit the Ryan house for a private dinner on their trip to America, and are the target for the second ULA attempt. Again Jack proves that he would have been a good Marine, and it is with a squad of Marines behind him that he finally encounters Sean MILLER aboard *COSTANZA*. MILLER lives to be executed only because RYAN stops short of killing in cold blood; it is enough that he has put the terrorist in fear for *his* life.

In *Cardinal*, Jack is special assistant to Admiral GREER and also the main CIA representative on the U.S. arms-negotiation team. In between trips to Moscow, he visits the TEA CLIPPER site, and is *not* happy when the chief negotiator puts SDI on the table in Moscow.

He is even less happy when he learns that FILITOV has been arrested and is doomed. However, with the backing of the senior men in the CIA (including RITTER, even if he thinks Jack has come along too fast), he carries out the bold blackmail of KGB chief GERASIMOV.

This saves NARMONOV as well as Colonel FILITOV, although Jack is wounded again (this time in the leg) in the confrontation with the KGB at Sheremetyevo Airport before the plane takes off. When it does, it leaves him behind, and only diplomatic immunity keeps him in one piece long enough for NARMONOV to provide first aid and promise to keep everything quiet.

In *Danger,* Jack is effectively Deputy Director (Intelligence), as GREER is in the hospital with terminal cancer. This keeps Ryan busy, and makes it easier for MOORE and RITTER to cut him out of any knowledge of the CIA's participation in the anti-drug operations. (They know his principles and his temper, and Admiral CUTTER needs delicate handling.)

He still has time for the first of several quarrels with Elizabeth ELLIOT. He resents her threatening him with dismissal; she thinks the worst of him as a "Cold Warrior."

When Jack pieces together a picture of what is going on, CUTTER is in the middle of betraying the covert-action troops. The FBI and CIA go to work establishing this connection, while Jack personally represents them on the rescue mission.

The mission is not one to convert a reluctant flyer. The helicopter lifts out of a HOT LZ, and Buck ZIMMER dies in Jack's arms after Jack promises to send his kids to college. Jack has also been a useful hand on one of the

MINIGUNS. He reaches *PANACHE*, flies to Washington from Guantánamo, and confronts the PRESIDENT over what he considers the man's lack of moral courage.

In spite of this, Ryan succeeds GREER as Deputy Director (Intelligence), and then is confirmed as Deputy Director of the CIA, a post he holds at the opening of *Sum*. He and his family are now living in the post–Cold War world—but there is still enough going on to keep a good intelligence man busy.

Ryan's joke (after the Temple Mount shooting incident) about the Pope's divisions leads to a serious proposal for Papal mediation of the Middle East situation. Jack's contacts help carry the proposal to Rome, and he also does much of the initial legwork in Rome, Tel Aviv, and Saudi Arabia.

Unfortunately he also has another argument with Elizabeth ELLIOT, which gives her a firm determination to remove Ryan. Soon Ryan faces persuading the NSA that U.S. diplomatic codes may have been compromised, the flood of intelligence from agents Musahashi and SPINNAKER, and a campaign to not only drive him out of government service but destroy his marriage as well. His Director, Marcus CABOT, is useless, and ELLIOT is using all her influence over President FOWLER and contacts in the media as well.

Matters come to a head when stress, exhaustion, and alcohol produce impotence, and his marriage comes under a severe strain. CLARK's intervention clears up that matter, Cathy settles the score with Elizabeth ELLIOT, and the Ryans are a united couple when the crisis hits.

During the crisis, Jack Ryan is really the man on the spot, the senior CIA official on duty. More and more appalled by the erroneous assumptions of FOWLER and ELLIOT and the way they are increasing the tension, Jack finally drives down to the Pentagon and breaks on to the hot line.

This bold step nearly gets him arrested, but it does help lower tension. After the bomb is known to be terrorist rather than Soviet, Jack flies to CAMP DAVID and has a confrontation with President FOWLER when FOWLER wants to bomb QUM. Jack's refusal to confirm the launch order prevents mass death but causes a constitutional crisis—which would bother Ryan more if he wasn't leaving government service.

His final trip before retiring to private life is to attend the execution of GHOSN and QATI in Saudi Arabia. He receives the executioner's sword as a gift of honor.

A good friend and ally, a wise and honorable adviser, and a dangerous enemy, John Patrick Ryan is a man who never forgets the question "If not now, when? If not me, then who?" when his country, his family, or his principles are in danger.

RYAN, JOHN PATRICK, JR.:   Son of John and Cathy RYAN. Conceived in London after the first encounter with the ULA, he is born in Annapolis at the time of the second. His godparents are the JACKSONs and the PRINCE and PRINCESS OF WALES.

He is in kindergarten by the time of *Cardinal* and thinks he is too old for "baby stuff" like his father kissing him goodbye. By the time of *Sum* he is old enough for Little League, and feels hurt that his father doesn't come to see him play or take him to promised Orioles games.

RYAN, OLIVIA (SALLY):   Daughter and eldest child of John and Cathy RYAN. Four years old at the time of *Games,* she is a bright, cheerful, extremely active child (a good rider), taking after her mother in appearance. She is also a complete daddy's girl and expert at getting her way with her father (such as a Skiing Barbie for Christmas in *Hunt*).

She has also been known to be a complete little hellion, leaving a trail of wreckage in her wake. Her high point was wiping out twenty thousand words of one of her father's books on the computer when she thought Wordstar was a game.

In *Games,* she and her mother are accommodated at Buckingham Palace. She thoroughly charms the QUEEN, who thinks that the stories of Sally's breaking things are nonsense and arranges for her to have private riding lessons.

In the ULA attempt on her mother, Sally is caught playing with her seat belt and is badly hurt from being thrown about inside the car. She suffers fractures and a ruptured spleen, and would have died if she'd reached the Shock-Trauma Center in Baltimore five minutes later.

She makes a complete recovery, although it is a long time before she is her usual cheerful self. (She learned the hard way that Daddy can't protect her from all the evil in the world.) Her parents' love, her doctors' care, and gifts like ERNIE the Labrador retriever and a huge stuffed bear in a Marine DI's outfit all bring her back to normal.

In *Cardinal,* she is attending a school called St. Mary's, and calls Dan MURRAY "Uncle Dan." In *Sum,* she knows that something is very wrong between her parents, but fortunately they are reconciled before she has to find out what.

S-3 VIKING: U.S. twin-jet carrier-based ASW aircraft; Lockheed. 500 mph; range 2,300 miles; ASW torpedoes and depth charges, HARPOON, MAD; crew of four. In service with U.S. Navy from 1974.

In *Hunt,* Admiral PAINTER proposes landing *KENNEDY's* F-18 HOR-

NETs to make room for twenty more S-3s; he needs the ASW assets more than he needs the striking power.

In *Storm,* S-3s from *NIMITZ* patrol for submarines as the battle group crosses the Atlantic. *INDEPENDENCE* launches hers in support of the Iceland landing.

In *Sum,* Robby JACKSON's Air Wing aboard *THEODORE ROOSEVELT* includes a squadron of S-3s.

S-76:   U.S. turbine transport helicopter; Sikorsky. In *Danger,* cartel leader UNITVEROS has one; it is destroyed in the first bombing.

SA-2 (NATO code name GUIDELINE):   Soviet SAM; in service 1957. Now obsolete, it was the main SAM encountered in Vietnam, and was extensively exported. In *Sum,* Mordecai ZADIN has to evade a dozen Syrian SA-2s.

SA-6 (NATO code name GAINFUL):   Soviet SAM. 1600 mph; range up to 25 miles; HE warhead; three-round mobile launcher; in service 1967.

In *Storm,* a battery of them defends the bridge attacked by Colonel ELLINGTON. In a brief, fierce engagement, the battery loses its radar to SHRIKE missiles, shoots down an F-111, but fails to save the bridge.

In *Sum,* the Israeli PHANTOM that causes so much confusion at ZADIN's base was hit by an SA-6 while escorting a reconnaissance mission over the Sinai. Later, ZADIN himself falls victim to Syrian SA-6s, although he destroys the battery that shot him down before his SKYHAWK disintegrates.

SA-7 (NATO code name GRAIL):   Soviet *Strela* shoulder-fired infrared homing AA missile. In service 1966; widely exported. Comparable in performance to the U.S. REDEYE.

In *Storm,* a panicky soldier firing an SA-7 from *JULIUS FUCIK* confirms the P-3's suspicions. A dozen more are fired at the HARPOON but none hit.

In *Cardinal,* the ARCHER first gained his name and reputation using captured SA-7s against Soviet aircraft.

In *Sum,* Günther BOCK rejects using a light aircraft armed with SA-7s to assassinate the U.S. President; the President's aircraft will have the best infrared jammers available.

SA-8 (NATO code name GECKO):   Soviet advanced SAM, comparable to the SA-6 but more capable against multiple targets; in service 1974 and widely used aboard Soviet warships as well.

Equivalent to the NATO ROLAND, as General ALEXSEYEV mentions in *Storm.* In *Sum,* they are used by the AA company of a Soviet tank regiment in Berlin against American aircraft supporting the BERLIN BRIGADE during the crisis.

SA-11 (NATO code name GADFLY):   Soviet mobile SAM. 2,000+ mph; range 15+ miles; HE warhead; four-round mobile launcher. In service from 1983, as a replacement for the SA-6.

In *Storm,* a battalion of SA-11s is aboard *JULIUS FUCIK,* but most of its missiles are ruined by salt water in the firefighting after the HARPOON hit; they were not the naval version. Forty replacement missiles restore the battalion's effectiveness.

Later, the SA-11s are sighted by EDWARDS, destroy a reconnaissance JAGUAR, and continue to be effective until they are expended or their launchers destroyed. It is discovered that the SA-11 has high acceleration, is almost smokeless, and has a backup infrared guidance system with a range of ten miles.

In *Sum,* they are used in Berlin; one of them shoots down an American F-16 whose pilot ejects but is killed landing on an apartment roof.

SA-N-8:   In *Hunt,* new Soviet shipboard SAM system, mounted in the cruiser *NIKOLAYEV;* its radar is studied by an EC-135 accompanying the B-52s the cruiser is tracking.

SAIL: The superstructure of a submarine, housing the bridge for surface maneuvering. (In U.S. submarines, the forward PLANES are mounted on the sail as well.)

In *Storm, PROVIDENCE's* sail is heavily damaged by the RBU rocket hit. In *Sum,* Captain RICKS stands on the sail to maneuver his ship out of the Trident base.

SAIPAN, **U.S.S.:**   U.S. *TARAWA*-class amphibious assault ship; in service 1977. In *Storm* she is one of the three amphibious vessels carrying Marines for Iceland and escorted by the *NIMITZ* battle group. In the missile attack, she receives several KINGFISH hits and blows up, with only 200 survivors.

SALYUT: Series of Soviet space stations launched from the late 1970s, using the Vostok three-man spacecraft. Several had military equipment aboard. In *Storm,* Mikhail SERGETOV wonders if the Salyuts compensate the average Soviet citizen for his or her lack of basic necessities.

SAM: Surface-to-Air Missile.

SANCHEZ, RAFAEL (BUD):   U.S. naval officer and F-14 pilot; a long-time friend of Robby JACKSON.

In *Hunt* Sanchez is flying F-14s from *KENNEDY* in VF-41. He is JACK-SON's wingman in the shooting incident with *KIEV's* FORGERs.

In *Sum,* he is a full commander and CO of VF-1 aboard *THEODORE ROOSEVELT.* He flies wingman with JACKSON in exercises against Marine F-18s before the carrier deploys to the Mediterranean. He is later JACKSON's wingman during the two engagements with MiG-29s in the crisis and shoots down one of the Russians with his gun.

SANDERSON, ERIK: In *Danger,* Alabama teenager, witness to the drug cartel's assassination of Ernie BRADEN, who was his baseball coach. Sanderson uses a .22 Marlin rifle against the assassins, shooting wildly but fatally wounding one of them.

SAPPERS: Another term for COMBAT ENGINEER TROOPS, used for the Soviet mine-clearing teams in *Storm,* working on the bridge at Alfeld. It is also used in *Sum* for the Swiss Guards' demolition sections.

SARATOGA, **U.S.A.:**   U.S. conventional aircraft carrier, *FORRESTAL* class; in service 1956.

In *Hunt,* she is in Norfolk with engine trouble, unable to go to sea. Her aircraft, however, are available to oppose the Soviet forces in the North Atlantic.

In *Storm,* she is one of the carriers in the *NIMITZ* battle group. Her radar is damaged but she can operate aircraft and takes aboard those from *FOCH* and *NIMITZ* unable to reach land. Later, Edward MORRIS sees her under repair in Norfolk.

In *Games,* a battle group built around *Saratoga* acts in support of the French raid on the *ACTION DIRECTE* camp.

SAVO ISLAND: Island in the SW Pacific, off Guadalcanal, Solomon Islands. Several World War II naval engagements were fought near it in 1942-43. In *Danger,* Admiral GREER says that some of his old shipmates died off Savo Island fifty years ago, so he's been lucky.

SCAMP, **U.S.S.:**   U.S. nuclear attack submarine, *SKIPJACK* class; in service 1961.

In *Hunt,* she is fitted in Norfolk with the DSRV *AVALON.* Her CO wonders about this, since the DSRV will slow his ship by at least ten knots. The only consolation is that they need fresh food after five weeks on patrol.

SCAMP takes *AVALON* to sea in support of *ETHAN ALLEN,* and launches the DSRV to evacuate the old BOOMER's crew to the attack boat. *SCAMP* then returns to port.

SCEPTRE, H.M.S.:   British Royal Navy *SWIFTSURE*-class nuclear attack submarine; in service 1978. In *Hunt,* Bart MANCUSO gives that identification for *RED OCTOBER* as she enters Norfolk Harbor, trusting that the real British submarine is nowhere around.

In *Storm,* she and *SUPERB* scout the route to be used by the American submarines in Operation DOOLITTLE.

SCOTT, SIR CHARLES: In *Games,* the doctor at St. Thomas's Hospital, London, who treats Jack RYAN after his first encounter with the ULA. Affable but firm, he advises RYAN not to be afraid of painkillers, in spite of his experience with them, or he will slow his recovery. He is competent enough to win Cathy RYAN's respect and send her husband back to her with no permanent damage.

SCRAM: The emergency shutdown of a nuclear reactor. In *Hunt,* MELEKHIN orders this to be done to *RED OCTOBER's* reactor when the alarm goes off for a radiation leak in the heat-exchange room.

SCRANTON, U.S.S.:   U.S. 688-class submarine; in service c. 1990. In *Sum,* it is mentioned that under Mike HEIMBACH's command she set the record for tracking an *OHIO*—4,000 yards.

SCUPPERS: Drainage troughs leading overside from the deck of a ship. In *Sum,* the water on *GEORGE MCREADY's* deck from the rogue wave drains overboard through the scuppers.

SEA CLIFF, U.S.S.:   U.S. deep-diving research submarine. 21 tons; 3 knots; crew of 2 plus one scientist/observer. In service 1968. Able to dive to 20,000 feet.

In *Hunt,* she operates from *AUSTIN,* taking Captain KAGANOVICH down to the wreckage of *ETHAN ALLEN* (supposed to be *RED OCTOBER*) to reinforce the cover story.

SEA KING: U.S. ASW helicopter. See SH-3.

SEA SPRITE: U.S. LAMPS helicopter. See SH-2.

SEA WOLF: British Royal Navy SAM; in service 1979. In *Storm,* H.M.S. *BATTLEAXE* mounts a Sea Wolf launcher and has killed a Soviet missile with it.

SEACOBRA: U.S. Navy/Marine Corps version of the AH-1 COBRA attack helicopter.

SEAHAWK: Soviet SLBM. See SS-N-20.

SEAHAWK: U.S. LAMPS helicopter. See SH-60.

SEAL: Sea, Air, and Land. U.S. Navy elite reconnaissance and raiding force, landing by small boat, helicopter, parachute, or underwater vehicle from a submarine. First recorded actions during the Cuban Missile Crisis, 1962. CLARK was a SEAL in Vietnam and in *Cardinal* still carries the distinctive SEAL tattoo.

SECRET SERVICE: Branch of the U.S. Treasury Department, charged with suppression of counterfeiting and the security of the President and other federal officials. Helen D'AGOSTINO, in *Danger* and *Sum,* shot a counterfeiter and is now on the White House detail.

"SEMPER PARATUS":   The Coast Guard anthem; title is the Coast Guard motto (English: "Always Ready"). In *Danger,* Dan MURRAY wishes they could sing it in honor of *PANACHE's* uncovering the drug-money-laundering operation.

SENTRY: U.S. and NATO AWACS aircraft. See E-3.

SERGETOV, CAPTAIN IVAN MIKHAILOVICH: In *Storm,* Soviet Army officer, elder son of Mikhail SERGETOV. Like his father he is short and stocky; he is also a specialist in the Middle East and speaks Arabic. He has a low opinion of Arab military skill, in spite of Afghanistan, and strongly supports the war (not suspecting the *maskirovka*).

Initially in command of a tank company, he is transferred to ALEK-SEYEV's staff because of his specialized expertise. When the move into the Mideast oil fields fails to materialize, he follows his general through his successive posts and fortunes.

This gives him a very lively war and a great deal of combat experience, during which he loses many of his illusions about the war. He wins promotion to major and the ORDER OF THE RED BANNER. He also has less agreeable experiences, including being shot down in the command helicopter, swimming for his life from the American counterattack at Alfeld, and confronting a KGB officer determined to denounce him as a deserter. His achievements are a great source of pride to his father.

He also comes progressively to share his father's and the general's views about the war. He acts as the indispensable link between the Minister and the General in the planning stages of the coup.

SERGETOV, MIKHAIL EDUARDOVICH: In *Storm,* Soviet official, in charge of energy production and distribution. A candidate member of the POLITBURO, he is technically highly competent and more than slightly disillusioned with the promise of Socialism. Father of Ivan SERGETOV.

After inspecting the Nizhnevartovsk oil fields, he reports on the disaster to the POLITBURO. He consents to, rather than supports, the decision for war, and does his best to guarantee adequate supplies of petroleum products for the armed forces in spite of the cost to the civilian economy. Outraged at the deaths of the children in the Kremlin-bomb *maskirovka*, he is deeply concerned about the fate of his son, Ivan, and envies General ALEKSEYEV, who has only daughters.

As the war progresses, he receives confidential reports on the failure of the Soviet plans for a quick victory from General ALEKSEYEV, both directly and through Ivan. He is immensely proud of his son's war record, but cannot avoid feeling that the war was a mistake.

The execution of seven high-ranking officers by the KGB and the proposal to use nuclear weapons make SERGETOV desperate. (He remembers the panic in the POLITBURO when the Operation DOOLITTLE TOMAHAWKs were reported as a "missile launch"—type unstated.)

He and ALEKSEYEV are already conspiring together when the Minister is approached by KGB chief KOSOV, eager to save his position amid the ruins of his country. This support is crucial to the success of the coup, allowing troops to be moved into Moscow without KGB interference.

After an initial protest over KOSOV's execution, Sergetov accepts the Army's refusal to obey the KGB, and assumes power as acting General Secretary. He divides key ministries among his supporters and plans a People's Court to try the civilian and military leaders of the war faction.

SH-2 SEA SPRITE: U.S. LAMPS helicopter; Kaman. 150 mph; range 400 miles; ASW torpedoes and MAD; in service (SH-2F model) from 1973.

In *Storm, PHARRIS* carries one, and it makes the final MAD contact on the Soviet FOXTROT sunk by the P-3. During a later missile attack (which sinks a destroyer and two merchant vessels), the helicopter launches in the hope of catching the Soviet submarine near the surface.

SH-3 SEA KING: U.S. carrier-based amphibious ASW helicopter; Sikorsky (license-built abroad). 150+ mph; range 500+ miles; ASW torpedoes, depth charges, antiship missiles (HARPOON, etc.), MAD, dipping sonar.

In service with U.S. Navy from 1961; widely exported and built abroad. Air Force versions of the SH-3 were the original Jolly Green Giant SAR helicopters of the Vietnam War, like the one flown by Colonel JOHNS (in *Danger*) winning his MEDAL OF HONOR.

In *Hunt, INVINCIBLE* operates Sea Kings and one of them detects *RED OCTOBER.* In *Storm,* a Sea King carries Robert TOLAND out to *NI-*

MITZ; another evacuates wounded from *PHARRIS* after she is torpedoed.

In *Games,* a Royal Navy Sea King helicopter delivers a flight surgeon to *CENLAC* after the MILLER rescue, then attempts to track the ULA dinghy with radar. Another helicopter joins the pursuit with armed Royal Marines aboard.

The Marine-crewed VH-3 helicopters which carry the President and other VIPs (including RYAN) in *Danger* and *Sum* are VIP-transport versions of the SH-3 series.

SH-60 SEAHAWK: U.S. LAMPS helicopter; Sikorsky. 170 mph; range 300+ miles; ASW torpedoes, MAD, airborne radar. In service from 1983; will eventually replace SH-2F and SH-3.

In *Storm,* all SEA SPRITES are committed when MORRIS takes over *REUBEN JAMES,* but the FFGs can operate the larger LAMPS Seahawk. A prototype of the Seahawk F with a dipping sonar and Jerry the Hammer O'MALLEY as pilot is sent aboard instead, and becomes the most effective weapon aboard *REUBEN JAMES* for the rest of the war.

SHABILKOV: In Hunt, Soviet *ALFA*-class submarine. She is stationed off Charleston when the Soviets receive word that a damaged *OHIO* is heading south along the coast.

SHACKLETON: British four-engined propeller-driven AWACS; converted from an ASW patrol aircraft in service since the 1940s. In *Storm,* they work with NIMRODs and American E-3s to provide warning against the Soviet air raids on Scotland.

SHAPIRO, DR. BARRY: In *Games,* Deputy Trauma-Surgeon-in-Chief at the SHOCK-TRAUMA CENTER in Baltimore. The son of a New York rabbi, he has picked up a southern drawl at Baylor University in Texas and loathes Edgar Allan Poe as much as his father loved him. Poe to him is a poet of death and darkness. Formerly an Air Force flight surgeon, he now owns a glider.

He is the surgeon in charge of Cathy and Sally RYAN and head of the team that saves Sally's life. He describes her condition to RYAN and JACKSON, and is promised a ride in a T-38 by JACKSON if he pulls Sally through.

SHARK, U.S.S.:   U.S. nuclear attack submarine, *SKIPJACK*-class; in service 1961. In *Hunt,* Skip TYLER remembers serving with Captain COLEMAN aboard her.

SHASTA, U.S.S.: U.S. ammunition ship; in service 1972. In *Danger,* she is carrying the weapons for *RANGER's* "Drop-Ex" (actually the two MEDELLIN raids).

SHAVROV, SENIOR LIEUTENANT VIKTOR: In *Hunt,* Soviet naval officer and FORGER pilot, assigned to *KIEV.* A veteran of Afghanistan, he prefers the risks of carrier aviation to the risks of what awaited shot-down Soviet pilots there. Young, aggressive, and somewhat hotheaded, he is looking forward to flying from a full-deck carrier.

He is assigned to make a stealthy approach on the E-3 AWACS monitoring the Soviet fleet. However, he is easily detected and intercepted by F-15s and threatened if he approaches too closely; the humiliation makes him lose his temper over the radio.

He returns to *KIEV* with a chip on his shoulder. This leads trouble later on, when he is with Kingfisher Flight, the FORGERs that intercept Robby JACKSON's F-14s. When the F-14s buzz Kingfisher Flight, Shavrov launches his ATOLLS by sheer reflex, hitting and damaging JACKSON's plane and nearly provoking a major incident. Neither Shavrov's flight commander nor *KIEV* approve.

SHAVYRYIN, MARSHAL ANDREY: In *Storm,* Soviet officer, Chief of the General Staff at the opening of the war. He does his job more than competently, but is not forgiven for the failures in Germany and is executed along with Marshal ROZHKOV.

SHAW, ENSIGN KEN: In *Sum,* U.S. naval officer, son of William SHAW. Married (wife's name Bonnie), with one son, Kenny Junior, born between the Dakota shoot-out and the crisis.

An Annapolis graduate, he is assigned to *MAINE* and leads a sonar tracking party in an exercise. Minor lapses in performance lead to a humiliating interview with RICKS. Shaw continues to be one of the Captain's hate objects, but survives *MAINE's* sinking.

SHAW, WILLIAM CONNOR: FBI agent and counterterrorist expert. A slender man with deep-set eyes, he is a sharp dresser and the father of at least two children. At the time of *Games* he is in his mid-forties, lives in Chevy Chase, Maryland, and is working sixteen-hour days. His daughter is a teenager.

In *Games,* he meets Jack RYAN after the attack on Cathy and Sally and informs him of the increasing danger of terrorist activity in the U.S. He continues to handle the Ryan case for the FBI throughout, coordinating with the British through Dan MURRAY in London.

In *Danger* he is Executive Assistant Director (Investigations), and the man most directly involved with the drug battle. Working most of the time with Dan MURRAY, he exploits the evidence gained from the *EMPIRE BUILDER* arrest.

After JACOBS's assassination, he becomes Acting Director of the Bureau. He and MURRAY trace the security leak to Moira WOLFE, then arrange for compassionate handling of her case after her suicide attempt. He leads the FBI in cooperation with the CIA in obtaining evidence against CUTTER, and has the Admiral under surveillance ready for arrest when the man commits suicide.

In *Sum,* he is Director of the FBI, and on Dan MURRAY's advice arranges for Walter HOSKINS's reassignment to Denver. Like many other VIPs, he is snowbound during the crisis, leaving the FBI largely in MURRAY's capable hands.

SHILKA: See ZSU-23-4.

SHOWBOAT, OPERATION: In *Danger,* code name for the program of ACTIVE MEASURES against the drug cartel, on the grounds that they represent a "clear and present danger" to the United States.

SHRIKE: U.S. ARM-45 antiradar missile; in service from 1963. Extensively used in Vietnam and also used by Israel. In *Storm,* F-111s attacking a bridge destroy the SA-6's battery's two radars with Shrikes.

SICARIO: Italian word meaning "hired killer." Dan MURRAY uses it in *Danger* to describe the *EMPIRE BUILDER* pirates to Mark BRIGHT.

SIDEWINDER: U.S. air-to-air missile. See AIM-9.

SIEGFRIED LINE: German World War II fortress system, on the Franco-German border. In *Danger,* the U.S. Embassy in Colombia looks like a cross between an office block and part of the Siegfried Line.

SIMS, **U.S.S.:** *W.S. SIMS,* 1052-class frigate; in service 1970. In *Storm* she is with one of *REUBEN JAMES's* convoys; her SEA SPRITE finishes off a Soviet CHARLIE damaged by O'MALLEY.

SKATE, **U.S.S.:** U.S. nuclear attack submarine; in service 1957. In *Storm,* she was once a target for both O'MALLEY and MORRIS in an ASW exercise.

SKI-JUMP BOW: Type of aircraft-carrier bow in which the flight deck slopes sharply upward, giving aircraft taking off extra lift and altitude. Both *INVINCIBLE* in *Hunt* and *KUZNETSOV* in *Sum* have this feature.

SKIPJACK, U.S.S.:   U.S. nuclear attack submarine. 3,100/3,500 tons; 35 knots; 6 TT; crew 120. In service 1959. Lead ship of a class of six, the first nuclear-powered submarines with teardrop hulls and high underwater speed.

In *Hunt,* Admiral GALLERY and the quartermaster steering *ETHAN ALLEN* away from the dock have served together aboard *Skipjack.*

SKYHAWK: U.S. jet attack aircraft. See A-4.

SLAVA: Soviet conventional missile cruiser; in service 1982. In *Sum,* she is one of *KUZNETSOV's* escorts.

SLBM: Sea-Launched Ballistic Missile, a BALLISTIC MISSILE designed to be launched from aboard ship (usually a submarine). The SS-N-20s aboard *RED OCTOBER* in *Hunt* and the TRIDENTS aboard *MAINE* in *Sum* are SLBMs.

SMART BOMB: Any bomb equipped with guidance systems (TV, radar, infrared, and laser are the most common) permitting it to be steered by the drop aircraft precisely to a target, or to home actively on that target. Such bombs are dropped in *Storm* in Operation DREAMLAND and on Iceland; the bombs used against the drug cartel leaders in *Danger* are also smart.

SMITH, SERGEANT JAMES: In *Storm,* U.S. Marine NCO. A clerk on duty at a Keflavik Marine headquarters, he still has basic infantry training and experience, like all Marines. He also has his CO's maps, which prove invaluable when he leads a squad of Marines south with EDWARDS.

Smith himself proves even more invaluable, accepting EDWARDS's authority in spite of the officer's inexperience with ground warfare and persuading the other Marines (including the air-dropped Royal Marine reinforcements) to accept it also. At the same time he politely guides EDWARDS in what to do and not to do—and recognizes when the lieutenant's mind is made up, as in the rescue of Vigdis AGUSTDOTTIR.

Smith is wounded in the patrol's final action but survives to identify and praise EDWARDS to the RECON MARINES.

SONAR: Sound Navigation and Ranging, an acoustic underwater detection and communications system. Sonars are divided into *active,* in which sound pulses are emitted and their reflection from the target recorded, and *passive,* in which the target's radiated noise is simply received.

Both kinds are used by surface ships, submarines, and aircraft (via SONOBUOYS) in ASW warfare, and may also be mounted in fixed locations (as in the SOSUS network used in *Hunt*). Passive sonar is increasingly preferred because it does not reveal the emittor's location—as in *DAL-LAS's* tracking of *RED OCTOBER* in *Hunt* and *MAINE's* work against *ADMIRAL DUBNIN* in *Sum.* The various measures for making modern submarines quiet (such as *RED OCTOBER's* CATERPILLAR drive) are intended to defeat passive sonar.

SONOBUOYS: Air-droppable, expendable ASW devices consisting of a compact SONAR and a transmitter to relay any contacts to a receiving aircraft. Standard with both Soviet and American fixed-wing ASW aircraft and those helicopters that do not carry a DIPPING SONAR.

Sonobuoys are dropped by Soviet ASW aircraft in the early stages of *Hunt;* by U.S. helicopters (including one from *PHARRIS*) and Soviet ASW aircraft (particularly against *CHICAGO*) in *Storm.*

SOROKIN, MAJOR ARKADY SEMYONOVICH: In *Storm,* Soviet paratroop officer, veteran of the Iceland campaign and father of Svetlana, one of the YOUNG OCTOBRIST victims of the Kremlin-bomb *maskirovka.*

He is first met consoling his wife at the funeral of the bomb victims. He then commands a rifle company in the attack on Iceland; he is wounded in the leg and receives the ORDER OF THE RED BANNER. Medevacked and convalescent, he is recruited by ALEXSEYEV to be a combined body-guard and tactical commander in the eventual coup.

Once the coup is successful, the Major executes KGB chief KOSOV, if not on ALEXSEYEV's direct orders then certainly with his approval. Svetlana is avenged, and her father is put in charge of guarding the arrested POLITBURO members.

SOVREMENNY: Soviet class of conventional-missile destroyers. 6,300/7,900 tons; 34 knots; 4 5″, 4 30-mm guns, AA and cruise missiles, helicopter; crew 380. At least twelve built; name ship in service 1981. Primarily antisurface and AA ships, with limited ASW capabilities.

In *Hunt,* five *Sovremennys* go to sea as part of the Soviet forces in the North Atlantic. In *Storm, CHICAGO* detects at least one with the *KIROV* group, but is not much concerned about her. In *Sum,* one is sighted escorting *KUZNETSOV.*

SPARROW/SEA SPARROW: U.S. AIM-7 radar-guided air-to-air missile. 2,000 + mph; range 40 + miles (later versions); HE warhead. In service with U.S. Navy from 1956; widely exported (including Britain).

In *Storm,* Sparrows are used by the F-15s from Iceland against the incoming Soviet missiles and by F-14s in raids on the Soviet-held island.

Other Sparrows (possibly borrowed from RAF stocks) are used by *NI-MITZ's* temporarily land-based F-14s against Soviet BACKFIREs attacking the convoys and BLINDERs raiding British air bases.

In *Games,* Robby JACKSON discusses the merits of the Sparrow and the PHOENIX with the PRINCE OF WALES. In *Danger,* Sparrows and SIDEWINDERs will be shot off against live targets during Robby JACKSON's cruise aboard *RANGER.*

Sea Sparrow is the U.S. Navy's standard Point Defense Missile System, consisting of eight Sparrows in a box launcher with its own radar. In *Storm,* it is carried aboard *PHARRIS* and damages a Soviet BEAR.

SPARTACISTS: German radical Socialist group, early 20th century. They attempted to seize power in 1919 but were ruthlessly suppressed. The grandfather of Manfred FROMM, in *Sum,* was one of the original Spartacists.

SPEARFISH: British Royal Navy submarine-launched, wire-guided heavy torpedo; in service 1987. Uses a turbine-driven water jet instead of propellers and is the world's fastest torpedo.

In *Storm,* it is newly in service. H.M.S. *TORBAY* carries them, and with one sinks the Soviet ALFA that sank *BOSTON* and *PROVIDENCE* and was evading *CHICAGO's* MARK 48.

SPECIAL AIR SERVICE (SAS):   British elite military unit, established during World War II for raids on enemy airfields in North Africa. It is currently the main British counterterrorist force.

In *Storm,* a one-eyed former SAS major is part of the team evaluating EDWARDS's situation and intelligence. In *Games* the PIRA representative refers to them as "assassins"; their Captain GREVILLE is assigned as bodyguard for the RYANs. In *Cardinal,* RYAN's driver on his second trip to Moscow is a former Australian SAS man.

SPECIAL BOAT SERVICE: Elite unit of the British Royal Marines, specializing in amphibious reconnaissance and raids. Founded during World War II; roughly equivalent to the U.S. Navy SEALs. In *Games,* the ULA terrorists escaping after MILLER's bloody rescue expect to be taken for an SBS training exercise.

SPECIAL FORCES: U.S. Army elite force, specializing in guerrilla operations and counterinsurgency. Established 1952; prominent in Vietnam War. All are airborne-qualified volunteers and undergo rigorous cross-training. Popularly known as Green Berets for their distinctive headgear.

They are not used as units in Operation SHOWBOAT in *Danger* for security reasons, but CHAVEZ's team has at least one Special Forces medic.

SPETSNAZ: *Spetsialnoye Naznacheniye* (Troops of Special Designation), the elite Soviet reconnaissance, raiding, sabotage, and counterguerrilla troops. Probably formed in the 1950s; selected from the fittest and most politically reliable conscripts and given rigorous training. Controlled by the GRU, they are its major asset for COVERT operations in foreign countries.

In *Storm,* Major CHERNYAVIN is a covert-operations *Spetsnaz* officer, a veteran of Afghanistan now commanding a planned operation against a major NATO headquarters. His operation is defeated by his involvement in a traffic accident that leads to his identification and interrogation, but other *Spetsnaz* missions have better luck, including one that blocks Hamburg harbor by sinking merchant vessels.

In *Danger,* CORTEZ knows that the Russians would have used a *Spetsnaz* company to retaliate for something like JACOBS's assassination—effective but crude.

SPINNAKER: In *Sum,* CIA code name for Oleg KADISHEV.

SPLASH: To shoot down a hostile aircraft into the sea. In the crisis in *Sum,* Robby JACKSON is ordered to splash the four Libyan MiG-29s, believed to be hostile.

SPRUANCE CLASS: U.S. class of conventional destroyers. 6,000/8,000 tons; 32 knots; 2 5″ guns, PHALANX, TOMAHAWK, HARPOON, ASW TT, ASROC, LAMPS; crew 330. Thirty-one in service 1975-83. They were the first gas-turbine-powered warships in U.S. service, and are primarily ASW vessels: *CARON* is the senior ASW ship of the *NIMITZ* group in *Storm* and is the largest ship to survive the missile attack undamaged.

SQUAD AUTOMATIC WEAPON (SAW): The U.S. M-249 light machine gun, a license-built version of the Belgian FN Miniman. 5.56-mm; 200+ rpm; effective range 600 yards; loaded weight 22 lbs. In service from 1979. Intended to provide the infantry squad with something lighter than the M-60 and more powerful than the M-16.

In *Danger,* SAWs are the heaviest automatic weapon of the covert-action troops, and prove highly effective in numerous firefights with cartel troops.

SQUADRON: Air service equivalent of a COMPANY, consisting of six to twenty aircraft, depending on service and type. Two or more squadrons make up a group, wing, or (in Soviet service) REGIMENT. The authorized strength of Robby JACKSON's VF-41 in *Hunt* would be fourteen TOM-

CATS; Commander JENSEN's A-6 squadron in *Danger* would have twelve planes.

SR-71 BLACKBIRD: U.S. strategic reconnaissance aircraft; Lockheed. 2,000+ mph; range 4,000 miles; extensive array of cameras and sensors. In service with U.S. Air Force 1964, it remained the fastest and highest-flying operational aircraft in the world throughout its career.

In *Storm,* TOLAND thinks an SR-71 will be needed to penetrate the heavily defended Soviet airspace over Norway. In *Cardinal,* an SR-71 is used as a launcher for a test of the point-defense ABM system, to simulate the performance of an incoming warhead more accurately than could be done with a PHANTOM.

SS-9 (NATO code name SCARP):   Obsolete Soviet ICBM, the basis for the F-series satellite launchers which in *Storm* launch many of the ROR-SATS and ASAT weapons.

SS-11 (NATO code name SEGO):   Soviet two-stage liquid-propellant ICBM; in service 1966. In *Storm,* a Soviet launch detected by NORAD could from its signature be either an SS-11 or an F-1 satellite launcher.

SS-18 (NATO code name SATAN):   Soviet three-stage liquid-fuel ICBM. Uses storable liquid propellants and cold-launch techniques; can carry either a single 20-25 megaton warhead or 10+ -warhead MIRVs. In service from 1974. The largest ICBM ever placed in service, it gave the Soviet Union a potential COUNTERFORCE capability that caused the U.S. great concern.

In *Hunt, RED OCTOBER's* SEAHAWK missiles carry the same MIRV as the SS-18, but with fewer warheads. In *Cardinal,* FILITOV considers a scenario in which the SS-18 REGIMENTs would be placed on alert for a first strike at the American MINUTEMAN force.

In *Sum,* many of the SS-18s are being dismantled, but not as fast as the treaties require. The Americans wonder if the Russians are dragging their feet; the Russians justifiably claim lack of facilities for handling the fuel and warheads (which helps American suspicions about missing nuclear weapons). The Russians are also perfectly happy to be rid of the SATANs, which were hard to maintain and dangerous to operate.

During the crisis, the Russians are continuing to dismantle SS-18s. The vehicles at one base give the appearance of preparations for launch. Then an accident leads to an SS-18 blowing up, which at first looks like a launch. NORAD establishes that the explosion wasn't a launch, but President FOWLER's already shaky nerves have been shaken further.

SS-19 (NATO code name STILETTO): Soviet two-stage liquid-fuel ICBM; in service 1975. In *Sum* three of them, along with five SS-18s, are targeted on Denver.

SS-20 (NATO code name SABER): Soviet IRBM. Solid fuel; two stages; three-warhead MIRV; mobile launchers. In service 1960s; considered a major strategic threat in the European theater. The PERSHING-2 was developed and deployed as a reply to it; both missiles were to be removed under the INF treaty of 1987.

In *Hunt*, Jack RYAN has made a previous visit to England to discuss SS-20 sites on the Chinese border. In *Sum*, leftover warheads from SS-20s (up to 500 kilotons) are a source of concern to the Americans.

SS-25 (NATO code name SICKLE): Soviet three-stage solid-fuel mobile ICBM; in service early 1980s. In *Cardinal*, an American satellite records an SS-25 blowing up shortly after launching. By the time of *Sum*, they have become more reliable—one reason why the SS-18s are being phased out.

SS-N-18 (NATO code name STINGRAY): Soviet two-stage liquid-fuel SLBM; in service 1970s. The DELTA III trailed by *CHICAGO* in *Storm* carries sixteen of them.

SS-N-19 (NATO code name SHIPWRECK): Soviet ship-launched supersonic CRUISE MISSILE. In service aboard *KIROV* battle cruisers and OSCAR-class submarines from 1981.

In *Storm*, an OSCAR attacks the Marine landing force off Iceland and launches two SS-N-19s; one is shot down and the other seriously damages *ILLUSTRIOUS*.

SS-N-20 SEAHAWK (NATO code name STURGEON): Soviet three-stage solid-fuel SLBM: multiwarhead MIRV. In service 1983 as the main armament of the TYPHOON-class submarines.

In *Hunt*, *RED OCTOBER* goes to sea with a full load of twenty-six SS-N-20s. One contains a range safety package, intended for sabotaging the ship in the event of defection or capture. Igor LOGINOV is setting the timer on the package when he is shot by RYAN, who thereafter disables the timer and package.

As an extra precaution, RAMIUS and RYAN agree to jettison the missile. This appears on *DALLAS's* sonar as a missile launch, but the panic subsides when the missile sinks. It is later discovered by *SEA CLIFF*, proving that *RED OCTOBER* was a missile submarine and that the Soviets have been lying about her.

STALIN: Historical character (1879-1953). Joseph Vissarionovich Stalin, ruler of the Soviet Union from 1929 to his death. A totally despotic ruler, he forcibly collectivized Soviet agriculture and conducting devastating purges of the Party and Army. He left a legacy of overcentralized government, rule by terror and repression, and fear of one-man rule. The CHAIRMAN in *Storm* and NARMONOV at all times must reckon with this last legacy.

STALLION/SEA STALLION/SUPER-STALLION: U.S. heavy-lift helicopters. See CH-53.

STANDARD: U.S. solid-fuel ship-based SAM. 1500 mph; range 30-70 miles (depending on version); HE warhead. In service with U.S. Navy from 1968. Exists in several versions, varying in range, some compatible with the AEGIS system and VLS.

In *Storm,* Standard is the main missile armament of the AEGIS cruisers defending the *NIMITZ* battle group and the Iceland landings. *REUBEN JAMES* also carries it, and uses it to shoot down a Soviet BEAR.

An air-launched ARM version of the Standard is used in *Storm* by the WILD WEASEL PHANTOMs against Soviet SA-11 radars during the first B-52 raid on Iceland.

STARLIFTER: U.S. strategic jet transport. See C-141.

STASI: Common abbreviation for *Staatssicherheit* (State Security), the East German secret police. Active supporters of terrorism in the West, they were abolished after the unification of Germany and their records confiscated.

In *Sum,* Jack RYAN is afraid of cooperation between ex-Stasi people and forcibly retired East German officers. Erwin KEITEL's work with BOCK proves those fears justified.

STINGER: U.S. shoulder-fired infrared homing SAM. 1300 mph; range 3 miles; system weight 33 lbs. In service 1981; widely exported, including to the Afghan resistance fighters, who used it with great effectiveness against Soviet helicopters. An improvement over REDEYE, being able to attack approaching targets.

In *Storm,* a Stinger kills a Soviet antitank helicopter that has just destroyed the tank of Sergeant MACKALL's troop commander.

The ARCHER in *Cardinal* is witness to the Stinger's effectiveness in Afghan hands. He has gained an even higher reputation with it than with the REDEYE or SA-7, and shoots down two Soviet aircraft with it.

STINGRAY: British lightweight ASW torpedo, comparable to the MARK 46; in service 1983. In *Storm,* Stingrays are carried by *BATTLE-AXE's* LYNX helicopter on the *REUBEN JAMES* convoy; two hits sink the PAPA tracked by O'MALLEY.

STRAKES: Longitudinal plates projecting from the hull of a ship, usually to prevent spray from reaching the deck. In *Storm,* 1052-class frigates in the stormy Atlantic (including *PHARRIS*) have them toward the bow.

STRATEGIC AIR COMMAND (SAC): Operational command of the U.S. Air Force, controlling strategic bombers and land-based missiles; established 1946. Headquarters at OFFUTT AIR FORCE BASE, Omaha, Nebraska.

In *Hunt,* SAC provides the missile-loaded B-52s that keep the Soviet surface ships in the North Atlantic under surveillance.

In *Storm,* it provides the B-52s for the Iceland raids. After the heavy losses of the first one, the faster FB-111s are preferred, but SAC is reluctant to part with enough of them to permanently cripple the Iceland airfields.

In *Cardinal,* RYAN considers the spectacle of Soviet officers visiting SAC missile silos if on-site inspections are allowed.

In *Sum,* it launches two bomber wings, one of B-1s and one of B-52s, and the "Looking Glass" airborne command post (a converted KC-135), and puts the MINUTEMEN on alert.

STRATEGIC ROCKET FORCES: Branch of the Soviet armed forces responsible for all land-based strategic missiles; established 1959.

In *Hunt,* the CIA agent betrayed through Peter HENDERSON was a colonel in the Strategic Rocket Forces. In *Storm,* SERGETOV suggests that the Strategic Rocket Forces might be enough to deter the West during the oil shortage (and ought to be, considering how much money has been spent on them!).

In *Sum,* the Strategic Rocket Forces are placed on alert, as the Soviets fear an American response to the Denver explosion. This has never happened before, as Elizabeth ELLIOT points out—and by making the Americans more nervous, makes the crisis worse.

STRIKE FLEET ATLANTIC: In *Storm,* the major NATO strategic naval offensive force, with at least three attack carriers assigned to it. In its first engagement with the Soviets, it loses *FOCH* sunk, *NIMITZ* heavily damaged, and Admiral BAKER KIA.

It later operates more cautiously but more effectively against Soviet raids on the Atlantic convoys, and with the flagship now *INDEPENDENCE,* supports the landings in Iceland. Robert TOLAND spends his sea time during the war on the staff of the CO of this force.

STUART, EDWARD: In *Danger,* Alabama attorney, defense counsel for the *EMPIRE BUILDER* pirates. Fluent in Spanish and a committed opponent of capital punishment, he suspects something when his clients describe the hanging aboard *PANACHE.*

Acting on these suspicions and drawing on his own experience as a Navy yeoman, Stuart approaches *PANACHE* crewmen, including Chief RILEY. Pretending to be an old shipmate of RILEY's, he is able to obtain full information about the hanging.

Stuart confronts the Federal authorities with this information and is able to obtain permission for his clients to plea-bargain. However, the Mobile police arrange for the pirates to be disposed of by the PATTERSON twins, and the influence of Senator BILLINGS (among other things) prevents any action against the *PANACHE* crew.

STUKA: German World War II single-engine two-seat propeller-driven dive bomber. The most widely used German dive bomber of the war. In *Hunt,* Yuri PADORIN remembers dodging Stuka bombs aimed at his gunboats.

STUMP, U.S.S.:   U.S. conventional destroyer, SPRUANCE class; in service 1978. In *Hunt* she is one of *NEW JERSEY's* escorts.

STURGEON: U.S. class of nuclear attack submarines. See 637-CLASS.

SU-24 (NATO code name FENCER):   Soviet twin-jet, two-seat supersonic attack aircraft; Sukhoi Bureau. 1500 mph; combat radius 750+ miles; 15,000+ lbs. ordnance. In service 1975. Variable-geometry wings give excellent low-altitude performance; the Fencer is probably the most formidable Soviet strike aircraft.

In *Storm,* Fencers are doubtless among the two hundred Soviet aircraft destroyed by Operation DREAMLAND; this would noticeably reduce the threat to NATO's rear areas.

In *Cardinal,* SU-24s destroyed the ARCHER's home village, leaving him alone and sworn to revenge. They strike again at the refugee camp on the Pakistani border, hitting and running too fast to be intercepted by Pakistani F-16s. Civilian casualties are heavy, and the ARCHER swears never to show mercy to a Russian again.

SUBMACHINE GUN (SMG):   Lightweight automatic weapon firing pistol rounds (usually 9-mm or .45); used in situations requiring heavy firepower at short range. The UZIs used by the ULA in *Games* and the

INGRAM and MP-5 used in *Danger* are among the most widely used SMGs.

SUBMUNITION: Small explosive charges carried within a larger bomb or warhead and scattered over the target area by the detonation of the carrying weapon in the air. The ROCKEYE cluster bombs and TOMAHAWK missiles in *Storm* use submunitions against Soviet vehicles and aircraft.

SUBROC: U.S. submarine-launched antisubmarine missile, consisting of a rocket-boosted nuclear depth charge; range 35 miles. In service 1965. In *Storm,* the officers of *CHICAGO* know that even Subroc can't reach the White Sea sanctuary of the Soviet BOOMERs.

SUPREME SOVIET: Highest legislative body of the Soviet government; nominally elects the Council of Ministers. In *Storm,* it is one of the numerous bodies that the POLITBURO can effectively ignore.

SURZPOI, KIRILL: In *Hunt,* Soviet naval officer, *RED OCTOBER's* assistant engineer. He is one of the defecting party and ably assists MELEKHIN in deceiving the crew. When examined by Doctor PETROV, his radiation badge is said to show the highest dosage.

SUSLOV: Soviet submarine, class unspecified (probably a BOOMER). In *Hunt,* Viktor TUPOLEV served under RAMIUS when he was in command of *Suslov.*

SVENSON, CAPTAIN SONNY: In *Storm,* U.S. naval officer, CO of *NIMITZ.* He is more worried than his admiral about the effects of the Soviet capture of Iceland but knows better than to argue with BAKER. He survives the missile hits with minor injuries, and gives Robert TOLAND the con while he takes charge of firefighting.

SVYADOV, LIEUTENANT: In *Hunt,* Soviet naval officer. A zealous junior engineer and KOMSOMOL member. He is one of the work party that checks the piping after the first sign of a radiation leak.

Nervous but conscientious, he is completely deceived by MELEKHIN. He returns to the Soviet Union and provides a KGB interrogator with an impressively convincing description of the developing crisis aboard *RED OCTOBER.*

SWIFTSURE, H.M.S.: British Royal Navy nuclear attack submarine. 4,000/4,500 tons; 28 knots; 5 TT; crew 120. Lead ship of a class of six; in service 1973. In *Hunt,* she was teamed with *DALLAS* in a NATO exercise; the two submarines used foul weather to penetrate surface formations.

T-34/76:   Soviet World War II tank. 30 tons; 30 + mph; 76-mm gun. One of the best tanks of World War II. Mikhail FILITOV saw most of his combat in them, beginning on the fourth day of the war (mentioned in *Hunt*).

T-38:   U.S. supersonic jet trainer; Northrop. In service from late 1950s. In *Games*, Robby JACKSON promises Dr. SHAPIRO a ride in one if he saves Sally RYAN.

T-55:   Soviet main battle tank. 36 tons; 30 mph; 100-mm gun. In service late 1950s.

Mikhail FILITOV's younger son was killed in one in 1959, in a training accident caused by a faulty breech mechanism. In *Storm*, ALEKSEYEV sees smashed and burning T-55s near Alfeld, the remnants of a counter-attack by CATEGORY C units after all the higher CATEGORY ones were shifted north.

T-62:   Soviet main battle tank. 40 tons; 30 mph; 115-mm smoothbore gun; in service from 1962. In *Sum*, Motti ZADIN is attacking some Syrian T-62s when he encounters the SA-6s.

T-80:   Soviet main battle tank. 43 tons; 45 + mph; 125-mm smoothbore gun with automatic loader and laser sights. In service from late 1970s, it has become the standard tank for Soviet CATEGORY A formations. Later versions have many further improvements, including possibly a composite-armor turret. Overall, it is the most formidable Soviet tank.

In *Storm*, ALEKSEYEV watches the training exercises of a regiment equipped with T-80s before the war starts. Later, Sergeant MACKALL and his comrades encounter them more often than any other Soviet tank.

In *Sum*, the Soviet GUARDS regiment in Berlin that BOCK and KEI-TEL trap into opening fire on the Americans is equipped with T-80s. They prove fast and formidable, but most of them are destroyed by M-1 and TOW fire once the BERLIN BRIGADE starts fighting back.

TAIT, CAPTAIN RANDALL: In *Hunt*, U.S. Navy Medical Corps officer. Forty-eight years old and a Mormon, he joined the Navy to see more of the world than Utah. A conscientious doctor, he observes the Mormon prohibitions against alcohol, tobacco, and caffeine.

In *Hunt*, he is transferred from BETHESDA NAVAL HOSPITAL to the Norfolk Naval Medical Center, to take charge of the care of Andrei KATYSKIN, the sole survivor of *POLITOVSKY*. He performs his medical duties with skill, and also keeps a watchful eye on the Soviet observers sent from Washington. This leads to a confrontation with PETCHKIN, when

Tait sees the KGB man apparently trying to murder the patient by lighting a cigarette in an oxygen-filled room.

TALBOT, BRENT: In *Sum,* President FOWLER's Secretary of State. Seventy years old, he is a longtime friend of FOWLER and a former professor of political science at Northwestern University. He is less an academic than an old-fashioned gentleman, and with his thin face and white hair looks the part.

He has, however, a well-developed killer instinct and many years' experience sitting on advisory commissions. He is now close enough to the seat of power to make his influence felt, and wants a share of whatever glory the changes in the world may produce for those who take advantage of the opportunities.

This means that while he has a well-developed sense of ethics and judgment and reservations about Elizabeth ELLIOT, he remains a player on FOWLER's team. He goes along with denying RYAN credit, although he does not actually participate in ELLIOT's campaign of disinformation.

Talbot and whatever advice he might have given die in the Denver bomb. He has, however, left behind some competent appointees, who are useful in the cleanup.

TALBOT, U.S.S.: U.S. conventional missile frigate; in service 1967. In *Storm,* she is with *PHARRIS's* first convoy and sends MORRIS a signal about the fall of Iceland.

TANGO (NATO code name): Soviet class of conventional submarines. 3,100/3,900 tons; 16 knots; 10 TT; crew 70. Eighteen built 1972-82.

In *Hunt,* the SOSUS monitoring of the Barents Sea reports one Tango.

In *Storm,* TOLAND analyzes a satellite photograph of three Tangos having a battery change. Later, the Soviets use Tangos for ASW patrol in the Barents Sea, and have a decoy device that sounds like one. Placed in the middle of a minefield, this device cost NATO H.M.S. *TRAFALGAR.* While escorting the damaged *PROVIDENCE, BOSTON* sinks one of the patrolling Tangos.

TARAWA, U.S.S.: U.S. amphibious assault ship. 25,000/39,000 tons; 24 knots; 2 5" guns, PHALANX; CH-46 and CH-53 helicopters; crew 1,400 plus up to 1,800 Marines. Lead ship of a class of five, in service 1976.

In *Hunt, TARAWA* is at the Little Creek Amphibious Base, near Norfolk. She is sent to sea with a complement of HARRIERs and ASW helicopters, to operate with the *NEW JERSEY* group until the end of the *RED OCTOBER* incident. In *Storm,* she participates in the Marine landings on Iceland.

TARPON, OPERATION: In *Danger,* code name for the FBI investigation of the money-laundering operation for which *EMPIRE BUILDER's* late owner was the American agent.

TAUSSIG, DR. BEATRICE: In *Games,* optical physicist at the TEA CLIPPER laboratory, colleague of Candi LONG, and (under the code name Livia) a Soviet agent controlled by Tania BISYARINA.

A brilliant but lonely woman, she is a lesbian with and all-consuming an unrequited passion for Candi LONG. She is convinced that GREGORY is totally unworthy of LONG, who is an altogether superior and nobler creature. This conviction leads her not only into espionage but into cooperation in the kidnapping of GREGORY.

When she declares her passion for LONG, however, she is rejected so thoroughly that the trauma makes her willing to confess. This provides valuable intelligence toward the recovery of the Major.

TEA CLIPPER: In *Games,* code name for the SDI ASAT laser project.

TECUMSEH, **U.S.S.:**   U.S. nuclear BALLISTIC MISSILE SUB-MARINE; in service 1964. In *Hunt,* Skip TYLER and Captain COLEMAN have also served together aboard her. Captain ROSSELLI in *Sum* did an excellent job as CO of her GOLD crew.

TENNESSEE, **U.S.S.:**   U.S. nuclear-missile submarine, *OHIO*-class; in service 1988. In *Sum,* Ronald JONES has been aboard her testing sonar at AUTEC.

TEXAS, **U.S.S.:**   U.S. battleship; in service 1914; now a historical monument in her namesake state. At the time of Pearl Harbor, James GREER was a seaman second aboard her.

THEODORE ROOSEVELT, **U.S.S.:**   U.S. nuclear-aircraft carrier, *NIMITZ*-class; in service 1986.

In *Sum,* she is assigned to the Sixth FLEET in the Mediterranean, as flagship of a battle group. Robby JACKSON is her CAG, "owning" the seventy-eight BIRDs of her AIR WING. With her escorts she proceeds through the Strait of Gibraltar, and is off the Libyan coast when the Denver explosion begins the crisis.

In the crisis, *TR* becomes a strategic nuclear delivery system, with A-6s and bombs assigned to Soviet naval targets. She is proceeding toward her launch position when her CAP encounters first Libyan, then Soviet MiG-29s; six are shot down without loss to the CAP.

A full-scale carrier vs. carrier showdown between *TR* and *KUZNETSOV* is averted only by the ending of the crisis. The battle group then engages in SAR and retrieves three Soviet MiG pilots.

THEROUX, FRANÇOISE: In *Games, ACTION DIRECTE* terrorist, responsible for at least three murders, including a friend of the President of France. As good looking as she is ruthless.

Examining satellite photographs, RYAN notices the figure of a girl in a bikini at a camp in Libya. The French identify the girl as Theroux and the camp as belonging to *ACTION DIRECTE.* She is arrested in the para raid on the camp, then interrogated, tried, and executed along with her associates.

THOMAS S. GATES, U.S.S.:   U.S. AEGIS cruiser; in service 1987. In *Danger,* she escorts *RANGER.* In *Sum,* she escorts *THEODORE ROOSEVELT;* the group air-warfare officer is aboard her, with the call sign Stetson.

THOMPSON, LIEUTENANT ROGER: In *Hunt,* U.S. naval officer, sonar officer of *DALLAS,* Annapolis graduate, and football hero. A competent officer, he makes good use of subordinates like Chief LAVAL and Ronald JONES—even if he doesn't quite understand JONES and envies his success with women.

TICONDEROGA, U.S.S.:   U.S. AEGIS cruiser; in service 1983. In *Storm,* she is an escort with the *NIMITZ* battle group. She engages the incoming KINGFISH with her VLS and STANDARD missiles, emptying her magazines in minutes and killing over 60 percent of the missiles.

Unfortunately, enough missiles survive to overwhelm the close-range defenses of the battle group. *TICONDEROGA* herself becomes a missile target, and has major damage and fires in her aft superstructure from a near-miss.

TIMMONS, MAJOR GENERAL CHUCK: In *Sum,* U.S. Air Force officer, Deputy Chief of Staff (Operations) of SAC. He is on duty at the "Hole" at OFFUTT AIR FORCE BASE at the time of the explosion, alerts the two ready WINGS, and launches the "Looking Glass" airborne command posts. He remains on duty through the crisis, ably backing up CINC-SAC through RYAN's refusal to confirm the launch order against QUM—which is a great relief to Timmons.

TITAN II: U.S. two-stage liquid-fuel ICBM; in service from 1963 to early 1980s. Its storable liquid fuels made it even harder and more dangerous to maintain than the SS-18, as several people (including RYAN) point out in *Sum.* Basis for the TITAN III series of satellite launchers.

TITAN IIID: U.S. military satellite–launching vehicle, consisting of a Titan II ICBM with two solid-fuel strap-on boosters for additional thrust. In service from early 1970s as launcher for BIG BIRD and KH-11 satellites.

In *Danger,* a Titan IIID is launched from Cape Canaveral with a hastily substituted payload, a communications satellite to support Operation SHOWBOAT.

TOFTE, HANS: Historical character. A veteran of the World War II OSS, he was an early field agent of the CIA. One major operation he conducted was the hijacking of a Norwegian shipload of medical supplies bound for the Chinese Army during the Korean War. In *Hunt,* it is mentioned that Judge MOORE participated in that operation.

TOLAND, COMMANDER ROBERT: In *Storm,* U.S. naval reservist and intelligence specialist. Happily married to the former Martha Keegan, he left active duty after a grounding incident made it clear his promotion chances were limited.

He begins as an NSA analyst. Adding data acquired on the job to what he learns about Soviet activity in a dinner with MORRIS and MCCAF-FERTY, he comes to the conclusion that the Soviets are preparing for war. After presenting this to COMSUBLANT, Admiral Pipes, he is called to active duty with the Intentions Section of CINCLANT Headquarters.

As tensions increase, he is reassigned to the staff of STRIKE FLEET ATLANTIC, aboard U.S.S. *NIMITZ.* Admiral BAKER dismisses his evaluations of the increased threat from Iceland and the possible decoy role of the first Soviet air strike.

Toland is slightly burned when the missiles hit, but escapes the CIC in shape to take the con of *NIMITZ.* He goes ashore when *NIMITZ* reaches Southampton, to serve on the staff of Admiral BEATTIE.

While ashore Toland helps plan several NATO offensive actions against the Soviet threat to the Atlantic convoys. He earns from the Admiral the tribute that it was a mistake for the U.S. Navy to retire him.

Going to sea again aboard *INDEPENDENCE,* the new flagship of STRIKE FLEET ATLANTIC, Toland spends the rest of the war at sea. He obtains vital intelligence about the origins of the war from the shot-down Major CHAPAYEV, which he transmits up the chain of command. At the end of the war, he is going over estimates of Soviet strength in preparation for a carrier strike on Murmansk.

TOLKAZE, IBRAHIM: In *Storm,* Soviet-trained oilfield engineer, of Azerbaijani descent, leader in the sabotage of the Nizhnevartovsk oil field. The grandson of a man who died in rebellion against Soviet rule, he has returned to Islam after a secular education and training. Now a religious fanatic, he carries a Koran as he enters the control room and uses his knowledge to start uncontrollable fires. He dies shouting *"Allahu akbar!"*— God is Great.

TOMAHAWK: U.S. AGM/BGM-109 CRUISE MISSILE: General Dynamics. Speed 500+ mph; range 300+ miles (longer with nuclear warhead); nuclear or HE warhead; advanced terrain-following radar and computers. In service from 1982. The first and to date most successful CRUISE MISSILE, the various versions of the Tomahawk can be launched from ground, air, surface ships, or submarines (688-class).

In *Hunt,* the *NEW JERSEY* group carries Tomahawks.

In *Storm, CHICAGO* has Tomahawks aboard on her first cruise, although she does not use them. Later, additional Tomahawks are flown in C-5s across the Atlantic and loaded aboard other 688-class submarines for Operation DOOLITTLE.

Fifty-eight of the sixty Tomahawks launched in the operation reach their targets, the Soviet airfields on the KOLA PENINSULA. Many BACK-FIREs are destroyed, and the Soviet attacks on the ATLANTIC BRIDGE receive a major setback.

TOMCAT: U.S. carrier-based jet fighter. See F-14.

TORBAY, H.M.S.: British Royal Navy nuclear attack submarine, *TRAFALGAR*-class; in service 1987. In *Storm,* her captain briefs the Operation DOOLITTLE COs on Soviet ASW operations they may face. Later she comes to the rescue of *CHICAGO* when the ALFA that sank *BOSTON* and *PROVIDENCE* is evading. The faster British SPEARFISH torpedoes overtake and sink the ALFA.

TORNADO: NATO twin-engined two-seat supersonic jet fighter-bomber; Panavia (an international aerospace consortium). In service with the British, West German, and Italian air forces from 1980. Variable-geometry wings give it exceptional low-altitude performance.

In *Storm,* Tornadoes are used against Soviet supply lines. Both strike Tornadoes and interceptors are used against Soviet forces in Norway, but suffer heavy losses; the survivors are retained for defense against Soviet air raids.

TOW: U.S. heavy antitank missile: Tube-launched, Optically tracked, Wire-guided. 600 mph; range 3,000 yards; HE shaped-charge warhead. In service from 1970; current version (TOW-2) from early 1980s. The standard U.S. heavy antitank missile and widely exported.

In *Storm*, American mechanized infantrymen use TOWs against Soviet tanks in front of Alfeld and in numerous other engagements. In *Sum*, BRADLEYs of the BERLIN BRIGADE use TOW-2s against the T-80s of the attacking Soviet GUARDS regiment.

TRAFALGAR, H.M.S.:   British Royal Navy nuclear attack submarine. 4,700/5,200 tons; 30 knots; 5 TT, HARPOON; crew 110. Lead ship of a class of seven; in service 1983.

In *Hunt*, RAMIUS considers the *Trafalgar* class a threat equal to the American *LOS ANGELES*. In *Storm*, she is on patrol in the Barents Sea when she detects what is thought to be a Soviet Tango. The Tango is actually an acoustic decoy in the middle of a minefield; *Trafalgar* strikes a mine and is lost.

TRENT, CONGRESSMAN ALAN: Liberal Congressman from Massachusetts, member of the House Select Committee on Intelligence. Openly gay, he is an intelligent and effective politician. He lost a lover to the KGB some years ago, so has a score to settle with them.

In *Cardinal*, Jack RYAN draws him into a public quarrel to lend credibility to the story of RYAN's being in trouble. After learning what is actually going on, Trent becomes one of RYAN's firmest supporters—a fact which surprises Elizabeth ELLIOT and Arnold VAN DAMM in *Danger*. It is no surprise to Ryan, who in *Sum* consults with Trent about appropriations for new diplomatic codes and support of the musahashi operation.

TRIDENT: U.S. three-stage solid-fuel SLBM. Range 4,400 miles (I); 6,900 miles (II). The Trident I entered service aboard existing missile submarines in 1979. The Trident II or Trident D-5 has equipped *OHIO*-class submarines (like *MAINE* in *Sum*) since 1990.

With a seven-warhead MIRV, the Trident D-5 is so accurate as to be considered a potential COUNTERFORCE weapon. (This fact influences Captain DUBININ's decision in *Sum* to engage *MAINE*, since her missile load alone could significantly reduce the Soviet ICBM force.)

TRIESTE: U.S. deep-diving exploration vehicle; in service from 1966. In *Hunt*, Lieutenant AMES of *AVALON* has dived to 20,000 feet aboard her.

TRITON, U.S.S.:   U.S. nuclear submarine; in service 1959. Originally designed as a radar-picket submarine, she had two reactors but was not successful as an attack boat. In *Hunt*, RAMIUS tracked her for twelve hours while in command of "The Vilnius Academy," the first CHARLIE, and claimed that his success led to *Triton's* retirement.

TRUXTUN, U.S.S.:   U.S. nuclear missile cruiser; in service 1967. In *Hunt,* she is one of *NIMITZ's* escorts.

TU-16 (NATO code name BADGER):   Twin-engined Soviet medium jet bomber; Tupelov Bureau. 550 mph; maximum range 4,000 miles; 20,000 lbs. ordnance, including bombs and KELT missiles. In service 1955; many remain in service for aerial refueling, electronic intelligence, and maritime strike and reconnaissance.

In *Storm,* the Badgers are nearly at the end of their useful lives, but play a vital role in the Soviet effort against the ATLANTIC BRIDGE. They launch a decoy strike from the north, using obsolete KELT missiles, which diverts much of the *NIMITZ* group's CAP until it is too late.

One formation of Badgers is intercepted by Amy NAKAMURA's F-15s. Her warning is not believed aboard *NIMITZ,* but she and her flight shoot down five of the Soviet bombers.

TU-22 (NATO code name BLINDER):   Soviet twin-jet supersonic bomber; Tupelov Bureau; in service 1962. In *Storm,* some attack British air bases, escorted by MiG-23s and carrying missiles, which they are not supposed to be able to do. They suffer losses and the attacks are progressively blunted.

TU-22M/TU-26 (NATO code name BACKFIRE):   Soviet twin-jet medium bomber and maritime strike aircraft; Tupelov Bureau. 1300 mph; combat radius 2,000 miles; 25,000+ lbs. ordnance, including bombs and missiles. In service late 1960s (22M); 1973 (26). Based on the TU-22 but with many improvements including variable-geometry wings, the Backfire is the most important Soviet Naval Aviation strike aircraft.

In *Storm,* Backfires have a major strategic role against the ATLANTIC BRIDGE. With the G.I.UK gap opened by the fall of Iceland, they operate freely against both NATO carrier forces (such as the *NIMITZ* group) and the convoys (*PHARRIS's* first convoy loses seven ships to Backfire-launched missiles). They initially suffer few losses, although six are shot down by French F-8s after the sinking of *FOCH.*

However, NATO countermeasures become progressively more effective. EDWARDS's intelligence from Iceland and AWACS surveillance give increased warning time and permit more interceptions. Finally, Operation DOOLITTLE destroys many Backfires on their home airfields and damages the fields themselves.

TU-95/142 (NATO code name BEAR):   Soviet four-engined turboprop strategic bomber and maritime reconnaissance/ASW aircraft; Tupelov Bureau. 500+ mph; combat radius over 5,000 miles; variety of bombs and antiship/CRUISE MISSILES. In service (as bomber) 1955; as ASW aircraft and missile launcher from 1970. Next to the B-52, the Bear is the most durable and versatile strategic aircraft in history. The Bear has also been in continuous production longer than any other military aircraft in history.

In *Hunt,* Bears are not used by the Soviets, as this would damage the credibility of their "submarine accident" cover story.

In *Storm,* Bears are the key Soviet maritime reconnaissance aircraft for locating the convoys and carriers, in spite of their vulnerability. One is damaged by *PHARRIS* but its mates have done their job of guiding the Backfires to the convoy; the damaged Bear lands safely in Iceland.

As NATO countermeasures increase, so do Bear losses. Several are shot down by missiles and F-14s around the *REUBEN JAMES* convoy.

CHICAGO has several encounters with ASW Bears, some supporting the *KIROV* group, others during Operation DOOLITTLE.

TUCKHACHEVSKY: Historical character (1893-1937). Mikhail N. Tuckhachevsky, Marshal of the Soviet Union, hero of the Civil War and the war against Poland, was executed on STALIN's orders in 1937. His death began the purge of the Red Army's leadership that eliminated it as a political force—a fact which NARMONOV in *Sum* thinks the Americans still do not grasp.

TULLIBEE, U.S.S.: U.S. nuclear attack submarine; in service 1960. The smallest operational U.S. nuclear submarine.

In *Hunt,* it is mentioned that she has a reputation for bad luck, and apparently was overdue on one occasion two years back. Lieutenant PARKER detected and "sank" her more recently during ASW exercises with his new two-seat HARRIER.

TUPOLEV, CAPTAIN SECOND RANK VIKTOR ALEKSIEVICH: In *Hunt,* Soviet naval officer, CO of the ALFA-class *V.K. KONOVOLOV.* Marko RAMIUS's star pupil and a man marked for advancement in the Soviet Navy, he regrets his teacher's behavior. He also knows that he must prove his own loyalty—and by successfully defeating RAMIUS, can succeed him as the mentor of Soviet submarine captains.

Originally intended to practice tracking *RED OCTOBER,* Tupolev is sent across the Atlantic with the other ALFAs. After *RED OCTOBER* is apparently lost, he is assigned to cruise off Norfolk in the hope of tracking the "damaged *OHIO*" detected in Maine and now heading south.

After contact with *RED OCTOBER* and her escorts is made, Tupolev identifies the distinctive signature of the CATERPILLAR drive. Overriding his *zampolit,* who wishes to await instructions from Moscow, he decides to engage.

Unfortunately for Tupolev, RAMIUS is still the master. Although he succeeds in damaging *RED OCTOBER,* Tupolev is effectively harassed by the American escorts. He also fails to change his ship's depth, relying instead on her speed and acceleration, and is rammed by *RED OCTOBER.* Instead of succeeding RAMIUS, Tupolev goes down with his ship.

TURBULENT, H.M.S.: British nuclear attack submarine, *TRAFAL-GAR*-class; in service 1984. In *Sum,* JONES is on his way to England to spend a few days aboard her.

TWENTY-MIKE-MIKE: 20-mm ammunition. In *Storm,* the F-15 EAGLES attacking *JULIUS FUCIK* have a full load of it.

TWIN BEECH: U.S. twin-engined propeller-driven light transport; Beech. The original Beech Model 18 entered service in 1937; numerous variations since then.

In *Sum,* LARSON's personal aircraft, which he and CLARK use on several key missions, is a Twin Beech. It has Continental engines with modified cooling systems for operations from high-altitude, hot-weather airfields.

TYLER, OLIVER WENDELL (SKIP): Former U.S. naval officer. An Annapolis graduate and football player (second-string All-American and looks it), he was assigned as CO of *LOS ANGELES* when he lost a leg in an automobile accident caused by a drunken driver.

Tyler has a doctorate from MIT, teaches engineering at the Naval Academy, and does extensive consulting work for the Navy. He and his wife, Jean, have five children (twins born during *Games*), with a sixth on the way at the time of *Hunt.*

In *Hunt,* he is called in to analyze the data on the MAGNETOHYDRO-DYNAMIC DRIVE aboard *RED OCTOBER.* Using a Cray computer and a modified version of ADA, the standard Defense Department computer language, he provides valuable conclusions about what to listen for.

He also draws most of the appropriate conclusions about *RED OCTO-BER* and what she is up to, although he has not been cleared for any of the background. After their initial shock, both James GREER and Admiral DODGE bring him fully into the picture.

This pays off as Tyler devises the basic scheme for bringing *RED OCTO-BER's* crew off without letting them know what happens to their ship. After the success of his scheme, he is offered a return to active duty and the command of a 688 boat. Instead of taking somebody else's place, he asks for a look at the Soviet BOOMER.

A longtime friend of RYAN's, he and his pregnant wife greet the RYANs in *Games* after they deplane from the CONCORDE. After the twins are born, Tyler jokes about being unable to walk them to sleep because of his artificial leg. He finds ERNIE, the Labrador retriever, for Sally.

In *Sum,* RYAN knows that he's not handling his situation well when he realizes that he hasn't even seen Tyler in a long time, let alone confided in him!

TYPHOON: Soviet class of nuclear BALLISTIC MISSILE SUBMA-RINES. 21,500/28,500 tons; 24 knots; 8 TT, 20 SS-N-20 SLBMs; crew up to 200. Six in service or under construction from 1983.

By far the world's largest submarines, these vessels may be intended to operate under the Arctic ice cap, close to Soviet home waters and under protection of Soviet ASW forces. Their size would make it easier for them to break through the ice to launch their missiles.

They have several unique features, including a seven-foot space between outer and pressure hulls, possibly capable of defeating most NATO torpedo warheads, and a missile compartment forward of the SAIL rather than aft. The original TYPHOONs are also believed to have a two-reactor plant.

RED OCTOBER is a modified and enlarged TYPHOON, with 26 instead of 20 missiles, extra silencing, and a single-reactor power plant.

TYURATAM: The Tyuratam Missile Test Center, the major Soviet space facility. Also known as BAIKONOR Cosmodrome.

U-2:   U.S. long-range high-altitude strategic reconnaissance aircraft; Lockheed. In service 1957; basis for the TR-1 used in *Storm.*

UDALOY: Soviet class of conventional destroyers. 6,700/8,100 tons; 30+ knots; SAMs and extensive ASW weapons, including missiles, RBUs, and helicopters; crew 250. At least eleven in service from 1981; name of lead ship means "Daring."

In *Hunt,* at least eight *Udaloys* of the Northern Fleet put to sea in pursuit of *RED OCTOBER.*

In *Storm,* CHICAGO has to reckon with the *Udaloys* in the *KIROV* group because of their ASW capabilities (including sonar and helicopters). One is the target for *CHICAGO's* HARPOONs, which hit and sink her, although MCCAFFERTY doesn't know that until he meets the CO of *KOBBEN* ashore.

In *Sum,* two *Udaloys* are part of *KUZNETSOV's* escort.

UH-1N: U.S. twin-turbine utility helicopter; Bell. In service from 1970s. In *Cardinal,* one carries members of the FBI HRT, who rappel from it onto the KGB safe house where GREGORY is being held. In *Sum,* an Army UH-1N gives Chief CALLAGHAN an aerial view of the site of the Denver bomb.

UH-60 BLACKHAWK: U.S. twin-turbine utility helicopter; Sikorsky. In service from 1978, it is intended as the replacement for the venerable UH-1 series, and is the basis for the SH-60 SEAHAWK ASW helicopter.

In *Danger,* Sergeant CHAVEZ's squad in the 7th Light Division rides in a Blackhawk during training exercises in California. In *Danger* and also in *Sum,* VH-60 versions of the Blackhawk transport presidents and other VIPs.

ULSTER LIBERATION ARMY (ULA):   Maoist offshoot of the PIRA, led by Kevin O'DONNELL; has ties to *ACTION DIRECTE.*

In *Games,* it is responsible for two attempts to kidnap the PRINCE and PRINCESS OF WALES and their son, as well as the bloody rescue of their chief of operations, Sean MILLER, and the attempted murder of the whole RYAN family. They are repudiated even by the PIRA, which has lost a number of members to O'DONNELL. Most of their hard-core members are killed or captured in the second attempt on Their Highnesses at the RYANs' house, and those captured are executed shortly before the opening of *Sum.*

UNITVEROS, ESTEBAN: In *Danger,* MEDELLIN cartel leader, owner of an S-76 helicopter. He and it are both blown up in the first air strike.

UNIVERSE IRELAND: 340,000-ton supertanker. In *Storm, CHICAGO* makes a practice attack on her, which both MCCAFFERTY and his XO agree was too easy—a slow target on a steady course.

USTINOV, DMITRI FEODOROVICH: Historical character; Soviet Minister of Defense from 1976 to his death in 1984. He rose through a series of managerial positions in the armaments industry and became a Marshal of the Soviet Union in 1976. He appears in his actual office in *Hunt* as a longtime friend of Mikhail FILITOV, whom he handpicked as an assistant. Ustinov first met FILITOV when the tanker, retired from combat by his wounds from KURSK, was inspecting factories. They worked together for many years thereafter, with FILITOV acting as Ustinov's hatchet man for quality control in weapons production.

In 1965 he offered FILITOV general's stars but the Colonel refused, as they would not have been earned in combat. The friendship survived in spite of FILITOV's personal tragedies and drinking problem, about which Ustinov is genuinely sympathetic.

Not knowing that his old friend is a CIA agent, Ustinov provides FILITOV with a steady flow of intelligence on the Soviet end of the *RED OCTOBER* crisis. This is made easier by the fact that neither of them has much use for PADORIN, GORSHKOV, or the Navy.

In the end, Ustinov survives the crisis with his power largely intact, while PADORIN and GORSHKOV have to kneel to the KGB. By the time of *Cardinal,* he has been succeeded first by the foolish Sergey Sokolov, then by Marshal YAZOV, whom FILITOV respects.

UZI: Israeli submachine gun. 9-mm; 25-to-40-round magazine; 100+ rpm; effective range 200 yards; loaded weight 7+ lbs. Developed in the late 1940s, the Uzi has been one of the world's standard SMGs for two generations, noted for accuracy, safety, and reliability. It is still in production in Israel and widely licensed for production abroad.

In *Hunt,* Judge MOORE's security man keeps an Uzi under the dashboard of the Director's limousine.

In *Games,* the ULA uses Uzis in the attempt on Cathy and Sally RYAN. One of the discarded SMGs is found in a quarry by the NEWTONs and turned over to the FBI; it is identified as one of a batch of Singapore-built weapons traded by Erik MARTENS and the gun that killed the Maryland state trooper.

In *Danger,* CHAVEZ thinks that the MP-5 lacks the "sexy compactness" of the Uzi; Jack RYAN is now entitled to a bodyguard with an Uzi under the dashboard.

The SECRET SERVICE White House detail carries them, in both *Danger* and *Sum.* In *Sum,* RYAN also sees Israeli reservists carrying them in the streets of Tel Aviv, on their way to or from meetings; he thinks this must do a lot for street crime if not for terrorism.

VALLEY FORGE, U.S.S.: U.S. AEGIS cruiser; in service 1986. In *Sum,* she is "sunk" during a Pentagon war game which Elizabeth ELLIOT does not join, although it's part of her job as National Security Advisor.

VAN DAMM, ARNOLD: Professional politician, aide, and later chief of staff to Robert FOWLER. About fifty, he is a casual dresser, with thinning hair and blue eyes, and doesn't try to impress people. He is not particularly likable, but so clearly honest and competent that even RYAN respects him—a respect which is returned.

In *Danger,* he is FOWLER's chief aide. He sympathizes with Elizabeth

ELLIOT after her first quarrel with RYAN, but doesn't like her, then or later.

In *Sum*, he is FOWLER's chief of staff. He tries to mediate between RYAN and ELLIOT, but this becomes impossible after Charles ALDEN's death and the beginning of the affair between the President and ELLIOT. He tolerates rather than supports the removal of ALDEN and the later planned easing-out of RYAN; he is not knowingly part of ELLIOT's disinformation campaign.

He is with FOWLER at CAMP DAVID during much of the crisis, is a moderating influence (insofar as anybody listens to him at all), and is definitely relieved when RYAN refuses to confirm the launch order against QUM.

He retains his post as White House chief of staff after Roger DUR-LING's accession to the Presidency.

VANEYEV, ILYA ARKADYEVICH: In *Cardinal*, Soviet POLITBURO member, supporter of NARMONOV, father of Svetlana VANEYEVA, and political moderate.

Sixty-three at the time of his appointment, a widower, he is a former minister of agriculture and CENTRAL COMMITTEE member, with a comparatively clean record. However, his appointment will give NAR-MONOV one more full member than the ALEXANDROV faction supported by GERASIMOV. It therefore becomes urgent for the KGB chief to find a way to undercut Vaneyev, and for the Americans to support him—which is made harder by Svetlana's being on Sir Basil CHARLES-TON's payroll.

Vaneyev is shocked and saddened by his daughter's being charged with treason. However, he ultimately displays the moral courage to promise NARMONOV his continued support in spite of GERASIMOV's blackmail. Thanks to RYAN the KGB threat (and CARDINAL as well) is removed, but NARMONOV is grateful nonetheless.

VANEYEVA, SVETLANA: In *Cardinal*, daughter of Ilya VANEYEV, British SIS agent, and key member of the CARDINAL chain.

An attractive blonde, divorced with one child, she works for GOSPLAN, and espionage seems to be as much a thrill or rebellion as a serious matter. She is identified by Eduard ALTUNIN after his arrest and is in turn arrested and taken to the LEFORTOVO PRISON by Colonel VATUTIN before Ed FOLEY can warn her.

At the prison she is interrogated using an experimental but sophisticated sensory-deprivation technique that gives the subject a desperate need for human contact. Providing this contact, VATUTIN is able to obtain substantial evidence from her against FILITOV.

She is then released, to provide more intelligence about the CARDINAL chain. The threat of rearrest is held over both her and her father, but is wiped out by GERASIMOV's defection.

VATUTIN, COLONEL KLEMENTI VLADIMIROVICH: In *Cardinal,* KGB officer in charge of investigating Mikhail FILITOV. Son of an NKVD colonel, he is a more old-fashioned *CHEKIST* than GOLOVKO, but a competent professional for all that.

He uses the same public bath as FILITOV, and knows and respects the old hero. He first becomes suspicious when he is called in after the arrest of ALTUNIN. ALTUNIN's DOUBLING leads to a case against Svetlana VANEYEVA, whom Vatutin arrests personally and orders subjected to the sensory-deprivation tank.

By this point Vatutin is aware of the need to proceed cautiously. High Party issues are involved, and he has already been subjected to pressure from the Defense Ministry not to embarrass the Army by arresting a three-time HERO OF THE SOVIET UNION.

Nonetheless, he is obliged to proceed. Evidence against FILITOV becomes overwhelming, and Mary Pat FOLEYs' efforts to warn him lead only to the FOLEY's expulsion from the Soviet Union and accelerate the Colonel's arrest.

Warned that FILITOV's age and heart condition would make the sensory-deprivation method fatal, Vatutin uses another method. He exploits the Colonel's habit of talking with long-dead comrades to simulate their reproaching him for his treason, in the hope that guilt will induce confession.

All appears to be going fairly well until RYAN intervenes with his blackmail of GERASIMOV, which takes matters out of Vatutin's hands. Too late, the Colonel compares notes with GOLOVKO and joins him in the mad dash to Sheremetyevo Airport and the confrontation with RYAN on the runway. After the plane's takeoff, Vatutin leaves matters in GOLOVKO's hands.

VC-10: British four-jet long-range jet airliner; in service 1962. In *Games,* an RAF VC-10 lands the PRINCE and PRINCESS OF WALES at ANDREWS AIR FORCE BASE, with much ceremony and extensive security precautions.

VDS: Variable Depth SONAR: SONAR in which the sound emitter or receiver is lowered over a ship's stern at the end of a cable, thus able to reach below sound-reflecting layers in the water.

In *Storm, CHICAGO* encounters a Soviet KRESTA using her VDS in defense of *KIROV. BATTLEAXE* also has one, but loses it to a near-miss from a torpedo on the convoy before she begins operating with *REUBEN JAMES's.*

VICTOR: Soviet series of nuclear attack submarines. 4,300-5,000/5,300-6,300 tons; 32 knots; 6-8 TT; crew 100 +. 40 + built from 1968, in three different classes; the first Soviet submarines with teardrop hulls. The Victor IIIs are in many respects comparable to U.S. attack submarines and are still in production.

In *Hunt,* it was a Victor II that revealed the new Soviet ability to navigate the Iceland passage at high speed, by evading a 688 boat whose CO was unwilling to run the risk of hitting an underwater mountain. Numerous other Victors are deployed in pursuit of *RED OCTOBER* and are tracked by American submarines and SOSUs.

In *Storm,* one Victor is among the submarines leaving the Mediterranean before the war. After the shooting starts, Victors are used both against the convoys and for ASW patrols in Soviet home waters, being the most capable Soviet submarines.

It is a Victor under a skilled and aggressive CO that torpedoes *PHARRIS.* MORRIS learns from O'MALLEY that the maneuverable Soviet submarine used the tactic of making a knuckle in the water that gave a SONAR return while the submarine herself evaded; a Victor had used it previously against an American carrier.

In *Sum,* Victors have been known to station themselves off the coast of Washington, to monitor U.S. BOOMERs entering or leaving Bangor.

VINCENNES, **U.S.S.:** U.S. AEGIS cruiser; in service 1985. In *Storm,* she is the main air-defense for the Marine landings on Iceland, fires off all her missiles against a Soviet attack, then maneuvers among the reefs at 25 knots. This tactic works; the Soviet missiles mistake the reefs and shoals for ships and are diverted.

VIRGINIA, **U.S.S.:** U.S. nuclear-missile cruiser; in service 1976. In *Storm,* she is one of *NIMITZ's* escorts, survives the missile attack undamaged, and accompanies the damaged carrier on her high-speed run to England.

V.K. KONOVOLOV: In *Hunt*, Soviet nuclear attack submarine, ALFA-class; her CO is Captain TUPOLEV, RAMIUS's star pupil.

She is already at sea when *RED OCTOBER* leaves Polyarny, assigned to run tracking exercises against the missile boat. Instead she is sent across the Atlantic at high speed, with the other ALFAs.

After the "sinking" of *RED OCTOBER*, she is assigned to watch for a "damaged *OHIO*" off Norfolk, and makes contact with *RED OCTOBER*. In spite of *RED OCTOBER's* damage and her own higher speed, the relative quality of the captains is decisive.

RED OCTOBER rams *Konovolov*, breaching two compartments and turning the smaller submarine upside down. She sinks in that position; the rescue buoy tangles in the SAIL, and if any of her crew survive the sinking they die from lack of air within days.

VON EICH, COLONEL PAUL: In *Cardinal*, U.S. Air Force officer, pilot of the VC-137 that takes the U.S. arms negotiators (including RYAN) back to Moscow and later serves as the escape vehicle for GERASIMOV and FILITOV. A skilled pilot, Von Eich convincingly simulates a major electrical failure that makes it impossible for him to obey any of the Soviet fighters' commands, while rapidly guiding his plane toward international air space. The frustrated MiG pilots are finally obliged to break off the pursuit.

VOROSHILOV: Soviet submarine, class unspecified, mentioned in *Hunt* as having had a fatal reactor accident in 1970.

VOYSKA PVO: *Voyska Protivovozdushnoy Oborony* (Air-Defense Forces). The Soviet branch of service controlling all air-defense radars and weapons (guns, missiles, and fighters) involved in the defense of Soviet territory or troops. Established 1948; centralized 1981.

In *Hunt*, the fact that neither this nor any other non-naval forces are on alert suggests to RYAN that the Soviets are having an exercise or at least not planning war.

In *Cardinal*, it has ultimate authority over the BRIGHT STAR project—thus the project's CO, General POKRYSHKIN, is a former PVO fighter pilot. PVO also provides the frustrated MiG pilots who vainly chase the VC-137 carrying GERASIMOV and FILITOV.

In *Sum*, it controls the satellites that first detect the Denver nuclear explosion and provides NARMONOV with his first report of the crisis.

VT PROXIMITY FUSES: Shell or missile fuses consisting of a miniature radio transmitter; reflection of the radio waves from a target detonates the weapon at the optimum distance. Developed during World War II for AA use.

In *Storm*, the battleships' 5″ secondary guns bombard the key Soviet position, Hill 914, with VT-fused shells bursting twenty feet up and spraying the ground with fragments.

VULCAN: U.S. M-61 20-mm cannon. A Gatling-type weapon, with six rotating barrels and an effective rate of fire of 2,000 rpm; in service 1958. It has been the standard U.S. aircraft gun for nearly two generations, arming the B-52 (tail turret), F-105, F-4, F-14, F-15, F/A-18, and A-7, among others. It is also the basis for the U.S. Navy's PHALANX CIWS, and a three-barreled version arms the AH-1 attack helicopter.

In *Storm*, the F-15s strafe *JULIUS FUCIK* with their Vulcans, inflicting heavy casualties on exposed personnel, including the ship's captain. In *Danger*, Bronco WINTERS uses his Vulcan to shoot down a drug-running BEECH KING AIR. In *Sum*, Commander SANCHEZ splashes the second MiG-29 from *KUZNETSOV* with his cannon.

WAINWRIGHT, U.S.S.:   U.S. conventional missile cruiser, *BELKNAP* class; in service 1966. In *Hunt*, she is one of *NEW JERSEY's* escorts, at first on radar picket duty. In *Storm*, she is escorting *INDEPENDENCE*. Hit by two Soviet missiles, she blows up.

WALKER: Historical character. John A. Walker, U.S. Navy chief petty officer and communications expert, was a Soviet spy for eighteen years prior to his arrest in 1985, and provided the Soviets with much vital intelligence on U.S. communications, submarines, and sonar. Most of the NSA codes were compromised, as RYAN mentions in *Sum*.

WARDROOM: The dining room and social center for the officers of a ship. Also used as a term for the officer complement of a ship: in *Danger*, Red WEGENER took over *PANACHE* with "an inexperienced wardroom."

WARSAW PACT: The Eastern European mutual-defense organization, nominally comparable to NATO but in fact dominated by the Soviet Union, which controlled all major commands and nuclear weapons. Established 1955.

Its non-Soviet forces play only a limited role in *Storm*. In *Sum*, the Arab states at the time of the Yom Kippur War have a better air-defense network than the Warsaw Pact.

WATER SLUG: The water in an empty submarine torpedo tube, expelled by a burst of compressed air as if it were a torpedo, and sounding remarkably like the firing of a torpedo. In *Sum,* Captain RICKS uses a water slug to shake up *OMAHA* during his tracking duel with her.

WATKINS, GEOFFREY: In *Games,* British Foreign Office official, liaison between his ministry and the Royal Family. He is nearing forty, six feet tall, graying, and looks like a diplomat.

He is also a traitor, passing information on the movements of the Royal Family to the ULA via Dennis COOLEY. He drifted into treason after becoming disenchanted with British policy in Northern Ireland while serving there as an Army officer. As his job requires him to know their itinerary and security arrangements, he is an invaluable asset to O'DONNELL.

Because of the large number of people who also have the same knowledge, it is a while before Watkins comes under suspicion. About the time of the ULA attack at the RYANs', Commander OWENS and Dan MURRAY are planning to visit Watkins. However, they find that he has committed suicide after seeing a report of the ULA failure, and "is now answering to a Higher Authority."

WEGENER, RED: In *Danger,* United States Coast Guard officer, the oldest lieutenant commander in the service, and CO of U.S.C.G. *PANACHE.* Red-haired and a pipe smoker, he was born in Kansas and joined the Coast Guard because it was as unlike his home state as possible.

He was thoroughly grounded in seamanship at Cape May, New Jersey, and acquired practical experience aboard a succession of motor lifeboats. Commanding the forty-eight-footer *INVINCIBLE,* he saved fifteen lives.

In a winter storm off the Oregon coast, he took his cutter *POINT GABRIEL* to sea to rescue the crewmen of the fishing boat *MARY KAT.* The stories a seasick reporter aboard filed won the reporter a Pulitzer Prize and Wegener the title of "King of SAR."

It also won him a commission, thanks to the influence of Senator BILLINGS (whose nephew was aboard *MARY KAT*). Three years later he was eligible for command.

This command turned out to be *PANACHE,* a one-off design of cutter with experimental diesels, an inexperienced crew, and many other problems including a shipyard on strike. Wegener's leadership got the ship to sea (winching out of the way a crane that blocked the exit from the drydock), found men able to handle most of the technical problems including the diesels, and restored morale.

Under Red Wegener's command, *PANACHE* has the reputation of a crack ship by the opening of *Danger*. She is on patrol in the Gulf of Mexico, intercepts *EMPIRE BUILDER* as a suspected drug smuggler, and discovers what has happened aboard.

Outraged that the pirates may escape scot-free, Wegener, RILEY, and OREZA devise the mock trial and mock hanging to intimidate the pirates into confessing. This ploy is later discovered by Edward STUART, but the PATTERSON twins take care of the pirates, and Senator BILLINGS prevents any action against Wegener.

He is at sea in *PANACHE* again at the time of the rescue mission into Colombia. Maneuvering his ship in the middle of a hurricane, Wegener provides a last-minute landing spot for the helicopter, and afterward treats the wounded in sick bay. *PANACHE* then proceeds to Guantánamo Bay with the survivors and the captured Colonel CORTEZ aboard.

A man who has always taken seriously the Coast Guard's motto, "You have to go out. You don't have to come back," even against enemies other than the sea.

WELLINGTON, ERNEST: In *Sum,* ambitious young Justice Department lawyer, honor graduate of Harvard Law School. Twenty-seven years old and with more ambition and talent than judgment or ethics, he and three assistants assemble the data that is the basis for Elizabeth ELLIOT's campaign against RYAN.

WERNER, SPECIAL AGENT GUS: FBI agent and HRT leader.

In *Games* he is alerted by Bill SHAW at the first report of the terrorists. He leads the helicopter-lifted HRT to the RYANs' house but is unable to engage the ULA because the helicopter is shot down by a REDEYE. After the flight of both terrorists and intended prey, he rallies his men and rejoins the pursuit, ending by taking command aboard *COSTANZA*.

By the time of *Cardinal*, he has been head of the HRT for five years, passing up a promotion to stay with the work he knows and loves. He is called into action for the rescue of Major GREGORY, with shoot-to-kill orders. He is one of the four men who rappel into action from the helicopter and break into the house. He personally shoots LEONID in the arm.

"WET WORK": Soviet intelligence term for assassination, the ultimate ACTIVE MEASURE, as Colonel CORTEZ knows in *Danger*.

WHITE, VICE ADMIRAL JOHN: In *Hunt,* British Royal Navy officer, commanding the *INVINCIBLE* group, and Eighth Earl of Weston. He and his Countess, Antonia, are friends of the RYANs' and the Countess and Cathy RYAN have played together in a group of amateur musicians (Cathy on the piano, the Countess on an antique violin). Tall, florid, and fifty, he is a gracious host and a thoroughly professional officer, whose rank owes little to his peerage.

He receives RYAN on his arrival, arranges for him to brief key officers of the staff, then lets him catch up on his sleep. He shows high tactical skill in maneuvering his Anglo-American force to intercept *RED OCTOBER* and a talent for improvisation when the helicopter with the U.S. intelligence team crashes and the team has to be replaced out of *INVINCIBLE's* resources.

WILD WEASEL: Military aircraft configured for the detection and suppression of enemy radars and SAM batteries, with special electronic equipment (detectors and jammers) and ARMs.

In *Storm,* Wild Weasel F-4s support the second B-52 strike on Iceland. In *Danger,* Colonel JOHNS won his MEDAL OF HONOR rescuing a Wild Weasel crew in Laos. (The standard Wild Weasel in Vietnam was a converted F-105.)

WILL ROGERS, **U.S.S.:**   U.S. nuclear-missile submarine; in service 1967. In *Hunt,* the quartermaster of *ETHAN ALLEN* served with Admiral GALLERY aboard her. In *Storm,* MCCAFFERTY was serving aboard her when he spotted a sailboat with a couple making love on the cabin roof.

WILLIAMS, OWEN: In *Hunt,* British Royal Navy lieutenant, serving aboard *INVINCIBLE.* He has a degree in Russian and has served aboard H.M.S. *DREADNOUGHT,* which makes him a logical candidate to accompany RYAN aboard *RED OCTOBER* after the original contact team is lost in the helicopter crash.

He boards the Soviet vessel, wearing an American uniform and concealing his knowledge of Russian. After the crew is evacuated, he and Lieutenant KAMAROV are ordered forward to secure all hatches. They encounter GRU agent LOGINOV; the Soviet officer is killed and Williams is shot in the chest.

He is discovered by RYAN and RAMIUS and given first aid after LOGINOV's death. A unnamed Soviet officer interested in medicine improvises a chest tube which keeps Williams alive long enough for Doctor NOYES to perform emergency surgery after *RED OCTOBER* reaches the Maine coast. Williams is a very sick young man when he leaves the submarine, but is expected to survive.

WILLOW: The security clearance for CARDINAL information in *Hunt* and *Cardinal.* At first only MOORE, RITTER, and GREER have it; RYAN gains it because of "need to know" during *Hunt.*

"WING-WIPER":   Uncomplimentary slang for air-service ground personnel like Lieutenant EDWARDS in *Storm*. His Marines are determined not to let one outmarch them; it is a surprise to Sergeant SMITH that EDWARDS has run marathons.

WINTERS, CAPTAIN JEFF (BRONCO):   In *Danger*, U.S. Air Force officer. A Black Air Force Academy graduate, his mother was killed in a druggie's mugging, so he has a personal score to settle with the cartel. An F-15 pilot, he got his nickname from a classmate who is now flying cargo planes.

Assigned to fly the air-intercept missions of Operation SHOWBOAT, he splashes a drug-running BEECH KING AIR. He also forces a DC-7B to land in Florida, where the crew are intimidated into confessing by RECON MARINES. After completing his antidrug missions, he is assigned to an F-15 in Germany.

WOLFE, MOIRA: In *Danger*, secretary to FBI Director Emil JACOBS; competent, loyal, and trusted. An attractive widow in her forties, she was happily married for twenty-two years, and has two children. Her husband, Rich, died of a sudden aneurysm two years before the events of *Danger*. The loss still hurts like an open sore.

Lonely and charmed by "Juan Diaz," she slips into a passionate affair with Felix CORTEZ, with the blessing of both colleagues and friends. She inadvertently provides him with crucial intelligence on Emil JACOBS's plans and movements. This intelligence, passed on to ESCOBEDO, is the basis for JACOBS's assassination.

After SHAW and MURRAY identify Moira as the leak, she refuses their reassurances and attempts suicide. After her narrow survival, the FBI continues to treat her as another victim rather than a criminal. She receives therapy and is given an equally good job in another government agency where she will have no access to classified material.

She is present when CORTEZ is handed over to the Cubans at GUAN-TÁNAMO BAY. The Colonel has the humiliation of knowing exactly what she thinks of him—and she has the satisfaction of seeing him get what he deserves.

WOOD, COMMANDER: In *Hunt*, CO of *POGY*. An able captain with a sense of humor (he asks a patrolling P-3 to send out some beer), he operates effectively against the Soviet submarines crossing the Atlantic. He later uses his boat's maneuverability and SONAR in cooperating with *DALLAS* to support *RED OCTOBER* against *KONOVOLOV*.

XO: Executive officer, the second-in-command of a ship or military unit: Lieutenant Commander CLAGGETT, XO of *MAINE* in *Sum;* Wally CHAMBERS, XO of *DALLAS* in *Hunt.*

YAK-36/38 (NATO code name FORGER):   Soviet Navy single-seat jet carrier-based VTOL fighter-bomber; Yakovlev Bureau. 700 mph; combat radius 250+ miles; 3,000+ lbs. ordnance including ATOLL missiles. Experimental Yak-36 tested from 1967; production version Yak-38 in service from 1975, aboard *KIEV*-class carriers. With separate lift engines, the Forger is generally inferior to the HARRIER—"a piece of junk," as an Air Force officer calls it in *Hunt.*

In *Hunt,* Forgers are aboard *KIEV.* They attempt to harass the American E-3 AWACS but are discouraged by the escort of F-15s. Later confrontations with F-14s from *KENNEDY* lead to the shooting incident in which Robbie JACKSON's plane is hit.

YANKEE (NATO code name):   Soviet class of nuclear BALLISTIC MISSILE SUBMARINES. 7,900/9,600 tons; 27 knots; 6 TT, 12-16 missiles; crew 120. Thirty-four built 1967-74. The first nuclear-powered Soviet BOOMERs capable of launching missiles while submerged, many have been scrapped or converted to attack/cruise-missile boats.

In *Hunt,* an early sign that the Soviets are not planning war is a Yankee heading north (instead of south, close to the American coast for her short-range missiles).

In *Storm,* the Russians' major disarmament initiative is the dismantling of the entire Yankee class.

One sank off Bermuda in 1986 after an explosion in her missile compartment, a highly publicized accident RYAN refers to in *Cardinal.*

YAZOV, DMITRI TIMOFEYEVICH: In *Cardinal,* historical character; Soviet Defense Minister from 1987. A Marshal of the Soviet Union, he works hard enough to earn Mikhail FILITOV's respect although he rose mostly due to Party influence.

An affable man, he has four grandchildren and chats with both RYAN and Mary Pat FOLEY at an embassy party. He is placed in an embarrassing position by the charges against FILITOV.

YORKTOWN, U.S.S.:   U.S. AEGIS cruiser; in service 1984. In *Storm* she is part of STRIKE FLEET ATLANTIC supporting the Iceland landings; she carries the fleet air-defense officer.

YOUNG OCTOBRISTS: Soviet youth group for children from seven years old. Six children from the Pskov chapter are killed in the Kremlin *maskirovka* bombing in *Storm,* including Major SOROKIN's daughter, Svetlana.

YOUNG PIONEERS: Soviet youth group for teenagers; formerly gave extensive paramilitary training. Marko RAMIUS was a member.

YP: Yard Patrol craft. 172 tons; 12 knots; crew of 7 plus 24 midshipmen. Wooden-hulled vessels assigned to the Naval Academy for seamanship training and security. In *Games,* Jack RYAN, the PRINCE OF WALES, and a squad of Marines board one to pursue the ULA terrorists to Baltimore.

YURI GAGARIN: Soviet space-monitoring ship; in service 1971. In *Sum,* she is within range of the disabled satellites during the crisis and is suspected of attacking them with microwaves from her high-gain antennas—another factor in increasing the tension.

ZIMMER, SENIOR MASTER SERGEANT BUCK: In *Danger,* U.S. Air Force senior NCO, veteran of SAR and Special Operations in both the Vietnam War and afterward, and for twenty years a friend and confidant of Colonel JOHNS.

In *Danger,* he is crew chief of the PAVE LOW helicopter used for the covert troop insertions, and later for the rescue mission. The rescue mission is a pleasure; he is another of those men who would rather die than betray subordinates. On the way, he gives Jack RYAN a quick course in the MINIGUN.

He is mortally wounded by ground fire from cartel troops as the helicopter lifts off with the rescued troops. RYAN takes over the gun and uses it effectively. Zimmer dies worrying about his children, with RYAN assuring him that they're going to college.

ZIMMER, CAROL: Wife (later widow) of Sergeant Buck ZIMMER. Thirty-six at the time of *Danger,* she is the daughter of a Hmong chief who fought on the American side in the Vietnam War. She was lifted off a Laotian hill at the last minute by Colonel JOHNS and ZIMMER, and is the only survivor of a family of ten. She and Buck have seven children, "the seven cutest kids in Florida."

In *Sum,* she runs a convenience store in Maryland, and her children have the benefit of an educational trust fund set up by Jack RYAN. CLARK and CHAVEZ have also intimidated local gang members from trying anything at the store. She has the classic Asian belief in education, and keeps the store so clean that Cathy RYAN could perform surgery on the counter. One son, Laurence, is in pre-med; a second, Peter, has been accepted at MIT.

After Ernest WELLINGTON discovers the "Zimmer" file in RYAN's data, he and Elizabeth ELLIOT conclude that RYAN is keeping Carol as a mistress and may be the father of her youngest child. This leads to the "sexual impropriety" part of the case against RYAN mentioned in the papers. A visit by RYAN just after daughter Jackie has spilled some of her mother's perfume makes matters worse, as Jack returns home to an already suspicious wife smelling of another woman's perfume.

Fortunately, CLARK's intervention saves the day. He arranges a meeting between Carol and Cathy, which tells Mrs. RYAN everything she needs to know—except who set her up.

ZSU-23-4 *(SHILKA)*:   Soviet self-propelled AA gun, consisting of four water-cooled 23-mm cannon on a tracked, radar-equipped chassis. In service 1966; widely exported and effectively used by the Arabs in the Yom Kippur War (including the Syrians on the Golan Heights in *Sum*).

ZSU-30:   Soviet self-propelled AA gun, consisting of twin 30-mm radar-controlled guns on a T-72 tank chassis. In service 1980s as a replacement for the ZSU-23-4 *SHILKA*.

In *Storm,* they are sent to Iceland, where they are sighted by EDWARDS and used against American air strikes. They are also with Soviet armored forces in Germany; General ALEKSEYEV sees one destroyed by the suicidal crash of a German ALPHAJET. Its Sergeant Lupenko will receive a posthumous ORDER OF THE RED BANNER.

ZADIN, CAPTAIN BENJAMIN (BENNY):   In *Sum,* Israeli police officer in command at the Temple Mount demonstration in Jerusalem. Traumatized by the desertion of his wife, he has returned to militant Judaism and sees the demonstration as a chance to avenge his brothers, both KIA in battle against the Arabs. He orders the police to open fire, then personally confronts and shoots Hashimi MOUSSA.

ZADIN, LIEUTENANT MORDECAI (MOTTI):   In *Sum,* Israeli Air Force pilot, brother of Benjamin ZADIN. An eighteen-year-old *sabra,* he is a keen and competent pilot.

In the Yom Kippur War he is an A-4 pilot assigned to deliver nuclear weapons. On runway alert, his flight is suddenly shifted to a conventional mission against the Syrian armored advance on the Golan Heights. In the confusion caused by the crash of a damaged F-4, no one has time to remove the nuclear weapon from his SKYHAWK.

Zadin takes off with the weapon still aboard, engages a Syrian SA-6 battery, destroys it, but is shot down and killed. The bomb falls on the land of the Druse FARMER, to become a terrorist weapon for GHOSN and QATI.

ZHUKOV: Historical character (1896-1974). Georgi K. Zhukov, Marshal of the Soviet Union, was the outstanding Russian general of World War II. One of his achievements was the counterattack around Moscow in 1941, which forced a German retreat; Mikhail FILITOV led a battalion spearheading that attack.

ZNAMIROWSKI, CHIEF BOSUN'S MATE MARY: In *Games,* U.S. Navy petty officer, in charge of the YP RYAN uses to pursue the ULA boat to Baltimore. She is a competent sailor, respected by her crew, and apparently a Clint Eastwood fan.

ZUNI: U.S. 5″ air-to-ground rocket; in service 1957. In *Sum* the A-4s of Motti ZADIN's flight are rearmed with Zunis for their strike on the Golan Heights; the rockets destroy the Syrian SA-6 battery.